Animal Activism On and Off Screen

ANIMAL POLITICS

Danielle Celermajer, Rick De Vos, Katie Woolaston & Chloë Taylor, Series Editors

The Animal Politics series provides a forum for animal studies scholarship that is grounded in and expands political and critical theory. Our understanding of "politics" is expansive, embracing work across disciplines and scales, including but also reaching beyond institutional, cultural, and relational dimensions of politics. We are especially interested in the work of critical animal studies scholars that is intersectional in approach, or that puts considerations of animals as political subjects in conversation with critical race and ethnicity studies, anti-colonialism and Indigenous studies, gender and sexuality studies, feminist and queer theory, critical disability and mad studies, labour, and critical poverty studies.

Animal Activism On and Off Screen
Ed. Claire Parkinson and Lara Herring

Animal Death
Ed. Jay Johnston and Fiona Probyn-Rapsey

Animal Dreams
David Brooks

Animal Welfare in Australia: Politics and Policy
Peter Chen

Animal Welfare in China: Culture, Politics and Crisis
Peter J. Li

Animals in the Anthropocene: Critical Perspectives on Non-human Futures
Ed. The Human Animal Research Network Editorial Collective

Australian Animal Law: Context and Critique
Elizabeth Ellis

Cane Toads: A Tale of Sugar, Politics and Flawed Science
Nigel Turvey

The Climate Crisis and Other Animals
Richard Twine

Decolonising Animals
Ed. Rick De Vos

Dingo Bold: The Life and Death of K'gari Dingoes
Rowena Lennox

Engaging with Animals: Interpretations of a Shared Existence
Ed. Georgette Leah Burns and Mandy Paterson

Enter the Animal: Cross-Species Perspectives on Grief and Spirituality
Teya Brooks Pribac

Fighting Nature: Travelling Menageries, Animal Acts and War Shows
Peta Tait

The Flight of Birds: A Novel in Twelve Stories
Joshua Lobb

A Life for Animals
Christine Townend

Meatsplaining: The Animal Agriculture Industry and the Rhetoric of Denial
Ed. Jason Hannan

Obaysch: A Hippopotamus in Victorian London
John Simons

Animal Activism On and Off Screen

Edited by Claire Parkinson and Lara Herring

SYDNEY UNIVERSITY PRESS

First published by Sydney University Press

Sydney University Press
Gadigal Country
Fisher Library F03
University of Sydney NSW 2006
AUSTRALIA
sup.info@sydney.edu.au
sydneyuniversitypress.com.au

A catalogue record for this book is available from the National Library of Australia.

ISBN 9781743329757 paperback
ISBN 9781743329764 epub
ISBN 9781743329740 pdf

Cover image: Shutterstock/Loredana Sangiuliano
Cover design: Miguel Yamin

We acknowledge the traditional owners of the lands on which Sydney University Press is located, the Gadigal people of the Eora Nation, and we pay our respects to the knowledge embedded forever within the Aboriginal Custodianship of Country.

Contents

Acknowledgements

Our thanks go to all those at Sydney University Press who have helped and supported us throughout the process of bringing this book to publication: Naomi van Groll, Fiona Probyn-Rapsey, Agata Mrva-Montoya, Susan Murray and Jo Lyons. The work of David Gould, Research Assistant with the Centre for Human Animal Studies at Edge Hill University, was indispensable to this project. Claire and Lara are grateful to Dave for all that he did to ensure the final manuscript came together. We are indebted to all the contributors to this volume. Our thanks to them not only for their thought-provoking and inspiring contributions to the book but for all they do to make change in the world for nonhuman animals.

Claire would like to thank her co-editor, fellow film enthusiast and very good friend, Lara. We have worked together on this and other projects over the last few years and I hope there will be many more collaborations in the future. Thank you for all the great chats, your support and friendship, and for the honour of letting me be a small part of your academic journey. I'm fortunate to have great colleagues at the Centre for Human Animal Studies, in the Department of English and Creative Arts and elsewhere at Edge Hill University. Thanks to all those who have supported me and this project in various ways over the last couple of years, especially Dr Richard Twine. Finally, special thanks to my family, human and nonhuman, for their love and good humour.

Lara would like to thank, first and foremost, her co-editor, mentor, friend and constant inspiration, Claire. It is one of the great privileges of my life to have met you and had the pleasure of your friendship, guidance and support throughout the years. The extent of my gratitude will perhaps never be adequately articulated but at least can be commemorated at times like these. I look forward to continuing our work together in the years to come and, of course, to the continuation of our much cherished and seemingly endless chats. I also wish to send my thanks to the Centre for Human Animal Studies at Edge Hill University; becoming a member of the centre has been a tremendous source of inspiration to me. Lastly, to my dad and Jack, to Romy and Michelle, and to all the glorious friends that have been an integral part of my journey; I thank you and I love you.

Introduction

Claire Parkinson and Lara Herring

Since the early 2000s there has been a growth in films that engage with themes of animal advocacy and veganism. The film *Earthlings* (2005) was widely dubbed "the vegan-maker" and was notable for being a feature-length animal rights documentary with a celebrity narrator (Joaquin Phoenix) and music by Moby. In addition, and highly unusual for an animal rights film, *Earthlings* won awards on the film festival circuit. Prior to this, animal rights films were often low- or "no-" budget productions, usually involving undercover filming, with short run times and produced predominantly by animal advocacy groups with little in the way of formal distribution routes open to them. *Earthlings* was financed by the filmmaker and, due to its subject matter, the film was rejected by 22 film festivals and struggled to get distribution. It was accepted at three film festivals and won key awards at each. Made available for free for online streaming, *Earthlings* garnered significant grassroots support through word of mouth. The film's public reach and lack of traditional distribution remains reflected in the film's rating on the aggregate website Rotten Tomatoes, which gives the film a 92 per cent positive audience score but has no critics' score due to a lack of reviews.

Earthlings marks an important moment in a history of animal advocacy filmmaking, demonstrating that a feature-length animal rights film could have an extensive reach, making use of newly available technologies that disrupted the traditional routes of distribution and enabling imagery of animal abuse, cruelty and exploitation to reach new audiences. Following *Earthlings* and from 2006 onwards, the number and availability of feature-length animal advocacy films has increased substantially and, importantly, new opportunities for financing and distribution have become more readily available. Coupled with this, there is now a more sophisticated understanding of impact campaigns that accompany films and which function to suggest relevant actions that can be taken by viewers interested in the issues that the films raise. Support from grassroots organisations is often important to the success of these films, helping to build word of mouth and audience interest, while the films can be used to promote an animal advocacy group's campaigns through public screenings, interviews with key personnel and reviews. As a result, more films that are regarded as having animal rights and/or pro-vegan themes reach mainstream audiences, who are enabled to undertake some type of action in response to the issues covered in the movie. Films such as *Cowspiracy: The Sustainability Secret* (2014), *The Ghosts in Our Machine* (2013), *Forks Over Knives* (2011), *Blackfish* (2013), *Vegucated* (2011), *The Game Changers* (2018) and *What the Health* (2017) have garnered awards and been cited by animal advocacy groups as important drivers in shifting public opinion and changing behaviours.

More recently, television has moved towards greater inclusion of pro-vegan content, primarily focused on cookery and lifestyle programs, an indicator that mainstream veganism remains connected to dietary choices and plant-based healthy lifestyles rather than being concerned with animal ethics. For example, promotion for the relaunch of the Plant-Based Network 3.0 reflected this emphasis, as seen in a statement on the lifestyle and entertainment network's website: "You told us what you want: More TV shows and movies on better health and a greener planet."[1] Factual television generally has witnessed a notable increase in vegan cooking shows and pro-vegan health and lifestyle programs, for example *Kirly-Sue's Global Kitchen*, *New Day New Chef*, *Jazzy Vegetarian*, *The Big Fat Truth*, *Dirty Vegan* and *Living on the Veg*. There have been "plant-based" episodes and challenges in

1 Plant-Based Network, 2022.

popular competitive cookery programs such as *The Great British Bake Off* (UK), *The Great British Baking Show* (US) and *MasterChef* (UK/Australia), with plant-based chef Teresa Colaco winning *MasterChef Portugal*, and the launch of an all-vegan-cast show, *Peeled* (USA). Yet, despite the mainstreaming of vegan eating practices, issues of animal ethics are more likely to be discussed in television fiction, cases in point being the BBC mockumentary *Carnage*, written and directed by comedian Simon Amstell, a 2019 episode of the animated sitcom *South Park* ("Let Them Eat Goo") and in various episodes that feature Lisa Simpson, a character in the long-running show *The Simpsons*, who remains vegetarian in the animated sitcom after bonding with a lamb in a petting zoo. However, narratives that include a positive pro-animal rights message remain few and while the animal welfare discourse continues to populate television, especially in reality animal rescue shows, representations of animal rights activists, post-9/11, are more likely to be negative.

There are some signs of change, though, and off screen there have been an increasing number of celebrities who openly advocate on behalf of animals and veganism, lending their support to animal rights groups, charities and actions. Receiving the Best Actor award at the 2020 Academy Awards, Joaquin Phoenix used his speech to openly criticise the animal-industrial complex and endorse the Academy's choice to serve plant-based food at one of the most important events in the film industry calendar. Phoenix is also well known for his involvement in campaigns, marches, protests and actions against animal cruelty and exploitation, as is a growing roster of other celebrities such as Pamela Anderson, Ricky Gervais, Peter Egan, Evanna Lynch, Peter Dinklage, Moby, Sadaa Sayed and Woody Harrelson, some of whom are discussed in this volume. While this suggests a new context for animal advocacy, there remain significant barriers to animal rights messages reaching mainstream audiences. The associations between animal rights, extremism and terrorism continue to shape the public discourse and media representations to such an extent that stereotypes of animal rights activists as unstable, violent and on the margins of society continue to populate on-screen fictions. Indeed, Phoenix's speech had a mixed response from the press, with some UK and US news outlets suggesting that the actor was rambling, had mental health problems or was simply misinformed. Such comments reflect that despite more mainstream visibility, animal rights and its connection to veganism remains marginalised in many spheres.

This book examines the relationship between animal activism and the screen industries in the 21st century, exploring three key aspects of this new context for animal rights: representations of activism on screen; activist texts and their reception; and celebrity vegans and animal advocates. Although aspects of online or digital activism are mentioned in some chapters, for reasons of focus, the volume is concerned with the overlapping screen industries of film and television. It is certainly the case that a majority of film and television that we might identify as animal activism texts is labelled as factual or documentary. An aim of this book was to ensure that we looked beyond factual media to explore what fiction can offer to our thinking about animal activism on screen. For this reason, fiction film or television is represented in each section of the book.

Across the chapters are connections between the three key strands that structure the book. Narrative, generic and aesthetic strategies and issues of audience and reception emerge as significant points of discussion in many of the chapters, which adopt a range of discursive critical and theoretical lenses through which animal activism is explored. To these ends, the volume includes chapters from leading academics in the fields of cultural studies, animal studies, critical animal studies, and film, communication, television and media studies, as well as contributions from activists and those working in the screen industries.

Mieke Roscher's chapter (Chapter 1) opens the first section on the representations of animal activism on screen. Roscher employs theories of cultural transfer to examine the representations of the animal liberation movement in English, German and American crime fiction television series between 1990 and 2010. Crime fiction has, Roscher reminds us, been central to the establishment, popularisation and normalisation of stereotypes of animal activists. Such representations emerge from a media backlash in the 1980s against animal liberation activists in the UK following a series of direct actions and the "Mars Bars hoax". Associations between animal liberationists and IRA bombers led to a new press discourse on activism that aligned animal rights with terrorism. The American Animal Liberation Front was included in the FBI's list of domestic terrorist groups from 1992. After 9/11 and the introduction of the *USA PATRIOT Act*, the classification was reinforced, and in 2006 the introduction of the *Animal Enterprise Terrorism Act* regarded threats of violence against businesses as acts of terrorism. In Germany, the media reported on British activism, and mainstream animal welfare groups, keen to avoid any association with animal liberationists, began to make the connections between animal rights and terrorism. Crime drama on television reflected this shift in the discourse and criminalisation of animal rights, and Roscher examines in detail episodes from *The Bill* (UK), *Law & Order* (USA) and *Tatort* and *Polizeiruf 110* (Germany) to examine how the representations of activists are culturally reinterpreted.

In Chapter 2, Núria Almiron, Laura Fernández and Olatz Aranceta-Reboredo take the focus from fiction to factual media and more specifically to US-produced animal advocacy documentaries over a 20-year period. They propose that despite the prevalence of a frame where activists are depicted as being involved in risky, dangerous situations that necessitate warfare-like tactics, there are a number of other frames which are evident across the range of advocacy films that they analyse. Twenty documentaries were analysed using a series of frames, leading to the proposition that activists were portrayed across the sample as using ethical arguments, with emotional and rational arguments also figuring strongly in the films studied. The chapter also looks at the prevalence of health and environmental arguments and the use of frames such as "hero", "convert", "freedom fighter" and "educated" in representations of activism. By studying a range of films over a period of two decades, Almiron, Fernández and Aranceta-Reboredo are able to chart the evolution of self-representation by animal activists and the strategic and ideological changes that have taken place over time. In their discussion, they explore the development of the health and environmental focus in animal rights films and argue that the meaning of veganism has been transformed and as a result there is a decreased prevalence of "direct action" and "freedom fighter" frames being used in these films. One result is, the authors propose, that it may become easier for non-vegan audiences to identify with vegan activists.

In Chapter 3, Emily Plec returns to an exploration of the alignment of animal activists with terrorists in an examination of *The Animal People*, a 2019 documentary that covers a 15-year period, and the activism and persecution of six animal activists affiliated with Stop Huntingdon Animal Cruelty (SHAC). Plec's focus is on the potential of the film to function as reconstitutive discourse through an analysis of the audience's perceptions of the rhetor (first persona) and the implied audience for the film (second persona). Plec argues that *The Animal People* succeeds as a film that supports free speech and animal rights. With Joaquin Phoenix as an Executive Producer, the film benefited from the actor's star power and from his receiving the Academy Award for Best Actor in 2020, shortly after the film's release. As Plec points out, Phoenix's association with the film strengthened audience perceptions of the credibility of *The Animal People.* While some of the audience will have watched the film due to Phoenix's name being attached to it, others, Plec contends, will have watched due to a pre-existing interest in veganism, animal liberation and animal rights. The second persona is intrinsically tied to the movement of an audience from a position of support to one of active engagement. This chapter explores how *The Animal People* reminds audiences of the asymmetries of power that exist between activists and corporations.

In Chapter 4, the imbalance of power between neoliberal corporate capitalism and activists is discussed through an analysis of the fantasy fiction film *Okja* (2017). Bong Joon Ho's film is a story of political resistance to corporate capitalism where the Animal Liberation Front are comic heroes with whom audiences are encouraged to identify. Made for the streaming service Netflix, it is a film that would not have been made within the Hollywood system due to its pro-animal rights and anti-corporate message. Claire Parkinson analyses the representation of animal rights activism by the fictional Animal Liberation Front (ALF) group and argues that Bong's signature use of genre-blending allows for audience identification with the position of the activists. Parkinson argues that, while there has been a focus on the importance of factual documentaries as a means to engage audiences with animal rights issues, there is a place for what she terms "advocacy fiction". The chapter examines Bong's use of anthropomorphism, fantasy and caper heist conventions as part of a "structure of sympathy" and analyses how allegiance to the ALF position is constructed through the moral system of the text. Parkinson examines the critical and audience reception to the film and concludes with the recommendation that animal advocacy should widen its repertoire of communication strategies to include anthropomorphism, fantasy and comedy.

While the first four chapters look at representations of animal activists, the second section of the book is concerned with activist films and TV shows and their reception. Paula Arcari's chapter (Chapter 5) opens Section Two with an essay that takes up the concern over tensions between pro-vegan films that engage with the realities of the animal-industrial complex and those that frame veganism as beneficial to human health and wellbeing. The survey of 45 films covers a 15-year period, and Arcari notes that over half of those included in the study make no reference to animals as subjects. Indeed, a little over one-fifth of the documentaries do not depict animals at all and some reinforce the normalisation of eating animals through the promotion of so-called sustainable options. Representations of animal suffering and the extension of moral concern to only certain animals is, Arcari argues, problematic in that it bestows contingent rather than inherent value on animals. The chapter concludes that current trends within pro-vegan documentary filmmaking do not do enough to counter the common understanding of animals as "usable", and narrative strategies should include consistent representations of the animal-industrial complex as well as accounts of the techniques of oppression, and should emphasise the inherent value of animals.

The remaining chapters in Section Two focus on individual films, beginning with Lorena Elke Dobbie's discussion of the documentary *The Ghosts in Our Machine*, a film on which she worked and is credited as Research Consultant. This chapter takes the form of a personal account of her life as an activist and her work on the film interwoven with reflections on theorisations of haunting, its relationship to emotion, grievability and where we might find the possibility of change. Elke applies these ideas to her own analysis of *The Ghosts in Our Machine* and explains how they influenced the making of the film and her own animal rights activist journey. The chapter deals with the experience of growing up and witnessing animal deaths as a child, the impact of the work of Avery Gordon, Sara Ahmed and José Esteban

Muñoz on her thinking about social movements, bearing witness and involvement in the Toronto Save Movement, and her work on *The Ghosts in Our Machine* with filmmaker Liz Marshall. Elke's chapter considers the inclusion of imagery of animal abuse, its impact on the viewer, the choices that can be made in a film, and how such imagery is dealt with in *The Ghosts in Our Machine*. In her chapter, Elke calls for diversification in the animal rights movement, arguing that the movement reproduces gaps of experience and creates silenced presences, all of which affect marginalised communities, including nonhuman animals. This chapter offers a highly personal and in-depth account of activism, education and filmmaking.

Lara Herring's chapter (Chapter 7) turns again to fiction films and asks what they can say about animal activism when read from a critical animal studies perspective. Taking the 2012 film *Cloud Atlas* as her example, Herring explores the film's implicit critique of carnism, drawing out the connections between the animal-industrial complex and the film's broader themes of cannibalism, slavery and exploitation. Informed by the work of Carol J. Adams, Herring contends that *Cloud Atlas*' depiction of human slavery, exploitation and liberation functions as a commentary on animal liberation and, in doing so, can be re-read as an activist text. In her analysis, Herring examines how the depiction of the lives of the "fabricant" characters mirrors those of the realities of industrially farmed animals. She identifies how the film handles species hierarchies and the rights of one sentient being to kill another with impunity. The chapter offers a thorough and detailed analysis of the film, drawing out the parallels between the depicted slaughter of the fabricants and the operations of commercial slaughterhouses and the practices of animal liberation and activism. It traces one fabricant's journey to being recognised as an "individual" and the revolution that resulted. In the chapter's conclusion, Herring argues that fiction film offers important opportunities for multiple readings and, in doing so, films can be re-read through an activist frame.

In Chapter 8, Debra Merskin and Carrie Freeman focus on the lessons that can be learned from the "*Blackfish* effect"; *Blackfish* is a documentary film about an orca named Tilikum that mobilised action among its audiences and resulted in severe economic and reputational damage to SeaWorld Orlando, Florida. Merskin and Freeman regard the outcomes of the film as an "animal advocacy phenomenon" and employ a critical animal and media studies lens to examine the factors that led to *Blackfish*'s success, its results, and whether there is a formula that can be drawn upon to inform future activism and filmmaking. *Blackfish* was made with a very small budget and employed fairly standard documentary conventions. What, then, Merskin and Freeman ask, made this film achieve such impact among audiences? The chapter applies accumulation theory to the *Blackfish* case study to explore the film's cultural momentum. In this case, the authors demonstrate the effect of a message that is told consistently and corroborated across media forms and propose that the film's success must be understood within a broader social and cultural context that takes account of the media landscape and public opinion at the time. From this analysis, Merskin and Freeman propose a series of recommendations and strategic tools for activists and filmmakers.

Chapter 9 is an interview with Liz Marshall, the award-winning filmmaker responsible for the influential *The Ghosts in Our Machine* (2012), *Midian Farm* (2018) and more recently *Meat the Future* (2020). In the interview, Marshall explains how and why she became a filmmaker and what inspired her commitment to social justice issues. The interview explores her identification as a filmmaker and an activist and the path that led to her making *The Ghosts in Our Machine*. The director reveals how she approaches filmmaking, discussing style, storytelling techniques and narrative choices and her motivations for focusing on particular stories and issues. The interview delves into the making of *Meat the Future* and offers a fascinating insight into the challenges faced, the reason behind certain directorial choices and techniques, and how Moby and Jane Goodall came to be involved in the project. Marshall offers a vital and valuable voice to the volume, giving her perspective as a filmmaker and activist.

The interview closes the second section of the book, and the third section moves to a focus on celebrity activism. Elizabeth Cherry's chapter (Chapter 10) asks what animal activists think of celebrity activists and how the utility of celebrity support differs in different cultures. Using data from in-depth interviews and nearly three years of participant observations with activists in France and the United States, Cherry's chapter examines the differences in media strategies and the extent to which they employ or pursue celebrity endorsement. Cherry argues that celebrities are a cultural tool that can either be deployed or not deployed to serve different purposes and bring public attention to issues. The chapter finds themes emerging from US activists, including the positive view that celebrities can make veganism "hip" and provide opportunities for the promotion of activism, but this was countered by concerns that celebrities can distract from the issue and in some situations can pose a reputational risk. French activists also thought celebrities could be used to promote animal activism and veganism but did not follow this route due to a variety of reasons including the concern that the bad behaviour of celebrities would become associated with animal rights issues. Cherry examines what the differences in activists' attitudes towards celebrities mean for their tactical "toolkits" and concludes with important insights into the question of appropriate tactics for different cultural contexts.

Brett Mills' chapter (Chapter 11) on celebrity chef activism focuses on a series of UK television "Food Fight" programs that campaigned for better animal welfare and featured Hugh Fearnley-Whittingstall, Jamie Oliver and Gordon Ramsay. Chefs are conduits through which debates about the morality of food systems can take place, acting as cultural and political intermediaries who are influential in the construction of categories of ethical and unethical consumption. Mills' chapter examines critically the issues surrounding the campaigns, which all called for better treatment of animals used in food production but did not question their systemic exploitation, slaughter and consumption. Mills argues that the programs and campaigns offered opportunities to promote veganism as a viable option, but in preserving the anthropocentric norms of animal consumption, the advancement of animal welfare in these programs, which invited audience outrage and disgust, offered only solutions that function to soften audience anger rather than make any real material changes to the lives of animals. The chapter concludes by placing the programs in historical context and compares their utilisation of shock and disgust with the tactics of contemporary vegan chefs who promote vegan practices as an identity-based lifestyle.

In Chapter 12, Toby Miller begins with an examination of how the industrial infrastructure of Hollywood is involved in the construction of the celebrity as "activist" and the wider context of environmental damage that is wrought by the film industry and the industry's engagement in "green" activities. The later focus of the chapter is on Pamela Anderson's relationship with PETA, which Miller situates within an environmental theories framework. Miller argues that consumerism is at the centre of PETA's narrative, pointing to the promotion of healthy vegan diets and cruelty-free shopping and the work that the organisation does with fast-food outlets and fashion brands. The companies that PETA endorses remain concerned with a relentless drive for profits and reputational capital that requires degrees of moral legitimacy. As a result, Miller argues, PETA is part of the neoliberal promotion of consumerism and vulnerable to co-optation by the business interests it seeks to influence. The chapter examines Pamela Anderson's association with PETA and the critical reception of PETA campaigns that feature the celebrity. Miller notes the longstanding critique of the racialised class structures of animal rights organisations and ecofeminist responses to the animalisation of women in advertising. Differing responses to Anderson's PETA campaigns illustrate the struggle for meaning that exists more broadly in relation to the use of celebrity bodies for activism. It is in this space that PETA occupies, Miller argues, where polysemic campaign strategies catch women in a set of contradictory meanings.

The media reaction to Joaquin Phoenix's Academy Awards 2020 speech is the topic of Loredana Loy's essay, the penultimate chapter in the volume. The Oscar ceremonies have long been used as a platform for celebrities to promote causes and social issues, notably Marlon Brando's refusal of the Best Actor Award delivered at the event by Native American activist Sacheen Littlefeather in 1973; Vanessa Redgrave's speech in defence of the Palestinian Liberation Organization in 1978; and more recently Leonardo DiCaprio's environmental message in his 2016 acceptance speech for Best Actor. In this chapter, Loy examines how the US media used Phoenix's speech for its news value and for its promotion of animal interests, and questions media industry personnel's responses to its critique of speciesism. The chapter explores the wider significance of the speech in which the actor explains that he is, by virtue of his position, obligated to be a "voice for the voiceless". Loy's chapter analyses the speech in detail and maps the responses from the liberal and conservative US media. Loy is interested in media ecologies, and in this case concludes that Phoenix's speech is taken up by an ecosystem that ultimately legitimates and promotes speciesism. The chapter concludes with a call for further research to explore how liberal and conservative audiences received the speech and the reactions of animal rights groups and proposes that such research would provide useful insights for the animal rights movement.

The volume closes with Eva Haifa Giraud's chapter, which draws on the concept of media ecologies to frame a case study of the actor James Cromwell, who is best known for the role of Farmer Hoggett in the 1995 film *Babe*. Giraud's analysis utilises media articles, films, interviews and web-based content to trace the different but connected expressions of vegan politics that are related to Cromwell's celebrity. The chapter explores the utility of understanding celebrity activism in media ecological terms, arguing that this provides a framework for considering the relationship between textual content and the platform of dissemination. Contextualising the analysis of Cromwell's celebrity, the chapter provides an overview of animal biographies, more specifically those that relate to pigs. Giraud argues that *Babe* is culturally significant as a text that disrupts the normalised narrative of pigs as food animals, although she points to the limitations of the political efficacy of the text long term. Fictional portrayals may play a role in awareness-raising, but such narratives do not develop into more sophisticated narratives that critique the systems of production for fear of alienating commercial audiences. Cromwell's celebrity activism does, Giraud argues, offer potential routes into navigating the popular terrain without sacrificing critiques of human–animal relations. Ecological approaches are, the chapter proposes, especially useful to identify how these more radical narratives can emerge.

Taken together, the chapters in this volume offer a close examination of the relationships between film and television industries and animal activism in the 21st century. Throughout the book, the authors offer valuable insights and arguments for tactics, tools, approaches and strategies that we believe have the potential to inform and benefit future academic work, media production, campaigns and activism.

Part One

Representations of animal activism

1

Animal rights activism is (not) a crime

Portraying violence and the animal rights agenda in German, American and British TV crime series (c. 1990–2010)

Mieke Roscher

Introduction

Already in the 1980s, animal rights activism was routinely used as a setting for dramatic storytelling in British entertainment TV shows. Crime fiction television in particular has seemed to not focus on the violence against animals but instead paint a picture of an irrational mob of animal lovers gone wild, more often than not linked to one pathological-minded killer.[1] As such, the topics presented in these shows did not mirror the discussion on the rights of animals per se, but rather focused on the alleged crimes of those who claimed to protect them. From the 1990s onwards, practices of cultural transfer brought such formats to audiences both in continental Europe and North America, where an animal liberation movement had also formed – albeit with quite different overall media attention. Inspired by concepts of cultural transfer analysis, this chapter will show how, from the 1990s forward, certain elements of how British animal rights activists were

1 Gold 1995.

portrayed did find their way to other cultural formats. However, animal liberation on the Continent did not evolve from a longstanding interest in animal welfare, but mainly from ideas communicated via the media. Therefore, it will be of interest to see how this played out in crime fiction formats.

But why look at crime fiction TV? "Stories about crime and law enforcement", as Chris Greer and Robert Reiner discuss, "have saturated television ever since it became the leading broadcasting medium in the 1950s".[2] They claim that at least 25 per cent of the most popular prime-time TV shows have been crime or police series. It should come as no surprise, then, that topics such as animal rights and animal liberation were absorbed as possible settings for this genre as they were routinely being taken up by the press.

Furthermore, as Margaret Rogers argues, the television police genre, as a special subcategory of the genre of crime fiction, is influenced by issues of historical moment, national attributes and cultural contexts.[3] John Tulloch, in turn, claims that this is shaped by national rather than global discourses.[4] So, in order to get a glimpse of how specific topics have determined the cultural discourse on animal liberation at a given time, one can look at fictional TV programs, even if this discourse, at first glance, seems to be somewhat specific.

In her analysis of translating crime fiction books, Karen Seago puts it this way:

> Crime and criminals are indicators of what a particular culture views as legitimate and crime fiction functions as a barometer of a society's values and morals reflecting and interrogating what is inscribed as crime. The central engagement with what, who and why a particular behaviour or action is deemed deviant gives insight into structures and ideologies of power and is indicative of cultural and social anxieties at a particular time in a particular culture.[5]

---

2 Greer and Reiner 2012; for a good overview on the research on the fictional representation of policing, see Colbran 2014, 8–20.

3 Rogers 2008, 78.

4 Tulloch 2000, 33–55.

5 Seago 2014, 2.

However, as I will show, there are certain aspects that were transported via cultural exchanges that do reflect globalised themes. Thus, Rogers' refinement of Tulloch's argument is more accurate. She writes that television police series share universal concerns regarding law and order and crime and punishment but that these concerns are then articulated through discourses shaped by national rather than global contexts. It is through familiarity with these discourses that these crime series are, if not universally, at least partially understood.[6] Crime fiction, furthermore, communicates via clear moral codes in which the culprit is (mostly) marked as evil and the police as good. Although such black-and-white dichotomies have in recent years been abandoned for a more realistic picture of police work, they still attend to a plot structure that tries to avoid contingency. It is, thus, the personalised communicative net of perpetrators and victims, witnesses and investigators at the heart of TV crime fiction that allows for this avoidance of vagueness and the interplay between stereotypes and innovation, clichés and variation, consistency and change.[7] In TV formats in particular, as criminologist Richard Sparks argues further, the common narratives are based on respectability, vice or threat.[8] Because threat is a narrative tool that allows producers to prolong the story's dramatic arc, it is the one mostly chosen for TV entertainment. Crime, the "most popular consumer products of our times",[9] as Moira Peelo and Keith Soothill have dubbed it, therefore was at the centre of most fictional portrayals of animal rights activists. As such, what we see in crime fiction is not so much a total distortion of reality but rather a (politicised) program that further provokes the argument of a debate that relies on at least a certain level of authenticity.[10] TV crime fiction series, which will be looked at in this chapter, thereby take on the role of popularising and normalising the (political) workings of a certain society at a given time by communicating knowledge on certain topics such as animal rights by reducing complexities and by defining

6 Rogers 2008, 82.
7 Bleicher 2014, 93.
8 Sparks 1995, 52.
9 Peelo and Soothill 2013, 35.
10 Colbran 2014, 3–5.

what is doable and sayable in mainstream discourses.[11] This chapter follows this development over roughly a 20-year period and argues that media negations and portrayals were necessary for the cultural shift that took place after the 2010s, even though they tended to be largely biased against the animal rights agenda. Starting with the 1990s, where the trope of animal liberation had reached many other countries besides Britain, this chapter looks at the portrayal of both humans and animals but concentrates on the portrayal of the animal rights activists. As the period after 2010 is characterised by an increasingly diversified media fiction market, where streaming services and a multitude of TV stations compete against one another for a more diversified audience, my analysis ends there.

By taking a cultural historical approach that identifies the different national discourses and tropes on violence and animal rights activism and regards them as both mirroring and producing historical realities, this chapter aims to identify the cross- and transcultural developments. Using the method of close contextualised reading of distinct episodes of the TV shows *The Bill* (UK), *Law & Order* (USA) and *Tatort* and *Polizeiruf 110* (Germany) that make animal rights activism the focal point of their plot, these discourses are then systematised in order to identify key elements of the cultural narration of violence and crime. These shows were chosen because, first, they were long-running shows that covered the whole period discussed in this chapter, and second, they focus on police and police work, not on other forms of crime settings such as the private investigator genre. This way, it is hoped that the distinct elements of cultural embeddedness can be extracted.

Preparing the stage: Animal liberation and the media backlash

Before looking at how animal liberation was portrayed in particular TV series after the 1990s, it is imperative to examine the specific cultural-political basis. This started in Great Britain. With animal liberation activities making headlines there from the early 1970s, the news media at first reacted rather positively. They portrayed animal

11 Hißnauer 2018, 364.

liberationists as dedicated animal lovers akin to other freedom fighters. Before 1986 especially, as Steve Baker points out, the hooded figure clutching a nonhuman animal to be liberated was seen as some kind of "heroic lone ranger" whose intention was to do good.[12] Some activists freed animals from their cages, while others just brought their cameras. Pictures of animals with screws and electrodes in their heads, skinned alive and imprisoned in small cages engendered fears of an unleashed scientific community.

But after some activists in Great Britain had taken to sending letter bombs to presumed animal abusers and placing incendiary devices in fur shops and the like, a radical shift took place in the British media. In 1984, Animal Liberation Front (ALF) activists threatened to have adulterated and poisoned Mars candy bars. They aimed to force the company to stop animal experiments. It was the Mars Bars hoax, especially, that led the media to draw another picture altogether, one that associated animal liberationists not with unsung heroes but with IRA bombers,[13] and defined them as terrorists.[14] What was striking here, however, was that this shift included almost all topics related to the freeing of animals, regardless of whether activists used violent techniques or labelled themselves as following radical agendas. The media no longer differentiated between animal lovers, animal liberationists or even common criminals. Just aligning oneself with the idea of animal rights was enough to be put in the corner of militancy and terror.[15]

This is in line with the portrayal of other political causes, where "politically subversive behaviours are depoliticised and assimilated to routine crime: both are portrayed as pathological conditions unrelated to wider social structures".[16] Of course, this is a hegemonic analysis of the news media, but I would argue that in terms of animal rights there is good reason to believe that, from the 1980s forward, there was a quite

12 Baker 1993, 196.
13 Baker 1993, 198.
14 Kew 2003, 30.
15 Roscher 2009.
16 Greer and Reiner 2012.

undifferentiated picture of animal rights, at least in the British news media.

Animal liberationists were portrayed as some kind of dangerous human-hating outlaw. All in all, what was being conveyed was what Stanley Cohen has famously defined as a moral panic. When "a condition, episode, person or group of persons emerges to become defined as a threat to societal values and interests", as Cohen has laid out, society is prone to becoming subject to a moral panic.[17] While the issues identified may be real, the claims are usually exaggerated and paint a picture of inevitable harm. Such images conveyed by mass media furthermore tend to create a typification of the deviant that contrasts with the normal, the normal here being the animal-using consensus.[18] Christopher Rootes, in his media analysis of environmental action in the 1980s, has also concluded that it was entirely dominated by the animal rights debate, although not focused on substance but rather on the alleged militancy. The reason he gives for this is striking: As those stories sold newspapers, they were used in spite of the fact that they only accounted for a few and rare instances in the spectrum of animal rights related activities, thus creating a very distorted image of reality.[19] But by only relying on depicting the action and not the rationale behind the action, the media was able to build on a scenario of danger that focused on animal liberation as a movement.

As Clare Molloy points out, more nuanced:

> animal activists received mixed press, with sympathetic reporting on early forms of direct action which was soon replaced by stereotypes and moral panics about deviant activities in the 1980s and labelled as terrorist practices after 9/11.[20]

She goes on to say that "often the characters are stereotyped as young, misinformed, angry, aggressive, sometimes insane".[21] And while I do

17 Cohen 1987, 9.
18 Kew 1999, 177; Sparks 1995, 51.
19 Rootes 2000, 38.
20 Molloy 2011, 18.
21 Molloy 2011, 38.

agree with these characterisations, I find that they are historically specific and can be narrowed down using a genealogical approach.

Setting the scene: British crime drama and animal liberation

It was the scenario of danger that was, as mentioned above, picked up by television more generally and by crime drama specifically. This is important insofar as there is a high percentage among the audience of such formats that "saw media fiction as a crucial source" about crime and policing.[22] Conversely, writers of such shows were equally influenced by (tabloid) newspapers as by the police themselves, who often worked as liaisons or advisers for the shows.[23] As Mark Gold specifies, in these shows:

> animal rights activists are usually portrayed as humourless, people hating, sexless anarchists who turn to caring about animals as a result of some inadequacy which leaves them unable to cope with people.[24]

This means that the themes presented must have been the result of both the police reporting and what the writers gathered from the headlines. Gold gives several examples from the late 1980s and early 1990s to support this observation, among them the popular ITV police drama series *The Bill*.

The Bill was the longest-running police procedural television series in the UK and ran from 1983 until 2010. Set in a fictional police station, Sun Hill, in South London, it showed the work of both uniformed and Criminal Investigation Department (CID) officers. In its first 15 years, its episodes did not tell an ongoing story but rather concluded themes that could be understood without ever having watched any other episode. This was achieved mainly by focusing on the day-to-day police work and not on the characters. Animal liberation seemed to

22 Greer and Reiner 2012, 34.
23 Colbran 2014, 78.
24 Gold 1995, 24.

have been one part of this everyday work. In an episode from 1991 titled "Cause and Effect", the officers attend a break-in at an animal testing research centre and make an arrest of a fully masked assailant in camouflage clothing, who turns out to be activist Josie Madden. At first it appears that only some paperwork has been stolen, until a member of the centre's staff is found bludgeoned on the floor. The police officers furthermore find out that a lab technician has been abducted by Josie's fellow activists, who then threaten to kill the technician should the animals not be released. When they check up on prior police records, they find nothing on the "national index" about Josie, referencing here the Animal Rights National Index established in 1986 to combat the movement. Much of the episode is dedicated to the interrogation of Josie by DI Frank Burnside, during which she calls her engagements "direct action", to which Burnside replies: "No, it is terrorism." Her explanations of equal value of animals and people fall on deaf ears. Later, and contradicting herself, she welcomes the death of vivisectors. Another telling feature is the police insistence in this episode that not only anarchists are involved in animal liberation but also the extreme right. Characterising animal rights as a fringe issue of the political extremes was a trademark of the British discourse especially.

In the 2002 episode "Protection", officers are called to a rally outside a research laboratory involving a group of pro-life activists protesting the use of foetal stem cells. The leader of the group Pro-Ethics, Ben Fletcher, is introduced as a "career-activist" who "used to be animal rights". When a bomb explodes under the car of the head of research, Peter Allen, that kills his wife, Fletcher becomes the primary suspect. What is narrated here is that the causes are interchangeable and that an anti-science position goes hand in hand with misanthropy. As it later turns out, it was Allen himself who planted the bomb, hoping to cash in his wife's life insurance money to help save his bankrupt laboratory.

Of course, all this falls back to the assumption that TV crime fiction must rely on crude stereotyping in order for roles to be immediately identifiable to the audience. This is achieved either through iconography – the visual elements of an individual identity, such as clothes, physical characteristics, social settings, material objects and so on – or by particular behaviour patterns such as violence, disloyalty, cowardice and irrationality.[25] Already in 1983, media studies scholar Philip Schlesinger and his colleagues had shown how in British television, political opponents of the state are often depicted as irrational and pathologically criminal terrorists, and the state itself becomes the saviour from harm, a narrative through which repressive action by the state is largely legitimised.[26] The media representation of the Animal Liberation Front and other such groups as terrorists was also a tool to practically ignore or even omit their historical evolution. A simplification of the animal rights agenda was the result of such a mischaracterisation that effectively turned the goals of the liberationists upside down.[27] As Schlesinger, Murdock and Elliott point out, the terrorism (or extremism) terminology helped to delegitimise any political or ideological goals of the whole movement. To be portrayed as an animal-loving activist in the British media context could thus be helpful until roughly the early to mid-1980s. After that, animal rights ideology was mostly read as one thing and one thing only: pure fanaticism. As Schlesinger, Murdock and Elliott have also analysed, the fictional media's definition of terrorism frequently followed inputs provided by the government. These, however, did not necessarily align with the law or the judicial interpretation of the law.[28]

In everyday mass media discourses, the terrorism label was passed on uncritically and, in turn, produced a version of reality that benefited those in power.[29] The same was also true for violence, as Schlesinger explains. As a flexible term, it helped to create a clear-cut definition of what passed as "legitimate" protest. Concurrently, the media's fixation on the "violent society", he goes on to say, made it easy to paint utterly different activities with utterly different ideological backgrounds with the same brush and to not only conflate terrorism with violence but equate it with different forms of political struggles.[30] More often than not, it was the IRA that was used as a stand-in for terrorism per se, only to be replaced by Islamic fundamentalism after the turn of the century.

25 Hurd 1981, 58.
26 Schlesinger, Murdock and Elliott 1986, 279.
27 Schlesinger, Murdock and Elliott 1983, 3.
28 Schlesinger, Murdock and Elliott 1983, 53.
29 Schlesinger 1991, 78.
30 Schlesinger 1991, 36.

A notable change in this clear-cut narration is presented in an episode called "Beasts", first aired in 2000. In it, PC Sam Harker infiltrates a group of animal rights activists whose leader, Ged Mannings, is suspected by Special Branch of planning a terrorist attack. Harker takes part in vigils, direct action and animal liberation actions at an abattoir, freeing some pigs. He begins to sympathise with the cause and defends some of the activities, even in front of his colleagues at the police station. At this point, he discovers Mannings' plan to firebomb a local department store that sells fur coats. His supervisors tell him to "push harder" in order to get evidence admissible before a court so they can arrest the group. They manage to catch the activists red-handed, planting incendiary devices in the store. In the end, however, they need to let them go because of a recording that documents Harker's active involvement in the planning of prior activities, making him some kind of agent provocateur. When released, Mannings stops to whisper in Harker's ear that he is a "dead man". So, while this means that generally a sense for the righteousness of the cause is communicated by Harker as well as the female activists in the group, the others are portrayed as dangerous criminals. However, the fact that animals are shown up-close and that their plight is discussed much more thoroughly marks a transitional change in the series' make-up. No longer an "absent referent",[31] the animals now are an object of sympathy that is used to explain Harker's emotional struggle.

The fight against the fur trade is also the theme of a 2007 episode called "A Model Murder". In the episode, detectives Kapoor and Stamp discover the body of a supermodel who had recently fronted an anti-fur campaign despite her lack of real conviction. What they note is that the crime scene had been arranged to resemble a shot from the campaign footage, suggesting animal rights activists may have resented her hypocrisy, only to find out later that a stalker had killed her.

Another notable narration revolves around the concept of class. In a 1997 episode titled "Animals", detectives Ackland and Blake, with the help of the RSPCA, rescue dogs abused in illegal dog fights. In an all too familiar manner, this episode aligns itself to the narration of the criminal working-class poor as the main culprits of animal abuse.[32]

31 Adams 2000.

Here, the police take on the role of the respectable class that, in unison with the even more respectable RSPCA with its bourgeois roots, take on the animal abusers. As Ben Lamb writes, *The Bill* was not interested in showing a benevolent police force that aims at easing class tensions.[33] Instead, what we see is a picture of a rather brutal lower class that is guided by a moral middle class (the police, RSPCA) or attacked by a misguided middle class (animal rights activists); a class that is also prone to commit not only crimes but acts of terror.

Animal liberation is a crime: The American way

The spectre of terrorism also revealed itself in the discussions about animal liberation in the United States. The ALF and other such groups were here, however, firmly placed on the left of the political spectrum, even if only as a single-issue movement.[34] From 1992 onwards, the American ALF was listed on the FBI's top ten list of domestic terrorist groups, with a first mention in 1987.[35] In 2001, this categorisation was reinforced with the passing of the *USA PATRIOT Act*, which was the result of the September 11 attack on the World Trade Center in New York. The new definition of terrorism included violence against property. Finally, the 2006 *Animal Enterprise Terrorism Act* regarded the threat of violence against any business connected with the use of animals as an act of terrorism.

These discourses about the criminality of animal liberation were picked up by the crime drama series *Law & Order*, which premiered on NBC in 1990 and ran until 2010. As an "important part of American culture", TV cop shows, as Roger Sabin writes, "tell us about our attitudes to crime" and, what is more, the complex "social contract" that exists between state and citizen.[36] In the United States, he goes on to say, they perform cultural work that is mostly aligned to a politically

32 Kean 1998.
33 Lamb 2020, 87.
34 Martin 2003, 327; Bai 1997.
35 Gale Research Inc. 2006, 131.
36 Sabin 2015, 1.

conservative outlook.[37] Although *Law & Order* did air episodes that featured topics of political controversy and introduced characters that were thinking and speaking outside the mainstream, the general format of a, at times, semi-documentary style exaggerated the seriousness of the crime.[38] The series is set in New York and narrates two things: the investigation of a crime by police detectives and the prosecution of the suspects in court. The series aims to portray real cases that made headlines, although they might have taken place elsewhere or with a different set-up. In a 1993 episode titled "Animal Instinct", a genetics researcher is found murdered in her vandalised laboratory at the Manhattan Institute, rats running loose all over the place, leaving the inspectors to believe a militant animal rights group was responsible for the killing. They arrest the leader of an underground group calling itself the Animal Rights Crusade, finding suspicious material like *The Anarchist Cookbook* and a lot of cats in his apartment. When he can offer a solid alibi, they have to let him go, although Detective Logan continues to refer to him as a lunatic. The detectives then discover that the culprit is the dead woman's husband's potential lover. With regard to language and stereotyping, the episode seems to have followed the blueprint provided by British TV.

In the 2001 episode "Whose Monkey Is It Anyway?" there is an almost identical first scene. This time the detectives are called to a research institute, where a biotechnician has died due to an anaphylactic shock after being bitten by an ape. This was after 17 monkeys, eight of them infected with a strain of Simian immunodeficiency virus, were freed from their cages. The detectives again speculate about a group of militant animal rights activists, this time All Living Creatures United, being behind the attack, but also acknowledge that since a person has died, they might not be willing to claim the attack. When the detectives narrow down their list of suspects, they settle on Barry Pratt, who has a history of assault and burglary, and then Maxine Walden, a dedicated activist who had started a friendship/romance with the security guard, George Peavy, who later confesses to having freed the monkeys and to having placed them in

37 Sabin 2015, 8.
38 Faucette 2015, 120–1.

an animal rescue centre. The following court proceedings are then, contrary to all other crime series discussed here, a presentation of arguments about why animals deserve rights. They are brought forward by an animal rights law attorney and a philosopher as expert witnesses. The defendant is portrayed as a caring human being. The resulting guilty verdict is described by the prosecution as the natural dominion of mankind having been restored, but it is an argument even his colleagues don't seem to accept.

What is apparent here is that, in contrast to *The Bill*, matters of class are not addressed nor is terrorism ever mentioned. At the same time, pictures of vigils and break-ins are presented that are very similar to those seen in British TV crime shows. However, the animals shown in *Law & Order* are clearly only there for content and are more likely portrayed as a danger themselves. The focus therefore is on the criminality of the acts. It is repeatedly stressed that there is no place for morality in the law. What is, of course, interesting is that no episodes with animal rights content were filmed after the passing of the drastic bills mentioned above, making the American case somewhat inconclusive.

German animal liberation: Same, same … but different

The same cannot be said for the German situation, where the history of the animal liberation movement seemed to mirror that in the United States. In 1983, there was an attack on the animal laboratory of the Free University of Berlin, an attack for which activist Andreas Wolff was charged. After confessing, he was granted parole having spent six months on remand. In front of the press, he claimed that it was the actions of the British ALF that served as an inspiration. As the news magazine *Der Spiegel* wrote, animal liberationists across the Federal Republic were in awe of what they saw playing out in the UK.[39] Similar accounts are delivered from the US.[40] Although planting incendiary devices and pursuing other acts of sabotage remained a rare feature of German animal rights activism, it was the German media reporting

39 *Der Spiegel* 1984, 55.
40 Finsen and Finsen 1994.

on British activism that led to the adoption of the name *Tierbefreiungsfront*.[41] The accusation of terrorism was not, however, a common feature of the discourse but rather adopted by more mainstream animal welfare organisations who feared for their own reputations.[42]

In a way, this sentiment was echoed by German TV crime drama series, the most popular of which, *Tatort*,[43] first aired an episode discussing animal suffering and animal rights in 1991. *Tatort* at this time had established itself as the most popular German crime fiction show and had, from the mid-1980s onwards, undergone "a thematic turn to topics of current political relevance".[44] As it is also the longest-running series on German television, having first aired in 1970 and still being produced, it gives a glimpse into the popular memory of German post-war culture.[45] Also, it is advertised by the ARD, the joint organisation of Germany's regional public service broadcasters, as a reflection of German society that also shows its potential development.[46] As such, the national specificity of German crime fiction is that "many basic constructions were replaced by new ones. Key concepts of the post-war period like authority, determination by conventions, conservative habit and so forth were destroyed by radical criticism."[47] Other than the shows in Britain and the US, the fact that *Tatort* runs on a public service broadcasting service, which made it much less dependent on commercial success and therefore more open to a broader kind of storytelling, must of course be considered.[48]

---

41 *Tierbefreiungsfront* is German for Animal Liberation Front.

42 Grasmüller 1985, 57.

43 *Tatort* (Crime Scene) is a television crime series that has been running continuously since 1970. Developed by the German public service broadcasting organisation ARD for their channel *Das Erste*, it is unique in its approach in that it is jointly produced by all of the organisation's regional stations, whereby every regional station contributes a number of episodes to a common pool.

44 Gräf 2010; Mattson 1999, 163.

45 Wenzel 2000, 7.

46 Hißnauer, Scherer and Stockinger 2014, 12.

47 Brück and Viehoff 1998, 9.

48 For the importance of commercial imperatives for *The Bill*, see Colbran 2014, 104–21.

What is strikingly different to what we have seen from the other programs discussed here is that it is also the animal rights activists who are targeted. In the 1991 episode titled "Animals", the two Munich detectives, Leitmayr and Batic, are investigating the death of a young female activist from the group Animals International. Only days before, she had approached the two urging them to explore a research facility of a cosmetic firm for which she used to work as a model and where cruel animal experiments were taking place. The investigators had informed her that the homicide division was not the right place and that she should try an animal welfare organisation. After the woman's death, the investigation leads them first to the "headquarters" of the activists, a flat share full of lazy hippies, then to the local media that had obtained and published some of the gruesome pictures, and finally to the head of the research facility, who is later convicted of the murder. Throughout the episode, the detectives serve as moral authorities, discussing the plight of animals in such institutions, watching and commenting on the material obtained by activists. However, those activists are at the same time depicted as hopeless and rather tragic figures and not as criminal masterminds, let alone terrorists. From their appearance, they do not resemble the stereotypical image of an animal liberationist; they are not masked up at any time during the break-ins, nor do they wear hoods. The message is clear: it is the state, represented here by the police, that should be relied on to right the wrongs perpetrated against animals.

In 2005, it was the *Tatort* investigators Starck and Ritter, a team from Berlin, who were to solve the next case involving animal rights as a topic. This episode, titled "Leiden wie ein Tier" ("Suffering Like an Animal"), appears to be more in line with a narration of the danger posed by animal liberationists. In an institute for experimental medicine called VIVITEST, the leading scientist is found dead on the dissection table of the animal pathology department. The cause of death at first remains a mystery, but there are some tubes and electrodes stuck in his outstretched body, reminding the viewer of well-known pictures of animals being experimented on. The professor's fiancée later states that there were always problems with animal rights activists. As a result, the professor's stepdaughter becomes a suspect as she is portrayed as a radical member of this scene and an outspoken critic of any kind of animal testing. Another suspect is a neighbour who had accused the professor of stealing his cat for animal experiments. Suspicions against the institute for experimenting with pets stolen from private individuals are reinforced when Starck's own neighbours' little dog disappears. Finally, a lab assistant is also thought to be a potential culprit as he has connections to the animal rights gang. After some twists and turns, it is revealed that it was the housekeeper who poisoned the professor because she wanted to secure the stepdaughter's inheritance, which would have been lost as a consequence of the marriage, a promise she had made to the girl's mother. The preparation on the dissection table was supposed to give him a taste of his own medicine. So even though the animal rights activists were not to blame, it is telling that not only are they the first suspects but animal rights are considered a potential lethal movement. However, given that other topics such as pet stealing and whistleblowing are addressed, a more nuanced picture of what the politics of animal liberation entailed in the new millennium is presented and is here following the *Tatort* trademark of "interweaving of the crime case with issues of social relevance".[49] Thus, *Tatort* tends to "focus on global themes and universal places"[50] while at the same time playing to a national audience with a focus on the regional.

The other popular German crime series, *Polizeiruf 110*, which was originally created in 1971 as a counterpart to *Tatort* by East German television and then, after reunification, integrated into the ARD, only took on animal rights as an issue well into the new millennium.[51] In contrast to *Tatort*, episodes of *Polizeiruf 110* were mainly situated in the country rather than the city.[52] Thus, it was not animal experiments but intensive farming that came into focus. In a 2009 episode titled "Schweineleben" ("Pigs' Life"), detectives Tellheim and Hinrichs of the Schwerin police department are investigating the death of a consultant to the animal rights organisation OINK that tries to stop the building of an animal feedlot for 100,000 pigs in the Mecklenburg lake district.

---

49 Eichner 2018, 182.

50 Eichner 2018, 174.

51 *Polizeiruf 110* (the title refers to the emergency telephone number of the German police) is a franchise similar to the *Tatort* series. Local members of the ARD produce their own episodes, which are aired by the ARD.

52 Guder and Wehn 1998, 19.

As it turns out, the consultant has had quite a history in the GDR's own ministry of agriculture and had then favoured intensive pig breeding. Therefore, pressured by the investor in the venture, a Dutch magnate, he had withdrawn his survey for OINK two weeks before it was due to be completed and one week before his death. That makes the animal rights activists, again represented by a fierce young woman, Irina Schramm, possible perpetrators. But here also there is much understanding for the causes that drive the activists. Indeed, one of the detectives, Hinrichs, a believer in organic farming, joins in the efforts to stop the building of the facility because he also has a love interest in Irina. In the end, it is a local business owner who was concerned about her newly opened spa-hotel suffering from an animal factory nearby who is responsible for the death of the consultant. The animal rights topic seems to be pushed to the side. The closing scene is particularly interesting, however. Here, Irina, defeated on the legal level (the site is being built), swears that she will liberate every single pig and then burn down the building. This statement is left undisputed by Hinrichs, who simply turns away so as to communicate that he is not with her in this deed.

Strikingly different to the British and American series are the gendered aspects communicated in the German series. Almost all activists in prominent roles are female. Some appear to be slightly irrational and thus playing to older tropes of the hysterical cat lover image that are common to portrayals of female activists.[53] Yet, they are also portrayed as very attractive and self-confident women and as the driving forces of their movements. This is remarkable insofar as crime series disproportionately present primarily higher-status, white, middle-aged males as offenders. In another episode of *Polizeiruf 110*, titled "Raubvögel" ("Birds of Prey"), which first aired in 2012, it is the dedicated ornithologist and director of a local nature conservation authority, Maria Wanka, who kills her estranged husband because he was trying to make use of her knowledge of the whereabouts of three nests of the highly endangered lesser spotted eagle in order to sell the eggs on the black market. Her violent behaviour is explained by the betrayal she suffered, not by an alleged fanatism for saving animal life.

53 Roscher 2011.

Only in the 2013 *Polizeiruf 110* episode titled "Wolfsland" ("Wolves Land") is the animal rights activist (and perpetrator) male. Stefan Waldner, who returns to his home in Brandenburg in order to save a newly settled wolf pack from local hunters and farmers, slays a local vet and violently attacks the father of his lover, who he catches in the middle of shooting the whole wolf pack in the hope of getting rid of both the troublesome animals and a potential son-in-law. It is the female detective Simon who prevents worse from happening, but who also characterises Waldner as being fanatically pro-animals and thus basically unfit for human society. She is thereby playing to the same accusations pitted against Anglo-American activists. This might, therefore, be regarded as a one-off narration given that later episodes of both *Tatort* and *Polizeiruf 110* have largely stuck to the theme of animal rights as a righteous cause. However, it does show that the transfer and adoption of themes across the English Channel were successful.

Conclusion

Cultural transfer must be understood as a varied exchange of material objects, information, symbols or meanings that are all based on multiple interpretations. Cultural exchange is, therefore, not the "circulation of objects and ideas as they already are, but their relentless reinterpretation, rethinking and re-signification".[54] This means that the ideas of animal rights and animal liberation as presented by the movement *and* the media were not the same but were reinterpreted according to situational contexts. As could be seen, these reinterpretations relied on different political backgrounds.

Formats such as those used in *Tatort* or *Polizeiruf 110* were adopting tropes such as violent break-ins into laboratories, lethal threats to animal abusers or vigils already familiar to British consumers. However, they also dared to look at the laboratory itself, thereby also portraying the second layer of violence, the one against animals. Even in the early episodes aired in the 1990s, there is no moral panic communicated; animal liberationists are not depicted as a threat to

54 Yakushenko 2014.

society. This is also true for the American context, where the philosophy behind animal rights is shown in much more detail while at the same time blaming the activists for their action, thus putting them in the same category as common criminals. As such, a general shift after 2000 towards also including the animal in the narration aligns with a more general trend in crime TV away from concentrating on law enforcement to focusing more on the victim of the crime.[55] How much room there was left for the depiction of the suffering animal varied significantly, though. The reason why the German series stood out could thus also be based on the fact that the length of each episode was 90 minutes, compared to *Law & Order*'s 40–48 minutes and *The Bill*'s 30–60. Despite this, it is still fair to say that a standard categorisation of animal rights constituting moral panics needs to be redefined, and there has been, of course, quite substantial criticism of Cohen's initial framework. This criticism highlights that those panics are very time specific and rely on a corresponding narration by the media *and* state actors.[56] To say that the output of the media invariably supports the status quo is, then, as Colbran rightly states, perhaps a bit simplistic.[57]

In essence, this means that even though animal liberation had become a global concept, the shows painted a picture of the different societal consequences of engaging in animal rights. The usual trope of a male perpetrator was enforced by British crime series, something that was not necessarily invoked on German television where the notion of animal activism as a largely female cause seemed to have struck a chord, probably at least to some degree also because the female activists made for good narrative pairings with the male detectives. When it comes to class, there are similar observations to be made.

A 2014 episode of the British series *Lewis* (2006–2015) titled "Entry Wounds" begins with an arson attack on a hunting lodge and apparent threats against a neurosurgeon, who is later found shot dead. One of (many) potential suspects is a young animal rights activist who is said to be the leader of the Oxford-based group Animal Rights Brigade. However, none of the usual defamatory accusations of lunacy

55 Colbran 2014, 18.
56 Marsh and Melville 2019, 24.
57 Colbran 2014, 24.

and misanthropy are directed against her. Quite the contrary. She is portrayed as a caring, if a bit naive, young woman and animal rights is portrayed as a multifaceted movement. However, classism seems to have passed the test of time as, again, university students are marked as the foreseeable go-to when it comes to identifying the activists, with Oxford being their natural breeding ground. That animal rights are a middle-class issue is widely proven, so the fact that also on German TV students are thought to be perpetrators in the 1991 episode of *Tatort* is not necessarily a surprise. It is the fact that class is made an issue that makes the British case stand out.

It can thus be concluded that there are globally recognisable tropes when it comes to using animal liberation as a setting for crime fiction and that these are used widely among the shows looked at in this chapter. It was demonstrated that these shows are embedded in other categorical cultural and societal tropes of class and gender and that they meander between seeing animal liberation as terrorism, crime or a moral expression of helplessness. The place of the animals in these shows is, however, rather off than on screen, because even if they are shown, they still serve more or less as “absent referents”. They might be victims, but they are not victims of the crime.

References

Adams, Carol J. (2000). *The Sexual Politics of Meat: A Feminist-Vegetarian Critical Theory*. Tenth Anniversary Edition, New York: Continuum.

Bai, Matt (1997). Breaking the cages. *Newsweek*, 29 September.

Baker, Steve (1993). *Picturing the Beast: Animals, Identity, and Representation*. Manchester: Manchester University Press.

Bleicher, Joan Kristin (2014). Der Tatort als Spiegel gesellschaftlicher Entwicklungen am Beispiel der Veränderung von Täterprofilen. In Christian Hißnauer, Stefan Scherer and Claudia Stockinger, eds. *Zwischen Serie und Werk: Fernseh- und Gesellschaftsgeschichte im Tatort*, 89–108. Bielefeld: transcript Verlag.

Brück, Ingrid and Reinhold Viehoff (1998). Crime genre and television. From *Stahlnetz* to *Tatort*: a realistic tradition. In Reinhold Viehoff, ed. *Stahlnetz,*

Tatort, Polizeiruf 110: Transitions in German Police Series, 3–11. HALMA 8. Halle: Universität Halle.

Cohen, Stanley (1987). *Folk Devils and Moral Panics: The Creation of the Mods and Rockers*. Oxford: Blackwell.

Colbran, Marianne (2014). *Media Representations of Police and Crime: Shaping the Police Television Drama*. New York: Palgrave Macmillan.

Der Spiegel (1984). *Grüne Zelle Lurch*, 10, 55.

Eichner, Susanne (2018). Crime scene Germany. In Kim Toft Hansen, Steven Peacock and Sue Turnbull, eds. *European Television Crime Drama and Beyond*, 173–92. Cham: Palgrave Macmillan.

Faucette, Brian (2015). *Law & Order* (NBC, 1990–2010). In Roger Sabin, Ronald Wilson and Linda Speidel, eds. *Cop Shows: A Critical History of Police Dramas on Television*, 116–23. Jefferson, NC: McFarland.

Finsen, Susan and Lawrence Finsen (1994). *The Animal Rights Movement in America: From Compassion to Respect*. New York: Twayne Publishers.

Gale Research Inc. (2006). *Extremist Groups: Information for Students*. Detroit: Thomson Gale.

Gold, Mark (1995). *Animal Rights: Extending the Circle of Compassion*. Oxford: Jon Carpenter.

Gräf, Dennis (2010). *TATORT: Ein populäres Medium als kultureller Speicher*. Marburg: Schüren.

Grasmüller, Andreas (1985). *Tierschutz-Terrorismus? Du und das Tier* 4, 57.

Greer, Chris and Robert Reiner (2012). Mediated mayhem: media, crime and criminal justice. In Rod Morgan, Mike Maguire and Robert Reiner, eds. *Oxford Handbook of Criminology*, 245–78. Oxford: Oxford University Press.

Guder, Andrea and Karin Wehn (1998). Polizeiruf 110: the transition from socialism to capitalism. In Reinhold Viehoff, ed. *Stahlnetz, Tatort, Polizeiruf 110: Transitions in German Police Series*, 12–24. HALMA 8. Halle: Universität Halle.

Hißnauer, Christian (2018). TV. In Susanne Düwell, Andrea Bartl, Christof Hamann and Oliver Ruf, eds. *Handbuch Kriminalliteratur*, 362–72, Stuttgart: JB Metzler.

Hißnauer, Christian, Stefan Scherer and Claudia Stockinger, eds. (2014). *Zwischen Serie und Werk: Fernseh- und Gesellschaftsgeschichte im Tatort*. Bielefeld: transcript Verlag.

Hurd, Geoffrey (1981). The television representation of the police. In Tony Bennett, ed. *Popular Television and Film: A Reader*, 33–70. London: British Film Institute.

Kean, Hilda (1998). *Animal Rights: Political and Social Change in Britain since 1800*. London: Reaktion Books.

Kew, Barry (2003): Appropriating liberation. *Society and Animals* 11(1): 29–49. https://www.animalsandsociety.org/wp-content/uploads/2015/11/kew.pdf.

Kew, Barry (1999). Fearsome truths: the challenge of animal liberation. PhD thesis, University of Durham, Durham.

Lamb, Ben (2020). *You're Nicked: Investigating British Television Police Series.* Manchester: Manchester University Press.

Law & Order (2001). Series 11, Episode 10: "Whose Monkey Is It Anyway?" Vincent Misiano (Dir.). Distributor: NBC.

Law & Order (1993). Series 3, Episode 18: "Animal Instinct". Ed Sherin (Dir.). Distributor: NBC.

Lewis (2014). Series 8, Episodes 1 and 2: "Entry Wounds". Nicholas Renton (Dir.). Distributor: BBC.

Marsh, Ian and Gaynor Melville (2019). *Crime, Justice and the Media.* London: Routledge.

Martin, Gus (2003). *Understanding Terrorism: Challenges, Perspectives, and Issues.* London: SAGE.

Mattson, Michelle (1999). *Tatort*: the generation of public identity in a German crime series. *New German Critique* 78: 161–81.

Molloy, Claire (2011). *Popular Media and Animals.* Basingstoke: Palgrave Macmillan.

Peelo, Moira and Keith Soothill (2013). *Questioning Crime and Criminology.* London: Willan.

Polizeiruf 110 (2013). "Wolfsland". Ed Herzog (Dir.). Distributor: Eikon Media.

Polizeiruf 110 (2012). "Raubvögel". Esther Wenger (Dir.). Distributor: Mitteldeutscher Rundfunk.

Polizeiruf 110 (2009). "Schweineleben". Eoin Moore (Dir.). Distributor: All Media Pictures.

Rogers, Margaret (2008). Arresting drama: the television police genre. *Studies in Learning, Evaluation Innovation and Development* 5(2): 78–84. https://tinyurl.com/5a26x2dz.

Rootes, Christopher (2000). Environmental protest in Britain 1988–1997. In Brian Doherty, Matthew Paterson and Benjamin Seel, eds. *Direct Action in British Environmentalism*, 39–75. London: Routledge.

Roscher, Mieke (2011). Gesichter der Befreiung. Eine bildgeschichtliche Analyse der visuellen Repräsentation der Tierrechtsbewegung. In Chimaira Arbeitskreis, ed. *Human-Animal Studies: Über die gesellschaftliche Natur von Tier-Mensch Verhältnissen*, 335–63. Bielefeld: transcript Verlag.

Roscher, Mieke (2009). *Ein Königreich für Tiere*. Marburg: Tectum.

Sabin, Roger (2015). Introduction. In Roger Sabin, Ronald Wilson and Linda Speidel, eds. *Cop Shows: A Critical History of Police Dramas on Television*, 1–14. Jefferson, NC: McFarland.

Schlesinger, Philip (1991). *Media, State and Nation: Political Violence and Collective Identities*. London: SAGE.

Schlesinger, Philip, Graham Murdock and Philip Elliott (1986). "Terrorism" and the State: a case study of the discourses of television. In Richard Collins et al., eds. *Media, Culture and Society: A Critical Reader*, 264–86. London: SAGE.

Schlesinger, Philip, Graham Murdock and Philip Elliott (1983). *Televising "Terrorism", Political Violence in Popular Culture*. London: Comedia Publishing House.

Seago, Karen (2014). Introduction and overview: crime (fiction) in translation. *The Journal of Specialised Translation* 22: 2–14.

Sparks, Richard (1995). Entertaining the crisis: television and moral enterprise. In David Kidd-Hewitt and Richard Osborne, eds. *Crime and the Media: The Post-modern Spectacle*, 49–66. London and East Haven: Pluto Press.

Tatort (2005). "Leiden wie ein Tier". Uwe Janson (Dir.). Distributor: Rundfunk.

Tatort (1991). "Animals". Walter Bannert (Dir.). Distributor: Rundfunk.

The Bill (2007). Series 23, Episodes 44 to 45: "A Model Murder". A.J. Quinn (Dir.). Distributor: ITV.

The Bill (2002). Series 18, Episode 45: "Protection". Declan O'Dwyer (Dir.). Distributor: ITV.

The Bill (2000). Series 16, Episode 9: "Beasts". Gwennan Sage (Dir.). Distributor: ITV.

The Bill (1997). Series 13, Episode 110: "Animals". Dominic Lees (Dir.). Distributor: ITV.

The Bill (1991). Series 7, Episode 97: "Cause and Effect". Jan Sargent (Dir.). Distributor: ITV.

Tulloch, John (2000). *Watching Television Audiences: Cultural Theories and Methods*. London: Arnold.

Wenzel, Eike (2000). "Tatort" – Deutschland. Eine Einleitung. In Eike Wenzel, ed. *Ermittlungen in Sachen 'Tatort'. Recherchen und Verhöre, Protokolle und Beweisfotos*, 7–18. Berlin: Bertz.

Yakushenko, Olga (2014). *What is cultural transfer?* European University at St. Petersburg, 22 September. https://eusp.org/en/news/what-is-cultural-transfer.

2

Inspiring animal liberation

The representation of animal activists in US animal advocacy documentaries (2000–2019)

Núria Almiron, Laura Fernández and Olatz Aranceta-Reboredo

Despite the diverse representations of animal advocates included in animal advocacy documentaries, most research on these films has focused on content and discourse analysis,[1] or on how human animal advocates frame nonhuman animal advocacy.[2] To our knowledge, no research has been conducted on animal advocates' profiles and how they have evolved, despite the potential utility of such an analysis for the communication strategy of the animal defence movement. The research we present in this chapter aims to fill this gap by examining the self-representation of animal activists in animal advocacy documentaries.

Although there are some earlier examples (e.g., *The Animals Film* [1981]), it was not until the 1990s that the animal advocacy movement began to make regular use of documentaries to spread its message, most notably with the release of *It's a Dog's Life* (1997), a film produced by Small World for Channel 4 in the UK, which exposed the abuse of animals at the Huntington Life Sciences animal testing centre. The documentary's main character and activist, Zoe Broughton, used warfare tactics such as infiltration, spying and undercover filming in her advocacy in the film. Since then, this frame of animal activists as

1 For example, Christopher, Bartkowski and Haverda 2018; Freeman 2012.
2 For example, Newman 2015; Scanlon 2012.

engaged in a kind of warfare has been a frequent resource in animal advocacy films.

Despite the prevalence of the warfare frame, animal advocates have been depicted in many other ways in animal advocacy documentaries. To inventory these frames, we conducted a content analysis of a sample of 20 US-produced documentaries,[3] including films from 1999, when the genre was born, and particularly from 2013, when the genre proliferated, up to 2019. We coded the different frames used in the portrayal of the animal activists' profiles and actions as they appear in the films with the aim of producing a categorisation of the typologies. We also sought to determine whether the profiles emerged at different stages in time or whether the evolution of the genre was non-linear. We used this classification to discuss how the findings can illuminate the field of strategic communication of animal defence. The analysis was conducted within the perspective of critical animal and media studies.[4]

Framing animal advocates: A literature review

To build a preliminary classification of frames for animal advocates as depicted in animal advocacy films, we conducted a literature review of works discussing documentary films on animal advocacy. This included discussion of non-fiction films focused on animal defence but excluded fiction films and documentaries of animals in nature such as those produced by *National Geographic* or the BBC.

Three general frames emerged from this review: (i) human advocates in relation to their personal profiles; (ii) human advocates in relation to their actions; and (iii) nonhuman animals as activists.

---

3 A non-fiction film, *Bold Native* (2010), was included for its relevant documentary footage and realistic, documentary-style portrayal of the complex issues facing animal rights activists today, including the wide range of advocacy positions that coexist in the modern animal rights movement.

4 Almiron, Cole and Freeman 2018.

The framing of human advocates in relation to their personal profiles

The literature finds that the documentaries largely frame animal advocates as converts, social justice advocates, grassroots people, the vegan elite and heroes.

The convert is a person who was previously an opponent of animal rights and/or former animal exploiter before a eureka moment that turned them into an animal advocate. This is the role depicted by, for instance, Ric O'Barry in the film *The Cove* (2009).[5] Lara Newman describes him as "former dolphin trainer turned activist",[6] while Carrie Freeman points out that he went "from dolphin trainer to dolphin activist/liberator … to dismantle the lucrative dolphin and whale captivity industry that he helped produce".[7] Carrie Freeman and Scott Tulloch also point out that the "protagonists in *The Witness* (2000), *Peaceable Kingdom* (2004) and *The Cove* narrate their own transformation from animal-eaters, farmers, trainers, or researchers, to newfound vegans and activists".[8] In *Peaceable Kingdom*, Howard Lyman is introduced as a "rancher-turned-vegan"[9] and in *The Witness*, Eddie Lama goes "from first cat-sitting for a girlfriend to rescuing strays, going vegan, and becoming an anti-fur activist".[10] As for the documentary *Moon Bears: Journey to Freedom* (2007), Chia-ju Chang reports on:

> Robinson's touching rite-of-passage story of how she became involved in the bear-rescue project in China … she speaks of the direct contact between a caged female bear and herself that marked the transformative moment triggering her life-changing decision.[11]

---

5 The references for all documentaries mentioned are available in Table 2.1.
6 Newman 2015, 79.
7 Freeman 2012, 106.
8 Freeman and Tulloch 2013, 123.
9 Freeman and Tulloch 2013, 123.
10 Freeman 2013, 111.
11 Chang 2017, 104.

The social justice advocate frame includes activists being defined similarly to human rights activists, as well as animal advocacy being either defined or portrayed as a type of social justice advocacy. For instance, Freeman states that in *The Cove* animal advocates are portrayed as being "implicitly similar to human rights activists in their willingness to take risks breaking laws (non-violently) in order to save victims suffering injustice".[12] Referring to *Behind the Mask* (2006), Freeman and Tulloch claim that "[t]he documentarian justifies animal activism by linking it to historic actions to help human victims of injustice, adding credibility to animal rescues" and including "frequent comparisons ... referencing Martin Luther King Jr, Harriet Tubman, and Nelson Mandela".[13]

According to the literature, animal activists are also framed in documentaries as grassroots citizens; that is, ordinary citizens who are also advocates and represent "actual vegans".[14] This frame includes activists arguing "for a more altruistic orientation aimed at reducing animal cruelty and environmental degradation", as can be found in *Vegucated* (2011).[15]

The fourth frame of advocates in relation to their profiles is the one related to the cultural creation of a vegan elite. Christopher, Bartkowski and Haverda found in *Vegucated* and *Forks Over Knives* (2011) that activists are depicted as "prominent advocates of this distinctive diet and lifestyle" and as those who "define authentic veganism as a cultural object".[16] This frame also seems to apply to the description that Katherine Lind offers of *The Cove*, with the documentary depicting "Westerners as heroes while degrading the Japanese government and fishermen",[17] which makes it possible for the producers to define morality and advocate for their distinctive worldview.

Finally, a number of scholars show how animal activists are portrayed as heroes in animal advocacy films; that is, as people fighting

12 Freeman 2012, 107.
13 Freeman and Tulloch 2013, 123.
14 Christopher, Bartkowski and Haverda 2018, 5.
15 Christopher, Bartkowski and Haverda 2018, 17.
16 Christopher, Bartkowski and Haverda 2018, 4.
17 Lind 2019, 638.

for freedom, enacting heroic actions, engaging in acts of self-sacrifice and conducting heroic rescues or heroic transformations, among others. Freeman and Tulloch, for instance, report that *The Cove* and *Behind the Mask* "are largely about humans enacting heroic rescues or experiencing moral development".[18] Taylor Scanlon points out that the animal liberator in *Bold Native* (2010) is referred to as "our hero Charlie" by the filmmakers.[19] For *Virunga* (2014), László Erdős speaks of the activists as "real heroes who risk their lives to protect mountain gorillas amidst war and unscrupulous economic exploitation".[20]

The literature also shows that the hero frame overlaps with several other profiles, including the saviour, the social justice advocate, the moral agent and the educated. In her analysis of the promotional content used by *The Cove* as another dimension of the documentary itself, Lind concludes that it portrays humans as saviours:

> while adding a religious intertextuality to the advocacy message … [which] facilitates a notion of moral authority and casts the filmmakers and activists as virtuous saviours whose actions to protect dolphins are unimpeachable.[21]

The hero and social justice frames also overlap. This framing creates a link between the heroic construction of animal rights advocates and other struggles for social justice. Freeman and Tulloch find that the link to social justice in *Behind the Mask* adds "credibility to animal rescues by framing activists as heroic, self-sacrificing freedom fighters in the familiar, culturally-accepted vein of civil rights, abolitionism, and women's rights".[22] As a result, they argue that "[f]ar from being 'objective' narrators, these documentarians serve as critical rhetoricians who construct storylines that promote and legitimise animal rights activism by framing activists as freedom fighters protecting the innocent".[23]

---

18 Freeman and Tulloch 2013, 120.
19 Scanlon 2012, 53.
20 Erdős 2019, 218.
21 Lind 2019, 633.
22 Freeman and Tulloch 2013, 123.
23 Freeman and Tulloch 2013, 112.

Heroism is also identified with moral agency. Kellie Evans argues that "animal rights activists portray the experience of animals in moral terms – that is, as a power struggle of good versus evil".[24] The director is said to argue that "the heroes of the animal rights debate are the activists who operate against the suffering of animals",[25] where moral virtue is established through heroic actions.[26]

The last common depiction the literature finds is that of animal advocate heroes as educated. That is, animal activists are portrayed as citizens with degrees, liberal careers and rational views while being heroic. Regarding *Bold Native*, Scanlon mentions that, despite the "anarchist desires or violent impulses" of the animal activist appearing in the film, he rather represents "the enlightened liberal straight white male in whom the viewer is meant to emotionally invest".[27] Moreover, Scanlon claims that he "is constructed by the film as a sympathetic yet rational and nonviolent animal activist".[28]

The framing of human advocates in relation to their actions

Previous examinations of animal advocacy documentaries also report a number of frames related to the actions carried out by the activists in the films. More specifically, animal advocates are found to be framed as terrorists, welfarists, moral entrepreneurs and people conducting risky actions.

The identification of "activists-as-terrorists" is a category provided by Scanlon to explain the framing of activism as violence in *Bold Native*. Regarding the animal advocate portrayed in the film, Scanlon finds that "Charlie is framed sympathetically as a character whose terrorist charges by the American government categorise him as an individual with motives and behaviours like those associated with the Feral Child movement".[29] Therefore, the film may portray the activist positively but still maintain the criminalisation.

24 Evans 2014, 66–7.
25 Evans 2014, 36.
26 Evans 2014, 6.
27 Scanlon 2013, 55.
28 Scanlon 2013, 61–2.
29 Scanlon 2013, 64.

Scanlon also points out that *Bold Native* portrays another activist as a "welfarist"; that is, as someone who is "taunted and ridiculed for her chosen position" even as she successfully campaigns for welfare reforms.[30] As a welfarist, "Jane is framed as doing little more than allowing people to feel better about consuming meat", and the film constructs her "as a flat and ineffectual character".[31]

Christopher, Bartkowski and Haverda consider the role of an activist depicted in *Forks Over Knives* to be that of a "moral entrepreneur for veganism, albeit health veganism",[32] who advocates "for a particular vantage point using techniques of persuasion" and produces "distinctive depictions of the vegan subculture".[33]

Finally, several papers identify documentaries framing animal activists as people who take risks despite the possibility of consequences such as their arrest, physical injuries or psychological impacts. Freeman and Tulloch describe the main advocate character of *The Cove*, Ric O'Barry, as being in "an 'Oceans 11' spy adventure format" since he and his volunteer team "risk arrest setting up underwater cameras".[34] Newman does not use the word "risk", yet it is implicit in the activists' prosecution in *Bold Native*, whose protagonist, Charlie Cranehill, is "a middle class, white, male animal rights activist who is being chased by the Federal Bureau of Investigation for crimes committed under the Animal Enterprise Terrorism Act".[35] In the case of *Behind the Mask*, Freeman and Tulloch describe the introduction of the Animal Liberation Front (ALF) to the audience as sympathetic, while the activists "risk arrest to liberate animals from labs and fur farms".[36]

The framing of nonhuman animals as activists

Interestingly, a third category of framing is found in the literature about animal advocacy documentaries: that of the nonhuman animals

---

30 Scanlon 2013, 63.
31 Scanlon 2013, 75–7.
32 Christopher, Bartkowski and Haverda 2018, 14.
33 Christopher, Bartkowski and Haverda 2018, 5.
34 Freeman and Tulloch 2013, 111.
35 Newman 2015, 79.
36 Freeman and Tulloch 2013, 112.

as activists. Burford and Schutten discuss this in relation to *Blackfish* (2013) and the orca starring in the film: "Tilikum, and the other orcas' stories discussed in *Blackfish*, were the first activists that initiated this particular environmental justice movement".[37] These authors provide the specific category of "whales-as-activists", which would lead "us to another potential understanding of captive orcas".[38]

In summary, in the literature on animal advocacy documentaries we were able to identify at least 13 different frames: animal advocates profiled as converts, social justice advocates, grassroots people, vegan elites, heroes, saviours, moral agents and educated people; animal advocates acting as terrorists, welfarists, moral entrepreneurs and people taking risks; and nonhuman animals portrayed as activists.

Methodology

For our research, we selected 20 documentaries (Table 2.1) that complied with four criteria: (i) they were non-fiction animal advocacy documentaries (excluding nature documentaries, health-oriented documentaries and fiction films); (ii) they depicted activists in a relevant way (excluding those documentaries that provided no explicit profiles for advocates despite being animal defence films); (iii) they had US producers (to comply with this chapter's focus); and (iv) they were accessible to the research team.

In order to develop our list of frames, we used the frames from the literature review as a starting point and conducted three pilot codings after which we ended up with 28 frames: 13 frames for the profiles of animal advocates, 14 frames for the actions they conduct, and one frame of nonhuman animals as activists. This last frame was not the focus of our analysis, being centred on the representation of human advocates, but we deemed it interesting to code it in any case since, in the end, it could have an impact on the global perception of animal advocacy. Table 2.2 shows all of the frames, their description and the number of documentaries in which they appear at least once. Frames

37 Burford and Schutten 2017, 9.
38 Burford and Schutten 2017, 9.

Table 2.1 List of analysed documentaries.

Film	**Year**
The Witness (Dir. Jenny Stein)	2000
Lolita: Slave to Entertainment (Dir. Tim Gorski)	2003
Peaceable Kingdom: The Journey Home (Dir. Jenny Stein)	2004
Behind the Mask (Dir. Shannon Keith)	2006
I am an Animal: The Story of Ingrid Newkirk and PETA (Dir. Matthew Galkin)	2007
The Cove (Dir. Louie Psihoyos)	2009
Bold Native (Dir. Denis Henry Hennelly)	2010
Vegucated (Dir. Marisa Miller Wolfson)	2011
Speciesism: The Movie (Dir. Mark Devries)	2013
Blackfish (Dir. Gabriela Cowperthwaite)	2013
Cowspiracy (Dir. Kip Andersen and Keegan Kuhn)	2014
Tyke Elephant Outlaw (Dir. Susan Lambert)	2015
Unlocking the Cage (Dir. Chris Hegedus and D.A. Pennebaker)	2016
Vegan: Everyday Stories (Dir. Glenn Scott Lacey)	2016
Food Choices (Dir. Michal Siewierski)	2016
73 Cows (dir. Alex Lockwood)	2018
A Prayer for Compassion (dir. Thomas Jackson)	2019
The Animal People (dir. Casey Suchan and Denis Henry Hennelly)	2019
Test Subjects (dir. Alex Lockwood)	2019
The Invisible Vegan (dir. Jasmine Leyva and Kenny Leyva)	2019

were merely coded for appearance (1) or non-appearance (0). The coding was conducted by the second and third co-authors of the paper and a third coder hired for the task. The piloting allowed us to achieve an intercoder reliability of .89 following Fleiss Kappa's equation, which is considered an excellent agreement between coders.[39]

Table 2.2 Framing advocates in animal advocacy documentaries from 2000 to 2019.

1. WHO ARE THE ADVOCATES (PERSONAL PROFILE)		
FRAME (shading represents aggregate groups)	**DESCRIPTION**	**Documentaries in which it appears (*N*=20)**
Converts	Activists were former oppressors or opponents (for instance, farmers) and experienced a eureka moment.	13
Advocates made in real time[40]	Filmmakers become animal advocates in front of the camera.	6
Heroes	Animal activists endorse heroic actions, self-sacrifice, heroic rescues, heroic transformations, etc.	11
Freedom fighters	Animal activists defined as fighting for freedom.	10
Social justice advocates	Activists defined as a type of social justice advocate or intersected with other social justice causes.	16
Grassroots people	Animal activists portrayed as grassroots citizens, that is, ordinary citizens.	16
Educated people	Animal activists portrayed as educated citizens with degrees, liberal careers, etc.	12
Vegan elite	Animal activists portrayed as representatives of authentic veganism, that is, as a morally superior community.	2

39 Allen 2017, 738–40.

40 By "real time" we mean when filmmakers appear as turning into advocates during the film shooting, in front of the camera. These are presented as live conversions within the filming.

Caregivers	Animal activists portrayed as caregivers of abandoned, traumatised or exploited nonhuman animals.	14
Healthy people healing the world	Animal activists presented as healthy people who eat a plant-based diet and who exercise, as well as being concerned for the health of the planet and other animals.	6
Showing ethical traits	Animal activists portrayed as moral characters or virtuous characters.	18
Showing emotional traits	Animal activists portrayed as emotional characters.	18
Showing rational traits	Animal activists portrayed as rational characters.	15

2. WHAT THE ADVOCATES DO (ACTIONS AS STRATEGIES, TACTICS ...)

FRAME	DESCRIPTION	Documentaries in which it appears (N=20)
Abolitionist activists	Animal activists portrayed as animal abolitionists, not just welfare defenders. *Abolitionism refers to the questioning of the use and exploitation of animals as a problem in itself, not just the conditions in which such use occurs.*	19
Welfarist activists	Animal activists portrayed as animal welfare defenders, not as abolitionists. *Welfarism refers to the improvement of living conditions of nonhuman animals under exploitation, within the industry, without questioning the use and exploitation of animals.*	8
Warfare	Activists depicted using warfare tactics (infiltration, spying, undercover filming, etc.).	9
Promoters of nonviolence	Animal activists portrayed as promoting nonviolence.	9

Direct action	Animal activists portrayed using direct action, including but not limited to actions such as breaking into private facilities to rescue NHA, engaged in civil disobedience, illegal actions, strikes, picketing, trespassing and mass occupation of land or buildings, perpetrating property damage and sabotage, along with a measure of agitation.	7
Violence/ Terrorism	Animal activists depicted using violence or terrorism through their association with the traits and actions usually attached to terrorists, such as the destruction of property, bombing, harassing, etc.). Similar to the frame of direct action, but with the additional element of criminalisation.	3
Using ethical arguments	Animal activists portrayed using moral arguments.	20
Using emotional arguments	Animal activists portrayed using emotional arguments.	19
Using rational arguments	Animal activists portrayed using rational arguments.	18
Using environmental arguments	Animal activists portrayed using environmental arguments.	10
Using health arguments	Animal activists portrayed using health arguments.	10
Using economic arguments	Animal activists portrayed using economic arguments.	7
Without risk	Animal activists conducting actions that involve no risk and that are portrayed as without risk: leafletting, demonstrations, marches, etc.	18
In risk	Animal activists taking risks (including arrest, physical injuries, psychological impacts, etc.) that could eventually involve risk to their lives.	11

3. OTHER		
FRAME	**DESCRIPTION**	**Documentaries in which it appears (*N*=20)**
Nonhuman animals as activists	The documentary portrays nonhuman animals as advocates because of their agency or because they simply trigger human advocacy with their attitude and character.	8

Figure 2.1 summarises the incidence of the 28 frames in the sample of documentaries as a percentage. Our main finding is that animal advocates were portrayed as developing ethical arguments in all films in the sample. Other arguments and traits were nearly as profuse: 19 documentaries also included portrayals of advocates using emotional arguments; 18 documentaries portrayed them with rational arguments; 18 films attached emotional and ethical traits to activists; and 15 films depicted them having rational traits. Therefore, despite the strong depiction of advocates as ethical characters endorsing ethical action, activists are also abundantly depicted as emotional and rational characters in animal advocacy documentaries.

The ethical arguments and traits uttered and articulated by animal advocates in the films mostly include concern for the suffering and death inflicted on animals, mentions of animals' sentience and agency, the ethical consequences of animal exploitation on world hunger and resource distribution, the unethical nature and vested interests of the system and industries exploiting animals, and the compassionate profile of advocates. As Jay puts it in *73 Cows*:

> I began to sort of feel conscious of the fact that the animals had feelings and [this] led to feelings of unease about actually eating them when we raise them. You realise that they do have personalities and they experience the world. They are not just, sort of, robots that eat and sleep.

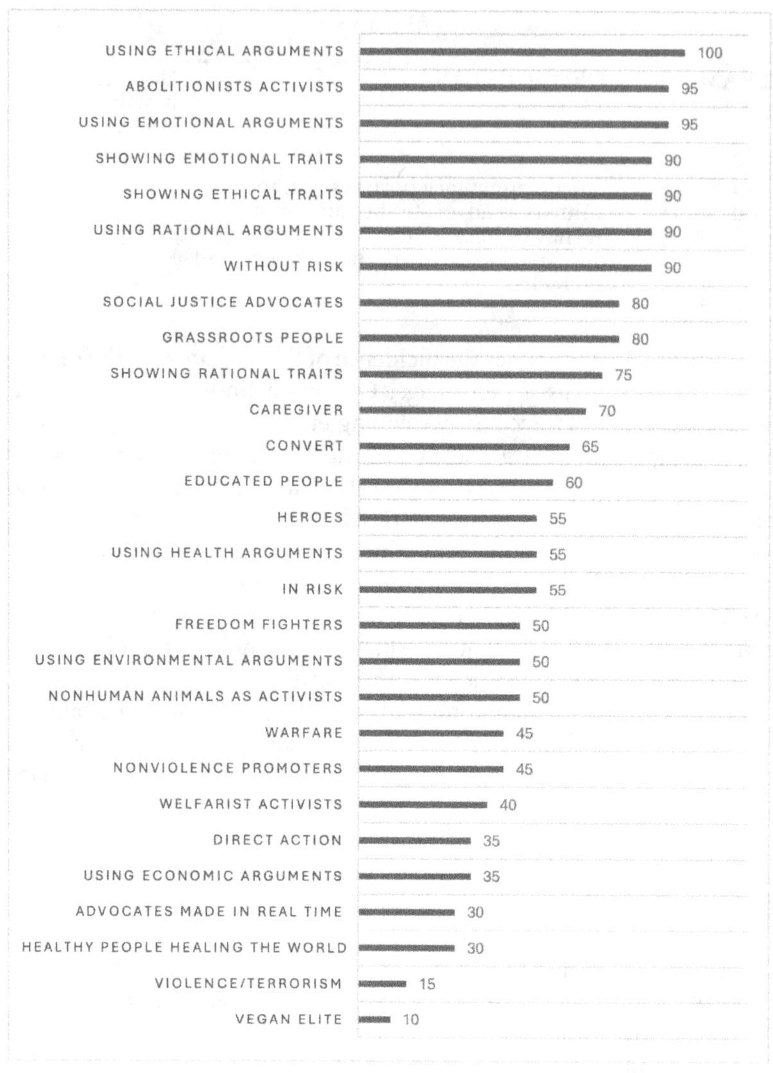

Figure 2.1 Incidence of frames.

The emotional arguments and traits of animal advocates as depicted in the films mostly include portrayals of the emotional bonds they hold with other animals, the emotional bonds nonhuman animals hold with each other, and direct depictions of animal advocates candidly expressing emotions (e.g., crying in sadness or concern), strong regret or compassion. As one character in *The Invisible Vegan* (2019) said, "Who with a heart can watch when a cow cries when its calf is taken away from it?"

The rational arguments and traits animal advocates are portrayed as holding in the films include logical and scientific claims against animal exploitation and its consequences, discussions of the effectiveness of advocacy, the erroneous perceptions humans hold, quotations by prominent people (the authority argument), and many instances in which activists invite the audience to reflect, such as when the advocate in *The Witness* says: "Question your brain."

Along with these arguments and traits that profile the advocates, the next most abundant frame in our sample (present in 19 of the 20 documentaries) is an action frame: that of advocates endorsing abolitionist strategies. In contrast, only eight films (40 per cent of the total) feature advocates involved in welfarist actions (some of which appear in films that also depict abolitionist action). This means that all but one of the films include claims to a complete end of the exploitation and killing of nonhuman animals. Probably the most illustrative example of this is in *Tyke Elephant Outlaw* (2015), in which the owner of the sanctuary in the film states that even there, in sanctuaries, animals should not be behind fences. An example of the few cases of welfarist strategies being associated with activists in the films is the portrayal of PETA's strategy with McDonald's in *Speciesism: The Movie* (2013).

In those documentaries in our sample with an action frame, more feature depictions of animal advocacy as having no risk (18 films) than those that do (11 films). Riskless advocacy actions portrayed in the films include leafletting, giving lectures, taking care of animals in sanctuaries, peaceful street protests and demonstrations, the distribution of stickers, documentary screenings, academic research, lawsuits, vegan street outreach, parliamentary lobbying and welfarist corporate alliances. As for actions involving risk, the documentaries include typical direct action and warfare tactics (rescues and animal releases, trespassing, property destruction, undercover investigation, blackmail) but also infiltrations, the refusal to participate in some acts (such as vivisection) that may lead to academic marginalisation; the consequences of some actions could involve police and legal repression and even death at the hands of corporate mafias.

A relevant number of documentaries (16 films) also profile advocates as grassroots, ordinary people engaged in a social justice cause that is equated with other human justice causes. In this regard, for instance, animal imprisonment is very often compared to human slavery (*Speciesism*, *Tyke Elephant Outlaw*, *Unlocking the Cage* [2016], *A Prayer for Compassion* [2019], *Bold Native*), including one comparison to the human holocaust (*Food Choices* [2016]). Other examples include reminders of past social justice advocates that were vegetarian for ethical reasons (*Vegucated*), including the use of quotations from human rights activists such as Martin Luther King Jr (*Cowspiracy* [2014]) and activists highlighting the intersectionality of all social struggles (*The Invisible Vegan*).

A relevant number of films (14) also depict animal advocates as caregivers, mostly in connection with rescue centres or sanctuaries. In these, activists report on the care the saved animals receive and images providing factual support of their words are provided – such as, for example, in *Vegan: Everyday Stories* (2016) when an activist speaks to a rescued hen who is falling asleep on her lap.

Approximately half of the documentaries (10 to 13) also include frames of advocates as heroes, freedom fighters, converts and educated people. In the case of heroes, advocates are explicitly described using this term, while for freedom fighters we coded this frame every time activists were presented as literally freeing nonhuman animals from bondage or arguing that they were fighting for freedom. Converts, in turn, were mostly former farmers, vivisectors, trainers or slaughterhouse workers. Educated people were coded every time the animal advocate was presented as having a higher education or training (e.g., university lecturers, researchers, PhD researchers, medical doctors, scholars, writers, journalists or psychologists).

Half of the documentaries also portrayed animal advocates as using health and environmental arguments. Most of the time, the health and environmental arguments are articulated in connection with the plight humans inflict on nonhumans, which can be summarised in the case of health with Christopher Sebastian's quote in *The Invisible Vegan*: "Having a healthy body is political." As for the environmental link, the documentaries include advocates observing that a plant-based diet prevents global warming, water scarcity, species extinction, the destruction of the Amazon rainforest, the depletion of the oceans and world hunger, among other issues.

The rest of the frames identified in the documentaries are found in less than half of the films. Of them, advocates explicitly depicted as nonviolence promoters – when the conductor, the activists or the images include an explicit mention of pacifism or nonviolence – are found in nine films. This frame is especially present in the documentary *A Prayer for Compassion*, which presents animal advocacy from a plural religious and spiritual approach. An example of this frame is Russell Simmons' linking of veganism and not harming (ahimsa) in *Vegan: Everyday Stories*:

> There's definitely a correlation between the spiritual practice of non-harming and veganism and the way I am living today compared to the way I used to live. The way I used to be was harmful to myself, to my body, to my loved ones. Essentially, I am trying to live a more spiritual life, and for me that involves trying to cause as little suffering as possible and to try to just do my best … so yeah, we don't want to cause any harm. So, if we really examine ahimsa, its meaning, or if we want to be people who practice ahimsa or cause less harm, the … first and most important thing we should do is get away from eating animal products.

Advocates using economic arguments, advocates made in real time (referring to the process by which the narrator or filmmaker becomes an animal advocate on camera) and advocates profiled as healthy people healing the world appear only a few times (in seven, six and six films, respectively), while activists depicted as violent people or as an elite are only anecdotal (in three and two films, respectively).

Finally, the frame of nonhuman animals as activists was found in eight documentaries, which is not a negligible number. In some cases, the activism of animals is more a kind of projection of humans, such as in *The Animal People* (2019) when the activist Kevin Kjonaas comments: "If Junior [the beagle rescued from a lab] is not gonna be defeated by animal testing, why the hell would I?" However, there are clear instances of agency by animals, such as the dolphin that commits suicide in the hands of Ric O'Barry in *The Cove* or, most strikingly, the case of the orca Tilikum in *Blackfish*.

As for the evolution of frames over time, our results show that the majority of the 28 frames found in our sample were equally distributed in time with five exceptions; three did not appear before a certain time period, and two did not appear after another period. Advocates made in real time, healthy people healing the world and the use of environmental arguments are frames that emerge mostly around 2009–2010. They were almost non-existent before then. The freedom fighter and advocates engaged in direct action frames nearly stopped appearing after 2010–2011. We discuss this and the rest of the findings in the final section.

Framing human activists in documentaries: A discussion

The evolution of frames in US animal advocacy documentaries over time provides some clues about the movement's ideological and strategic changes and may help us better understand the relationship between the representation of activists and current discussions and events taking place within the animal liberation movement and critical animal studies. The analysis of the representation of activists guides us towards a deeper examination of the (un)shared meanings of concepts such as veganism, antispeciesism and activism, which are deeply ideological. For instance, some questions that emerged during our research process were: How is veganism defined? What kind of actions are considered activism, and why? What are the disputes around ethical, political and strategic choices in the representation of animal advocates in documentaries?

In our exploration, we have noticed an increase in the "advocates made in real time" frame in recent years, which, as stated earlier, refers to the process in which the narrator or filmmaker becomes an animal advocate on camera. This rise could be seen as being connected with the social need for vegan and animal advocate role models, especially in a world where veganism and activism are still minority phenomena. Identification with the characters through storytelling and personal experiences are key in attempts to popularise veganism.

The increased prevalence of the "healthy people healing the world" frame could be related to the emergence of the idea of health beyond individual physical health. The narrow health focus has been challenged by more holistic perspectives that integrate individual, collective and environmental health into a whole. Within the animal defence movement, this paradigm change can be considered as informed by an anti-racist, anti-capitalist and intersectional approach that considers food access, justice and sovereignty, labour rights, environmental destruction, animal exploitation and structural racism all together. Particularly in the US, access to fresh fruit and vegetables is not granted to everyone, and "food deserts" affect predominantly impoverished communities, especially people of colour, as scholars and social justice projects have pointed out.[41]

The proliferation of the use of environmental arguments in animal advocacy documentaries may be explained by the general increase in the social merging of environmental and animal ethics arguments, especially with respect to food industries. We have previously supported the inclusion of environmental arguments and pluralistic approaches in animal advocacy for strategic and ethical reasons.[42] At this point, however, we believe that the ethical arguments against speciesism should be kept at the core of representation efforts in order to avoid removing nonhuman animals from the centre of the struggle and the movement.

We believe that the decreased prevalence of the "direct action" and "freedom fighter" frames in recent years can be explained by Richard J. White's analysis of "activist veganism" and "lifestyle" or "corporate"

41 Food Empowerment Project 2021; Harper 2010.
42 Almiron 2019; Fernández 2019.

veganism.[43] For White, *activist veganism* refers to "one which inspires a more radical vision for veganism, encouraging greater critical reflection, awareness, and commitment to social justice issues", while *lifestyle* or *corporate veganism* is concerned with acquiring greater mainstream attention and is:

> focused almost exclusively around questions of food ... which, crucially, is uncoupled and detached from related actions relevant to inter-species social justice. Deprived of any ability to challenge capitalism, lifestyle veganism is very much endorsed and promoted by corporate interests and investment.[44]

This transformation of the meaning of veganism cannot be separated from the professionalisation of animal rights organisations, which has increased the distance between nonprofits and grassroots collectives and disempowered the latter, which tend to promote more radical ideas and actions, as pointed out by Wrenn.[45] Undoubtedly, this polarisation has de-linked *lifestyle veganism* from more political approaches such as support for direct action for animal liberation, in this case especially the activities of the Animal Liberation Front. From our point of view, this paradigm change in activist representation may have taken place for several reasons. As we argued with reference to the increased prevalence of the "animal advocates made in real time" frame, this change may be linked to the need to make veganism accessible and to frame vegan activists as common people who are more easily identified with by non-activist audiences. Images of hooded people liberating nonhuman animals from their cages could be a distant, even hostile, referent for certain audiences with no prior political engagement. In addition, given the rise of *lifestyle veganism*, direct action generally implies a broader questioning of justice, legality, the establishment, power structures and industrial complexes.[46] The omission of such questioning in the most recent documentaries could also be rooted

43 White 2019.
44 White 2019, 4.
45 Wrenn 2019.
46 Best and Nocella 2004.

in a desire to avoid earlier hegemonic representations of vegans that could trigger "vegaphobia"[47] and/or activist political criminalisation and repression among the audiences, considering that "media stories on ALF actions ... often turned the animal oppressors into victims".[48]

Several issues can be considered to be signs of increasing moral consideration of other animals by humans. These are mostly related to the increased adoption of plant-based diets in Western countries, the decline in the use of other animals for labour, accessories or entertainment, and the problematisation of vivisection or animal experimentation, including the emergence of public discussion of their eventual full abandonment. These signs are also related to ever more frequent calls for the liberation and care of animals under exploitation, for the return and restoration of natural habitats, for the provision of aid and assistance to other animals in nature, and for the acknowledgement of the agency of all sentient beings. These are only some of the most prominent examples of indications of moral progress by humanity – or, as Gandhi famously put it, "for nations". Sadly enough, in all cases the progress is excruciatingly slow, when there is any. For some people, this is a sign that animal advocacy is failing. Since advocacy documentaries are a prominent tool used in animal advocacy, as a consequence this would mean that these films are not sufficiently effective. Since a relevant hostility towards animal defence remains prevalent among certain segments of the population, we could also infer that the impact of these films does not compensate for the vested interests and psychological barriers raised by the capitalist industrial order, which prevent ethics from advancing.

The opposite, however, could be equally true. Without animal advocacy, moral progress in society and the situation of other animals could be even worse. We know that a relevant portion of current animal advocates joined the movement precisely because of a documentary. After all, in the Vomad 2019 global survey, which explored why and how people go vegan, the most-voted answer to the question "What was the first thing that made you seriously consider going vegan? (even if it didn't make you go vegan yet)" was "a feature-length documentary".[49]

---

47 Cole and Morgan 2011.

48 Dawn 2004, 215.

In theory, we could measure the success of documentaries in terms of effectiveness if we had an objective measure of how many people turned into animal advocates after viewing them. Meanwhile, data from research such as the analysis we have presented here is at least illustrative of the kinds of results we could expect from such a study.

At the UPF-Centre for Animal Ethics – to which the three authors of this chapter belong – in recent years we have been compiling a list of animal advocacy documentaries that we have deemed as relevant for animal liberation.[50] Despite the fact that such a list can only be incomplete, we have been able to identify up to 47 documentaries with direct or indirect benefits for animal liberation, of which 70 per cent (33 films) were launched between 2013 and 2019. Most of these documentaries are US productions, and so our analysis of 20 of them here may be considered quantitatively relevant. In this regard, our findings clearly show that the documentary films have strongly followed the rule that the best strategy is to follow a pluralist approach (making a combination of ethical, rational and emotional claims) with an emphasis on ethical arguments.

Our findings also suggest that a profound sense of social justice and a desire for the abolition of animal exploitation is highly present in the analysed sample. The depiction of activists as grassroots people is also noteworthy, as well as the relevance of activists' role in taking care of individuals from other species. The "convert" frame was and still is a common resource in documentaries, as it opens the possibilities for 180-degree change, where the animal liberation goal is taken up by former exploiters who dedicate themselves to animal liberation and social transformation. We also recognise the abundance of activist representation as taking low-risk actions and find it important for audience identification with diverse forms of activism, which tend to be less glamorised than other more spectacular actions. However, at the same time, we deem the representation of nonviolent direct action in animal advocacy documentaries as still highly important and necessary, as these strategies have historically been, and still are, a core element of the international animal liberation movement and its success. An

49 McCormick 2019.

50 https://tinyurl.com/5rcxnth9.

ethical representation of direct action is needed to show the bigger picture of animal advocacy and to promote political awareness and solidarity with activists involved in this kind of action, who frequently suffer from criminalisation and state repression.[51] As Steven Best and Anthony J. Nocella observe:

> Resolved not to harm living beings, motivated by love, empathy, compassion, and justice, animal liberationists are the antithesis of the "terrorists" that government, industries, and mass media ideologues impugn them to be. They are not violent aggressors against life; they are defenders of freedom and justice for any enslaved species. They uphold rights not covered by law, knowing that the legal structure is defined by and for human supremacists.[52]

To conclude, we celebrate the representation of nonhuman animal agency and resistance in the "nonhuman animals as activists" frame, because who else but nonhuman animals can better represent their own fight for liberation? Nonetheless, in a world where their voices are still silenced, underestimated and ignored, in these documentaries, human advocates for animal liberation speak their minds against speciesist violence and oppression and show their personal transformations and daily actions, thereby becoming allies with nonhuman animals' daily struggles as victims of imprisonment, exploitation and murder. Animal advocates compel society to recognise the injustices perpetrated against nonhuman animals and communicate the urgent need for an antispeciesist and compassionate social transformation. This is why activist representation in documentaries matters: because animal advocates are role models and speakers that inspire compassion, truth, nonviolence and justice. They are the ones asserting the ineluctable message of animal liberation.

51 Potter 2011.
52 Best and Nocella 2004, 12.

References

Allen, Mike, ed. (2017). *The SAGE Encyclopedia of Communication Research Methods.* Los Angeles: SAGE. https://doi.org/10.4135/9781483381411.

Almiron, Núria (2019). Greening animal defense? Examining whether appealing to climate change and the environment is an effective advocacy strategy to reduce oppression of nonhumans. *American Behavioral Scientist* 63(8): 1101–19. https://doi.org/10.1177/0002764219830466.

Almiron, Núria, Matthew Cole and Carrie P. Freeman (2018). Critical animal and media studies: expanding the understanding of oppression in communication research. *European Journal of Communication* 33(4): 1–14. https://doi.org/10.1177/0267323118763937.

Best, Steven and Anthony J. Nocella, eds. (2004). *Terrorists or Freedom Fighters?: Reflections on the Liberation of Animals.* New York: Lantern.

Burford, Caitlyn and Julie K. Schutten (2017). Internatural activists and the "Blackfish effect": contemplating captive orcas' protest rhetoric through a coherence frame. *Frontiers in Communication* 1, January: 1–11. https://doi.org/10.3389/fcomm.2016.00016.

Chang, Chia-ju (2017). Global animal capital and animal garbage: documentary redemption and hope. *Journal of Chinese Cinemas* 11(1): 96–114. https://doi.org/10.1080/17508061.2016.1269483.

Christopher, Allison, John P. Bartkowski and Timothy Haverda (2018). Portraits of veganism: a comparative discourse analysis of a second-order subculture. *Societies* 8(3), 55: 4–21. https://doi.org/10.3390/soc8030055.

Cole, Matthew and Karen Morgan (2011). Vegaphobia: derogatory discourses of veganism and the reproduction of speciesism in UK national newspapers. *The British Journal of Sociology* 62(1): 134–53. https://tinyurl.com/56spj26z.

Dawn, Karen (2004). From the front line to the front page – an analysis of ALF media coverage. In Steven Best and Anthony J. Nocella, eds. *Terrorists or Freedom Fighters?: Reflections on the Liberation of Animals*, 202–12. New York: Lantern.

Erdős, László (2019). *Green Heroes: From Buddha to Leonardo DiCaprio.* Cham: Springer.

Evans, Kellie S. (2014). The valorous, the villainous, and the victimized: the melodramatic framework of animal rights documentary. Master's thesis, University of Akron, Akron, Ohio.

Fernández, Laura (2019). Using images of farmed animals in environmental advocacy: an antispeciesist, strategic visual communication proposal. *American Behavioral Scientist* 63(8): 1137–55. https://doi.org/10.1177/0002764219830454.

Food Empowerment Project (2021). *Food Empowerment Project*. https://foodispower.org.
Freeman, Carrie P. and Scott Tulloch (2013). Was blind but now I see: animal liberation documentaries' deconstruction of barriers to witnessing injustice. In Anat Pick and Guinevere Narraway, eds. *Screening Nature: Cinema Beyond the Human*, 110–26. New York: Berghahn Books.
Freeman, Carrie P. (2012). Fishing for animal rights in *The Cove*: a holistic approach to animal advocacy documentaries. *Journal for Critical Animal Studies* 10(1): 104–18. https://tinyurl.com/3zy7jucx.
Harper, A. Breeze (2010). *Sistah Vegan: Black Female Vegans Speak on Food, Identity, Health and Society*. Brooklyn, NY: Lantern.
It's a Dog's Life (1997). Film. Justyn Jones (Dir.). Distributor: Small World.
Lind, Katherine D. (2019). Flipping the script: developing an intertextual dialogue for dolphin advocacy in *The Cove*. *Environmental Communication* 14(5): 628–40. https://doi.org/10.1080/17524032.2019.1699134.
McCormick, Benjamin (2019). Why people go vegan: 2019 global survey results. *Vomad*, 4 March. https://bit.ly/3vD0rZJ.
Newman, Lara (2015). The effects of The Cove and Bold Native on audience attitudes towards animals. *Animal Studies Journal* 4(1): 77–98. https://ro.uow.edu.au/asj/vol4/iss1/6.
Potter, Will (2011). *Green Is the New Red: An Insider's Account of a Social Movement Under Siege*. San Francisco, CA: City Lights Books.
Scanlon, Taylor M. (2013). Opening cages and ending the world: the representation of animal activism-as-terrorism in *Bold Native* and *28 Days Later*. Master's thesis, The University of British Columbia, Canada.
The Animals Film (1981). Film. Victor Schonfeld and Myriam Alaux (Dirs.). Distributor: Beyond the Frame.
White, Richard J. (2019). Looking backward, moving forward: articulating a 'yes … BUT!' response to lifestyle veganism. *Europe Now*. https://bit.ly/4aZgwJa.
Wrenn, Corey Lee (2019). *Piecemeal Protest. Animal Rights in the Age of Nonprofits*. Ann Arbor: University of Michigan Press.

3

The Animal People

Reconstituting identity in the animal liberation movement

Emily Plec

Fifteen years in the making, the 2019 documentary film *The Animal People* chronicles the activism and persecution of six Americans affiliated with an animal rights effort known in the UK and US as Stop Huntingdon Animal Cruelty or SHAC. Huntingdon Life Sciences (HLS) performed contract work for corporations and was Europe's largest contract animal testing laboratory, testing products such as household cleaners, pesticides and food additives "on approximately 75,000 animals every year – from rats to wild baboons".[1] After the company moved to the US, SHAC challenged HLS' profits and business practices through protests that targeted employees, affiliates and supply chain companies.

That the actions of a handful of animal liberation activists prompted one of the largest Federal Bureau of Investigation (FBI) investigations in history is itself alarming. How the SHAC website, campaigns and the otherwise protected speech of these activists were legislatively transformed into terrorist activities is even more troubling. *The Animal People* exposes the system that framed SHAC activists as terrorists for their disruption of capitalist practices and, at the same time, calls attention to the ongoing torture and exploitation of animals for commercial purposes. Contrary to popular perceptions, the vast

1 Center for Constitutional Rights: https://bit.ly/3vKssOM.

majority of animal experimentation, as Peter Singer pointed out half a century ago, does not yield any medical or human health-related benefit. Rather, it is consumer product testing practices that have created the impetus for much of the systematic breeding, experimentation and euthanising of laboratory animals.

This chapter examines *The Animal People* in terms of its potential to function as reconstitutive discourse. John Hammerback and Richard Jensen propose a three-pronged model for examining the capacity of activist discourses to reconstitute audience member identities, altering character in a way that builds community.[2] Following a rhetorical analysis of the first persona, second persona and substantive message of *The Animal People*, I discuss the extent to which the film encourages a subjectivity that is strongly supportive of both animal rights and free speech. The film's graphic exposure of the abusive practices of HLS, along with political discourse affording greater protections to corporations than to the activists or the animals they seek to protect from harm, function to remind audience members that company profit trumps nonhuman lives (and activists' rights) in the value system of our late consumer capitalist societies.

I am also interested in how the film contributes, if at all, to the reconstitution of what Carrie Packwood Freeman (2020) terms a "human animal earthling" identity. Freeman's concept is "a new, more humble and integrated identity for humans" in which we identify "not just egocentrically with our own species but with the animal kingdom as a whole and the mutual status we share as living beings on the planet".[3] Understanding how a documentary film such as *The Animal People* can persuade viewers, (re)constitute identity and influence actions is especially important in this cultural and historical moment, when the principles of democratic praxis and the foundations of environmental sustainability are being so profoundly threatened by industry and government collusion, enabled by citizen inaction and the human–animal divide.

---

2 Hammerback 2001; Hammerback and Jensen 1998.

3 Freeman 2020, 29.

The first persona: Proponents of animal and human rights

In the model of reconstitutive discourse, and in rhetorical theory generally, the "first persona" refers to the image the audience holds of the rhetor. For instance, Black community leader and entrepreneur Marcus Garvey, through his rhetorical adoption of themes of election, captivity and liberation, evoked a "Moses" persona.[4] The first persona can be a preconceived idea the audience has of the rhetor, an image cultivated through the rhetor's discourse, or a combination of the two. In the case of *The Animal People*, the rhetor includes several people including the directors, Casey Suchan and Denis Henry Hennelly, producers Mikko Alanne, Ari Solomon and Joaquin Phoenix, and most importantly, the protagonists known as the SHAC 7 – the US-based activists, six of whom stood trial for their efforts to shut down HLS.[5]

The film's impetus was the news image of the six defendants outside the New Jersey courthouse where they were tried; Alanne and Solomon felt the story needed to be told. Suchan and Hennelly "had already explored the subject of breaking the law for animals in their dramatic feature film 'Bold Native'" and were "immediately drawn to the project".[6] *Bold Native*, a fictional film about an animal liberation activist who is wanted by the FBI, emphasises the importance of activism at a time when animal liberators are being targeted as domestic terrorists by law enforcement agencies.[7] Thus, the producers' empathy for SHAC, along with the filmmakers' knowledge of and commitment to a subject matter common to both films, likely contribute to audience members' perceptions of the rhetor as credible and also left-leaning in terms of the politics of animal liberation. This dimension of the first persona is further reinforced by the involvement of a well-known celebrity.

Award-winning actor Joaquin Phoenix, an outspoken animal rights activist and vegan, joined as Executive Producer when the film was

---

4 Ware and Linkugel 1982.

5 Charges were not pursued against John McGee, presumably due to a lack of evidence of his involvement and concern that his inclusion would weaken the prosecution's case. The six who stood trial are: Jake Conroy, Darius Fullmer, Lauren Gazzola, Josh Harper, Kevin Kjonaas and Andy Stepanian.

6 Lo 2019.

7 Del Gandio and Noella 2014.

in post-production, lending his influence to a documentary "about fundamental questions concerning free speech, social change, and corporate power that have never been more urgently relevant in our world".[8] Shortly after the film's release, Phoenix, accepting the 2020 Academy Award for Best Actor, called upon the audience to "create, develop, and implement systems of change that are beneficial to all sentient beings and to the environment".[9] By adding his voice to the public conversation about animal rights and liberation, using his platform as a famous actor and celebrity vegan, Phoenix further strengthened the perception of the rhetor as credible.

Unlike these "behind the scenes" figures, the six defendants affiliated with SHAC are known to most audience members entirely in terms of their representation in the film. When they are not depicted speaking for themselves, narration is provided by award-winning investigative journalist Will Potter, whose book *Green Is the New Red* details the FBI's use of anti-terrorism resources to target animal rights and environmental activists.[10] Potter's narration, as well as his appearance as the sole witness for the opposition in hearings on the counterterrorism legislation known as the *Animal Enterprise Terrorism Act* (AETA), furthers audience perceptions of the rhetor as sympathetic to SHAC, or at least critical of the FBI's persecution of environmental and animal rights activists.

The opening scene introduces the main protagonist, Kevin Kjonaas. Special Agent James Anderson is heard stating his intent to record a telephone conversation, which is followed by a loud dial tone, quiet sounds of dialling and a man's voice answering "SHAC USA". The caller responds, "Hi, is Kevin there?" The footage then cuts to an aerial view of a quiet midwestern community. Kjonaas describes seeing FBI agents moving in and out of his house. Jake Conroy then describes his interaction with a law enforcement officer, who got upset when Conroy laughed at him: "This guy … got in my face" and said, "you tell Kevin, we're going to get him", to which Conroy responded, "Yeah, I'll get right on that." The plotline is then laid out in typeface across the screen:

8 Phoenix, quoted in Lo 2019.
9 Phoenix 2020.
10 Potter 2011.

"In 2004, following one of the largest investigations in FBI history, the United States government charged six Americans with terrorism." A diagram of SHAC leaders' photos and names appears with voiceover from Josh Harper:

> We're six activists who are indicted under federal terrorism laws. We didn't break anything. We didn't burn anything, we didn't beat anyone, we didn't even so much as trespass. Our crime is doing exactly what I'm doing right now, speaking.

Will Potter then describes the group's target, HLS ("and companies that did business with it") before the footage cuts to a congressional hearing in which SHAC is described as engaging in "a campaign of fear" and "an international conspiracy". Lauren Gazzola's first appearance occurs at this juncture. She says, matter-of-factly, "Corporations get to do what they want ... We challenged the right of this corporation to exist."

The documentary then cuts back to Kevin Kjonaas, shown in his kitchen giving his dog, Willie, a treat. He describes his passion for public policy and social change, as well as his childhood growing up with Barney the Beagle as his best friend. When he learned that beagles are used extensively in animal experimentation, he began to get involved and helped organise a club at the University of Minnesota to oppose animal researchers. Depicted as an idealistic young college student who believes in the power of the people to right a moral wrong, Kevin describes demonstrations outside the home of Marilyn Carroll, a university researcher who uses rhesus monkeys and rats as test subjects for drug addiction research. Kevin was further energised to be a spokesperson for radical actors such as ALF after a break-in at a university building housing research animals. Shortly after the break-in, Kevin's home was searched by the FBI and the Minnesota Senate attempted to pass a law criminalising any person who would "promote, advocate, and take responsibility for criminal acts", even attempting to make the law retroactive. In the film, he reflects upon his willingness to take such risks: "Maybe it was hubris and being young and full of oneself but I felt like repercussions weren't going to be an issue for me." These events are depicted as catalysts for Kevin's move to the UK to lead SHAC's efforts against HLS during the 2002 jailing of

SHAC founders Greg and Natasha Avery and Heather Nicholson (née James).

Throughout the film, Kevin is shown as a principled person whose straightlaced manner contrasts with the image many audience members may have of animal rights activists. For instance, he describes his dissatisfaction with the disorganised nature of the groups he sought out: "I believe in hierarchy and leadership. I believe in authority," he says early in the film. He is also sympathetic to the tenet of ALF to not criticise any act undertaken with the intent of furthering animal liberation. In fact, SHAC's online communication and tactics aimed at financially restricting the ability of companies to harm animals for profit, along with Kjonaas' refusal to condemn others' property crimes, would become central to the prosecution's case against him and other SHAC members.

The film's opening sequence emphasises the FBI's persecution of activists at the behest of corporations, which is a key part of the substantive message. State and federal agencies also targeted Josh Harper and Jake Conroy, whose politicisation and experience with the anti-whaling movement is presented as their entry point into SHAC. Harper talks about the influence that leaked footage from the animal testing facility had on him, presumably referencing a Channel 4 exposé that galvanised public protests against HLS. He describes witnessing "what was supposed to be a necropsy on a primate that was clearly still living and breathing. A man callously cutting open his chest." Harper expresses the importance of recognising that change occurs because people are willing to fight, to sacrifice, and even willing to suffer to make it happen. Later in the film, Conroy describes going to work in the SHAC office: "I was only supposed to go for three months. And I never came back." From the producers to the protestors, the first persona in *The Animal People* is presented as informed, intelligent, compassionate, energised by the injustices of animal experimentation and committed to the cause.

Due to SHAC's success in the UK, HLS is forced to seek government support and new financial backers. Warren Stephens, the CEO of Stephens Inc., the US company that backs HLS after the UK campaign succeeds, insists that "The animals are treated as humanely as they possibly can be." Josh Harper's "mission" on a trip to Stephens

Inc. headquarters in Arkansas, is "to show that there would be consequences for Stephens' decision to support HLS". In newsreel footage, a reporter describes the protests outside Stephens' home in a way that highlights the media's collusion with law enforcement and corporate interests: "As the members of … leaders of this gang try to terrorise … I'm sorry, they're trying to show their threat of what they're going to do today." These discourses of terrorism and threat, wielded awkwardly by the reporter, reveal how the mainstream media aligned with government and industry. Though intended to demonise the protestors, the way the footage is deployed in the documentary encourages greater sympathy for the activists.

Like Kjonaas and Harper, Jake Conroy is deeply committed to animal liberation and opposed to experimentation. In one scene, we hear audio of a phone conversation with his mother. He is telling her that HLS kills 500 animals a day. In response, she asks, "Are you a terrorist?" His stunned reaction leads audience members to the conclusion that the media representations, and collusion between industry and government, have even shaped the perceptions of his closest family members.

At the same time, the film does not shrink from the realities of radical protest and acknowledges its limits in terms of activists' ability to challenge capitalist enterprises. The filmmakers point out that, while the lawful "above-ground campaign" against Stephens Inc. continued, an uncontrollable element began to take over and use underground sabotage. For instance, $100,000 was charged to Warren Stephens' credit card and his apartment was painted red. Later in the film, Harper distances himself from such actions while also praising those who committed them, saying "some of the things I really despise about the campaign, I love the people who did these things … People need to develop the skills to resist these multinational organisations." Ultimately, the campaign succeeded and Stephens sold the stock. In the next frame, Kevin Kjonaas says bitterly, "Somebody bought the damn shares." The audience, having been positioned to identify with the first persona, feels the disappointment and frustration of the activists.

Lauren Gazzola is the other SHAC member depicted prominently in the interview footage. Gazzola is portrayed as intelligent, tactical and committed to staying within the realm of protected speech. In an excerpt from her interview she says, laughing, "Some people are good at sports, I'm good at the law, including following it, I might point out. Some would disagree." The film cuts to footage of Gazzola protesting outside a residence and challenging an officer who is attempting to silence the demonstrators. She says to the officer, "I'm not here to be considerate, I'm here to follow the law. So what's the law that says that?" Gazzola, in the interview, discusses the "incitement test" and the standard that speech must "set fire to reason". When Gazzola receives an indictment in the mail, she admits, "Everything they've said in here is true!" Her attorney argued that "burn the house down" was protected speech, that nothing in her actions indicated an intent to burn down anyone's house. The court agreed but it was only the beginning of Gazzola's legal battles and an indication of the capacity for law enforcement and government prosecutors to intimidate and silence animal rights activists by charging them as terrorists.

The narration, individual reflections and file footage hint at a youthful naiveté yet the group, on the whole, is depicted as clever, committed, hardworking and deeply dedicated to their cause. This depiction is set against that of the vindictive and petty Federal Bureau of Investigation, state law enforcement agencies, corporations and the US government that passed legislation to criminalise effective direct-action tactics and expanded the use of counterterrorism resources to surveil and prosecute activists whose campaigns are perceived as threatening by corporations. For instance, one scene shows footage of FBI domestic terrorism section chief Thomas Carey talking about taking "a look back" to see what they can "potentially charge people with". He says, "We're going to take every tool in our toolbox and use it."

The activists describe how it started out with "two well-dressed men rifling through their garbage" and even joke about letting the FBI know when they were going out to run errands when the surveillance began. Josh Harper points out: "Anybody who studies resistance movements in the United States knows that the FBI has always been an enemy of people attempting to effect change." The video cuts to Kevin Kjonaas talking about his hatred of the FBI: "I think they're perverse, pathetic bullies", then cuts back to an official saying, "We're going to be as creative as we possibly can to charge them with a violation." Such statements further paint the SHAC members as being aggressively and unreasonably persecuted by law enforcement.

Additional credibility is lent to the rhetors in the form of expert interviews. Philosophy professor Steven Best offers some historical context, suggesting that the SHAC members are part of a long history that people want to revise. He highlights examples of civil disruption and disobedience from Gandhi and Martin Luther King Jr, pointing out that significant social change is catalysed by social forces and collective action. "Violence and sabotage, and property destruction, threats of violence and coercive change of various kinds," says Best, "is what moves history." Heidi Boghosian, Executive Director of the National Lawyers Guild, summarises the film's central concern: "They have pinpointed boycotts and traditional forms of protest and criminalised it so that any threat to cause a loss of profit to a corporation is now considered an act of terrorism." From conception to direction, narration and depictions, *The Animal People* constructs a rhetor committed to exposing this very undemocratic reality. As the conviction of the six members of the US-based SHAC unfolds in the film's story, so does the audience's sense that a deep injustice has occurred. The extent to which the audience is also urged to identify with the cause of animal liberation, a cause that continues to motivate the SHAC activists to this day, is addressed in the next section.

The second persona: Constructing a human animal earthling identity

In an essay in *Rhetoric Review*, John Hammerback argues that:

> rhetors who incarnate their messages and who depict their audiences in ways to facilitate identification with themselves open an avenue to persuade and in some cases, to reconstitute those audiences.[11]

11 Hammerback 2001, 21.

Whereas the "first persona" is a concept intimately linked to the audience's perceptions of the rhetor, the "second persona" refers to the audience that is envisioned by the rhetor.[12] It is the role assumed by the audience in response to the rhetor's discourse. This "implied audience" includes all those capable of being reconstituted by the discourse. The second persona can also be understood as the audience called into being by being constructed anew.[13] In their study of the rhetoric of Cesar Chavez, for instance, Hammerback and Jensen show how Chavez constructed a "new man" who was fearless and optimistic and willing to act as an activist and advocate.[14] In *The Animal People*, several key moments give insight into values and worldviews ideally held by audience members.

Though some audience members may have watched the film because of its promotion by a celebrity such as Joaquin Phoenix, most were likely exposed to the film because of a pre-existing interest in animal rights, animal liberation, veganism (the film was reviewed on a number of vegan websites and publications), or through networks promoting values associated with these topics. Thus, it is safe to assume that many of the audience members targeted by the filmmakers are, themselves, budding or committed activists, or at least potentially inclined to take further action. Hammerback talks about the "added importance of fitting the audience into its 'second persona'",[15] which, in this case, entails moving the interested audience from a place of tacit support to active engagement. Thus, the second persona of *The Animal People* is the animal rights and free speech activist. As Edwin Black, theorising the second persona, points out, discourse provides us with "enticements not simply to believe something, but to *be* something".[16] He goes on to say that "the discourse will exert … the pull of an ideology".[17]

12 Black 1970.
13 Hammerback 2001; Hammerback and Jensen 1998.
14 Hammerback 2001, 18.
15 Hammerback 2001, 19.
16 Black 1970, 119, emphasis in original.
17 Black 1970, 113.

The ability to play an active role in the liberation of animals as well as the fight to restore legal rights for humans engaged in agitation is critical for Freeman's "human animal earthling" identity and the ideologies that constitute it. Freeman argues that the rights of humans can be "encompassed within the broader category of animal rights", providing a "bridge between human rights and environmentalism".[18] She identifies the following "common opponents identified by activists", all of whom play an integral role in shaping the audience's response to *The Animal People*:

> Exploitative corporations
> The global economic system
> Corrupt or weak governments
> Societal discrimination
> Selfish people[19]

HLS is the exploitative corporation, supported by a global economic system, that depends on animal experimentation purportedly to ensure product safety and develop new pharmaceutical interventions. That global system allowed HLS, when effectively shut down due to protests in the UK, to simply "move shop" to the US and later to morph into Envigo (which has over 20 locations in North America and Europe, according to the company website).

HLS' exploitative practices involving animals are highlighted in contrast to the rhetoric of the corporation. A member of the senior management team says, "Huntingdon was doing everything right. Everything." In the next shot, viewers are informed about a Channel 4 undercover investigation that showed workers abusing and mistreating animals, whose audible whimpers, cries and screams reinforce the irony of the executive's statement. The film paints HLS as a company less interested in preventing animal abuse than making sure the media doesn't find out about what actually goes on in their labs. Efforts to blame a single individual (who was allegedly fired, along with their supervisor) and minimise the harm ("One technician out of 600

18 Freeman 2020, 35.
19 Freeman 2020, 225.

slapped a dog") are contrasted with descriptions of widespread abuse by an undercover investigator. She describes being in the US lab when the UK case broke and says that "the message that came to the workers in the US lab was 'Don't get caught doing anything like that'". She concludes, "The animals are treated awfully. There's no regard for them. Their suffering doesn't matter at all. It's just about the dollar bill. It's all true."

After presenting HLS as one of many institutional villains, the narrative shifts to the effectiveness of SHAC's targeting of secondary and tertiary groups – those financing HLS and those upon whom HLS depends but are themselves not dependent on HLS for financial stability. A UK banker tells representatives from HLS that they are at the "leading edge of high risk". CEO Brian Cass affirms that the company soon faced difficulty getting a bank account or insurance coverage and even lost several shareholders. Barclays and the Royal Bank of Scotland pulled their financial backing as pressure from the SHAC campaign mounted. As mentioned previously, HLS then turned to an anonymous US backer, Stephens Inc., to purchase their debt. Kjonaas says Stephens was "the crutch Huntingdon was leaning on to survive". If Stephens could be pressured into severing ties with HLS, the activists hoped, then HLS could not continue to operate.

The Animal People reveals how the "war on animals" has been escalated by "neoliberalism and global capitalism".[20] After all, the "weak government" of the UK bowed to HLS once (providing insurance services after a SHAC campaign against private insurer Marsh succeeded). Now, the film stresses, the corrupt US government is using the power of the FBI to surveil animal rights activists and using industry-friendly counterterrorism legislation to criminalise dissent that threatens corporate profits.

Presumably, the historical and cultural orientation of the audience is important to their willingness to accept the veracity of this narrative. After all, both the free speech issues and the animal rights issues addressed in the film are topics about which most people are poorly informed, or at least significantly less informed than the members of SHAC. Therefore, it is necessary for *The Animal People* to construct the

20 Best 2014, 160.

story in such a way as to educate viewers while also inviting audience identification with the activists, a feature of reconstitutive discourse that is addressed in more detail in the next section.

Audience members are led to the conclusion that governments are colluding with industry to maintain the status quo regarding animal experimentation. Moreover, this collusion is aimed at criminalising environmental activism that has the potential to economically destabilise harmful and exploitative industries by classifying those activities as ecoterrorism. Societal discrimination against radical environmentalists and animal rights activists enables the curtailment of democratic rights by "selfish people", exemplified in the film by Senator James Inhofe, the FBI, and the billionaire CEOs of HLS and its affiliates.

To counter such opponents, Freeman argues that solidarity needs to be built around core "project areas" such as: "democratic reforms", "economic system reforms" (that emphasise stakeholders over shareholders), "abolition of enslavement of sentient beings" and "freedom from unfair imprisonment of sentient beings", among others.[21] *The Animal People* entreats audience members to join in these projects by forging identification with the brave, persecuted activists and against the greedy industry leaders, cruel animal experimenters and complicit HLS employees. In case the audience missed the message, it is driven home by primate researcher Dr Stuart Zola who says in the legislative hearings, hyperbolically, "If this continues, the animal extremists will have won and the loser will be humanity." Zola's statement comes at a point in the film when audience members have been well informed about the nature of most animal experimentation and presented with reasoning, discussed in the next section, that indicates that the vast majority of animal experimentation does not lead to beneficial advances for humanity but is, rather, cruel and unnecessary. The narrative, in fact, begins to beg the question of what such large-scale experimentation upon animals for consumer purposes does to our humanity and why a humane ethic demands that we end it.

Audience member identification with SHAC, particularly for audience members who may view themselves as politically moderate, could be limited by the description of radical tactics which might either

21 Freeman 2020, 225–32.

entice or offend someone sympathetic to the cause. Kjonaas talks about placing ads with titles like "Learn to Recognize Gang Members" and holds up a flier depicting different types of police officers. He laughs about a mock advertisement for a brick with the tagline: "A smashing idea in the war on vivisection!" The film also highlights SHAC's efforts to keep businesses, from custodial and cafeteria services to internet providers, from working with and for HLS. Activists used denial of service attacks and demonstrated against service providers and shareholders (someone even "vomited on" one of HLS' display tables at an event). As the activists themselves put it, "We're going to be a royal pain in the ass and then a rude embarrassment to any company that is connected to Huntingdon." Viewers who are offended by such tactics are less likely to find their identities transformed by the relationship between the first persona and the substantive message, though they will likely still be uneasy about political efforts to criminalise some of the more innocuous forms of protest.

The substantive message: The prosecution of a political movement

In the model of reconstitutive discourse, the substantive message is articulated through argument and explanation. When merged with the first and second persona, it can:

> induce auditors (1) to act out their self-perceived qualities of character, (2) to animate their latent qualities, and (3) to reorder their qualities of character and thereby alter their self-definition.[22]

Hammerback goes on to say that this "synergistic interaction of message and personae creates multiple and overlapping layers of identification"[23] that are critical for audience reconstitution. Identification is achieved in this case through negative portrayals of HLS (forging a common enemy held by both SHAC and now viewers), sympathetic depictions of SHAC members (discussed in the first

22 Hammerback 2001, 20.
23 Hammerback 2001, 20.

section) and credible arguments about the effectiveness of their direct-action campaigns.

The enthymematic reasoning that undergirds all of this rests on the major premise that HLS' experimentation on animals is unnecessary and cruel. Left implicit are the reasons why people who care about animals should not allow unnecessary and cruel things to happen to them. The filmmakers need only draw audience members to the conclusion that people who care about animals should oppose HLS. By showing how SHAC went about doing just that, *The Animal People* highlights the extent to which they were persecuted and prosecuted because of their effectiveness as well as the desire by those with financial and political power to protect the economic interests of corporations, including but by no means limited to HLS. As a result, the substantive message moves from an argument about animal rights and the illegitimacy of much animal experimentation to a case study in political persecution.

The breadth of the implications of the *Animal Enterprise Terrorism Act* (AETA) and the FBI's surveillance suggests to viewers that citizens who engage in direct-action tactics, particularly those that undermine the ability of corporations to do business, will be pursued and punished for flaunting their rights and challenging capitalist practices that depend on the exploitation of animals and nature. Legal scholar Kim McCoy writes: "The real targets of this legislation are above-ground activists who seek to abide by the law."[24] During the congressional deliberations, the potential for harm to the timber and fossil fuel industries is raised by Senator Inhofe as additional justification for criminalising such direct-action tactics.

That SHAC's campaign in the US intensified just as the World Trade Center attacks of 2001 occurred is also highlighted in the film and informs audience members' understanding of the political context leading up to the AETA. Jake Conroy says there was optimism among animal rights activists that law enforcement would have a focus other than targeting political activists, "but obviously, it was the opposite". A clip of President George W. Bush saying that the war on terror begins with Al-Qaeda "but it does not end there" is followed bypolice

24 McCoy 2014, 33.

surveillance footage from SHAC's Little Rock protests against Stephens Inc. Animal rights activist Daniel Andreas San Diego is charged with a night-time bombing at the Chiron building (and the group taking credit for the act claims the action was motivated by Chiron's ties with HLS), after which he appears on the FBI most wanted list "alongside Osama bin Laden and others" and featured on *America's Most Wanted*. The film also suggests that gubernatorial candidate Chris Christie's political ambitions fuelled the effort to hold SHAC accountable for radical underground animal liberation actions.

"All the police in the world can't protect their finances"[25]

Throughout the documentary, police officers are shown in often violent confrontations with protestors and as a protective force for corporate interests. Midway through the film, Darius Fullmer's description of the "free speech zone" that was set up by law enforcement to contain the protestors in Arkansas drives home the point the film is making about First Amendment rights and police protection:

> The police had set up this free speech zone, which makes you wonder, you know, if this is like the free speech zone, then what's everything outside of the free speech zone? The whole country is supposed to be a free speech zone.

As activists begin shaking the barricades of the "free speech zone", police threaten force and then use pepper spray and rubber bullets against the protestors, before arresting Harper and others.

In addition to demonstrations, the film presents a wide range of direct-action tactics that were used to persuade other companies to disinvest and disengage from HLS. Activist leaders from across the country describe the creativity and effectiveness of campaign efforts. The diversity and national distribution of leadership presented in these clips, along with the information about some of SHAC's creative and disruptive tactics, further contributes to the potential for audience

25 Slogan shouted by Kjonaas at a rally.

reconstitution. Viewers get a sense of how widespread the movement is as well as how diverse the approaches to social and institutional change can be. From divestment campaigns to property crimes, viewers who are sympathetic to the cause of animal liberation can presumably find a place to plug into that movement through SHAC and the campaign against HLS (now Envigo). But will they?

The Animal People's message presents a complicated tension. On the one hand, viewers are presented with a rational argument for opposing HLS and corporations like it for their animal experimentation practices. Yet they are also presented with evidence that shows how their potential actions have been criminalised by governments and the extent to which animal rights activists will be persecuted for actions that threaten corporate profit. McCoy points out the problem the AETA causes, which the film fails to resolve, which is that "people who are sympathetic to animal rights are encouraged to distance themselves from animal advocates for fear of guilt by association".[26] The ability for audience members to be reconstituted as "animal people" hinges in part on their willingness to overcome that distance. It also depends on the belief that activist campaigns can make a meaningful difference, which is another complicated tension given that SHAC won numerous victories but failed in their ambition to halt animal experimentation. The film aims to "ignite public discourse" and "provide an opportunity to connect with advocacy issues".[27] Because of the intersection of animal rights and free speech issues, the film has the capacity to connect audiences to advocacy across pre-existing lines of interest.

Potter's narration of the film, emphasising the history of First Amendment case law, is supplemented by legal experts whose testimony reinforces the view that the SHAC members engaged in constitutionally protected speech. "The First Amendment protects advocacy," says attorney Matthew Struger, "including advocacy of illegal actions unless it meets the incitement test." Heidi Boghosian of the National Lawyers Guild points out that unless the speech targets a "specific individual" for "imminent harm", it is protected by the First Amendment.

26 McCoy 2014, 33.
27 Loy 2020, 221.

Underscoring the film's focus on the persecution of the activists, footage from a Senate hearing shows James Inhofe claiming that "there is a need for tighter legislation to curb this criminal activity that up to date has been impervious to law enforcement authorities". He goes on to describe SHAC as "the most serious domestic terrorist threat today". Barry Sabin from the Department of Justice's Counterterrorism Division testifies and asserts his department's support for amending the federal counterterrorism legislation to include "economic disruption to animal enterprise". Multiple industries rallied behind the AETA and it was ushered through using obscure rules and with minimal opposition.[28]

Later in the film, viewers are introduced to MIT Researcher Ryan Shapiro who, through *Freedom of Information Act* requests, uncovers the FBI's "Operation Trailmix", an effort to break the animal rights movement. He shows how, due to their inability to capture those responsible for the underground, illegal direct actions, the FBI refocused its energies on prosecuting the above-ground elements, namely the SHAC 6, for their advocacy. The prosecution used witnesses who had been targeted by SHAC actions to construct what Josh Harper describes as a "parade of victims" and they presented HLS as a corporation that was engaging in animal research to purportedly "save children's lives". While the prosecution could speak about the life-saving research of HLS, the defendants were prohibited from speaking about the abuse and mistreatment of animals inside the facility. Thus, the jury was presented with a narrative in which the youthful activists engaged in disruptive activity, perceived as life-threatening and intimidating by HLS employees and their families, for no justifiable reason.

ACLU Foundation of California Chair Stephen Rohde says, "There was no direct evidence of any unlawful conduct so know you're in the area of either inciting unlawful conduct, or conspiring to commit unlawful conduct." Both Kjonaas and Gazzola, in separate interview footage, justify their support for activists who engaged in property damage (vs. damage to people and animals). Kjonaas says, "Property destruction is not violence, it's sabotage" and Gazzola says, "It's just

28 Del Gandio and Nocella 2014.

not the same kind of harm to break a window as to break an arm." Nonetheless, at trial, a guilty verdict is issued against all six members. Bob Obler, Darius Fullmer's court-appointed lawyer, states that the case was never about putting them in jail, it was about "appeasing the appropriate business interests and making a statement". The point of the trial was to show pharmaceutical and biomedical industries that the government "had their back and would have their support".

The film mentions that, upon appeal, the judge found that the rights of the defendants to say what they said was constitutionally protected, but then went on to say that same speech was sufficient to get Harper convicted of terrorism. According to the film, Harper was sentenced to three years at Sheridan Federal Prison, Fullmer received a sentence of one year for calling Kjonaas to tell him about a protest, Stepanian received a three-year sentence, Conroy four years, and Gazzola four and a half years. Kjonaas, unsurprisingly, was sentenced to the longest term – six years – and was released after almost five. Footage reminds audience members that animal experimentation is still rampant, as HLS merges with numerous other facilities to become Envigo.

The film closes with both doubts and affirmations of the effectiveness of their activism. Kjonaas is praised in a Fox segment with Tucker Carlson for the legislative reforms associated with his Beagle Freedom Project. The potential for positive change is reinforced in clips from Kjonaas' and Harper's speeches after incarceration, where they urge others to commit to the cause. The importance of rising up is further emphasised by scenes of civic uprisings around the globe. Harper seems to be addressing the audience directly when he offers these closing words:

> I can't in good conscience turn my back on what history has told me. And that is that without struggle, there is not progress. And that unless you are willing to rise up and to fight with your hands, nothing changes.

Conclusion: "The animal people are coming"[29]

Rhetorician and radical activist Jason Del Gandio writes: "Animal liberationists seek to save the lives of nonhuman animals, and as a consequence, improve the human condition."[30] *The Animal People* shows how members and supporters of SHAC challenged a major corporation. Portraying the activists as courageous, committed, inspirational figures who were, and still are, willing to put their freedom at risk to end animal experimentation contributes to audience reconstitution in two major ways. First, it reminds audience members of the power imbalance between corporations and activists. HLS/Envigo was able to leverage the support of the US Congress, FBI and local law enforcement, and ultimately the court system, to silence dissent and continue to engage in animal experimentation. Clearly, animal liberationists are at a major disadvantage. Second, the portrayal of the activists helps to forge identification. The first persona, combined with the activist orientation into which audience members are interpellated (the second persona) and blended with the substantive message (about cruel and unnecessary experimentation on animals as well as undemocratic persecution of activists), has the potential to reconstitute audience members as "animal people".

The challenge with this identification is in considering how audience members respond to their reconstitution. For audience members who were previously unaware of the AETA and surveillance of animal rights activists, the reconstitution is complicated by the dangers that come with being associated with terrorism. Audiences may hold greater fear of taking action as a result of SHAC's persecution by law enforcement. At the very least, they may be more inclined to confine their activism to mainstream actions such as voting, supporting legislative reforms and financially supporting animal rights organisations. For audience members who already held a liberationist stance and view the US government as more an instrument of capitalism than democracy, the film has the potential to strengthen

29 Testimony from a HLS employee/parent whose child allegedly feared, "The animal people are coming" to get them, as reported in the film.

30 Del Gandio 2014, 210.

their resolve to continue the fight to end animal experimentation, restore First Amendment freedoms and overturn the AETA.

One shortcoming of *The Animal People* has to do with the film's ability to reconstitute identity by engaging the second persona, the reconstituted audience. Largely omitted from the film but pervasive in Freeman's *The Human Animal Earthling Identity* are examples of the kind of coalitional organising that can produce meaningful change by engaging in democratic, economic and liberatory praxis. Although the conclusion of the film places the animal rights movement in the context of other liberation struggles through video clips of protests and police repression, these are presented in a way that, like the first persona, focuses attention on the heroic human activists. Effective in inspiring other individuals to emulate their tactics, the depictions nonetheless fail to articulate those heroic humans to the suffering animals and broader environmental and social contexts that are part of the nexus of power relations inhibiting animal liberation.

Freeman points out that "caring for animals' wellbeing correlates with stronger empathy and justice concerns for other humans".[31] The human animal earthling identity she proposes draws upon values that are life-supporting, and grounded in fairness, responsibility and unity. It recognises that animal liberation and rights movements must also be anti-racist and committed to economic and gender equity. The struggle to save animals confined to facilities cannot be divorced from issues of climate-caused extinction or intensive animal agriculture. We need to listen to other animals when they give us hints as to how we might also save ourselves. We are all earthlings and share one planetary habitat. *The Animal People* presents one small sliver of that planet, geographically and historically. The UK and US activists who have been leading the fight to end animal experimentation for decades have made strides and improved conditions for innumerable animals, by "making visible what is routinely made invisible".[32]

Animal experimentation is something most people do not think about or, if they do, they tend to accept company rhetoric about medical necessity and humane treatment. But, as Jerold Friedman points out,

31 Freeman 2020, 24.
32 Linné 2020, 255.

"advocates rely on media to report on their campaigns to attract public sentiment" and "media occasionally defy business pressures".[33] A television exposé showing violent and cruel treatment of animals initially catalysed SHAC and prompted their campaign against HLS. The documentary film *The Animal People*, itself prompted by news coverage of SHAC, will hopefully contribute to continued and creative efforts to end animal experimentation and institutionalise animal rights. Whatever form that activism takes, companies like Envigo and governments around the world can be sure that the animal people are coming.

References

Best, Steven (2014). *The Politics of Total Liberation: Revolution for the 21st Century.* New York: Palgrave Macmillan.

Black, Edwin (1970). The second persona. *Quarterly Journal of Speech* 56(2): 109–19. https://doi.org/10.1080/00335637009382992.

Del Gandio, Jason (2014). The rhetoric of terrorism. In Jason Del Gandio and Anthony Nocella II, eds. *The Terrorization of Dissent: Corporate Repression, Legal Corruption, and the Animal Enterprise Terrorism Act*, 203–19. New York: Lantern Books.

Del Gandio, Jason and Anthony J. Nocella II (2014). Introduction: situating the repression and corruption of the AETA. In Jason Del Gandio and Anthony Nocella II, eds. *The Terrorization of Dissent: Corporate Repression, Legal Corruption, and the Animal Enterprise Terrorism Act*, xix–xxix. New York: Lantern Books.

Freeman, Carrie P. (2020). *The Human Animal Earthling Identity: Shared Values Unifying Human Rights, Animal Rights, and Environmental Movements.* Athens: University of Georgia Press.

Friedman, Jerold D. (2016). Adidas's black market goes to court: media and animal advocacy lawsuits. In Núria Almiron, Matthew Cole and Carrie P. Freeman, eds. *Critical Animal and Media Studies: Communication for Nonhuman Animal Advocacy*, 234–50. New York: Routledge.

Hammerback, John (2001). Creating the "new person": the rhetoric of reconstitutive discourse. *Rhetoric Review* 20(1): 18–22.

33 Friedman 2016, 235.

Hammerback, John and Richard Jensen (1998). *The Rhetorical Career of Cesar Chavez.* College Station: Texas A&M University Press.

Linné, Tobias (2020). Tears, connection, action! Teaching critical animal and media studies. In Núria Almiron, Matthew Cole and Carrie P. Freeman, eds. *Critical Animal and Media Studies: Communication for Nonhuman Animal Advocacy*, 251–64. New York: Routledge.

Lo, Sandy (2019). Joaquin Phoenix documentary "The Animal People" gets distribution. *Starshine Magazine*, 16 November. https://starshinemag.net/joaquin-phoenix-documentary-the-animal-people-gets-distribution/.

Loy, Loredana (2020). Media activism and animal advocacy: what's film got to do with it? In Núria Almiron, Matthew Cole and Carrie P. Freeman, eds. *Critical Animal and Media Studies: Communication for Nonhuman Animal Advocacy*, 221–33. New York: Routledge.

McCoy, K. (2014). The Animal Enterprise Terrorism Act: protecting the profits of animal enterprises at the expense of the first amendment. In Jason Del Gandio and Anthony Nocella II, eds. *The Terrorization of Dissent: Corporate Repression, Legal Corruption, and the Animal Enterprise Terrorism Act*, 3–34. New York: Lantern Books.

Phoenix, Joaquin (2020). Acceptance speech. Academy award for best actor. *92nd Oscars*, 11 March. https://youtu.be/qiiWdTz_MNc.

Potter, Will (2011). *Green Is the New Red: An Insider's Account of a Social Movement Under Siege.* San Francisco: City Lights Books.

Singer, Peter (1975). *Animal Liberation: A New Ethics for our Treatment of Animals.* New York: Avon Books.

The Animal People (2019). Film. Casey Suchan and Denis Henry Hennelly (Dirs.). Distributor: Finngate.

Ware, B.L. and Wil A. Linkugel (1982). The rhetorical *persona*: Marcus Garvey as black moses. *Communication Monographs* 49(1): 50–62. https://doi.org/10.1080/03637758209376070.

4

Anti-capitalism, animal rights and advocacy in *Okja*

Claire Parkinson

Directed by Bong Joon Ho, *Okja* is a Netflix original film that had its theatrical premiere at Cannes in May 2017 followed by a Netflix release in June of the same year. The film tells the story of a genetically modified super pig named Okja created by the Mirando Corporation who is sent to live for ten years with a South Korean farmer and his granddaughter, Mija (Ahn Seo Hyun). With 25 other super pigs, Okja is part of a public relations stunt designed to soften public resistance to genetically modified (GM) products. In part a rescue story, alongside the main protagonist, Mija, *Okja* features fictional representations of Animal Liberation Front (ALF) activists. The radical animal liberation movement emerged in 1960s Britain with the establishment of the Hunt Saboteurs Association (HSA) and later in the 1970s with the formation of the Animal Liberation Front: "Direct action for animals is associated with the formation of the ALF in 1976, although such tactics were developed during the 1960s within the HSA."[1] The ALF's aims were set out in guidelines which explained that the group sought to: liberate animals from places where they were abused; inflict economic damage on those who exploited animals for profit; and reveal the cruelty and

1 Boisseau 2019, 46.

atrocities committed against animals.[2] Describing ALF practices, Steven Best and Anthony J. Nocella write:

> ALF activists operate under cover, at night, wearing balaclavas and ski masks, and in small cells of a few people. After careful reconnaissance, skilled liberation teams break into buildings housing animal prisoners in order to release them (e.g. mink and coyotes) or rescue them (e.g. cats, dogs, mice, and guinea pigs). They seize and/or destroy equipment, property, and materials used to exploit animals, and they use arson to raze buildings and laboratories. They have cost the animal exploitation industries hundreds of millions of dollars.[3]

Branded by the UK government as "extremists" and as a "serious domestic terrorist threat"[4] by the US Federal Bureau of Investigation, *Okja* depicts the ALF characters as comic heroes.

This chapter analyses the representations of animal rights activism in, and public and critical responses to, *Okja*. It places *Okja* in the context of Bong's wider body of work and discusses the relationship between the film's critique of corporate capitalism and a pro-vegan message, then examines *Okja*'s narrative of resistance identifying how Bong's signature genre-blending merges fantasy and caper heist conventions with depictions of contemporary realities to align the viewer with the ALF position. I note the narrative devices which are used to encourage audiences to identify with the activists and argue that while there has been a focus on documentaries as an important mechanism to reach large audiences with animal advocacy messages, fiction films have an equally important role to play. To explore aspects of the film's public reception, I examine parents' and children's responses to the film to argue that what I term "advocacy fiction" is a useful means by which children and young people can engage with the complicated realities of the animal-industrial complex and resistance to

2 Best and Nocella 2004, 8.
3 Best and Nocella 2004, 12.
4 Lewis 2004.

its practices. I conclude that elements such as anthropomorphism and comedy can be highly effective narrative choices for advocacy fiction.

Okja is a rescue story, a film that reinterprets the child-and-their-loyal-pet story as a narrative of political resistance to corporate capitalism and a critique of the animal-industrial complex. For director Bong Joon Ho, the film was his sixth feature and the third film in a series of fantasies to deal with contemporary ecological concerns. Four years before the release of *Okja*, Bong directed *Snowpiercer* (2013), his first English-language film, based on the French post-apocalyptic climate fiction graphic novel *Le Transperceneige* (1982) and, before that, *The Host* (2006), a monster film about a giant amphibious creature – the result of dumping chemicals in the Han river – that attacks and kills people. In *Okja*, Bong turns his attention to neoliberalism and the greed of corporate capitalism which puts profit before ethics. Netflix financed the film with the sole condition that he shoot it using a digital format. Bong stated: "Netflix guaranteed my complete freedom in terms of putting together my team and the final cut privilege, which only godlike filmmakers such as Spielberg get."[5] The autonomy that Bong had in making *Okja* would be unusual in the US commercial film industry where such freedoms are reserved for a small cadre of Hollywood auteurs. However, in this case, Bong was one of a number of high-profile directors that Netflix recruited to write and direct original films for the streaming service.[6] In addition to full creative freedom, Netflix offered Bong USD $50 million to finance *Okja*. While this gave the director an opportunity to make a studio-style film and despite being premiered at the Cannes Film Festival, *Okja* only had a limited theatrical release in UK, US and South Korean cinemas, being primarily watched on television and laptop screens via the Netflix streaming service. As critics were quick to point out, *Okja* was a game changer for Netflix: a blockbuster film that would never have been made by the studios due to its anti-neoliberal stance and pro-animal rights sentiment.[7]

---

5 Kil 2017.

6 Other directors included Martin Scorsese, David Fincher and Alfonso Cuarón. For a discussion of directorial autonomy in US cinema, see Molloy 2017.

7 See, for example, Nelson 2017. It is also important to note that studio development is still focused on profitability from the theatrical market whereas

The film was developed from an original story by Bong who co-wrote the screenplay with British American journalist Jon Ronson. During interviews, Bong explained that the idea for the film originated from his seeing a large sad-looking pig beneath a bridge:

> I kept wondering why the pig was so big and then I thought of the food industry's cruel perspective on animals where they view these creatures not as living things but as food products and of course, for them, size is directly tied to product value. And then I ended up thinking about why the pig looked so sad and depressed and repeatedly thinking about this led me to the very strange story of Okja.[8]

Bong undertook research into slaughterhouse operations before completing the screenplay. To begin, the director initially watched films that depicted animal slaughter practices – *La Parka* (2015) and *Our Daily Bread* (2005) – but these did not prepare him for the realities of a commercial slaughterhouse. With producer Dooho Choi, Bong visited a slaughterhouse in Colorado, which he pointed out in interviews was never named as such: "They never call it a slaughterhouse. They call it a 'beef plant' and they're very proud of it."[9] Despite the facility he visited being recognised for its "humane" methods and for being "well-functioning", it was, Bong stated, "very scary being there".[10] According to the director, it was the smell that remained with him and led to his decision that the slaughterhouse scenes in *Okja* should be "disturbing" for the viewer.[11] Following the slaughterhouse visit, both director and producer became vegan for two months, although the film was not intended to promote veganism. A self-proclaimed "animal lover", dog owner and believer that "everyone should eat less meat",

---

streaming services such as Netflix need to keep a pipeline of new content to grow their subscriber base. As a result, studio films tend to be "safer" projects while streaming services can maintain more intense and constant development activity. See Greenwald and Landry 2022.

8 Santa Barbara International Film Festival (SBIFF) 2020.

9 SBIFF 2020.

10 SBIFF 2020.

11 Kohn 2017.

Bong insisted that the film's message was not that everyone else should become vegan. Instead, it was a critique of the system that profits from exploiting animals and seeing them only as products. In this regard, Bong's position on capitalism was unequivocal:

> All our problems arise because of capitalism. It brings pleasure but also so much pain and unhappiness. The questions I ask in my films about why we harm the environment or animals all come down in the end to capitalism.[12]

The intention to try to separate a critique of the industry from a vegan message was not, however, successful. Despite Bong asserting that the focus of the film was the commentary on corporate capitalism and the animal-industrial complex, reception of the film suggested otherwise. For example, one film critic claimed that they had stopped eating meat for a few days after seeing *Okja*,[13] *The Hollywood Reporter* headlined its review of the film "'Okja' just might convince you to go vegetarian",[14] and other news outlets reported that Google searches for the term "vegan" had increased by between 58 per cent and 65 per cent in the week following the release of the film.[15] Indeed, it is interesting to note that the increase in Google searches for "vegan" (~60 per cent) exceeded the increase in searches for the term "vegetarian" (10 per cent) during the same time period by six times. Taking the trends in these search terms as an index for public interest and given that neither term is actually used in *Okja*, the difference between the intention of the film – to critique neoliberal corporate capitalism which sustains the animal-industrial complex – and the reception of a pro-vegan message reveals the extent to which the two are entwined, and how veganism has entered the mainstream and become an important proxy for a range of positions that oppose the consumption of meat.

In *Okja* the contemporary realities of corporate capitalism – the drive to profit from the exploitation and death of nonhuman animals

---

12 Sharf 2019.
13 Niazi 2017.
14 O'Neill 2017.
15 Philip 2018; Starostinetskaya 2017.

– and slaughterhouse practices are merged with fantasy iconography. Highlighting the generic mix on its Facebook page prior to the film's release, Netflix posed the question: "Okja: Like a Disney movie, for adults?"[16] The question is pertinent to this discussion both in terms of the audience reception of the film (which is discussed later) and in relation to how generic elements are employed to cue audiences to identify with certain characters. There is no doubt that the film defies easy genre classification, which is unsurprising as genre-blending is characteristic of Bong's signature style. Recognised as a mainstream commercial filmmaker, Bong is known for subverting genre conventions, the most prominent element of which is the lack of a Hollywood "happy ending";[17] in this regard, *Okja* is no exception. His films usually pit a socially marginalised individual against a political or corporate power and, as Nam Lee points out, Bong "localizes 'conventional' (i.e., Hollywood) genres within Korean stories, realities, and sensibilities".[18] Bong's films address real-world issues and in the case of *Okja*, the film draws on elements of action, fantasy, family and horror genres to deliver a form of political filmmaking that I refer to as "advocacy fiction". In other words, *Okja* is a fiction film that engages with the cruelty and horrors of the animal-industrial complex with the intention of raising awareness and mobilising public debate and action.

In the film, Okja is a genetically modified pig with a hippo-like body, gentle expression and large floppy ears. Intelligent, empathetic, with a playful personality, she behaves like an enormous puppy and, at times, a protective maternal figure. A CGI creation, Okja is a fantastical anthropomorphised animal, the explanation for which draws on the contemporary scientific realities of genetic modification and selective breeding practices. While this might suggest that Okja is more science fiction than fantasy, it is useful to consider Katherine A. Fowkes' distinction between fantasy and science fiction as "ontological rupture", which she defines as "a break between what the audience agrees is 'reality' and the fantastic phenomena that define the narrative world".[19] Although

16 Netflix 2017.
17 Lee 2020.
18 Lee 2020, 5.
19 Fowkes 2010, 5.

Okja's physical being is explainable by scientific principles, her personality, behaviours and relationship with Mija provide the ontological rupture – "the fantastic phenomena … understood to really exist *within* the story-world".[20] Okja, the character, owes much to a Disneyesque style of anthropomorphism. As I have discussed in *Animals, Anthropomorphism and Mediated Encounters*, anthropomorphism, including that associated with the "Disneyification" of animals, should not be disregarded by animal advocacy.[21] Instead, I propose that anthropomorphism can engage audiences in effective empathy and mobilise meaningful action. In the case of *Okja*, the anthropomorphic creature is one aspect of the fantasy elements of the film that are important because, in part, they function as cues for the audience to identify with (or not) particular characters. For the purposes of this chapter, I begin with an analysis of the film's first two scenes, which introduce the characters Lucy Mirando (Tilda Swinton), Dr Johnny Wilcox (Jake Gyllenhaal), Mija and Okja. As I will discuss, these scenes which employ anthropomorphism and fantasy conventions are crucial to the audience's identification with the ALF activists later in the film.

The film opens with Lucy Mirando, the head of the Mirando Corporation, at a press conference in her grandfather's old factory, a place where we are told atrocities were carried out and the walls are stained with the blood of working men. Lucy wants to "reclaim the space" and tell a new story about the Mirando Corporation. She explains, in a voice that lurches from soft and lilting to loud and harsh, that following the discovery of a single "super piglet" on a farm in Chile, her company has humanely bred 26 super piglets that will be sent to live with farmers in different countries around the world. With the animated words "eco-friendly", "natural" and "non-GMO" projected behind her, the CEO explains that the company's intention is to reduce the carbon footprint of animal agriculture, revolutionise the livestock industry and address global food poverty. The 26 farmers are in competition with one another to raise the ultimate super pig, and the judge of the contest will be a beloved television zoologist, Dr Johnny Wilcox, whose on-screen antics with animals reveal him to be an

20 Fowkes 2010, 5, emphasis in original.
21 Parkinson 2019, 1–14.

eccentric and absurd character. After claiming that the pigs will be big, beautiful and leave a minimal environmental footprint, Lucy Mirando's eco-sensitive ethos is undercut when she declares "and most importantly, they need to taste fucking good". The erratic delivery of Lucy's message, her family's appalling history, her swearing, emphasis on the taste of animal bodies over any supposed environmental concern, and the ridiculous figure of Wilcox establish them as the corporate villains who are revealed, by the ALF activists in a later scene, to have lied about the super pigs. Bong's satirical swipe at corporate capitalism is conveyed, in part, through Swinton's exaggerated performance, which parodies the emotionally unstable villain and plays against Lucy's appearance – blonde, pristine, wearing a white wraparound dress and elegant high-heeled shoes. The stylised overacting recalls fantasy – at times pantomime – villains but is used to deliver the realities of contemporary real-world issues – food poverty, the environmental impacts of animal agriculture and GM foods. Typical of Bong's films where satire or parody is used to make the powerful look ridiculous or incompetent, the exaggerated performance is used to underscore the irony of corporate "care" for the environment and animals.

The next scene introduces Okja and Mija, the sequence borrowing tropes from child-and-their-loyal-pet narratives where Okja is friend, protector, maternal figure and confidant: a special relationship with an animal which fulfils the needs of the human protagonist that are not being met by other humans in the story. The setting for this relationship is idyllic – a sun-dappled woodland and a waterfall-fed natural lake on a mountainside where super pig and child play, romp and swim together and where, at one point, Okja saves Mija from falling off a cliff. The setting is enhanced by the sounds of birdsong and the gentle rustle of wind in the trees, which combine to contribute to the sense of Mija and Okja's peaceful happy existence. Ahn Seo Hyun's performance is naturalistic, and Okja delivers some gentle comedy moments when she rolls down a hill into an apple tree, jumps into the lake and defecates on demand when Mija pats her bottom. The contrast between this and the opening scene reinforces the differences between the two worlds. Lucy Mirando's press conference is a promotional performance, set in a place where horrific acts have been perpetrated, aided by computer-animated trees and animals, where real animals are reduced to superficial taste preferences. In Mija's world, nature is "real" and beautiful, Okja is a fantastical creature and a thinking, feeling individual. With Mirando's greenwashing and the close bond between child and anthropomorphic "pet" established in the film's early scenes, when Okja is reclaimed by Lucy's corporation, the viewer is cued to empathise with the child's loss and to identify with Okja's rescuers: the ALF activists.

Our first introduction to the ALF activists is when the group attempt to rescue Okja from a Mirando Corporation truck. Pink petals stream from a hand that appears mysteriously from the window of a black haulage truck in front of the vehicle taking Okja on the first leg of her journey from Seoul to New York where she will be used to promote Mirando's super pig project. As the Mirando truck draws alongside, the camera moves along the black truck and up to the window, a smiling young man, his head and face covered by a black balaclava, shouts into a loudspeaker microphone: "Nice to meet you. We're not terrorists!" The shot cuts back to the Mirando truck and the shocked face of the Mirando Corporation employee responsible for the safe transport of Okja (who is being held against her will in the back of the vehicle). "What?" yells the Mirando employee, cupping his ear with his hand. "We don't like violence!" exclaims the balaclava-wearing man. "We don't want to hurt you. Stop … stop the truck!" Still unable to comprehend what is happening, the Mirando employee shouts back "What?" as the camera cuts back to the black truck, pulling focus from the first masked man to a second man in the truck. The second man is also masked, but what can be seen of his unblinking eyes and relaxed mouth reveals a quiet, composed demeanour. A close-up of his face confirms his controlled disposition before he turns to look forward and reaches up to hold a grab handle above the window as the truck accelerates away, passes in front of the Mirando truck and then slows down again. A side door opens. Four masked people stand in the doorway and wave: three men and one woman. They urge the Mirando employee to put on his seatbelt, which he does as his bewilderment begins to give way to a dawning realisation that something is going to happen to his truck.

The activists force the Mirando truck to come to a halt against the side wall of a tunnel. Mija, who has managed to cling on to the moving truck, is thrown from the vehicle. As the masked group jump from their truck, the upbeat trumpet-led "Balkan music melody" begins and shifts the tone of the scene from action movie to caper heist. The activists free Okja, who gallops to Mija, and the two attempt an escape running through busy streets and eventually ending up in an underground shopping mall. Mayhem ensues as Okja crashes and slides through displays and shelves until finally crashing in slow motion to the floor. Mija is injured, her eye swollen and bruised, her face scratched. The music changes from the fast-paced Balkan folk music to the romantic country folk rendition of "Annie's Song" as the slow-motion action continues and men armed with dart guns shoot at Okja, who is squealing, clearly in pain. The activists protect her using umbrellas as shields before grappling with the men to prevent them getting to Okja. The action cuts to Mija, who watches Jay (Paul Dano), the ALF group's leader, gently remove a piece of broken ceramic from Okja's foot; his expression shows distress as he looks at the blood-soaked fragment. The shot pulls focus to Okja's face, as she looks away from him, tears running down her cheek. The ALF leader's action mirrors an earlier moment in the film where Mija removes a large thistle from Okja's foot. The camera then cuts away from the shopping mall and back to the Mirando truck, where the driver has noticed "ALF" spraypainted across the front of the vehicle. He searches on his phone and finds "Animal Liberation Front" and an image of masked activists with rescued beagles in front of an ALF banner. Cut back to the shopping mall and one of the activists lifts their top to show a tattoo on their waist of an ALF activist with large angel-like wings holding a rescued animal: "We are good people. On your side," the activist declares. Apologising to the men with the dart guns, the activists then make their escape with Mija and Okja. During the getaway, "Annie's Song" fades out as the activists throw ball bearings on the floor causing the police to slip, slide and fall, the movie returning to its caper-like conventions. Only the Mirando employee manages to evade the slip hazard and chases the truck. Mija pats Okja's bottom, causing her to defecate from the back of the truck covering the chasing man. The scene closes with a couple of verbal gags about having a "shitty day" and the Mirando employee phoning his partner to ask about bodywash.

What is notable about this representation of direct action is the use of humour, caper heist and action movie conventions to construct a non-threatening form of activism: the umbrella "shields" opening in slow motion are visually strange but benign "weapons"; the use of ball bearings to stymy the police chase is a slapstick trope; and the caring (telling the Mirando employee to put his seatbelt on) but sometimes amateurish and apologetic manner of the activists recalls the humorous anti-establishment elements of traditional caper movies. The audience has already been cued to sympathise with Okja and Mija in the early scenes, and Jay's attending to Okja's hurt foot as she lies vulnerable and unable to get up serves to reinforce identification with the activists as Okja's rescuers and protectors. Slow-motion shots and the change in music shifts the rhythm and affective spectacle of the sequence; a transition from the action of a fast-paced chase to a slow contemplative moment among the chaos as the activists protect Okja and deal with her injury. Slow-motion aesthetics have been used in Hollywood and other commercial cinemas to emphasise violence or give a poetic beauty to explosions, shootout scenes and bloodshed since the 1960s.[22] The slow-motion confrontation between the activists and the gunmen and the attention to Okja's injured foot against the strains of "Annie's Song" employs the slow-motion violence aesthetic, but there is a distinct lack of gore, bloodshed or the carnage usually associated with the convention. The only blood is that of Okja's on the broken piece of ceramic. The effect of this subversion of the action-violence aesthetic is to reframe the ALF group's direct action as an act of compassion. Moreover, the narrative is structured so that the Animal Liberation Front identity of the activists is only revealed after the action sequence has been reframed in this way. At this point in the narrative, only the viewer is given access to the truth of the activists' identity through the cut to the shot of the driver in the tunnel searching for "ALF". When the sequence cuts back to the activists in the shopping mall, both Mija and the viewer (who may or may not be familiar with the ALF) are reassured of the activists' intentions through dialogue and image: "We are good people" one of the activists says when he shows the tattoo

22 Liu 2018, 63.

of an ALF activist with angel-wings as proof of his claim. The rest of the sequence returns to the caper heist conventions as the activists, Mija and Okja escape. With the activists now firmly established as the compassionate rescuers, the film returns to one of Bong's signature narrative moves, making those in power look absurd. The visual and verbal gags at the end of the scene, which all revolve around Okja's defecation, add to the slapstick humour. The audience is able to identify with the rescuers and to laugh at the Mirando employee, a representative of corporate power. At this point in the narrative, the line between the good and compassionate but socially marginalised heroes (a child *and* a group of animal activists) and the absurd but evil corporate power is firmly established.

Okja recalls the "Animal Liberation Front Guidelines"[23] when, after their escape from the shopping mall, Jay explains to Mija:

> We are animal lovers. We rescue animals from slaughterhouses, zoos, labs, we tear down cages and set them free. This is why we rescued Okja … We inflict economic damage on those who profit from their misery. We reveal their atrocities to the public and we never harm anyone, human or nonhuman. That is our 40-year credo.

The film also uses images that have become synonymous with the radical animal liberation movement: activists with liberated beagles; a masked activist with bolt cutters and the slogan "Until every cage is empty"; and activists with rescued lambs. In the context of the film, the images are used to reinforce Jay's claims about the ALF, shown to Mija on a tablet in the back of a truck as the group explain their actions and motivations. Mija is shown pictures of the laboratory where Okja was "created" and a realistic-looking newspaper article about GM foods accompanied by images of "experimental" mice, fish, a pig and turkeys. A photograph of Lucy Mirando in a news article about the super pig project, an image of a disguised Lucy in the laboratory selecting the 26 "prettiest" GM animals and another news image of Lucy at the press conference accompany Jay's revelations that Okja is one of a

23 Best and Nocella 2004, 8.

group of experimental animals who are being used as a publicity stunt to manipulate the public into eating GM animals. Jay explains that the ALF want to get video footage of the laboratory which they will release to the public but explains that the security is impenetrable. This statement is accompanied by a murky image of a large, locked metal door. He asks Mija to consent to the group returning Okja to the Mirando Corporation and assures her that they have a plan for her release once the footage has been secured. Mija says she wants to take Okja back to the mountains, but the activist who has been translating – K (Steven Yeun) – lies to the rest of the ALF group, saying that Mija has agreed to the plan. At this point, only the viewer and K know the truth of what has transpired. This is an important plot point in the film and a moment where the viewer is asked by the narrative to make judgements about the activists. During the scene, Jay's translated conversation is interrupted by a disagreement among the activists who dispute the need for Mija's consent. They argue that the ALF credo was written in the 1970s – a point that is historically accurate – and that their mission, which will save many more animals, can't be ruined by Mija's decision. Jay rebukes them, saying that if they refuse to adhere to the credo and don't get Mija's agreement then they are not true ALF. This disagreement provides the motivation for K's deception, which the viewer is led to understand comes from a moral conviction that more animals will be saved by Okja's return to Mirando.

The viewer has already been cued to identify with Okja's rescuers through the earlier scenes where Okja has been established as worthy of rescue. Murray Smith proposes that this orientation of the spectator emerges from a "structure of sympathy" that is composed of three tenets: the spectator identifies with stable agents through a process of recognition; a process of alignment occurs by the narration filtering story events through a character's experience; alignment cues the spectator to evaluate characters morally; and a process of allegiance.[24] Sympathetic allegiance is determined by an "underlying evaluation of the character's moral status within the moral system of the text".[25] Being aware of K's deception of both Mija and the rest of the ALF group, the

24 Smith 1995, 62–3.
25 Smith 1995, 62.

moral structure of the film is constructed to cue the viewer to make a moral evaluation of the character who, while perhaps having a noble motivation, is nonetheless morally worse than the rest of the ALF group who are unaware of the lie. In this way, the moral system of the film allows the viewer to continue to identify with the ALF activists, who it now transpires are not actually Okja's rescuers but want to return her to Mirando. Jay establishes the link between Mija's consent and being true to the ALF credo, making K's deception a non-ALF act. In this way, when the group abandon Mija, leaving her and Okja to be recaptured by the authorities, their actions are not "bad" within the moral structure of the film.

Images are used in the film as narrative devices to provide evidence of the activists' legitimacy, which the viewer discovers alongside Mija. Including what appear to be real images from the radical animal liberation movement, the film blurs the boundaries between fact and fiction. Re-created for the film, the images are almost identical to archival photographs and, as such, function as a signpost of realism for the viewer. Google Trends indicate that there was a surge of interest in the Animal Liberation Front in the week following the Netflix release of *Okja* on 28 June 2017. Searches for Animal Liberation Front increased significantly, reaching peak popularity between 2 and 8 July. The top related queries – that is, searches by users who also searched for Animal Liberation Front – were for "Okja" and "animal liberation front okja", suggesting that the film substantially increased public awareness of the organisation. The film and the representation of the ALF attracted commentary in the form of articles and blog posts from People for the Ethical Treatment of Animals (PETA), which encouraged viewers to acquaint themselves with the real ALF:

> While Okja is computer-generated, the ALF – which is simply the name adopted by people who take action to rescue animals from the cruel conditions of laboratories and factory farms – is real. The ALF never hurts humans or animals. It breaks inanimate objects, such as stereotaxic devices and decapitators, in order to save lives. It burns empty buildings in which animals are tortured and killed.[26]

PETA's support for the film focused on its realism, both in terms of its representation of ALF activists and the depiction of animal cruelty, breeding, containment and slaughter. An article titled "These 12 photos will show you that 'Okja' is more real than you think" compared images from the film with real images of animals exploited and killed by the animal-industrial complex.[27] The article ended with an option to claim a free vegan starter kit. Other PETA content provided links to a vegan pledge and a list of animal rights films for viewers of *Okja* to watch. It has become widespread practice for advocacy documentaries to have an associated impact campaign: content and resources for viewers who want to find out more about a film's topic or feel compelled to action. In the case of *Okja*, PETA filled the impact campaign "gap" by offering additional guidance and content for viewers keen to access more information about animal exploitation, veganism and the ALF. Indeed, a number of PETA articles about *Okja* included a link to purchase *Free the Animals*, a book about the ALF written by PETA president, Ingrid Newkirk. Much of the PETA content on *Okja* focused on the realities that the film depicted, using its authority as an animal rights organisation to reframe the fantasy of the film as being rooted in truths about the animal-industrial complex.

Positive reception of the representation of the ALF was not, however, universal. Bong, who had researched the Animal Liberation Front prior to writing *Okja*, was open about his support for the group. At a Cannes Film Festival press conference, where *Okja* was due to premiere, the first question to the director was from a British journalist concerned with the depiction of the Animal Liberation Front in the film. The journalist stated that the ALF was classed as an extremist organisation with a history of threats, hate campaigns and leaving explosives outside houses. Bong replied that his research on the Animal Liberation Front led him to conclude that while he did not fully agree with all their methods, he nonetheless regarded them as:

26 O'Conner 2017.
27 PETA 2017.

> people of good will; their intention is to ensure that man and animals live in harmony. This is a good idea, so this is why I included this association in my film.[28]

The journalist later published an article in *The Times* with the headline, "Animal rights extremists are Cannes stars", stating:

> An extremist animal rights group with a history of burning down shops and planting bombs outside people's homes has been lionised in a film competing for the Palme d'Or at the Cannes Film Festival.[29]

Elsewhere, there was some reluctance by critics to be seen to fully endorse the on-screen actions. One reviewer noted:

> Despite gentle mockery of the activists' self-righteousness and tendency to announce their beliefs melodramatically, and an unfortunately unexamined strain of fanaticism exhibited by the group's leader Jay, the movie is very much on the ALF's side.[30]

A review in the *New Yorker* referred wryly to the ALF action as a "terrorist pig-napping"[31] and a positive review in *Newsweek* described them as an animal rights group with a "militant-minded leader".[32] However, the critical response to the film was overwhelmingly positive, with reviewers' comments focused primarily on the strength of the pro-vegan and anti-corporate message.

There was less agreement among critics over whether the film was suitable for children. Netflix had initially given the film a PG rating, which was later revised to MA 15+. Some of *Okja*'s marketing focused on the cartoonish antics of the eponymous character and the caper-style action, which led to criticisms that the film's promotion

---

28 Festival de Cannes 2017.

29 Malvern 2017.

30 Seitz 2017.

31 Lane 2017.

32 Schonfeld 2017.

did not adequately prepare audiences for the bleak horror of the slaughterhouse scenes, the depiction of Okja being forcibly penetrated, or the ending, in which only Okja and one piglet are rescued and the rest of the super pigs are left behind to face a horrific death. The website for Common Sense Media, a conservative nonprofit organisation that reviews and rates media to provide parents with guidance on suitability for children, said of *Okja*:

> Parents need to know that *Okja* isn't a movie for kids. Despite the family friendly poster of a giant pig and a little girl, and though it has many comic elements, it's an extremely intense, violent film about cruelty to animals in a world in which corporations wreak havoc on the planet.[33]

Reviews of the film by parents and children on the same website offer an interesting snapshot of the public reception of the film. Of the 19 reviews by parents, 12 agreed that the movie was not suitable for children. However, 26 out of 32 reviews from children were positive, with many noting that the film was scary *because* it depicted the realities of industrial farming and slaughter but that should not stop adults and children watching it for both entertainment and educational reasons. While this offers a highly selective snapshot of the film's public reception, it is nonetheless valuable to consider that *Okja* might provide a template for advocacy fictions that are aimed at children and adults.

Discussion about animal advocacy films more often than not turns first to documentaries. *Okja*, I propose, demonstrates that there is a place for fiction films within the arsenal of tools available to animal advocacy. Popular fiction films can reach audiences that documentaries cannot. Moreover, as *Okja* demonstrates, narrative strategies can effectively utilise anthropomorphism, fantasy and comedy to align viewers with an animal rights position. Although it is not possible to quantify the impact of *Okja*, there are indicators that the film raised awareness and mobilised viewers to take action. Google Trends indicated an increased public interest in both veganism and the ALF. PETA reported that it had received over 21,000 requests for vegan

33 Common Sense Media 2017.

starter kits in the month following the film's release.[34] There was an upsurge of public support for the ALF on the film's social media channels as well as comments from people who, after watching the film, had decided to go vegan, and reports across blogs and other social media of similar kinds of transformational stories including an increase in Korea of people trying out vegan restaurants for the first time.[35] The extent to which people have managed to sustain a transition to veganism after watching *Okja* is unknown, but there are strong indicators that the film had meaningful impact on some audiences. It is unreasonable and unrealistic to expect one film to propel the animal liberation movement forward to a tipping point where a majority of public views are in support of the rights of animals. *Okja* is, however, part of an incremental awareness-raising that expands public understanding of the horrors of the animal-industrial complex and leads to behaviour change. The film employs narrative strategies that are sometimes eschewed by animal advocacy: anthropomorphism, fantasy and comedy. However, as *Okja* demonstrates, such strategies can be effective and have the potential to be applied to narratives other than films. In future, it may become important for animal advocates to consider utilising these narrative tools more widely in campaigns and other forms of advocacy content to expand the reach of their message.

References

Best, Steven and Anthony J. Nocella, eds. (2004). *Terrorists or Freedom Fighters: Reflections on the Liberation of Animals*. New York: Lantern Books.

Boisseau, Will (2019). Animal liberation. In R. Kinna and U. Gordon, eds. *Routledge Handbook of Radical Politics*, 42–52. New York and London: Routledge.

Common Sense Media (2017). Okja. *Common Sense Media*. https://bit.ly/48VN4BZ.

Festival de Cannes (2017). Okja: Press Conference – EV – Cannes 2017. *Festival de Cannes (Officiel)*, 19 May. https://bit.ly/420ID6H.

Fowkes, Katherine A. (2010). *The Fantasy Film*. Chichester: Wiley Blackwell.

34 Starostinetskaya 2017.

35 Lee 2020, 125–6.

Greenwald, Stephen R. and Paula Landry (2022). *The Business of Film: A Practical Introduction*. London and New York: Routledge.
Kil, Sonia (2017). Bong Joon-ho on working with Netflix and the controversy over "Okja" at Cannes. *Variety*, 16 May. https://bit.ly/3tKTmpt.
Kohn, Eric (2017). "Okja": how one visit to a slaughterhouse turned Bong Joon Ho into a vegan. *IndyWire*, 7 June. https://bit.ly/3U7EGeu.
Lane, Anthony (2017). "A Ghost Story" and "Okja". *New Yorker*, 3 July. https://bit.ly/3HjVpDP.
Lee, Nam (2020). *The Films of Bong Joon Ho*. New Brunswick, NJ: Rutgers University Press.
Lewis, John E. (2004). Before the Senate Judiciary Committee Washington DC. fbi.gov, 18 May. https://bit.ly/3U7EHz4.
Liu, Yong (2018). *3D Cinematic Aesthetics and Storytelling*. Cham: Springer International Publishing.
Malvern, Jack (2017). Animal rights extremists are Cannes stars. *The Times*, 20 May. https://bit.ly/3TVNjJh.
Molloy, Claire (2017). Indie cinema and the neoliberal commodification of creative labor. In Geoff King, ed. *A Companion to American Indie Film*, 368–88. West Sussex: Wiley Blackwell.
Nelson, Alex (2017). Why Okja – unlike previous Netflix films – is worth the two-hour binge. *inews*, 29 June. https://bit.ly/48D96tF.
Netflix (2017). Okja. Video. https://bit.ly/3tUH9yl.
Niazi, Amil (2017). "Okja" used a super pig to link capitalism and consumption. *Vice*, 28 June. https://bit.ly/48RFmJo.
O'Connor, Jennifer (2017). Who are the real-life counterparts of the ALF heroes seen in "Okja"? *PETA*, 18 July. https://bit.ly/3vsDSqn.
Okja (2017). Film. Bong Joon Ho (Dir.). Distributor: Netflix.
O'Neil, Shana (2017). "Okja" just might convince you to go vegetarian. *The Hollywood Reporter*, 28 June. https://bit.ly/3HmwNul.
Parkinson, Claire (2019). *Animals, Anthropomorphism and Mediated Encounters*. London and New York: Routledge.
PETA (2017). These 12 photos will show you that "Okja" is more real than you think. *PETA*, 11 August. https://bit.ly/3HhAL7g.
Philip, Tom (2018). The people who say "Okja" and become vegetarians. *GQ*, 26 January. https://bit.ly/3O0LCGs.
SBIFF (2020). SBIFF 2020 – Bong Joon Ho discusses "Okja". *officialSBIFF*, 24 January. https://bit.ly/3HhAMbk.
Sconfeld, Zach (2017). "Okja" review: the Netflix movie is a brilliant and scathing satire of corporate evil. *Newsweek*, 28 June. https://bit.ly/3RWHjND.

Seitz, Matt Zoller (2017). Okja. *rogerebert.com*, 28 June. http://tinyurl.com/4df93vek.
Sharf, Zac (2019). Is Bong Joon Ho's "Okja" our new reality? China begins breeding giant pigs. *Indy Wire*, 7 October. https://bit.ly/3NYdE5p.
Smith, Murray (1995). *Engaging Characters: Fiction, Emotion, and the Cinema*. Oxford: Oxford University Press.
Starostinetskaya, Anna (2017). *Okja* release spikes "Vegan" Google searches by 65 percent. *VegNews*, 6 August. https://bit.ly/49cg9cT.

Part Two

Activist texts and reception

5

(More than) food, farms and freedom

Turning exclusions in "pro-vegan" documentaries into productive interventions for animal advocacy

Paula Arcari

Introduction

Anat Pick has stated that animal advocacy documentaries "must find ways to articulate the fundamental conditions and mechanisms of humans' crushing power over nonhuman animals".[1] Only then, she says, can specific uses be properly considered. Given that this "crushing power" is being exercised with ever-greater intensity and reach, and with increasingly dire and potentially irreversible consequences for terrestrial and marine environments, the climate and all life,[2] the urgency of this imperative for on- and off-screen animal advocacy grows stronger each day. This chapter therefore looks back over 15 years of "pro-vegan" documentaries to assess the extent to which they articulate the "fundamental conditions and mechanisms", or violent relationalities,[3] that shape, legitimate and reinforce humankind's domination of other animals.[4] Finding that, as a collective, these films largely fail in this

1 Pick 2016, 98.
2 Ripple, Wolf et al. 2021.
3 Wadiwel 2009.
4 For the remainder of the chapter, "animals" is used in place of other (than human) animals or nonhuman animals, and free-living animals is used in place of wildlife.

endeavour, it transposes three observed exclusions into interventions that could assist advocacy efforts in addressing movement-wide tendencies that may be hampering and even countering progress for animals.

Before defining "pro-vegan" documentaries and explaining the chapter's methodology, it is important to emphasise some key points relevant to the films' wider social context. Media discourses of dietary veganism/vegans have exhibited a dramatic turnaround in the last 15 years. From unequivocal denigration,[5] including warnings of "Children 'harmed' by vegan diets"[6] and "Death by Veganism",[7] we now hear of "The unstoppable rise of veganism"[8] with the *Economist* dubbing 2019 "The year of the vegan".[9] This mainstreaming of awareness and acceptance of pro-vegan narratives has dovetailed and been aided by the rapid democratisation of digital skills and the launches of YouTube, Facebook, Twitter[10] and Instagram between 2005 and 2010.[11] Together, these have facilitated the sharing and curation of all kinds of information relating to animals, food and its production. Alex Lockwood notes the critical role of social media in the "vegan revolution",[12] while Instagram has been implicated in "veganism's PR overhaul".[13] These developments have been paralleled by a steady increase in "pro-vegan" and animal advocacy documentaries (Figure 5.1).

However, over the same time, global "meat" consumption increased annually by between 0.5 per cent and 2.8 per cent per capita from 2005 to 2013, and between 1.2 per cent and 1.8 per cent by volume from 2013 to 2018.[14] Global meat and dairy production figures for the

5 Cole and Morgan 2011.
6 Roberts 2005.
7 Planck 2007.
8 Hancox 2018.
9 Parker 2019.
10 At the time of this book's publication, now called X. "Twitter" has been used throughout book to reflect the colloquial and historical context.
11 Doyle 2016; Pendergrast 2016.
12 Quoted in Anon. 2018.
13 Petter 2018.
14 Ritchie and Roser 2017; Statista 2021. Reliable global per capita consumption data post-2013 could not be obtained. Hence the use of volume data post-2013.

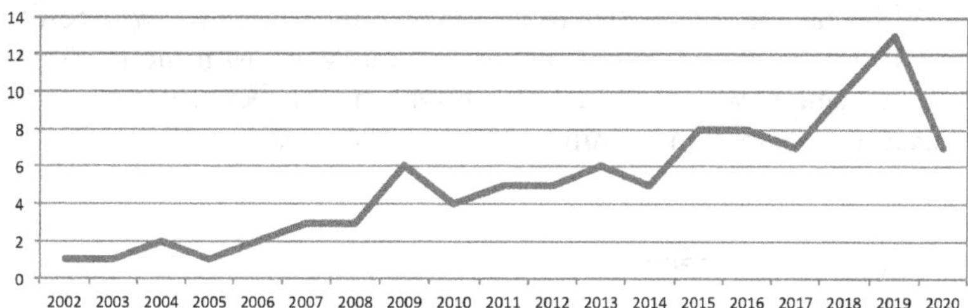

Figure 5.1 Increase in the number of English-language pro-vegan and animal advocacy documentaries (y-axis) released between 2002 and 2020.

period 2005 to 2018 similarly rose each year by between 1.2 per cent and 3.25 per cent.[15]

During the lockdown phase of COVID-19, these upward trends were somewhat checked. However, there is no reason to assume this deceleration was a result of increased concern around the use of animals, or that it will sustain over the longterm.[16] In fact, the COVID pandemic underscores longstanding questions relating to the efficacy of animal advocacy more broadly, notably: Why have decades of critique of "meat" production and consumption, approached from various angles, not had greater impact? And, why are connections between animal uses still not being made? The last 15 years supposedly signals a growing openness to vegan diets and lifestyles, and yet animal exploitation is intensifying while remaining sidelined in mainstream discourses, even amidst a zoonotic pandemic. Blame for the lack of more critical perspectives cannot solely be directed at mainstream media, major organisations and academia (see Arcari 2021). Critical animal scholars have expressed concern that traditional approaches to animal advocacy are not as effective as they could/need to be, and are not succeeding in spreading a sufficiently politicised understanding of, and opposition to, the use of animals.[17]

15 Ritchie and Roser 2017 (updated in 2019).
16 Arcari 2021.
17 Donaldson and Kymlicka 2013; Pick 2016; Sorenson 2014; White 2018; Woodhall and da Trindade 2016.

This chapter contributes to understanding why this might be the case. It builds on and complements previous work with the intention of identifying how animal advocacy might more effectively stimulate a radical transformation in animal–human relations.

"Pro-vegan" documentaries

My identification of films as "pro-vegan" draws on The Vegan Society's definition of veganism, which is arguably the go-to definition for a digitally connected general public:

> A philosophy and way of living which seeks to exclude – as far as is possible and practicable – all forms of exploitation of, and cruelty to, animals for food, clothing or any other purpose; and by extension, promotes the development and use of animal-free alternatives for the benefit of animals, humans and the environment. In dietary terms it denotes the practice of dispensing with all products derived wholly or partly from animals.[18]

Accordingly, any documentary that opposes animal exploitation and cruelty, and/or promotes animal-free alternatives, including dietary, is regarded as pro-vegan to the extent that it touches on one or more dimensions of veganism as a philosophy and set of everyday practices.[19] This admits a wide range of documentaries under the "pro-vegan" banner, from those that problematise multiple uses of animals or focus on single-issue activism to those that endorse plant-based diets or

---

18 The Vegan Society 2015.

19 In contrast to Dutkiewicz and Dickstein's (2021) conception of veganism as a practice limited to dietary conduct, this chapter upholds a more inclusive and politicised conception that encompasses all practices involving animals. Connections between animal uses and the practices that consume their lives – visually, emotionally and metabolically (see Wadiwel 2018) – are therefore emphasised rather than encouraging further exclusions that diminish the magnitude and scope of the animal-industrial complex.

oppose factory farming. Whatever the approach, veganism need not be explicitly mentioned.

"Pro-vegan" is therefore a contestable term, and I acknowledge the longstanding tensions and debates over goals, strategies, definitions and identities across a heterogeneous animal movement.[20] However, my critical focus in this chapter is less each film's approach and rather what these documentaries commonly exclude – "the entities, practices, and ways of being that are foreclosed" as others are materialised.[21] For, while exclusions are inevitable and not always negative, it is, nevertheless, important to make them visible "to foster meaningful forms of responsibility for and obligation toward them".[22] With the focus on the nature and implications of these exclusions, and articulating a response to them, the content of each documentary is not discussed in detail except to clarify the exclusions.

The next section describes the film selection process followed by a brief summary of their primary focus and framing. The remainder of the chapter focuses on the three overlapping and co-constitutive exclusions/interventions: (1) animals commodified and used for purposes other than food; (2) ontological violence associated with oppression; and (3) the inherent value of animals. These sections build my case for a more consistent and assertive mobilisation of the animal-industrial complex (A-IC)[23] as both a discursive framework and a practical tool. This could help communicate the fundamental conditions and mechanisms of all animal uses (exclusion 1), including those widely understood as less problematic or even benign (exclusion 2), and support arguments for ending animals' oppression based on their inherent value (exclusion 3).

20 Arcari 2022; Fitzgerald 2019; Stallwood 2012; Woodhall and da Trindade 2016, 25; Wrenn and Johnson 2013.

21 Giraud 2019, 2.

22 Giraud 2019, 4.

23 Noske 1989; Twine 2012.

Methodology

Treating pro-vegan documentaries as one representation of the evolving animal zeitgeist – an aggregation of understandings and intentions coalescing around questions of animal use – I conduct a broad and necessarily shallow review of 45 films, as opposed to an in-depth analysis of a smaller selection. Akin to a literature review, the intention is to highlight trends and themes, but more importantly narrative gaps that over time are potentially being reinforced. I consider the disruptive potential of these exclusions as indicating marginalisations that remain socially normalised, but also, more importantly, how centralising and politicising them is "vital in carving out space for intervention".[24]

Almost all of the reviewed documentaries are available free or for rent (for a small fee) through online streaming services including Vimeo, YouTube, iTunes and Amazon or subscription services such as Netflix. Although general screenings, festivals and community-funded events still take place, private streaming now dominates, and distributors rely on digital media to generate awareness of and interest in their films. Reflecting this shift, the collation of "pro-vegan" documentaries began with a Google search for both "pro-vegan" and "vegan" documentaries and films released since 2006 (four separate searches conducted in July 2020).

The first ten results for each of the four searches linked to listicles of 5 to 45 films. Some listicles appeared in more than one search result, giving a total of 18 separate listicles. After collating all listed documentaries, I noted the number of times each was mentioned in a listicle. To be included in this review, a film had to feature in at least three listicles and be US-facing in terms of production, funding and distribution. This includes the content being primarily, though not always entirely, drawn from US locations, events and practices, and/or the narration and framing (e.g., data references, comparisons and examples) being oriented to a North American audience. Most documentaries with a wide release on popular media platforms are US-facing and they are arguably the ones that reach the largest

24 Giraud 2019, 3.

international audience. This resulted in 20 eligible films, excluding three films released pre-2006.

To address bias due to algorithms and cross-referencing, I also conducted a wider search for documentaries associated with "animal advocacy". Many of the same films appeared, but an additional 25 post-2005, US-facing films were identified that focused on a wider range of issues than the pro-vegan lists, including exotic animals as pets, cruelty involving dogs and animal testing. Of these films, only six are mentioned once in a pro-vegan listicle, which is noteworthy in terms of the dominant "vegan" narrative. Yet as far as these films seek to end certain forms of exploitation and cruelty (though this message is not always explicit), then by raising awareness they are as equally "pro-vegan" as films such as the more widely known *Eating Animals* (2017) – arguably more so as they do not condone "less harmful" models of animal use. Table 5.1 provides a list of the 45 reviewed films, including their year of release, primary focus (in terms of animal use) and availability (in the UK as of July 2020). A master list of 100 pro-vegan and animal advocacy films released between 1996 and 2020, not restricted to a US-focus, was used to chart the growth in these films over time.

Table 5.1 Chronological list of 45 reviewed documentaries (post-2005, US-facing, and available in the UK). Highlighted films appear in at least three pro-vegan listicles.

Film	Year	Primary focus/Animal use*	Availability
Behind the Mask (S)	2006	Research, activism	Free on YouTube
Dealing Dogs (S)	2006	Dogs, dealing, research, activism	Free on YouTube
Your Mommy Kills Animals! (S)	2007	Research, activism	Free on YouTube
Meat the Truth	2007	Food	Free on YouTube
A Sacred Duty (S)	2007	Food	Free on YouTube
The Cove (S)	2009	Food (and entertainment)	Free on YouTube

Film	Year	Primary focus/Animal use*	Availability
Death on a Factory Farm (S)	2009	Food, activism	Free on YouTube
Fowl Play (S)	2009	Food, diet	Free on YouTube
Fat, Sick, and Nearly Dead	2010	Diet	Free on YouTube
Planeat	2010	Food	Free on YouTube
A Fall From Freedom (S)	2011	Entertainment	Free on YouTube
Forks Over Knives	2011	Diet	No longer available (July 2020)
Vegucated (S)	2011	Diet, food, fashion (primarily leather)	Free on YouTube
Maximum Tolerated Dose (S)	2012	Research	Rental
One Nation Under Dog (S)	2012	Pets	Free on YouTube
The Superior Human?	2012	Human superiority	Free on YouTube
Bear 71	2012	Wildlife surveillance	Free online
The Paw Project (S)	2013	Pets and entertainment (including exotic)	Free on YouTube
Live and Let Live (S)	2013	Food, diet	Rental
Speciesism (S)	2013	Food, diet	Rental, Amazon Prime, or purchase DVD
Blackfish	2013	Entertainment	Netflix
The Ghosts in Our Machine (S)	2013	Fashion, food, research (briefly entertainment)	Purchase DVD. No streaming options
Cowspiracy: The Sustainability Secret	2014	Food	Free on YouTube. Netflix
PlantPure Nation	2015	Diet, food	Free on YouTube
Tyke Elephant Outlaw (S)	2015	Entertainment	Rental. Amazon and iTunes
Racing Extinction	2015	Food, medicine	Free on YouTube

Film	Year	Primary focus/Animal use*	Availability
Unity (S)	2015	Food, entertainment	Free on YouTube
Food Choices (S)	2016	Diet, food	Rental
Before the Flood	2016	Food	Free on YouTube
Meathooked & End of Water	2016	Food	Free on YouTube
Called to Rescue	2016	Food, fashion, research (re. farm animals)	Free on YouTube
Vegan: Everyday Stories	2016	Diet, food (briefly circuses and vivisection)	Free on YouTube
Eating Animals (S)	2017	Food	Rental
What the Health	2017	Diet, food	Free on YouTube. Netflix
The Game Changers	2018	Diet	Free on YouTube
Dominion (S)	2018	Food, research, clothing, pets, entertainment, pharmaceuticals	Free on YouTube. Netflix
Eating You Alive	2018	Diet	Free on YouTube
H.O.P.E. What You Eat Matters (S)	2018	Food, diet	Free on YouTube
Let Us Be Heroes	2018	Food, diet (briefly leather and fur)	Free on YouTube
The Animal People (S)	2019	Research, activism	Rental. Netflix
Diet Fiction	2019	Diet	Rental. Amazon
A Prayer for Compassion (S)	2019	Food (briefly research)	Rental. Amazon
The Invisible Vegan (S)	2019	Diet, food	Rental
The Farm in My Backyard (S)	2019	Fashion (fur)	Free on YouTube
Test Subjects	2019	Research	Free online

* Primary animal uses include for food, research, pharmaceuticals, medicine, entertainment, fashion/clothing and as pets. Films that do not focus on animal use are primarily concerned with diet. Film titles suffixed with (S) indicate those whose narrative is based on animals' physical suffering (see Exclusion/Intervention 2 below).

Film summary

Of the 45 documentaries, 27 (60 per cent) focus almost exclusively on farming, food (i.e., "meat") and/or "food" animals.[25] Narrowed to the 20 films promoted across at least three pro-vegan listicles, this increases to 80 per cent (or 16 films) – 17 if *Racing Extinction* (2015) is included (addresses the hunting of marine animals primarily for food) and 18 if *Dominion* (2018) is also included (where "food" animals occupy the majority of the film). Animal testing is the subject of five films (three appear in one pro-vegan listicle each);[26] four are concerned with marine life as entertainment and food (all included in at least three pro-vegan listicles);[27] three tackle issues associated with free-living/exotic species as entertainment, pets and for conservation (one mentioned in one listicle);[28] two focus on dogs for research and as pets (neither feature in pro-vegan listicles);[29] and one looks at fur farming (*The Farm in My Backyard* – mentioned in one vegan listicle). Two films (*The Ghosts in Our Machine* and *Dominion*) narratively (if not equally visually) highlight a range of animal uses encompassing food, fashion, sport, entertainment and research (both included in four and five vegan listicles respectively), and one (*The Superior Human?*) challenges the logic of human superiority (not on any lists).

Animals do not feature at all in eight films concerned with "meat" and diets.[30] Of these, six appear in at least three pro-vegan listicles and three are among the most widely promoted documentaries, included in 14–17 lists each (*Forks Over Knives*, *The Game Changers* and *What*

25 Three of these films make very brief references to the use of the same animals in entertainment (*The Cove*) and fashion (*Vegucated* and *Let Us Be Heroes*). A further two make fleeting references to other topics – circuses (*Vegan: Everyday Stories*) and animal testing (*A Prayer for Compassion*).

26 *Behind the Mask* (2006), *Your Mommy Kills Animals!* (2007), *Maximum Tolerated Dose* (2012), *Test Subjects* (2019) and *The Animal People* (2019).

27 *Fall From Freedom* (2011), *The Cove* (2009), *Blackfish* (2013) and *Racing Extinction* (2015).

28 *The Paw Project* (2013), *Tyke Elephant Outlaw* (2015) and *Bear 71* (2012).

29 *Dealing Dogs* (2006) and *One Nation Under Dog* (2012).

30 *Meat the Truth* (2007), *Fat, Sick and Nearly Dead* (2010), *Forks Over Knives* (2011), *PlantPure Nation* (2015), *What the Health* (2017), *The Game Changers* (2018), *Eating You Alive* (2018) and *Diet Fiction* (2019).

the Health). For 91 per cent (41) of the 45 documentaries and 95 per cent (19) of the 20 most frequently promoted, the case for reducing or eliminating the use(s) of animals in question is predominantly framed in terms of benefits to human health, the environment and/or freeing animals from acute suffering.[31] For both the full list of films and the top-promoted list, 89–90 per cent (40 and 18 respectively) can be described as single-issue documentaries, being focused on one form of animal use (e.g., food) and/or one species or category of animals (e.g., "farm" animals).

The dominant exclusions that emerge include: (1) animals other than those typically used to produce "meat" (e.g., horses, dogs, free-living animals, aquatic animals, amphibians and reptiles)[32] and their associated (interlinked) practices (e.g., racing, zoos, trafficking, breeding, trading, hunting, pet-keeping); (2) forms of oppression other than physical use and mistreatment; and (3) animals' inherent rather than contingent value. The next three sections address each exclusion in turn and explore the space they offer for intervention.

Exclusion/Intervention 1. More than "meat": Mapping the animal-industrial complex

Considering the dominance of "meat" and "dairy" products, especially in the minority world, the growing numbers of animals used to provide these products that are exploited and killed, the associated environmental impacts and the derision historically directed towards vegetarians and vegans, the exclusive focus of the majority of these documentaries (particularly the most frequently promoted) on "meat" vs plant-based foods and dietary veganism, also (though not always) encompassing farming and "food" animals, appears justified. However, from the perspective of animals' total liberation,[33] such a focus is ill

31 *Blackfish* is the exception here, where the mental states and emotional capacities of orcas are forefront.

32 Aquatic animals, reptiles and amphibians comprise the majority of the live animal trade with their primary market being the European and US pet industries: see Smith, Zambrana-Torrelio et al. 2017, 30.

advised for one key reason. As long as other uses of animals are not also problematised, justifications for continuing to use "farm" animals, especially in "better" ways more aligned with uses conceived as benign and even benevolent, remain available to be mobilised at any time. This scenario is no less, and perhaps more, likely (based on evidence to date) than the more common reverse argument that recruiting people to plant-based or vegan diets can act as a gateway to ethical concern for "farm" and then all animals.[34] Critically, when other animal uses are excluded, the foundations of human supremacy that unite all practices involving animals cannot be fully articulated.

Of the 45 reviewed films, only two cover a spectrum of animal uses. Using the same approach as *Earthlings* (2005), *Dominion* (2018) introduces a parade of animals (mostly traditional "food" animals, including fish but also horses, foxes, dogs, mice and "exotic" animals) with a list of their associated uses – as pets, food, clothing, scientific research, pharmaceuticals and/or entertainment. Each segment is between 1.5 and 20 minutes long. This is the only film to include greyhound racing, horse racing, rodeos, circuses, zoos and aquariums among the examples of animal abuse and mistreatment. While *Dominion* highlights different dimensions of the A-IC and shows how one species can be put to multiple uses, it falls short of identifying each use as a highly organised industry and the extent of integration between the uses – how they rely on, support and leverage off each other. In *The Ghosts in Our Machine*, photographer Jo-Anne McArthur documents the suffering, neglect and abuse of animals used for food, clothing, research and, more briefly, entertainment. Pick and Drew commend this film for drawing attention to the wider cultural and economic context of the "war against animals".[35] While it is powerful viewing, I do not believe it offers the "broader structural critique[s] of the centrality of animal domination to our economy" that Drew claims.[36] This is primarily because what comprises that structure is not clarified, but

33 Pellow 2014.
34 Christopher, Bartkowski and Haverda 2018.
35 Drew 2016; Pick 2016.
36 Drew 2016, 207.

also because of the dominant focus on "horrors", as discussed in the next section.

Behind the Mask (2006) also covers more than two animal uses, focusing predominantly on one group of activists and their direct actions against animal testing, fur farming and animal agriculture. However, while the subjects of the film are understood as "animal activists", their actions are not contextualised in terms of other (less violent) human–animal relations and the scope of, and links between, these industries are not indicated. Both *Unity* (2015) and *The Superior Human?* (2012) challenge the human–animal binary more broadly, though specific uses of animals, other than as food in *Unity*, are neither represented nor challenged.

Across the remaining 40 films, there is no contextualisation of the single issue/use they focus on, and thus no pathway offered for the viewer to critically reflect on, and draw connections between, all human–animal relations. The transformational capacity of these films is therefore limited because they "fail to address the *power dynamic* that naturalizes extreme [or all] forms of violence against animals".[37]

By failing to account for this larger picture, and limiting the purview of "issues", pro-vegan documentaries tend to depoliticise, and implicitly excuse, a wide range of animal uses and permit an extended network of practices that constitute the entire complex to continue unchallenged in any coherent or meaningful way. Often these are practices that hold fewer negative associations, these generally being outweighed by positive associations (e.g., with entertainment, education or companionship). Part of the problem is that extreme violence and suffering is widely understood, and presented in these documentaries, as the primary, and sometimes the only, dimension of animal oppression that needs to be addressed, where there are of course multiple dimensions.

37 Pick 2016, 98, emphasis added.

Exclusion/Intervention 2. Violence is more than physical

Animal suffering and/or physical mistreatment feature prominently in 25 (67 per cent) of the reviewed documentaries (excluding the eight that do not include animals) (see Table 5.1). In eight of the remaining 12 films, the main concern remains the environmental, health, ethical and even spiritual impacts of physically using, killing, consuming and/or eradicating animals primarily in relation to food production and also scientific research.[38] If consideration is given to animals' subjective experiences, the narrative is still based on avoiding or eliminating their physical suffering, or rescuing them from such situations. That is, 90 per cent of films that include animals attend primarily or exclusively to the physical harms they are subjected to.

Regarding the 25 films in which animal suffering and/or physical mistreatment is foregrounded, the same footage often appears in several films and, as Carrie Freeman also notes in relation to US food advocacy campaigns, this tends to focus on the worst cruelties in factory farming.[39] Pigs and chickens are most frequently depicted as the subjects of the most horrific forms of abuse. Indeed, these animals are widely understood as enduring the worst conditions in animal agriculture. However, if the now commonplace graphic footage of conditions in which chickens and pigs are raised and killed, and the treatment they endure along the way, has not thus far prompted a reduction in their rates of consumption (rather, the opposite), should this approach be prioritised to the extent that it is? Or is it that it needs to be better contextualised to locate physical violence as just one of several forms of violence inflicted on and experienced by animals?

Ontological violence is described as the distortion of the phenomenological basis of an animal's existence.[40] Depending on its scale and duration, this distortion can disrupt phylogenetic (long-term, generational) as well as ontogenetic (lifetime) knowledge and, in the case of farmed animals, constitutes no less than ontological

---

38 *Planeat, Cowspiracy, Vegan: Everyday Stories, Let Us Be Heroes, Before the Flood, Meathooked & End of Water, Racing Extinction, Test Subjects.*

39 Freeman 2010, 169.

40 Weisberg 2015, 41.

genocide.[41] This notion of culturally severed and compromised lives resonates at an individual level with Marx's notion of alienation from species-being, and at a species level with Deborah Bird Rose's concept of "double death".[42]

While currently given less attention in advocacy, ontological violence is perhaps the most pervasive and insidious form of harm inflicted on animals, even as part of relations that may be conceived as "thoughtful and compassionate".[43] Exercised primarily through the repeated disruption, manipulation and severing of intersubjective attachment relations, ontological violence leads to often profound and interminable experiences of loss, grief[44] and, as *Blackfish* and *Tyke Elephant Outlaw* illustrate, also frustration and anger.

A number of films depict specific causes of ontological violence, such as baby cows and pigs being separated from their mothers, or portray its psychological effects, for example in the stereotypes of confined animals. However, it is typically the more obviously horrific techniques of physical violence that are the focus. While these may be identified as "systemic", their relation to, and dependence on, other techniques equally routinely used to oppress animals are obscured. Yet, physical violence is "merely" the outward manifestation of the oppression that is the defining condition of most animals' entire existence and experience, epistemically and legally inscribed on their sub-humanised bodies.

In terms of scale and return on investment, advocacy organisations can certainly justify targeting the practices responsible for the largest volume of killing and the most routinised violence. However, both for individual animals and moving towards the end of animal oppression, psychological and ontological harms must also be part of the narrative. For one, physical violence and acute suffering, which I would argue almost every person would oppose, are too easily framed as welfare issues – the result of practices that can be improved and made more "humane". Emphasising other forms of violence radically unsettles the

41 Brooks Pribac 2021.
42 Rose 2012, 2013.
43 Gruen 2015, 284–5.
44 Brooks Pribac 2021.

sense of fait accompli that can accompany welfare wins. It could also help advocacy organisations to elucidate the oppression underpinning all animal uses and situate the large-scale abuse and extermination of "food" animals as just one, albeit significant, component of the A-IC.

Collectively, animal advocacy on and off screen pays little to no regard to the ontological violence endured by animals separated from their ecologies, communities, cultures and their own sovereign selves. However, a recognition of ontological violence foregrounds the fundamental power imbalance that shapes all human–animal relations and brings the A-IC into relief by encompassing relations that are as yet not sufficiently problematised.

Indeed, non-physical violence (in the sense of not causing immediate physical harm) is integral to the A-IC and intimately linked to its success. Part of the reason for its under-representation across the reviewed documentaries may be that the different forms of violence experienced by animals, and the techniques that mobilise them, have only recently started to be clearly articulated (Arcari 2023).

In sum, these documentaries help shape a certain understanding of animal oppression as defined primarily by routinised physical violence and acute suffering. In so doing, a vast complex of exploitations are implicitly construed as acceptable by comparison, or at least not problematic enough to warrant concern. This is more especially the case with practices steeped in positive associations that prove more difficult to critique from traditional perspectives. This leads to my final point, and another reason why it is important to shift the advocacy narrative towards an acknowledgement of ontological along with physical violence.

Exclusion/Intervention 3. Behaviour trading: Inherent over utilitarian value

As discussed, extreme suffering, and freedom from that suffering, are the primary measures by which on-screen advocacy seeks to generate ethical concern for animals. However, as Twine explains, an ethic based on the "utilitarian language of suffering" leads to a (welfarist) focus on ameliorating animals' experience "without fundamentally calling into question the systemic nature of commodified human–animal relations".[45] Similarly, utilitarian promises of improved health and fitness, and/or environmental benefits are the primary and often the only arguments presented for reducing meat consumption and adopting plant-based or vegan diets. If animals are recognised at all, such arguments are even less likely to view their consumption critically, as part of a broader matrix of oppressive relations.

And yet, these three themes – health, the environment and animal suffering – constitute the main pillars around which over 90 per cent of documentaries formulate their appeals for change. This includes films in which one pillar is the sole or primary focus,[46] and those offering two or three potential justifications for changing behaviour.[47] This in itself is not necessarily a problem. However, the absence of a broader problem context,[48] and also of arguments based on animals' inherent value as "teleological centres of life",[49] leaves these narratives vulnerable to critique, counter-arguments or simply not achieving their potential in terms of the depth, scope, impact and endurance of their appeals.

Over half (23) of the 45 reviewed films make no reference to animals as centres or subjects of their own lives. This includes the eight films that do not feature animals at all or only minimally.[50] *Before the Flood*, *Meathooked & End of Water* and *Eating Animals* actually reinforce the objectification of "food" animals by promoting more "sustainable" options including "chicken" and pasture-raised "meat".

45 Twine 2010, 26.

46 Films focused solely on health include *Eating You Alive*, *The Game Changers*, *Diet Fiction*, *Forks Over Knives* and *Fat, Sick and Nearly Dead*. Those primarily concerned with the environmental impacts of animal agriculture and "livestock" include *Meat the Truth*, *Cowspiracy*, *Eating Animals*, *Meathooked & End of Water* and *Before the Flood*. Films where animal suffering constitutes the core narrative include *Dominion*, *The Ghosts in Our Machine* and *Fowl Play*.

47 Including *Vegucated*, *Live and Let Live*, *Food Choices*, *Vegan: Everyday Stories*, *H.O.P.E. What You Eat Matters* and *The Invisible Vegan*.

48 Arcari 2022.

49 Taylor 1986, 119.

50 Among the additional films (besides these eight) are *Dealing Dogs*, *A Sacred Duty*, *Eating Animals*, *The Farm in My Backyard*, *Let Us Be Heroes* and *The Invisible Vegan*.

There are implicit nods of varying degrees towards the notion of animal subjectivity in a further 13 films.[51] However, it is typically the pain and suffering of one species (e.g., pigs) or one group of animals (e.g., "farm" animals), their right *not* to experience that suffering, and the need to liberate them from it, that constitutes the narrative core. This is the case for *The Ghosts in Our Machine* where, just 30 seconds from the end credits, an unidentified voice describes animals' rights to "bodily integrity and liberty" as existing inherently rather than being bestowed by humans. It is also the case for *Dominion*, where narrator Joaquin Phoenix speaks of animals' desire to be seen as individuals and as beings in their own right, yet this line comes at the very end of the film after nearly two hours of graphic images of violence and suffering considered so difficult to watch that the film's website hosts advice from a clinical psychologist on post-viewing self-care. *Unity* appeals for the moral consideration of all beings, but as part of an evolutionary pathway towards "Homo Spiritus" – "the highest expression of man".

The majority (80 per cent) of reviewed documentaries (36 of the total, and 16 of those in pro-vegan listicles) thus prioritise utilitarian expressions of care or compassion that "simply extend the privileged category of the rational human master by admitting [some] animals within the sphere of moral consideration to the extent that they are like us"[52] – commonly with respect to their capacity to suffer and feel emotion. Alternatively, and also a form of extensionism, they draw equivalences (typically relating to intelligence) between one terribly exploited animal (e.g., pigs) and another less exploited (e.g., dogs) with the aim of evoking compassion for the former's differential treatment. Such framings bestow contingent rather than inherent value on animals, underscoring the urge to establish measures of anthropological sameness (or continuity) and difference, rather than encouraging a more inclusive, ahuman perspective grounded in what

51 Including *The Ghosts in Our Machine*, *Dominion* and the four focused on specific acts of activism (or more particularly the individual activists involved): *Behind the Mask*, *Your Mommy Kills Animals!*, *Death on a Factory Farm* and *The Animal People*.

52 Alloun 2015, 163. Therefore framing it as a duty we owe to "humanity" or the idea of "humanity" more than to the animal herself (see Steiner 2016).

Calarco calls indistinction.[53] Of the remaining nine films, two (*A Fall From Freedom* and *Blackfish*) depict the reduced and compromised lives of ocean mammals held captive to perform in aquaria, and five[54] allocate varying amounts of time, from just a few minutes (*Vegucated*) to the majority of the film (*Called to Rescue*), to the subjective experiences of "food" animals. These films, to varying degrees, do recognise (some) animals as subjects of their own lives, although this inherent value still tends to be predicated on human measures of emotional complexity, intelligence and the capacity for intra/interspecies community.

Only two single-issue documentaries exhibit some openness to a less human-centred indistinction, which is achieved primarily through a close attentiveness to biography over biology.[55] The films follow the predictably tragic journeys of an elephant named Tyke used for entertainment in circuses (*Tyke Elephant Outlaw*) and a free-living, electronically tagged grizzly bear named Bear 71. Both problematise the ways in which these animals' ecological, cultural and subjective worlds have been stripped away for human purposes using many of oppression's techniques[56] and ultimately leading to their premature deaths – Tyke being shot in a Hawaiian street after escaping from the circus, and Bear 71 being hit by a freight train.[57]

For the animal advocacy movement, utilitarian approaches to behaviour change and their alignment with market-based solutions have helped leverage important changes in farm animal welfare and a wider uptake of plant-based foods.[58] However, this success comes at

---

53 Calarco 2015; MacCormack 2020.

54 *Vegucated, Live and Let Live, Called to Rescue, H.O.P.E. What You Eat Matters* and *A Prayer for Compassion.*

55 Regan 2010. Regan's account still reflects an anthropocentric conception of "biographical animals" – being those that "share with humans a family of cognitive, attitudinal, sensory, and volitional capacities" (see 2010, 37).

56 Gruen 2015.

57 *Bear 71* raises surveillance, often a tool for "transparency", as another, more covert, technique of oppression whereby "the act of making the hidden visible may be equally likely to generate other, more effective ways of confining it" (Pachirat 2011).

58 It is worth noting that other animal uses, including for sport, entertainment, fashion, research and companionship, do not lend themselves so well to

a cost in terms of the unpredictable longevity of these changes and their limited capacity to benefit all animals. Moreover, with reference to the comparable "ecosystems services" model in conservation, Taylor, Chapron et al. stress that appeals based on human self-interest and anthropocentric values rely on people remaining convinced that the exchange is worthwhile.[59] Yet history demonstrates that "knowledge" relating to health, the environment and animal suffering, on which the majority of the reviewed documentaries depends, is constantly evolving, contestable and therefore unstable. Value perceptions can shift, conceivably to a point where there is sufficient "better" health, improved sustainability and reduced suffering such that the limits of these arguments are reached, whereupon their effects stall or even reverse.

The hollowing out of the philosophical and political context of animal advocacy for fear it will alienate the "self-interested" public[60] only compounds this risk. Aside from being refuted by empirical research,[61] the claim that foregrounding nonhuman interests/inherent value is not strategically effective "fails to appreciate the distinction between marketing and morality".[62] It also, Batavia and Nelson continue, "misconstrues nonhuman [intrinsic value] as only a rhetorical tool to be evaluated by its effectiveness, rather than a moral proposition to be judged by its justification".[63] There is a risk that without this moral foundation, a certain popularised and friable brand of "cheery-pop veganism"[64] defined by an anthropocentric vegan identity[65] will continue to erode the notion of veganism as a social movement as opposed to a lifestyle, diverting attention and energy from the goal of ending animal oppression.

---

quantifiable metrics of benefits associated with their reduction or elimination. They are also perceived as having more limited alternatives (Fitzgerald 2019, 45).

59 Taylor, Chapron et al. 2020, 1092.

60 Hopwood, Bleidorn et al. 2020.

61 Taylor, Chapron et al. 2020.

62 Batavia and Nelson 2017, 372.

63 Batavia and Nelson 2017, 372.

64 Wrenn 2017.

65 Hamilton 2019.

Complementing the push for intrinsic valuations of nature,[66] "pro-vegan" filmmakers (and other animal advocates) ought to consider foregrounding animals' inherent value and decentring the utilitarian elements of their narratives. With the inclusion of inherent value, advocacy aimed at reducing or eliminating animal use would be based not only on (potentially precarious) utilitarian exchanges – better health, improved environment, reduced animal suffering – but also, and more reliably, on animals' right to live their lives on their own terms, with no justification required. This counters potential defences of use based on variable assessments of suffering or harm by asserting animals' first and foremost right to be teleological centres of their own lives.

Conclusion

It is too soon to know whether the current plant-based trend will continue gathering pace and contribute to the eventual demise of all animal agriculture (including "seafood") or whether these industries will continue in some reduced, "ethical" and socially acceptable form alongside a more robust and legitimated vegan food industry. This review of 45 "pro-vegan" documentaries suggests that dominant approaches to vegan and/or plant-based advocacy do not pose a sufficient challenge to understandings of animals as usable to prevent the latter pathway prevailing. However, the elements that are currently absent/excluded from on-screen "pro-vegan" advocacy are also those that could attenuate this situation and help avoid the vegan revolution becoming a short-lived "fad".[67] These elements are: (1) a coherent and consistent representation of the animal-industrial complex; (2) a comprehensive account of oppression and all its violent techniques; and (3) an emphasis on the inherent value of animals.

This is not to negate the value of documentaries (and campaigns) that focus on food, farming (or other single issues) and freedom (from suffering). But additionally incorporating the three elements discussed

66 Batavia and Nelson 2017; Taylor, Chapron et al. 2020.
67 Jallinoja, Vinnari and Niva 2019, 174.

here would increase the odds that observed dietary trends could become more ideologically and politically grounded. This grounding in Pick's "fundamental conditions and mechanisms"[68] of animal use would provide the movement the resilience it needs to weather passing trends and maintain a core narrative regardless of which issues came to the fore. It would also explicitly extend limited critiques of one animal use to all uses, signalling the kind of comprehensive shift in perspective that could ripple through all dimensions of oppression. In this way, an animal advocacy movement united in its mobilisation of the A-IC, oppression and inherent value as core concepts could more effectively generate understanding and support for substantive change at pivotal moments (such as zoonotic pandemics) when the extent to which the experiences of marginalised others, human and nonhuman, are bound together under the same global institutional order becomes brutally evident.

Pro-vegan documentaries can be influential and often viral vehicles for calls to change. They can also provoke equally strong opposition aimed at invalidating veganism and maintaining supremacist conceptions of, and practices involving, animals. To increase the legitimacy and resilience of their respective messages, and echoing Pick in the opening of this chapter, I therefore argue that both on- and off-screen advocacy efforts should, and indeed need to, be collectively building a much more coherent, inclusive and powerful platform for all advocacy – one that mobilises a unified conception of animal use under the A-IC, embraces all forces and techniques of oppression, and withdraws from anthropocentric constructs of value, refusing the impulse to base animals' total liberation from oppression on anything more, or less, than that they are.[69]

Acknowledgements

Many thanks to Claire Parkinson and Lara Herring for their insightful guidance during the editing process, and also for bringing this fantastic

68 Pick 2016, 98.

69 MacCormack 2020, 31.

volume to fruition. Thank you also to Iris Bergmann and Shae Hunter for their wonderful feedback on a first draft of this chapter, and their suggestions for improvement.

References

Alloun, E. (2015). Ecofeminism and animal advocacy in Australia: productive encounters for an integrative ethics and politics. *Animal Studies Journal* 4(1): 148–73. https://ro.uow.edu.au/asj/vol4/iss1/9.

Anon. (2018). Social media and the rise of the vegan. *University of Sunderland, News*. 28 June. https://tinyurl.com/mptt43z.

Arcari, P. (2021). The Covid pandemic, "pivotal" moments, and persistent anthropocentrism: interrogating the (il)legitimacy of critical animal perspectives. *Animal Studies Journal* 10(1): 186–239. https://tinyurl.com/44njcbwh.

Arcari, P. (2022). (Animal) oppression: responding to questions of efficacy and (il)legitimacy in animal advocacy with a new collective action/master frame. *Animal Studies Journal* 11(2): 69–108. https://ro.uow.edu.au/asj/vol11/iss2/4.

Arcari, P. (2023). Slow violence against animals: unseen spectacles in racing and at zoos. *Geoforum* 144: 103820. https://doi.org/10.1016/j.geoforum.2023.103820.

Batavia, C. and M.P. Nelson (2017). For goodness sake! what is intrinsic value and why should we care? *Biological Conservation* 209: 366–76. https://doi.org/10.1016/j.biocon.2017.03.003.

Brooks Pribac, T. (2021). *Enter the Animal: Cross-species Perspectives on Grief and Spirituality*. Sydney: Sydney University Press.

Calarco, M. (2015). *Thinking Through Animals: Identity, Difference, Indistinction*. Stanford, CA: Stanford University Press.

Christopher, A., J. Bartkowski and T. Haverda (2018). Portraits of veganism: a comparative discourse analysis of a second-order subculture. *Societies* 8(3): 55. https://doi.org/10.3390/soc8030055.

Cole, M. and K. Morgan (2011). Vegaphobia: derogatory discourses of veganism and the reproduction of speciesism in UK national newspapers. *The British Journal of Sociology* 62(1): 134–53. https://tinyurl.com/56spj26z.

Donaldson, S. and W. Kymlicka (2013). *Zoopolis*. Oxford: Oxford University Press.

Doyle, J. (2016). Celebrity vegans and the lifestyling of ethical consumption. *Environmental Communication* 10(6): 777–90. https://tinyurl.com/2dwj9xph.

Drew, J. (2016). Rendering visible: animals, empathy, and visual truths in The Ghosts in Our Machine and beyond. *Animal Studies Journal* 5(2): 202–16. https://ro.uow.edu.au/asj/vol5/iss2/10.

Dutkiewicz, J. and J. Dickstein (2021). The ism in veganism: the case for a minimal practice-based definition. *Food Ethics* 6(1). https://tinyurl.com/2uwuzefu.

Fitzgerald, A.J. (2019). *Animal Advocacy and Environmentalism: Understanding and Bridging the Divide*. Cambridge, UK: Polity Press.

Freeman, Carrie P. (2010). Framing animal rights in the "Go Veg" campaigns of US animal rights organizations. *Society and Animals* 18(2): 163–82.

Giraud, E.H. (2019). *What Comes After Entanglement?* Durham, NC and London: Duke University Press.

Gruen, L. (2015). The faces of animal oppression. In S. Asumah and M. Nagel, eds. *Diversity, Social Justice, and Inclusive Excellence: Transdisciplinary and Global Perspectives*, 281–94. Albany: State University of New York Press.

Hamilton, C.L. (2019). *Veganism, Sex and Politics: Tales of Danger and Pleasure*. Bristol, UK: HammerOn Press.

Hancox, D. (2018). The unstoppable rise of veganism: how a fringe movement went mainstream. *Guardian*, 1 April. https://tinyurl.com/5n9xcph8.

Hopwood, C.J., W. Bleidorn, T. Schwaba and S. Chen (2020). Health, environmental, and animal rights motives for vegetarian eating. *PLoS One* 15(4): e0230609.

Jallinoja, P., M. Vinnari and M. Niva (2019). Veganism and plant-based eating: analysis of interplay between discursive strategies and lifestyle political consumerism. In M. Bostrom, M. Micheletti and P. Oosterveer, eds. *The Oxford Handbook of Political Consumerism*, 157–79. New York: Oxford University Press.

MacCormack, P. (2020). *The Ahuman Manifesto: Activism for the End of the Anthropocene*. London and New York: Bloomsbury Academic.

Noske, B. (1989). *Humans and Other Animals: Beyond the Boundaries of Anthropology*. London: Pluto Press.

Pachirat ,T. (2011). *Every Twelve Seconds: Industrialized Slaughter and the Politics of Sight*. New Haven, CT: Yale University Press.

Parker, J. (2018). The year of the vegan. *Economist*, 22 November. https://tinyurl.com/yufr2vam.

Pellow, D.N. (2014). *Total Liberation: The Power and Promise of Animal Rights and the Radical Earth Movement*. Minneapolis: University of Minnesota Press.

Pendergrast, N. (2016). Environmental concerns and the mainstreaming of veganism. In T. Raphaely and D. Marinova, eds. *Impact of Meat Consumption on Health and Environmental Sustainability*, 106–23. IGI Global. https://doi.org/10.1016/10.4018/978-1-4666-9553-5.

Petter, O. (2018). The surprising reason why veganism is now mainstream. *Independent*, 10 April. https://tinyurl.com/3jdkpp3u.

Pick, A. (2016). Animal rights films, organized violence, and the politics of sight. In Y. Tzioumakis and C. Molloy, eds. *The Routledge Companion to Cinema and Politics*, 91–102. London: Routledge.

Planck, N. (2007). Death by veganism. *New York Times*, 21 May. https://tinyurl.com/9az8cctb.

Regan, T. (2010). Animal rights. In M. Bekoff ed. *Encyclopedia of Animal Rights and Animal Welfare*, 36–8. Santa Barbara, CA: Greenwood Press.

Ripple, W.J., C. Wolf, T.M. Newsome, P. Barnard and W.R. Moomaw (2021). World scientists' warning of a climate emergency. *BioScience* 70(1): 8–12. https://doi.org/10.1093/biosci/biz088.

Ritchie, H. and M. Roser (2017). Meat and dairy production. *OurWorldInData.org*. https://ourworldindata.org/meat-production.

Roberts, M. (2005). Children "harmed" by vegan diets. *BBC News*, 21 February. https://news.bbc.co.uk/1/hi/health/4282257.stm.

Rose, D.B. (2012). Multispecies knots of ethical time. *Environmental Philosophy* 9(1): 127–40.

Rose, D.B. (2013). Anthropocene noir. *Arena Journal* 41/42: 206–19.

Smith, K.M., C. Zambrana-Torrelio, A. White, M. Asmussen, C. Machalaba, S. Kennedy et al. (2017). Summarizing US wildlife trade with an eye toward assessing the risk of infectious disease introduction. *Ecohealth* 14(1): 29–39.

Sorenson, J. ed. (2014). *Critical Animal Studies: Thinking the Unthinkable*. Toronto: Canadian Scholars Press.

Stallwood, K. (2012). Animal rights: moral crusade or social movement? In C. Calvert and J. Groling, eds. *Critical Perspectives on Animals in Society*, 19–24. Exeter: University of Exeter.

Statista (2021). Meat consumption worldwide from 2010 to 2021, by meat type (in million tons). *Statista*. https://tinyurl.com/bdhtd2e6.

Steiner, G. (2017). Animal rights and the distorting power of anthropocentric prejudice. In A. Woodhall and G.G. da Trindade, eds. *Ethical and Political Approaches to Nonhuman Animal Issues*, 177–99. Switzerland: Palgrave Macmillan.

Taylor, B., G. Chapron, H. Kopnina, E. Orlikowska, J. Gray and J.J. Piccolo (2020). The need for ecocentrism in biodiversity conservation. *Conservation Biology* 34(5): 1089–96. https://doi.org/10.1111/cobi.13541.

Taylor, P.W. (1986). *Respect for Nature: A Theory of Environmental Ethics*. Princeton, NJ: Princeton University Press.

The Vegan Society (2015). Definition of veganism. *The Vegan Society*, 19 December. www.vegansociety.com/go-vegan/definition-veganism.

Twine, R. (2010). *Animals as Biotechnology: Ethics, Sustainability and Critical Animal Studies*. London: Earthscan.

Twine, R. (2012). Revealing the 'animal-industrial complex': a concept & method for critical animal studies. *Journal for Critical Animal Studies* 10(1): 12–39.

Wadiwel, D. (2009). The war against animals: domination, law and sovereignty. *Griffith Law Review* 18(2): 283–97.

Wadiwel, D. (2018). Chicken harvesting machine: animal labor, resistance, and the time of production. *South Atlantic Quarterly* 117(3): 527–49. https://doi.org/10.1215/00382876-6942135.

Weisberg, Z. (2015). Biotechnology as end game: ontological and ethical collapse in the 'biotech century'. *NanoEthics* 9: 39–54.

White, R.J. (2018). Looking backward, moving forward: articulating a 'Yes, BUT…!' response to lifestyle veganism. *EuropeNow* (20). https://tinyurl.com/4a2xkxhy.

Woodhall, A. and G.G. da Trindade (2016). Saving nonhumans: drawing the threads of a movement together. In G. da Trindade and A. Woodhall, eds. *Intervention or Protest: Acting for Nonhuman Animals*, 23–56. Wilmington, DE: Vernon Press.

Wrenn, C.L. (2017). Trump veganism: a political survey of American vegans in the era of identity politics. *Societies* 7(4): 32. https://doi.org/10.3390/soc7040032.

Wrenn, C.L and R. Johnson (2013). A critique of single-issue campaigning and the importance of comprehensive abolitionist vegan advocacy. *Food, Culture & Society* 16(4): 651–68.

6

"Please don't look away"

The ghostly intersections between seeing and feeling in documentary film

Lorena Elke Dobbie

Introduction

I write this chapter as I currently locate myself on the traditional territories of many Indigenous nations including the Mississaugas of the Credit, the Anishnabeg, the Chippewa, the Haudenosaunee and the Wendat peoples on Treaty 13 lands of so-called Toronto, Canada. I am grateful for the opportunity to live, love and learn on lands that are not my own. My reflections in this chapter draw on both academic and activist teachings I have experienced in my life, yet mostly this chapter centres on my work of building right relationships with other animals. I move between identifying other animals as "nonhuman" and "other" as a way of showing how my own thinking continues to process and evolve as I continue to set things right with them.

In 2010, I began working on the documentary *The Ghosts in Our Machine*, directed by Liz Marshall. At that time, Liz and I were in a creative partnership as well as a life partnership. Since 1987, I have been an animal rights activist and vegan. I came to this consciousness about other animals because I was haunted. As a little girl, I was raised in the country in a province in Canada called Manitoba where I lived with extended family that were poor yet self-sustaining as we lived largely from the land. As a child, my exposure to animal slaughter was very confusing and emotional. I was the only child in the house and from a very young age I developed relationships with the animals. Animals were my friends, literally. When the little chicks would arrive in the mail in the spring I would be so excited, yet I didn't see the dead ones among them as my child eyes were gazing upon the fluffy lives that I loved. I cared for the chicks by feeding them and as they grew I also played with them. As seasons changed and fall came so did slaughter time, and it was brutal. I remember as a little girl being aghast at what was happening, and as a child, I had no agency around it. I remember it so vividly; the smells, the witnessing of slicing of throats and the chickens running around with no heads. As a child I never wanted to disconnect, yet the cognitive dissonance started at that point of slaughter because I was fed what my family ate. Still, there was always a recognition of that pain in the chickens and I believe that's where my animal consciousness began. That's also when the hauntings started. I became vegetarian when I was about 20 and vegan eight years after that. The politics of animal liberation began sinking in then and that's when the affective floodgates opened.

Emotion and hauntings

I started my undergraduate degree in women and gender studies in 1985 but left in my final year to take on a frontline streetworker job, working with disenfranchised people working in the sex trade. I went back to university and finished my degree in women and gender studies at the same time we were starting to conceptualise *The Ghosts in Our Machine*. Jo-Anne McArthur had been a long-time friend of mine, so I introduced Liz Marshall to her, and Liz started to work on the film and brought me on as a consultant and researcher. I'd been an animal rights activist and so the intersection of feminism and animal rights activism coupled with my childhood memories started to emerge both theoretically and practically. I was trying to make sense of it through my academic work, but also then applying it to the work we were doing on the film. That process was a very emotional journey and I was still at the place of wanting to scream to people "wake up" because the state of life and death for other animals was an emergency. Liz favoured a more nuanced message and wanted to expand on that emotion and instead invite people into the issue in a way that didn't alienate them. At the time, it caused tension about the film's message; however, now, I totally understand the approach. It was an effective strategy that allowed for creativity to emerge through the cinematography and for a strong message to be communicated about animal sentience.

It was interesting to me to note the invisibility of nonhuman animals within the political discourses about oppression, intersectionality and change as I continued with my degree at university. I was working on *The Ghosts in Our Machine* and recognised this invisibility as "hauntings". Avery Gordon's work on how we make sense of things in the world and the ideas of "ghostliness" and "hauntings" gave validity to that which I had experienced and was experiencing around my animal activism. At the same time as reading Gordon's work, I was introduced to speculative fiction writers such as Octavia E. Butler. Butler's work incorporates so many different identities, including the nonhuman animal identity, and these intersections continued to expand my thinking and writing. I was being exposed to all this, all the while trying to formulate ideas around the animal question and feminism, but then it expanded into "How do we think through change? How do we start/engage with social movements? Where do we find hope?" Ultimately, I was looking for hope. That's when I was introduced to queer utopian theorist José Esteban Muñoz. By drawing together the work of these different writers, the ensuing conversation between theorists began to reveal the invisibility of nonhuman animals, the "absent referent", as Carol Adams speaks to so well throughout her body of work.[1]

The Ghosts in Our Machine held opportunities to also talk through some of those ideas, to explore how we make an impact through film. I've always felt film is my art form. It's where I go when I want to escape, when I want to learn, when I want to feel. So, as a medium and as a way of making change in the world, I think it's such an important modality. It made sense to try to look at some of the theories I was immersed in and incorporate them somehow into discussions we were having. As a creative director, Liz is also very immersive and understands the importance of validating the affective responses to her films.

1 Adams 2010, 13.

Sara Ahmed's work gives a voice to the politics of emotion and the idea that it's not always an essentialising exercise – that in fact we all are emotional creatures.[2] Emotionality is part of this idea of the ghostliness of nonhuman animals in spaces where we violate them. Emotionality is also the haunting nature and the lingering of experience connected to animal rights work and film. It's a space of possibility to extend and expand how we conceptualise things. There are also some common tropes that attempt to disavow emotions, like the "angry vegan" or the "overly sentimental animal rights person". I don't discount these stereotypes because I can see that, if we don't feel anger about something, then what is it that we're actually feeling when we bear witness to animal cruelty? I think the challenge is to not stay in spaces of anger, solely; we're not one-dimensional. Anger can become comfortable and familiar as a space to try to rectify our love for other animals. Anger transformed into rage lives in me. That's often when the hauntings happen as well, and those images emerge; in the night when we are alone, when we are really one with ourselves. For me, this is the time when the images reappear. For a very long time they were violent images. How do we talk about that? How do we make sense of that? How do we work through that? When I found Avery Gordon,[3] her work anchored these ideas in art, in photos, and thinking about how we view haunting images felt liberating. It enabled the creation of a space to grieve – it could open the cracks, and find a vocabulary and a language for what I was feeling.

Avery Gordon speaks about the experience of lingering; visuals coming back and reappearing, the haunting. In *Ghostly Matters: Haunting and the Sociological Imagination*, Gordon writes:

> The ghost or the apparition is one form by which something lost, or barely visible, or seemingly not there to our supposedly well-trained eyes, makes itself known or apparent to us, in its own way, of course. The way of the ghost is haunting, and haunting is a very particular way of knowing what has happened or is happening. Being haunted draws us affectively, sometimes against

2 Ahmed 2004.
3 Gordon 1997.

> our will and always a bit magically, into the structure of feeling of a reality we come to experience, not as cold knowledge, but as a transformative recognition.[4]

The idea of images or audio coming back is a theme throughout the *The Ghosts in Our Machine* film. For example, consider the image of the cow being slaughtered. That scene depicts the devices Temple Grandin created to supposedly address animal welfare in the slaughter system, which she named the "stairway to heaven". That scene was also a moment where there is a tension between how long the camera lingers and how long we bear witness to that moment between life and the ending of life in a violent way for a nonhuman animal. How long is enough? How long is the discomfort before people disconnect? That was a tension and a moment that required a great deal of care and attention because it spoke the truth and we knew it would be hard. We also knew that it needed to be honest. That balance of the time spent there and what leads up to it and what comes after was incredibly significant. We move from that violent image into a moment of calm at Farm Sanctuary in New York state. We hear the sounds and see the images of live cows. That space between what we've just seen, which we know will come back to haunt us, moves into the reminder of possibility. I would argue that it is a space of possibility. The effectiveness of the haunted moment is that we are reminded of it consistently. It haunts us and yet, at the same time, it is juxtaposed with the possibility of rescue. I think both can live in us at once. That's what is important about the choices Liz made as a director; that trope runs throughout the film. Those moments of transition that allow for movement and breath also allow us to engage deeply with not only where we are but where we came from and where it is possible to go.

Possibility in the cracks

When we speak about images or ideas aloud, it affords us a different kind of agency. Author Anat Pick says of her experience of coming to

4 Gordon 1997, 8.

the animal question that, in fact, the ghosts accumulate in us, and they accumulate from the residues of violence.[5] Pick goes on to say:

> To truly ponder the enormity of animal death, through mass extinction or mass killing, is to find oneself in a world populated by nothing but ghosts. These hauntings, on the other hand, are shorthand for the complex realities of contact with the ordinary creatures that surround us.[6]

And that's the sad truth. We live in a world where largely – at least in the Global North – industrial farming is still the norm. That means all those ghosts accumulate in us. By acknowledging that we are haunted and thinking about how we honour those ghosts that currently live with us and all that will come next, there's a crack of opening there too. José Esteban Muñoz talks about those cracks, and that wherever those cracks exist, there's a space of possibility. He expands this concept when he describes concrete utopias in his book *Cruising Utopia: The Then and There of Queer Futurity*. He writes:

> Concrete utopias are relational to historically situated struggles, a collectivity that is actualized or potential ... Concrete utopias can also be daydream-like, but they are the hopes of a collective, an emergent group, or even the solitary oddball who is the one who dreams for many. Concrete utopias are the realm of educated hope.[7]

Utopian theory can be so readily dismissed in academia, yet I appreciate the distinction he makes between historically and contemporary situated struggles. It anchors all the intersections of oppressions, but also reminds us that there are those potential spaces, those cracks where hope lives. It's in that way of thinking and of conceptualising things that we can move, and movements can move.

---

5 Pick 2019.
6 Pick 2019, 230.
7 Muñoz 2009, 3.

When we consider these notions of ghostliness and haunting, we are inevitably accepting that there have been deaths of nonhuman animals. One of the tasks of *The Ghosts in Our Machine* was to deal with the emotional component related to death. In her work on pain and suffering, Sara Ahmed writes:

> The impossibility of feeling the pain of others does not mean that the pain is simply theirs, or that their pain has nothing to do with me. … an ethics of responding to pain involves being open to being affected by that which one cannot know or feel.[8]

I argue that in *The Ghosts in Our Machine*, the idea that we can connect through pain and suffering or grief is a space of possibility. I also propose that it's important to consider the idea of collective grief. Academic scholar Judith Butler talks about "the grievable bodies" and how there is a significance to public commemoration of things.[9] That's an important space for animal activists and animal rights movements to remember, in that there's a history of collective spaces of grief and of public mourning. We can adopt the tools and the ways of healing, connecting and relationality that can move us forward in our collective grieving for other animals. Judith Butler says:

> It is only by challenging the dominant media that certain kinds of lives may become visible or noble in their precariousness. … The tacit interpretive scheme that divides worthy from unworthy lives works fundamentally through the senses, differentiating the cries we can hear from those we cannot, the sights we see from those we cannot, and likewise at the level of touch and even smell.[10]

So it is important to think about lives and the concept of which bodies are grievable. This is highlighted in *The Ghosts in Our Machine* when the activists are bearing witness to the transport of pigs to the slaughterhouse. There is no voiceover in that scene. We are located

8 Ahmed 2004, 30.
9 Butler 2009.
10 Butler 2009, 51.

within the space of the activists and we hear the pigs first. Audio can be powerful – and it is haunting. First we hear them and then *we observe* and *we watch* as the activists bear witness to the pigs. We are with both the pigs and the activists in a long scene. We experience the pigs' arrival, and it's in that arrival that we know they are alive while at the same time we know they are going to die. We know they are about to become ghosts, and we are in that space with them. We are connecting with them. You hear some of the activists saying, "You're so beautiful" and "I love you". We see Jo-Anne taking the photos; we see the pigs through the slots of the transport truck. We are there with them viscerally. So even though we are not them and their bodies are not ours, we are experiencing that *with them*. It doesn't mean we're the same as them, but we are there in that space, watching, among them.

The initial development of the Save Movement was based on the idea that by bearing witness to animals on their way to slaughter, we recognise their lives *are* grievable. As they become the ghosts and haunt us, we acknowledge that their lives are grievable. I've personally experienced this in Toronto, Canada, at two slaughterhouses. The moments are so otherworldly, they are filled with emotion. At the same time, there is a communing that happens, which is unspeakable. The fact that there is no spoken language for that part of the film captures the essence of what it's like to bear witness. Tolstoy says:

> When the suffering of another creature causes you to feel pain, do not submit to the initial desire to flee from the suffering one, but on the contrary, come closer, as close as you can to him who suffers, and try to help him.[11]

That's the ethic of the Save Movement. For my final thesis paper in women and gender studies at the University of Toronto, I wrote about my experience of bearing witness and the concept of grievable lives and of how to bring this forward. How do we grieve together? How does grief become an acceptable emotion in relation to nonhuman animals, especially the animals that we eat? To bear witness to the suffering of cows, pigs and chickens in transport on their way to slaughter is

11 Tolstoy 1997.

perhaps one of the most intense and life-altering experiences that cuts to the emotional core of our being. There's a natural urge to flee the site of violence as it's overwhelming. The tendency to avoid or make invisible the suffering located at the slaughterhouse site is exacerbated by the inability to articulate the emotions and politics entangled within the space. Once you see the reality of what occurs on the slaughterhouse site it is virtually impossible to unsee it; the images become embodied. And yet at the same time, the injustice of what we see can become unsayable. While bearing witness to nonhuman animals at slaughter sites is deeply emotional, it is also a political action that interrupts the invisibility of their suffering through being seen.

In *The Ghosts in Our Machine*, the lingering on that scene and the centring of the animal experience along with the activists bearing witness to the animal experience of life leading to death, to their ghostliness, is about interrupting the invisibility of the suffering. It is powerful and there was always a great deal of response from viewers to that scene. The fact that Liz chose to keep the entire experience of it without significant edits was important and symbolic. It's almost a moment of reverence. That's why I think I've searched for a different kind of language – a different way of understanding the implications of the violence inflicted upon bodies of other animals. I was in a space at one point, even before working on *Ghosts*, where that sense of hopelessness for our own species was hard to shake. When you are immersed in the reality of what we do to nonhuman animals, to Indigenous and racialised people, to the planet, at one point you have to think, is this who we are; are we naturally violent, colonial people? Is that true? Those are the moments I go to José Esteban Muñoz and others to remind myself that there's a crack somewhere – to seek out those understandings because the violence gets almost incomprehensible. When I found theorists that were writing about what I was feeling and experiencing, it was such a sense of relief because I felt less alone. *The Ghosts in Our Machine* allows us to engage differently with these questions as well.

Ghosts and ghostliness

The Ghosts in Our Machine builds those relationships between viewer and nonhuman animal by lingering on the nonhuman animal bodies themselves. It starts in the opening shot of the film: the close-up on the animals, the close-up of their eyes and the slow dissolve from one animal to another. The lingering in those spaces helps the emotional state settle. Then we move to Jo-Anne and the human voiceovers while the visual is of the animals, always centring *them*. During the end credits the names of all of the animals are listed. That idea of agency for the ghosts reminds us that they live on in this film and represent the millions of others who continue to suffer. It's these affective approaches to the filmmaking itself, through the cinematography and in the editing choices, that enable this understanding of connection.

It is hard for most people to look at or watch imagery related to animal abuse and violence. *The Ghosts in Our Machine* grapples with difficult choices related to "seeing". Nonhuman animals are visually at the centre of this film. When we enter the fur farm, for example, we are there *with* them. There is no voiceover; there is no human dialogue. But we hear *their* voices. They are not silent. They are present both visually and auditorily. In relation to the exploitation, cruelty and suffering we witness, the cinematic choice allows for the potential of agency, even though it's in their suffering. Those are the voices that haunt me. It's their voices that remind me of their right to be. That kind of haunting is a reminder that we're not done yet. We are with Jo-Anne, watching the still images as she takes the ghosts with her. They are alive in still photographs, yet they are likely dead by now, we don't know. In this way, they are the ghosts. They are the apparitions that we can return to in Jo-Anne's book of her photographs. There's a pathway through, where the ghosts remain, the ghosts return, the ghosts remind us. That trope of the ghosts and the possibility of remembering what our work is, comes through the animals, always.

The concepts of "ghosts" and "ghostliness" affect how we see systems of nonhuman oppression while offering another way to think through the pain. I have questioned why I am so drawn to these concepts. What does that say about me? But it is my way of paying homage to their lives and deaths and believing and knowing that their lives are grievable. There's a line that Jo-Anne says in the film when we're first introduced to the fur farm. She says, "Leaving is why I'm haunted." That idea of leaving is hard for me to grapple with also. The ghosts and the haunting of the images allow that to return; therefore, in one way, we don't leave them. We are accountable to and for them in our continuing work. I look at Jo-Anne's work as a way to make sure that the ghosts don't leave. I was struck by Jo-Anne's words in the film. That seemingly simple phrase (which rationally makes sense) has an affective tone due to where it's situated in the film. Her rationale, of course, is that saving them doesn't change the system and that's the point of exposing the horrors: to ultimately change the system. That sense of grief and responsibility comes from the choice she has to make. In the moment, to liberate animals would feel like the best choice, yet when you're trying to change an entire system based on violence inflicted on other animals, it may only show the system where the gaps are located. That decision to leave them is an almost impossible one to make. Situated at the beginning of the film, that scene sets the tone for what's at stake for her as the protagonist; that she's entering these spaces and as difficult as it is to enter, it's even harder to leave. Acknowledging publicly the post-traumatic stress disorder (PTSD) she experiences gives legitimacy to her credentials as a war photographer and as a photojournalist. We also are witness to what she faces during her meeting at the agency where it is acknowledged that people don't want to see these images. As Jo-Anne says, images of wildlife and pets are accepted in the mainstream, but the animals that we use and exploit are not. The agents explain that it's a "PG 13 world". Sadly, that's where things were in 2011.

When I started to bear witness to animal slaughter, I realised that I was on a *site* of violence: violence towards the animals, but violence towards the slaughterhouse workers as well. When you start to look at who the workers are, they're often racialised and classed people. They live with PTSD, addiction, repetitive injuries that they are never compensated for as they have little to no workers' rights. When you start to examine the entire geography of a slaughterhouse site through the lens of intersectionality and oppression, you realise how many beings are impacted. When you observe and when you bear witness to the animals, it's as if you enter a space of ghostliness. The animals are about to be invisibilised. They are about to leave one space (the earth) and they don't fully know that yet. They are experiencing fear. And in *their* space of not knowing, you are trying to commune and relate and offer up some kind of compassion in the moment. There's something that happens in that space. It was something that happened in me that was different from the protests I've attended, different from the actions of disobedience. It was similar to how Avery Gordon talks about those moments when you think about ghost stories as a kid, or you watch them in a movie. The air around you becomes different or still and the ghost appears. It was that feeling in that moment; it felt like a different space and time. So being on that site of violence in that moment, communing with those that were about to die, there's something inexplicable created in that space. It also aligns with what Avery Gordon speaks about in relation to our imagination which, when we engage with it, offers a different understanding of things that could be. In thinking through how to grapple with the idea of graphic images, for example, if we're telling the truth about the nonhuman animal story on our planet, we have to grapple with these moments. So how do we then, as educators or filmmakers, proceed with these moments? As I discussed earlier, *The Ghosts in Our Machine* adopted a strategy of ebb and flow; the deliberate decision of how long to keep difficult graphic imagery in the film, followed by dissolves into breathable moments. Jo-Anne's photographs were used to elongate the difficult moments. Rather than seeing a moving picture, you're led to a still photo. The stills in the film resonate with Gordon's idea of the apparitions and of the hauntings; the returnable moment is always in those photos. It was also a way of showing images in different forms within a film that helped to transition people into being able to see things from different vantage points.

Another way of conceptualising how to navigate the challenges of showing graphic images comes from Lauren Corman and Tereza Vandrovcova. In their chapter, "Radical humility: toward a more holistic critical animal studies pedagogy", they explore the question of how, as educators, you grapple with challenging visuals, knowing that students will shut down emotionally to pain and suffering. They talk about the balance between, and the importance of, showing images but also of ensuring there is support and an environment of open dialogue, no matter the differing opinions. They write: "CAS pedagogy requires that attention be paid to that which is invisibilised in the name of profit, convenience and tradition".[12] It's important to not look away, but it's also how the images are shared that is critical. By incorporating the different levels of support for students, by encouraging dialogues that are challenging including critiques of the discourses themselves, Corman and Vandrovcova focus on links between oppressions, including speciesism. They write:

> the shared forms of domination and suffering experienced by humans and nonhuman animals serve as major points of solidarity. CAS should retain its intersectional orientation, while also taking the lead from Third World feminisms, that stress resistance, agency, and richer forms of subjectivity that do not position women strictly as victims.[13]

From here, we can more directly conceive of ourselves as animals' allies, rather than their saviours. These are new points of solidarity. It's interesting how the approach of intersectional analysis within teaching about critical animal studies opens the possibility of dialogues because it incorporates the other experiences of the students involved.

One of the interesting spaces that animal activists must navigate is around the saviour complex. One of the dominant tropes in animal rights movements is that we have to be "their voice" or the "voice of the voiceless". I have never felt comfortable with that because we aren't giving agency to animals – they already have voices, it's just that they are disavowed. In *The Ghosts in Our Machine* there is a focus on audio throughout the film so that we hear their voices; we hear their voices in the difficult moments in the transport truck, in the slaughterhouse scenarios, in the fur farm. Their voices are there; they're not voiceless. It becomes more about what we are and are not doing with their voices and also what we must learn from their voices. Rather than viewing other animals as victims all the time, how we reframe them creates a different possibility that reimagines liberation – and

12 Corman and Vandrovcova 2014, 136.
13 Corman and Vandrovcova 2014, 137.

challenges us to be in right relationship with other animals that creates environments that allow for their liberation in the first place. Corman and Vandrovcova talk about this and suggest "we must strive to more fully integrate marginalised human and nonhuman animal voices into CAS pedagogy".[14] They are critiquing that concept of the voiceless, which has also historically and continually been mapped onto marginalised communities including Indigenous and racialised people. In this instance, in relation to *The Ghosts in Our Machine*, it's also a reflective moment for the viewer to think about how we do the same for nonhuman animals. The strategies will differ, but Black and Indigenous communities are moving towards talking about the context of solidarity with nonhuman animals, much like vegan and animal rights people. I argue that it is critical for the animal rights movement, which has historically been white and male, to not only embrace diversification within the movement but also support leadership and methodologies that bring different understandings of how justice can be achieved for other animals that will only serve to benefit us all.

In a book chapter titled "Prophetic Labrador: expanding (Black) theology by overcoming the invisibility of animal life and death", theologian Christopher Carter describes learning from his relationship with his dog companion. He talks about the idea of the silenced presence and writes:

> In my case, silenced presence describes my realization that parts of me, if not all of me, remain unseen by those in power because they are more comfortable seeing the idea of me that they have created within their worldview rather than my reality.[15]

He links that to the nonhuman animal situation when he explains:

> What I want to suggest is that the traditional ways of delineating who gets to be a member of the community, who is allowed to be visible and heard (rather than a silenced presence), and who possesses agency is steeped in colonial white supremacist

14 Corman and Vandrovcova 2014, 139.
15 Carter 2019, 91.

> logic that defines a narrow "human" category that excludes many people as well as animals and nature.[16]

He points out that when we hear about disasters, such as hurricanes, commentators rarely mention the millions of nonhuman animals that are affected or abandoned. They also fail to mention the psychological trauma experienced by those who live near farmed animal factories, who are often poor Black or Brown people. He connects the need to interrogate how animals are rendered invisible with the situation of people in the surrounding communities who experience a silenced presence as well. We can consider that in relation to how we view and think about images. As Corman and Vandrovcova suggest, without that intersectional lens, we reproduce gaps of experience and create silenced presences, which affect marginalised communities, including nonhuman animals. Importantly, all these ideas emerged from Carter's experience with his dog companion. It's critical to have an intersectional lens to work from and through in order to hear the voices of other communities that are also grappling with the nonhuman animal question.

Conclusion

It's not cliché to talk about the common ground of grief, pain and suffering that communities feel. However, different communities feel it, grieve it, manage it and work through it, differently. I would add, as a white settler on Indigenous land, I also have different considerations and responsibilities to injustices perpetrated on different bodies, differently. Yet when it comes to the question of nonhuman animals, I think the approaches to and the understanding of suffering, pain and grief are examples of those cracks that Muñoz describes as a space of possibility. How can we create spaces where we can speak to one another truthfully? Can it be spaces where we can learn about one another? Is it a space where we can come together in mutual understanding? When it comes to nonhuman animals, where's the

16 Carter 2019, 97.

commonality? The focus in my work is always around the emotional context of things. My hope is there might be a shared space of knowledge production, and of dissemination and compassion. But I think when it comes to animal activism, we ought to begin in the spaces that we can have some say over, and then extend out and that means those of us with privilege need to step back and give up power in activist movements. It's not a punishment; rather it is an opportunity to enhance movements for justice, especially when it comes to nonhuman animals. More accountability around the diversification of films and filmmaking must come from within the industry but also from activists. There's work to be done there. Yet in coming together as activists or folks who are concerned about how we live on the planet with other beings, let's share where we can.

We have to grapple with our own fears around things. When you think of ghosts or haunting it conjures up that feeling of fear, because that's what the media has contextualised and historicised. Avery Gordon gives us a way to face death differently. And in the case of nonhuman animals, it gives us the opportunity to let ourselves go there, not skip over that part, as animal activists or as vegans. It's painful to imagine, yet it's important that we allow those spectres or ghosts to present themselves, because then we can think about the system of living differently. So, when the ghosts appear in our minds there's an interesting flicker or presence that I'm always curious about; that flickering moment of recognition that is like a haunting that can sometimes feel dreadful and at other times act as a reminder of how they were once alive. In *The Ghosts in Our Machine*, the haunting is of the horribleness we see that we inflict on animals, but it's also the beauty we can create through spaces such as sanctuaries.

I am haunted in a different way by the beauty of the eyes, by the beauty of the rescued animals, by seeing their bodies whole. That's also a presence. It's a haunting of a different kind. I'm taken by this notion and that word, and of reframing that word, and of reconsidering that word, but not denying it. I think when we deny it, we're skipping over a part of the death process, and the after-death process. I let those flickers happen now. Whether it's the flicker of a brutal moment in *The Ghosts in Our Machine* that is there and gone, like an apparition, or the flicker of Fanny and Sonny, the rescued cows, and their first moments at Farm Sanctuary. Their moment is also a haunting but of a different kind. It's haunting in that they represent the others; they were the chosen ones, they were the rescued ones of billions. Their safety and their security are that flickering in that moment, and I hang on to that. There's something about that space and the flickering that offers up hope. When we consider how ghosts have been represented or talked about in media, it's often like a flicker when people think they might have "seen" something. I think it can help us through the difficulties of the violence of nonhuman animal death. There's a potential if we can think about them as still being among us. It might help us to work with those who are continuing to suffer in the systems that need dismantling. Coming back to *The Ghosts in Our Machine*, use of dissolves enables us to experience sitting with the sparkling moments of the rescued animals in the sun dappling through the trees – as a flickering hope of possibility for change. Those are the cracks of possibility that Muñoz talks about. So then how do we better collectively mobilise, moving towards the concrete utopian way of being in the world which includes other animals as equals? I think even to say that that's possible is quite remarkable. *The Ghosts in Our Machine* offers us opportunities to think otherwise about an impossible situation for other animals.

References

Adams, Carol J. (2010). *The Sexual Politics of Meat: A Feminist-Vegetarian Critical Theory*. New York: Continuum.

Ahmed, Sara (2004). *The Cultural Politics of Emotion*. Edinburgh: Edinburgh University Press and Routledge.

Butler, Judith (2009). *Frames of War: When Is Life Grievable?* New York: Verso.

Carter, Christopher (2019). Prophetic Labrador: expanding (black) theology by overcoming the invisibility of animal life and death. In Brianne Donaldson and Ashley King, eds. *Feeling Animal Death: Being Host to Ghosts*, 91–103. New York and London: Rowman & Littlefield.

Corman, Lauren and Tereza Vandrovcova (2014). Radical humility: toward a more holistic critical animal studies pedagogy. In Shirley R. Steinberg, Anthony J. Nocella II, John Sorenson, Kim Socha and Atsuko Matsuoka, eds. *Defining Critical Animal Studies: An Intersectional Social Justice Approach for Liberation*, 135–58. New York: Peter Lang Publishing Inc.

Gordon, Avery F. (1997). *Ghostly Matters: Haunting and the Sociological Imagination*. Minneapolis: University of Minnesota Press.

Muñoz, José Esteban (2009). *Cruising Utopia: The Then and There of Queer Futurity*. New York: New York University Press.

Pick, Anat (2019). Ghosts at a glance: four animal fragments. In Brianne Donaldson and Ashley King, eds. *Feeling Animal Death: Being Host to Ghosts*, 229–42. New York: Rowman & Littlefield.

Tolstoy, Leo (1997). *A Calendar of Wisdoms: Daily Thoughts to Nourish the Soul*. New York: Scribner.

7

From carnism to cannibalism

Intersectional speciesism in the fiction film *Cloud Atlas*

Lara Herring

Academic analyses of animal activist films tend to focus on non-fiction genres such as documentary. This chapter explores what a fiction film can say about animal activism when read from a critical intersectional perspective. Fiction films provide the filmmaker with far more control over their subject matter, with the ability and freedom to create fictional stories about fictional characters and fictional worlds. Not being bound to the constrictions of "reality" in this way offers a level of autonomy and creative expression to the filmmaker that is not possible to the same extent in non-fiction filmmaking. This level of creative control affords the filmmaker more opportunities and methods of encoding their film texts with meaning, metaphor and subtext. This chapter takes as its case study the 2012 fiction film *Cloud Atlas*. In 2012, *Cloud Atlas* was released to surprisingly little fanfare, garnering mixed reviews and underperforming at the box office.[1] The film, based on a novel of the same name often described as "unfilmable" (see, for example, Cain 2019; Gore 2013; Konnikova 2012 and Lambie 2013), comprises several interweaving stories that foreground issues of race, gender, class and sexuality. The film serves to identify the superficiality of these social constructs and highlight the principle of interconnectedness that

1 A film is considered to have "underperformed" at the box office when it does not make a profit.

unites us all as "one tribe", that binds us beyond the reductive process of labelling. Intersectionality plays a crucial role in the film's portrayal of these constructed distinctions and the critical response to the film focuses on this perceived complexity. For example, a review in the *New York Times* notes that:

> the filmmakers try so hard to give you everything – the secrets of the universe and the human heart; action, laughs and romance; tragedy and mystery – that you may wind up feeling both grateful and disappointed.[2]

While *Empire* film magazine suggests: "If you're trying to encompass the entire human story, there's sure to be as much ridiculous as sublime."[3] However, what is less acknowledged is the aspect of the film's story that focuses on speciesism. In his short history of speciesism, Peter Singer establishes that the practical matter of "the rule of the human animal over other animals" can only be properly understood as "the manifestations of the ideology of our species – that is, the attitudes which we, the dominant animal, have toward the other animals".[4] Singer notes that our attitudes towards animals are formed when we are very young and that "we eat animal flesh long before we are capable of understanding that what we are eating is the dead body of an animal".[5] With its depiction of meat-farming human bodies, *Cloud Atlas* makes a direct comparison between the dead bodies of humans, as abhorrent, and the dead bodies of animals, as widely accepted. In doing so, the film draws attention to the "invisible belief system" that Melanie Joy refers to as carnism: the theory that "we eat animals without thinking about what we are doing and why because the belief system that underlies this behaviour is invisible".[6]

This chapter seeks to address, through contextual analysis, the way in which *Cloud Atlas* critiques carnism by simultaneously connecting

2 Scott 2012.
3 Nathan 2013.
4 Singer 2015, 185.
5 Singer 2015, 214.
6 Joy 2010, 29.

the meat industry with cannibalism, human slavery and sexual exploitation. Carol J. Adams, in her work *The Sexual Politics of Meat*, draws attention to the relationship between meat-eating and issues of gender, class, race and power.[7] I contend that this relationship is likewise highlighted in *Cloud Atlas*. The spirit of connected souls and the belief that we are all united which underpins the film's morality is emulative of Ryder's ethos of speciesism:

> We want people to open their eyes and to see the other animals as they really are – our kindred and our potential friends with whom we share a brief period of consciousness upon this planet.[8]

To this end, this chapter addresses four key themes raised by the film.[9] The first theme looks at the framing of a fabricant (synthetic human) as metaphor for animal, positioned as what Adams (2015a) refers to as an "absent referent". Then, the wider discourse on cannibalism and cognitive dissonance is evidenced through the film's focus on the "survival of the fittest" mentality. Next, the construct of animal liberation is explored in the revelations of Sonmi-451. Finally, the ways in which the filmmakers represent and construct the wider intersectionality that underpins the film's ambitious message is explored. The chapter concludes with an examination of the fiction-film-as-activist by identifying the unique opportunity that fiction films offer to convey otherwise contentious and divergent messages.

---

7 Adams 2015a.

8 Ryder 2000, 250.

9 The author acknowledges that the film *Cloud Atlas* is an adaptation of a novel by the same name. However, since this chapter is a study of fiction film as a tool for animal activism and not an adaptation study, it does not address or consider the adaptation process or the adapted text as it would detract from the matter at hand.

Sonmi-451: Absent referent

Fiction film and non-fiction film rely on and utilise the same underpinning characteristics of form and style including mise-en-scène, cinematography, editing and sound. The crucial distinction between fiction and non-fiction filmmaking is of course that the latter deals with real people, real events and/or histories and presents a version of "truth" that we understand as being "real" in the literal sense of the word. Conversely, fiction film creates fictitious characters and fictitious events and worlds that, while they may resemble our "reality" to a greater or lesser extent, are not designed to be "truthful". Creating fictitious characters is fundamental to the fiction film mode of storytelling. Creating fictional characters and worlds allows the filmmaker to stray beyond the narrative limitations of our reality. Taking this liberty, one of the main characters in *Cloud Atlas* is Sonmi-451 (Bae Doo-na), a human clone known in the film as a "fabricant", who resides in the fictitious, futuristic, post-apocalyptic world of Neo Seoul. Sonmi is referred to as both Sonmi-451 and Sonmi. The former represents her model's name and issue number. The latter is the name she is known by later in the film after she is liberated and when she is revered as a revolutionary and a god. The story of Sonmi-451 serves as a metaphor for the lived experience of animals as objects to be used and consumed. More importantly, Sonmi's narrative arc offers a depiction of "animal" liberation. The notion of animal liberation put forward by Peter Singer is a call for the end of discriminatory and prejudicial treatment of animals.[10] Singer uses the term liberation in direct comparison with the Black Liberation, Gay Liberation and Women's Liberation movements, asking readers to recognise that "attitudes to members of other species are a form of prejudice no less objectionable than prejudice about a person's race or sex".[11] Although Sonmi-451 is not technically an animal, as a fabricant she is othered from the human species who are referred to as "purebloods" in the film. Not only is a fabricant distinguished from a pureblood, but fabricants are subservient to the latter; in *Cloud Atlas*

10 Singer 2015.
11 Singer 2015, xix.

fabricants were created by purebloods as an "engineered labour force". Sonmi-451's native language is called "sub-speak" and the English language is known to her as "consumer". Her food is delivered in a carton called a sub sack. Every aspect of her existence is characterised by subservience and subsistence. Sonmi-451 is a server at a fast-food chain known as Papa Song's. If Sonmi is an animal, her master is capitalism. Indeed, the first "law" (so-called catechism) of fabricants is "honour thy consumer".

In addition to serving as the metaphorical animal, Sonmi is overtly animalised in several ways, by way of issues of ownership and captivity. When we are introduced to Sonmi-451 at the start of the film, she is in captivity; the first shot of her is in handcuffs. As a Papa Song server, Sonmi-451's life is entirely restricted. Sonmi describes a "typical twenty-four-hour cycle" at the Papa Song restaurant where she is stationed: wake, eat (sub sack), sanitise, dress (in uniform), work (for 19 hours), eat (sub sack), sleep. This highly restricted and repetitive schedule can be likened to the restricted and repetitive existence of animals in captivity, particularly those who are also forced into labour. Papa Song servers like Sonmi-451 never leave the confines of the restaurant which, outside of service hours, resembles a run-down, rusty, windowless metal warehouse that looks like a prison. During service hours holograms and projections transform the space into a bright, clean and colourful eatery. This stark example of the difference in the quality of lives between the consumers (purebloods) and servers (fabricants) is evocative of the contrast between the experiences of (free) humans and animals in captivity.

Sonmi-451 wears and is controlled by a steel collar, which is responsible for waking her up in the morning and sending her to sleep at the end of each day. Moreover, in addition to the connotations that collars have with pets and slaves, the collar is directly responsible for her captivity; each collar is fitted with an explosive remote-controlled device rigged to sever the carotid artery of the wearer to ensure the fabricants' obedience. Indeed, during the film Sonmi's "sister" Yoona-939 (Zhou Xun), another fabricant model, is killed in this manner when she tries to escape the restaurant. The only time a collar is removed from the wearer is at the "end of their contract", during a pseudo-religious ceremony called "Xultation", which will be covered later in the chapter. Sonmi-451's collar is removed by the rebel alliance that rescue her from captivity, an act that symbolises her emancipation and reveals a birthmark that links her with several other characters in the film who share the same mark,[12] which also acts as an indication of her "humanity" through her connection with other human souls.

Sonmi and her "sisters" (other fabricant servers) are highly sexualised and treated poorly by both the manager of the restaurant and the customers. Papa Song servers wear extremely short, tightly fitted dresses with red shorts underneath that are indistinguishable from underwear. All the servers, though some are different fabricant models, are designed to look almost identical. All sport a short bob and wear high heels. Their attire is impractical for long working days, further suggesting the disregard for their comfort or welfare, and further establishing that their appearance, like everything else about them, is designed to attract or satisfy pureblood consumers. It is no coincidence that these servers, dressed the way they are and being of Eastern Asian heritage, are reminiscent of the stereotypical sex worker found in inner-city red-light districts. Representation of Eastern Asian women in Western media has historically cast Eastern Asian women as objectified, Orientalised objects of desire whose purpose is defined by servitude.[13] Aki Uchida notes that "the mainstream media in the United States provides a … concrete and powerful depiction of the Oriental Woman who is exotic and sexy".[14] Uchida explains that:

> the Oriental Woman has a certain place among the different categories of women. The submissive, domestic, docile, and exotic image may be used to characterize Asian women in comparison to other women of colour; in one aspect the Oriental Woman could be put on a pedestal as "feminine ideal," for example, while in

12 There are six main storylines in the film. Each of the main characters, all of whom play multiple roles, share a matching birthmark that resembles a shooting star.

13 Uchida 1998.

14 Uchida 1998, 162. Uchida uses the term "Oriental Woman" to refer to images and stereotypes of Asian women, to distinguish such representations for the referent from the actual Asian women who are objectified through Orientalisation.

> other aspects she could be seen as passive, apathetic, self-effacing, and content to serve men.[15]

The aesthetic of Papa Song servers, where we take the fabricant as metaphor for animal, embodies the notion of the absent referent put forward by Carol Adams, who notes:

> the animals have become absent referents, whose fate is transmuted into a metaphor for someone else's existence or fate. Metaphorically, the absent referent can be anything whose original meaning is undercut as it is absorbed into a different hierarchy.[16]

In this case the fate of the animals is absorbed into a species-focused hierarchy, where the pureblood species is dominant, and the fabricant species is subservient. Of course, Sonmi's gender and her appearance are not coincidentally pornographic. In her work on the pornography of meat, Carol Adams explains how "pornography uses butchery to say something about women's status as mass terms: women are as meat; not only that, women deserve to be treated as meat – butchered and consumed".[17]

Sonmi's journey of liberation begins with the death of her friend and sister "the infamous Yoona-939". It is revealed that, for some time, the boss of this particular Papa Song restaurant, Seer Rhee (Hugh Grant), has been "waking" Yoona-939 during sleep hours for the purpose of his sexual gratification; he gets "drunk" on Soap (sub sacks), a nutritional drink made to sustain fabricants, which we later find is made from reconstituted protein from butchered fabricants, meaning that while Seer Rhee is raping Yoona-939 he is also consuming her. This alludes to the relationship between violence towards animals and rape and, as identified by Margo DeMello, the link between domestic abuse and bestiality.[18] One such night, Sonmi is awakened during sleep

---

15 Uchida 1998, 172.
16 Adams 2015a, 21–2.
17 Adams 2015b, 25.
18 DeMello 2012.

hours. It is unclear whether Yoona-939 wakes Sonmi to witness her treatment by Seer Rhee or if it is an accident, but either way Yoona takes the opportunity to show Sonmi "forbidden" things while Seer Rhee is passed out on Soap. Yoona shows Sonmi the wonders of the items left behind by customers and asks "forbidden" questions, such as questions about the nature of their existence. Sonmi reminds her that the third catechism forbids fabricants from thinking about what it would be like to be free.

Yoona-939 shows Sonmi a "secret" room containing lost property. These are discarded items that are evidently worthless to the original owner, yet to the sisters they are treasures and offer a rare glimpse outside of their incarcerated lives. The crown jewel among them is a broken handheld video device that is stuck on a loop, playing the same fragment of a scene over and over. In the fragment, taken from a film (within the film), a man (played by Tom Hanks) is arguing with a hotel desk clerk and shouts, "this is a ruddy violation of the criminal incarceration act", defiantly adding, "I will not be subjected to criminal abuse". This scene reverberates across multiple storylines in the film and the line "I will not be subjected to criminal abuse" is a defining statement of the film. Yoona-939 has clearly watched this clip many times as she recites this line along with the film. It is highly unlikely, if not entirely impossible, that Yoona understands the meaning of these words, so its irony and potency is perhaps lost on the characters but has a complex and deeply significant meaning for the viewer. Yoona-939 finally "snaps" after she is degraded sexually by a customer (a young male who pretends to ejaculate over her with a condiment in a bottle). In response, Yoona strikes the customer, causing everyone in the establishment to stop and stare, at which point, in her moment of rebellion, she recites the line, "I will not be subjected to criminal abuse". This moment offers a disruption of cognitive dissonance, when onlookers are forced to acknowledge a fabricant as an autonomous sentient being, one that has feelings, one that is aware of her unfair treatment. Yoona takes the opportunity to attempt an escape, but Seer Rhee activates the detonation device inside her collar, severing her carotid artery, killing her. The reality, of course, is that the treatment of fabricants, their imprisonment, their forced labour and, ultimately, their death, is not considered a criminal offence. Viewing this through the lens of fabricant as metaphor for animal, it offers an example of the double standards inherent to carnism; the death of certain types of nonhuman animal for the purposes of meat, dairy or other animal products is not considered murder, just as their poor treatment and living conditions are at best regrettable but also unavoidable.[19] As a viewer, it is obvious that the treatment of fabricants is inhumane, and therefore this moment in the film offers an interruption of cognitive dissonance not only for the onlookers in Papa Song's but also for the film's audience. More importantly, this scene sets up Sonmi's journey from server to revolutionary, which is triggered by her sister's extreme act of self-sacrifice and desperation.

Cognitive dissonance, cannibalism and survival of the fittest

The revelations of Sonmi-451 are by no means the film's only reference to complex attitudes towards carnism. One of the major themes that runs throughout each of the film's timelines is the notion of "survival of the fittest". Each of the main storylines is characterised by a David-and-Goliath dichotomy of the weak versus the strong, encountering and battling prejudices based on race, class, gender and species. One of the most overt examples of this dichotomous relationship is in the futuristic 2321 timeline where Zachry (Tom Hanks) and his peaceful tribe live in fear of cannibal warriors that hunt them. When we are first introduced to Zachry, he and his brother-in-law are beset by cannibals. Old Georgie – an apparition that Zachry sees, like a devil-on-your-shoulder – persuades him not to help his family and instead to hide. Old Georgie (Hugo Weaving) reminds Zachry: "You say all the time: the weak are meat and the strong do eat" – implying that it is inevitable that his family may be eaten by a cannibal and that he shouldn't feel bad for not helping, since it is an inevitability. This line is repeated in another timeline – 1849 – when Dr Henry Goose (Hanks) reveals to Ewing (Jim Sturgess) that he has been poisoning him. He explains: "There is only one rule that binds all people, one governing principle that defines every relationship on

19 Joy 2010.

God's green Earth: The weak are meat and the strong do eat." This is an example of the cognitive dissonance that enables carnism. As Joy notes, carnism is made possible by the invisibility of its ideology and the "vast mythology" surrounding meat, that relies on the justification that eating meat is "normal, natural, and necessary".[20] Such justifications are "so ingrained in our social consciousness that they guide our actions without our even having to think about them".[21] When the cannibals catch Zachry they say, "Now you're meat", implying an animalisation of the human body.

There is another allusion to cannibalism when Timothy Cavendish (Jim Broadbent) attempts to escape a prison-like senior home, Aurora House, where he is being held against his will. Cavendish calls to his fellow residents, quoting a line from *Soylent Green* (1973): "Soylent Green is people! Soylent Green is made of people." The film *Soylent Green* is a dystopian thriller that, like *Cloud Atlas*, focuses on social inequalities and the issue of slavery and dehumanisation. It is revealed in the film *Soylent Green* that a food source called "Soylent Green" is made from dead and incarcerated humans, making the population unwitting cannibals. Cavendish's recitation of this line is not actually related to the action in his timeline, he just wants to say something dramatic as he leaves, but its inclusion is far from "unrelated" in the wider context of the film.

The most potent example of the film's critique of the meat industry, however, comes from Sonmi's revelation regarding the annual rite of passage known as "Xultation". The word "exultation", of course, is defined as a feeling of triumphant elation or jubilation. Indeed, everything about this ceremony has been designed to make fabricants think it is not only a positive event but also one that they should look forward to and aspire towards. Asked whether she ever thought about the future, Sonmi tells the Archivist:

> "Papa Song servers have just one possible future."
> "You mean Xultation? Can you describe this annual rite of passage?"

20 Joy 2010, 96.
21 Joy 2010, 97.

Sonmi explains that servers get a stamp on their collar (reminiscent of loyalty cards and their consumer-driven rewards) and "twelve stars meant an end to our contract". Sonmi describes feeling "excited" when her "sisters" "ascended". She says, "I was happy for them. But envious as well". In the Xultation ceremony the sisters sing a hymn and watch in joy as the ascending sister is given a "robe" that resembles a hospital gown; something to be disposed of. The poor quality of her outfit is in stark contrast to the robes worn by the "priests", who wear red hooded robes. Significant lengths have been taken to promote this false happy ending, evocative of Temple Grandin's "humane slaughter". Grandin contends that "slaughterhouses can be operated with a high level of humane treatment"[22] by using the appropriate handling and stunning methods and confirming that the animal is "insensible to pain and permanently unconscious before hoisting, skinning, or other invasive dressing procedures".[23] The slaughterhouse workers in *Cloud Atlas* employ Grandin's techniques such as "low-stress handling",[24] and the fabricant is stunned and left presumably insensible to pain before the comparatively brutal hoisting of her unconscious body.

The revelations of Sonmi-451: Animal liberation

The climax of Sonmi's narrative arc acts as an analogy of the animal-industrial complex and relies heavily on the use of metaphor to do so. Shortly after Yoona-939's death, Sonmi-451 is saved by a group called the Union Rebellion whose mission it is to "create a free-willed fabricant" and Sonmi is their last hope. Sonmi's saviour, Hae-Joo Chang (Jim Sturgess), gives her access for the first time to pureblood food and clothes and exposure to information using an internet-like futuristic technology. At first Sonmi is scared to engage with the technology, explaining that "fabricants can be excised for this", to which Hae-Joo tells her, "Our survival often demands our courage." We can tell Sonmi is a quick study as she is shown deftly using the technology that she

22 Grandin 2013, 506.
23 Grandin 2013, 504.
24 Grandin 2013, 497.

has only just been introduced to; she is examining physics, fabricant evolution, fabricant violence, biology (DNA), Union Rebellion history and other (future) world history and philosophy. Sonmi says of the experience, "Knowledge is a mirror and for the first time in my life I was allowed to see who I was and who I might become." Her new knowledge, freedom and respectful treatment inspires the "revelations" of Sonmi-451, which go on to inspire future civilisations in the film world. There is a metaphor here for the carnist argument that assumes animals "do not have feelings", are not sentient, or are simply lower on the food chain. This is the same assumption that purebloods have about fabricants. This story is proving the opposite to be true; that the only thing stopping fabricants from feeling, thinking and being is their subjugation and restriction by purebloods. When Sonmi is briefly captured after her escape, her captor informs her that there is a disagreement about what to do with her; whether to euthanise her as a deviant, study her or dissect her brain. He concludes, "however, the problem you create is a political one". He tells her:

> I find it intriguing to imagine that beneath these perfectly engineered features are thoughts that terrify the whole of Unanimity. I am not afraid of such thoughts because I do not fear the truths. There's a natural order to the world, fabricant. And the truth is this order must be protected.[25]

By way of a response, Sonmi looks him in the eye, which unnerves her captor. The suggestion is that he is shocked and unnerved by her apparent sentience. Her existence as a free-willed fabricant calls all his previous assertions into question.

When An-Kor Apis (Keith David), leader of Union (the resistance group), tells Sonmi she is proof their efforts were not in vain, she says she is not capable – or "genomed" – to "alter reality" and that she cannot do what they are asking. An-Kor responds: "Before you call your decision final, there is one last thing I would like you to see in order to fully understand what we are fighting for." Hae-Joo takes Sonmi to a warehouse (essentially an abattoir) where she watches a

25 "Unanimity" is the name of the government in Neo Seoul.

herd of fabricants in their ceremonial gowns walking towards their fate, looking ecstatic, singing. Watching the scene from behind a chain-link fence, Sonmi instinctively knows what is happening. Sonmi observes: "They believe they are going to Xultation, but they are not, are they?" We are then shown the reality of Xultation; a Sonmi model fabricant is led on her own into a room with plastic slaughterhouse-style curtains. It is particularly important that it is a Sonmi model fabricant because the audience have already witnessed Sonmi's humanity. The Sonmi fabricant is welcomed by two individuals wearing hair nets who tell her to "take a seat. Just relax" and as they attach a headpiece with wires, they inform her "this is to remove your collar". But instead of removing her collar, the device kills her with a stun bolt gun, like those used in abattoirs. Then the seat reclines, turning into a slab, and after a device is used to pierce through both ankles she is dragged, by her ankles, onto a conveyor belt. The whole process is highly mechanised and designed to fool the fabricants until the last second, just like the "humane slaughter" principles used in abattoirs that include low-stress handling and stunning weapons that are used to "fool" the animals on their way to slaughter. As the Sonmi model fabricant is dragged away, her arms are involuntarily raised, resembling a Christlike figure on a crucifix. The piercing of the ankles recalls narratives of the crucifixion, suggesting that the Sonmi fabricant, likened to Christ, has died for the sins of humanity. The filmmakers are able to use the narrative freedom and creative control afforded by the fiction form to create this detailed and subtextual allegory. This level of control over the detail and nuance of the narrative as well as the performances, the mise-en-scène, editing, sound and cinematography thus offers the fiction film even more – or at least distinct – opportunities for engaging with and communicating animal activism.

Sonmi is taken behind the proverbial and literal curtain; another plastic abattoir curtain that features the logo of a happy fat buddha-like character. The irony of this logo is reminiscent of the "happy" chickens and cows that iconise meat products. Sonmi is horrified when confronted with a slaughterhouse stacked full of human (fabricant) bodies – strung up by their ankles with their heads, hands and feet removed. This is a striking image not only for Sonmi but also for the audience. There is no mistaking the similarity between the fictitious fabricant slaughterhouse and the realities of contemporary abattoirs. The only difference here is that instead of animal bodies hanging skinned and butchered, it is a human (fabricant) body. Thus, by replacing the nonhuman animal with the body of a human animal, the audience is confronted by the barbaric nature of meat-farming. Hae-Joo explains that "the genomics industry demands a huge quantity of bio matter for womb tanks. But more importantly, to sustain their engineered labour force. Recycled fabricants are a cheap source of protein." Upon realising that Soap – her food source – is made from fabricant bodies, she acknowledges: "They feed us to ourselves." This wording is particularly important because it directly implicates cannibalism. Faced with this horrific reality, Sonmi reaches the same conclusion as the Union revolutionaries:

> Sonmi: That ship. That ship must be destroyed.
> Hae-Joo: Yes.
> Sonmi: The systems that built them must be torn down.
> Hae-Joo: Yes.
> Sonmi: No matter if you were born in a tank or a womb, we are all pureblood.
> Hae-Joo: Yes.
> Sonmi: We must all fight, and if necessary, die, to teach people the truth.
> Hae-Joo: This is what we have been waiting for.

This short exchange encapsulates Sonmi's revelations, and these principles form the basis of her teachings in the film's future timelines when Sonmi is revered as a prophet and a book titled "The Revelations of Sonmi-451" is treated as a bible.

The revelations of Sonmi-451 are further revealed in her interview with the Archivist. We are first introduced to Sonmi-451 as a prisoner at the start of the film. At this point, she is being interviewed by the Archivist. The essence of Sonmi's message (and the film's overarching message) is one of unity; of an understanding that "we are all the same". One of Sonmi's revelations – a quote repeated across timelines – is: "No matter if you were born in a tank or a womb, we are all pureblood." Of course, she is referring to the difference between fabricants (who are created in a tank) and purebloods (who are created in a womb), but this has additional meaning as it is a way of differentiating between species at birth; an irrefutable division. At the end of the film when she is broadcasting her revelations, Sonmi says:

> To be is to be perceived and so to know thyself is only possible through the eyes of the other. The nature of our immortal lives is in the consequences of our words and deeds that go on a'pushing themselves throughout all time.

There are two key suggestions here: firstly that fabricants, as metaphor for animals in the meat and dairy industry, are invisibilised, just as they (fabricants-as-animals) are not allowed to know themselves. They are denied this vital self-awareness. Secondly, it is the responsibility of purebloods (humans) to "see" and to enact change through words and action. Melanie Joy foregrounds "the power of witnessing"[26] as a means for acknowledging and addressing carnism. Joy states:

> When we bear witness, we are not merely acting as observers, we emotionally connect with the experience of those we are witnessing. We empathize. And in so doing, we close the gap in our consciousness, the gap that enables the violence of carnism to endure.[27]

In her book, Joy uses an anecdotal reference to a story about Emily the cow who, in 1995, escaped an abattoir and, aided by local residents, was eventually rescued and rehomed in a sanctuary. Emily's story was widely reported, the rights to which were sold to a filmmaker, and a statue in her likeness stands at her grave. The parallels between Emily's story and Sonmi's are stark and meaningful. Joy writes: "Emily, once an anonymous dairy cow, came to be an individual who inspired compassion in the many lives she touched."[28] Sonmi-451, an

26 Joy 2010, 137.
27 Joy 2010, 138.
28 Joy 2010, 136.

anonymous fabricant, came to do the same. Moreover, Joy notes that Emily's life journey:

> reminds us to refuse to allow the violent system that is carnism to blind us to the truth, the truth of the needless suffering of billions of animals – and the truth that we care.[29]

This is precisely the nature of Sonmi's revelation and the purpose of her story. Individuation is crucial when trying to create compassion. As Claire Molloy notes in her work on popular media and animals, animals who are "individuated and named" are more likely to be understood by humans as sentient and "like them" and are therefore considered "worthy" of being saved.[30]

In the post-apocalyptic timeline that takes place hundreds of years after Sonmi's death, she is worshipped as a god: there are statues of her, her teachings – "The Revelations of Sonmi-451" – are revered as a bible. At one point the Abbess tells Zachry: "Let Sonmi guide you." The revelations of Sonmi-451 comprise the recorded conversations between Sonmi and the Archivist in Neo Seoul. In her own timeline, in Neo Seoul, Sonmi recounts her final testimony with the Archivist. Sonmi tells the Archivist what happened after she was shown the abattoir; she was taken to a Union-controlled satellite link where she broadcast her "revelation". Shortly after, they were attacked by "Enforcers" who were trying to stop her message from being broadcast. There is a resonance here with animal rights activism and protests more broadly in the desperate attempt on the behalf of the Enforcers, who can easily be substituted by real-world politicians and policy makers who seek to protect the cognitive dissonance necessary for guilt-free meat-eating. Animal activism is often based on interrupting this invisibilised ideology. Anat Pick notes that "animal rights films, whatever their formal properties, must find ways to articulate the fundamental conditions and mechanisms of humans' crushing power over nonhuman animals".[31]

29 Joy 2010, 137.
30 Molloy 2011, 4.
31 Pick 2016, 98.

At the film's climax, when all the film's timelines intersect to drive home the overarching message, the Archivist asks Sonmi why she went along with the Union plan when she "must have known" it was "doomed to fail" and that she would be executed. She replies, "If I had remained invisible, the truth would stay hidden. I couldn't allow that." The word "invisible" is important here. In critical animal studies (CAS), the invisibility of the nonhuman animal is a topic often explored. Not only are the animals invisibilised, but so are the beliefs and institutions that invisibilise them. Melanie Joy identifies the invisible belief system that underlies the consumption of animals as an entrenched unspoken ideology that makes the reality of the carnistic system.[32] In *Cloud Atlas*, Sonmi has seen through this invisible system and so poses a significant threat to the status quo. At the climax of the film, amid the intersecting storylines, the Archivist asks Sonmi, "What if no one believes this 'truth'?", to which she replies, "Someone already does." She is referring to each of the main characters across the intersecting storylines who have all had similar revelations regarding racial, gender, class and species inequality and the nefarious powers that both capitalise on and promote these inequalities.

Screening intersectionality in *Cloud Atlas*

Fiction films, which are not bound by the need to represent "factual reality" and which can afford a greater degree of narrative control than non-fiction films, are able to use this freedom and control to create complex narratives that use allegory, linking different storylines and drawing parallels that connect them. *Cloud Atlas* explores, as its primary objective, the intersectionality between race, gender, class and species to gain an understanding or awareness of the intrinsic link between all beings. The notion of intersectionality is of course a fundamental concept that underpins CAS. Taylor and Twine assert that intersectionality is "possibly the most important concept for analysing human–animal entanglements", noting that CAS "subverts the humanist assumptions of intersectionality theory by bringing animals

32 Joy 2010.

and animality into these areas and also into other potentially kindred fields".[33] In his seminal work on animal welfare, Peter Singer uses comparisons with sexism and racism to introduce the notion of speciesism. Singer explains that:

> the basic element – the taking into account of the interests of the being, whatever those interests may be – must, according to the principle of equality, be extended to all beings, black or white, masculine or feminine, human or nonhuman.[34]

It is important to note that while *Cloud Atlas* deals directly with the intersecting values and power dynamics inherent in issues of race, gender, sexuality, class and species, the "animal" is mostly absent and is dealt with almost entirely through metaphor or represented as fabricants. The film sets out the social hierarchy in an early scene while discussing a proposed law (the "Incarceration Act") designed to address the legality of slavery. The discussion makes it apparent that white men are at the top of this hierarchy, followed by non-white men, then women and finally animals. In fact, while the characters discuss the first three directly, the animal is not dealt with directly but rather by way of the fact that they are eating lamb. Dr Goose explains that the "natural order" that the Incarceration Act is designed to protect "makes a compelling case as to why we're sitting here enjoying this divine lamb while Kupaka [a black male slave] stands there content to serve". This scene employs irony to represent the notion of intersectional oppression, what Taylor and Twine refer to as "the interconnected oppression of people and animals",[35] thus exploring how "the material and symbolic exploitation of animals intersects with and helps maintain dominant categories of gender, 'race' and class".[36]

The film's intersectional theme traverses between different stories and timelines. The plot is organised so that each storyline, though spatially and temporally separate from one another, appears to follow

33 Taylor and Twine 2014, 5.
34 Singer 2015, 5.
35 Taylor and Twine 2014, 12.
36 Taylor and Twine 2014, 14.

a singular narrative arc. Specific motifs are used to connect characters both explicitly and implicitly: a piece of music that resonates throughout time, a specific birthmark inexplicably shared by all the main characters, and the line, "I will not be subjected to criminal abuse", are just a few examples of these narrative elements that echo across the timelines. The decision to cast actors in multiple roles, often playing different races, genders and classes, is further proof of the (in this case literal) drive towards intersectionality. The film identifies and promotes an "unspoken connection" between all beings and examines the notion of reincarnation and connections between souls throughout time. During the film's climax, Robert Frobisher narrates a letter written to his lover, his voiceover linking the action in several storylines. Frobisher writes:

> all boundaries are conventions waiting to be transcended. One may transcend any convention if only one can first conceive of doing so. In moments like this, I can feel your heart beating as clearly as I feel my own, and I know that separation is an illusion. My life extends far beyond the limitations of me.

The filmmakers use emotive music and crosscutting between the different narrative strands to highlight the poignancy of this message made evident by the collective nature of the experience, felt across time and space between characters and spaces that are interconnected. Frobisher's sentiments epitomise the film's message. Moreover, these notions of unspoken connection, the illusion of separateness and the concept of thinking beyond our "self" are all qualities, principles and ideologies put forward by Joy, Singer, Ryder and others as remedies for carnism, speciesism and animal exploitation.

The film's resolution lays bare its underpinning moral story; when Ewing destroys the Incarceration Act contracts and announces his intention to join the abolitionists, his father-in-law tells him:

> There is a natural order to this world, and those who try to upend it do not fare well. This movement will never survive. If you join them, you and your entire family will be shunned. At best you'll exist as a pariah to be spat on and beaten. At worst lynched or

> crucified … And for what? For what? Whatever you do it will never amount to anything more than a single drop in a limitless ocean.

Ewing replies, "What is an ocean but a multitude of drops?" This dialogue alludes to the notion of collective action. According to Sidney Tarrow, "conscientious collective action" is "the irreducible act that lies at the base of all social movements, protests, rebellions, riots, strike waves, and revolutions".[37] Ewing's revelation also speaks to the transformational power of witnessing that Joy refers to in her work on carnism. Joy makes a connection between witnessing carnism and witnessing other systems, stating:

> the ability to witness extends beyond carnism because witnessing isn't merely something one does; it is how one is. Witnessing isn't an isolated practice, but a way of relating to oneself and the world. It is a way of life that informs our interactions with ourselves and others.[38]

Ewing's father-in-law in this case represents the systems of power that are set up to fortify the status quo, while Ewing – after his journey, both physical and literal – has seen the truth for what it is. Although Ewing's revelation is not explicitly connected to carnism or speciesism, the film's intersectionality holds his revelation true for both. Ewing's narrative arc thus navigates the complex mechanisms of the politics of sight, wherein hidden realities are exposed to bring about political change.[39] Anat Pick notes that "the politics of sight requires reflexivity and nuance cognizant of the ideological mechanisms that govern sight".[40]

---

37 Tarrow 2011, 7.
38 Joy 2010, 148.
39 Pick 2016.
40 Pick 2016, 100.

Conclusion: The fiction film as activist

While animal activism in film and television is more traditionally served by non-fiction formats, a CAS reading of *Cloud Atlas* provides a rare and valuable example of how fiction filmmaking can help to engage audiences with complex and contentious issues like carnism and animal cruelty. Fiction films offer filmmakers a far greater degree of control over their subject, their characters and their visual style that is not always possible in non-fiction filmmaking. Fiction filmmakers are also afforded the liberty of creating fictional characters and worlds that they can imbue with meaning, drawing on the medium's form (editing, sound, cinematography, mise-en-scène) to create meaning through metaphor and subtext. The animal in *Cloud Atlas* – a fabricant – looks like us. The abattoir is full of "human" bodies. The audience does not distinguish between pureblood and fabricant because that is a distinction created beyond our experience or understanding. The audience simply sees a woman: subjugated, mistreated, sexually exploited and killed. Sonmi's existence as a server fits perfectly as an example of Adams' "formula for the absent referent"; "nonhuman/or human substitute + butchering = 'meat'/consumable flesh/mass term/ destruction of subject status".[41] Sonmi, ultimately, is executed. However, her execution is a far cry from the factory style killing in the Xultation ceremony. Instead, Sonmi's execution resembles a coronation, and she smiles at the moment of her death, knowing that her life has served a purpose.

Fiction film is able to use techniques at its disposal to convey animal activism through metaphor. This is, arguably, a more effective approach than is possible in non-fiction documentaries as it allows for a subtlety and subtext that requires the audience to make their own connections. Scholars have suggested that fiction in literature can inspire empathy and kindness towards others (see Hunt 2008; Keen 2010) and I contend that the same can be said for fiction films. Certainly, inspiring empathy and kindness was an intention made clear by *Cloud Atlas*. Crucially, the film was able to draw together in one story the intersectional experiences of six evocative stories that all share the same underpinning

41 Adams 2015b, 25.

message. In doing so, the audience is confronted with connections between issues surrounding race, sexuality, gender, class and species.

Cloud Atlas received mostly positive reviews, with the main criticism being the film's "complexity" (generally considered so due to the jumping back and forth between timelines) and was referred to as "ambitious" and "daring".[42] This suggests that critics struggled to grasp the interconnectedness between each timeline. Overall, critics appreciated the weighty intentions of the film to encourage audiences to think about how all lives are connected. A review in *The Guardian* suggested:

> One major role of culture is to offer spiritual consolation, especially in times of doubt and chaos, and *Cloud Atlas* clearly belongs alongside such mystical works as *The Life of Pi* and the films of Terrence Malick that aspire to answer such needs at a higher, more sophisticated level than sentimental comfort.[43]

Another criticism levelled at *Cloud Atlas* was an accusation of whitewashing and yellowface. The film uses prosthetics and make-up to transform various cast members' gender and race. This led to a backlash after the release of the trailer and promotional materials in advance of the film's release. The directors responded to this accusation, with Lilly Wachowski saying:

> That's good that people are casting a critical eye. We need to cast critical eyes toward these things. … But our intention is the antithesis of that idea. The intention is to talk about things that are beyond race.[44]

Lana Wachowski added:

> Their suggestion is that our tribes have to always remain separate. That the things that make us different are essential elements to

42 Ebert 2012; French 2013; Nathan 2013; Quinn 2013; Scott 2013.

43 French 2013.

44 Lilly Wachowski in Rosen 2012.

> our representation and our identity. Why we were attracted to the book is that the book has a bigger perspective. The book suggests that there is a humanity that is beyond our tribe, our ethnic features. A humanity that is beyond our gender. A humanity that unites all of us and transcends our tribal differences. As long as we continue to build these intractable and insurmountable walls between us to make these distinctions, we will continue to have an intellectual apparatus that allows us to make wars and that allows us to dominate, exploit and destroy others. Because we don't think of them like we think about our own kind, our own tribe.[45]

These sentiments are in line with the questions and concerns about the carnist belief system and speciesism more generally. The backlash appeared to dissipate after the film was released, which is a promising sign that the message was not lost on audiences after all.

Sonmi-451's first words in the film are, "Truth is singular. Its 'versions' are mistruths." The apparent malleability of "truth" is the essence of cognitive dissonance, which in turn underscores carnism. In her work on carnism, Melanie Joy says, "we avoid the truth" when we do not name the carnistic system.[46] Joy attests:

> The carnistic system is riddled with absurdities, inconsistencies, and paradox. It is fortified by a complex network of defences that make it possible for us to believe without questioning, to know without thinking, and to act without feeling. It is a coercive system that has cultivated in us an elaborate routine of mental gymnastics that keep us from being grounded in our truth.[47]

Sonmi's story serves to draw attention to this invisible belief system, although the filmmakers do not call it carnism. Joy suggests that one of the key ways that the carnistic system is enabled is by the invisibility of the animal-industrial complex. Sonmi-451's life as a server is likewise made invisible. However, through her liberation and revelation, Sonmi

45 Lilly Wachowski in Rosen 2012.
46 Joy 2010, 40.
47 Joy 2010, 133.

becomes individualised, and in so doing inspires a revolution. The audience bears witness to this *fictional* journey, interwoven with *fictional* stories of overcoming racism, sexism, classism and bigotry, and in doing so, *Cloud Atlas* offers and encourages the possibility of change in the *real* world.

References

Adams, C.J. (2015a). *The Sexual Politics of Meat: A Feminist-Vegetarian Critical Theory.* London: Bloomsbury Academic.

Adams, C. (2015b). *The Pornography of Meat.* New York: Lantern Books.

Cain, S. (2019). The Sandman, Catch-22, Cloud Atlas … is there such thing as an 'unfilmable' book? *Guardian,* 3 July. https://bit.ly/47D2pq4.

Cloud Atlas (2012). Film. Lana Wachowski, Lilly Wachowski and Tom Tykwer (Dirs). Distributor: Cloud Atlas Productions.

DeMello, M. (2012). *Animals and Society.* New York: Columbia University Press.

Ebert, R. (2012). Castles in the sky. *Rogerebert.com,* 24 October. https://bit.ly/47DiWum.

French, P. (2013). Cloud Atlas – review. *Guardian,* 24 February. https://bit.ly/3Sl7K18.

Gore, W. (2013). First Life of Pi, now Cloud Atlas. Why keep trying to film the unfilmable? *Spectator,* 2 March. https://bit.ly/48ujCmW.

Grandin, T. (2013). Making slaughterhouses more humane for cattle, pigs, and sheep. *Annual Review of Animal Biosciences* 1(1): 491–512. https://bit.ly/3SkaZ8P.

Hunt, L. (2008). *Inventing Human Rights.* New York: Norton.

Joy, M. (2010). *Why We Love Dogs, Eat Pigs and Wear Cows.* San Francisco: Conari Press.

Keen, S. (2010). *Empathy and the Novel.* Oxford: Oxford University Press.

Konnikova, M. (2012). The 'Cloud Atlas' question: when is an 'unfilmable' book actually filmable?. *Atlantic,* 15 October. https://bit.ly/48ACsbZ.

Lambie, R. (2013). Cloud Atlas review. *Den of Geek,* 22 February. https://bit.ly/3StMMgF.

Molloy, C. (2011). *Popular Media and Animals.* Basingstoke: Palgrave Macmillan.

Nathan, I. (2013). Cloud Atlas review. *Empire,* 26 July. https://bit.ly/3Skqaiv.

Pick, A. (2016). Animal rights films, organized violence, and the politics of sight. In Y. Tzioumakis and C. Molloy, eds. *The Routledge Companion to Cinema and Politics,* 91–102. London: Routledge.

Quinn, A. (2013). Film review: time-travellers reach for the sky in Cloud Atlas. *Independent*, 22 February. https://bit.ly/48x0PY5.
Rosen, C. (2012). "Cloud Atlas": Andy & Lana Wachowski and Tom Tykwer On The Problem With Hollywood. *Huffpost*, 22 October. https://tinyurl.com/52z9hmvm.
Ryder, R.D. (2000). *Animal Revolution*. Oxford: Berg.
Scott, A. (2012). Souls tangled up in time. *New York Times*, 26 October. https://nyti.ms/4bAPU19.
Singer, P. (2015). *Animal Liberation*. London: The Bodley Head.
Soylent Green (1973). Film. Richard Fleischer (Dir.). Distributor: Metro-Goldwyn-Mayer.
Tarrow, S. (2011). *Power in Movement*. Cambridge: Cambridge University Press.
Taylor, N. and R. Twine (2014). *The Rise of Critical Animal Studies*. New York: Routledge.
Uchida, A. (1998). The Orientalization of Asian women in America. *Women's Studies International Forum* 21(2): 161–74.

8

Animal activism formula for success

Lessons for capitalising on the "*Blackfish* effect"

Debra Merskin and Carrie Freeman

In 2013, a documentary film was released that would create a public stir and change policies and practices in the treatment of orcas (*Orcinus orca*) used for entertainment: *Blackfish* (2013). When *Blackfish* was presented on cable TV, it became CNN's most watched show for all of 2013 – with its biggest share in history of the valuable audience demographic of 18–23-year-olds.[1] Focusing on the 2010 death of SeaWorld Orlando trainer Dawn Brancheau, the film critiqued not only the safety conditions of the trainer/workers but also the conditions in which marine mammals, like 6.7 metre, 5.4 tonne Tilikum, are kept at entertainment parks. Importantly, it humanised orcas, and audiences could see them as individuals and, in a pivotal scene, as mothers who loved their offspring. In this way, the anthropomorphism in *Blackfish* productively serves as a cinematic example of "an affective and effective means of mobilizing empathy" between humans and other animals to materially improve their lives.[2] According to Loretta Rowley and Kevin Johnson:

1 Hargrove 2015, 229.
2 Parkinson 2020, 5.

> The anthropomorphic construction of orcas in *Blackfish* may well be a story that is more about what it means to be human than a story about what it means to be orca.[3]

And this may very well be what motivates viewers to change attitudes and behaviours when it comes to caring about animals other than humans. But there's something more going on in relation to media portrayals that seem to have reach not only in generating empathy for a species but also have real impact on industries.

This chapter explores what has come to be called the "Blackfish effect", defined as "the public outcry", the "tectonic shift in late-20th century public opinion regarding animal rights", and "kairotic backdrop"[4] resulting in the "financial struggles that SeaWorld faced after the 2013 documentary *Blackfish*".[5] This shift is an animal advocacy phenomenon "at the intersection of documentary storytelling, grassroots activism, multi-platform distribution and media strategy".[6] This film and its corresponding animal activism brought enough critical attention to orca captivity that it altered the nature of the way aquarium trainers engaged with the captive individuals, changed the keeping of them in tanks that, to us, would be no bigger than living in a bathtub, spawned anti-captivity legislation, and prompted an unprecedented crisis management and eventual rebranding campaign by SeaWorld as ticket sales and financial support plummeted.

Utilising a critical animal and media studies lens,[7] we posit answers to the following questions: (i) What key factors seemed to work in terms of the *Blackfish* film's content and promotion?; (ii) How have animal activists capitalised on the film's success?; (iii) Have there been similar successes for other documentary films intended to raise public consciousness about the rights and welfare of captive whales and dolphins?; and (iv) Is there a discernible "*Blackfish* effect" formula that can be used to guide animal activism and filmmaking going forward,

---

3 Rowley and Johnson 2015, 825.
4 Waller and Iluzada 2020, 227.
5 Hassan 2018.
6 Chattoo 2016.
7 Almiron, Cole and Freeman 2016.

where activists can strategically "use the momentum created by a blockbuster"[8] to catapult their existing campaigns? Accumulation theory[9] is used as an analytic tool that places this analysis in the context of media effects theories so that the Blackfish effect is not considered a solo victory of one documentary, and we account for the longer-term media messages accumulating public sympathy with/for whales and dolphins, thanks in large part to decades of animal rights activism (including other cetacean freedom documentaries) before and after *Blackfish*.

To set the background context, the following sections briefly discuss the advocacy nature of documentary films, the composition and promotion of *Blackfish* (2013) and theories of media effects including accumulation theory. We then answer our research questions, including reviewing media effects in an analysis of eight related documentary films on cetacean freedom. Based on our analysis, we conclude with recommendations for animal activists and filmmakers in continuing to utilise the power of documentary narratives (in terms of both content and strategic marketing) to facilitate justice for captive nonhuman animals.

Documentaries and advocacy

The term "document" originates in the Latin word *docere*, which means to teach. According to the *Oxford English Dictionary*, documentary is "factual, realistic, applied … based on real events or circumstances and intended primarily for instruction".[10] This educational goal sets this film genre apart from those designed to primarily entertain, from the purely fictional to some mixture of fact and fiction. The "current Golden Age of documentaries began in the 1980s. It continues unabated."[11] Documentary films are created to present a point of view; they "challenge assumptions and alter perceptions".[12]

8 Loy 2016, 225.
9 DeFleur and Dennis 1994/1996.
10 *Oxford English Dictionary* 2021.
11 Nichols 2010, 1.
12 Nichols 2010, 1.

Unlike some forms of media, particularly journalism, which are created to present multiple points of view with an effort towards "balance", documentaries have intention. Caty Borum Chattoo writes:

> At their core, documentaries are a form of art that supplies a civic and narrative imagination that is vital – well beyond simply knowing facts and information – to shaping a culture in order to understand the full spectrum of human experience and the lives we live.[13]

Blackfish is no exception as it provides facts and information but also "unashamedly wears its heart on its sleeve"[14] and stands apart from feature and other films that have performing animals (e.g., *Free Willy* [1993], which popularised whale watching in natural settings). *Blackfish* de-popularised whale watching in entertainment facilities: "It is less common for a film to influence people to turn away from a previously popular tourism choice."[15] In addition, it "has led to a series of notable societal, corporate, and policy changes, in several countries".[16] Thus, the central intention of *Blackfish* is to educate viewers on the harms inherent in keeping whales captive, as well as provide tools by which viewers can turn their elevated consciousness into action to prevent the exploitation of whales for entertainment.

Media effects

What gained traction as a phrase in academic and popular literature is the "*Blackfish* effect", used to describe the film's impact on viewers and subsequent activism via boycotts, word-of-mouth education and economic effects on the entertainment giant SeaWorld. There have been other popularly coined "effects", not necessarily based in media theory but that sound catchy and have gained traction in academic and

13 Chattoo 2020, 6.
14 Brammer 2015.
15 Parsons and Rose 2018, 74.
16 Parsons and Rose 2018, 74.

scholarly spheres. The "CNN effect", for example, "asserts that global television networks, such as CNN and BBC World, have become a decisive factor in determining policies and outcomes of significant events".[17] Johanna Neuman wrote of a curve such that:

> when CNN floods the airwaves with news of a foreign crisis, policymakers have no choice but to redirect their attention to the crisis at hand. It also suggests that crisis coverage evokes an emotional outcry from the public to "do something" about the latest incident, forcing political leaders to change course or risk unpopularity.[18]

The CNN effect originally meant the effect was on governments and politicians, but it can also apply to audiences. Other examples include the effect of instantaneous 24-hour news coverage of natural disasters or global pandemics. With the expansion of channels, networks, outlets and social media, the potential for reach and effects, both short- and long-term, has also expanded.

The "*CSI* effect" refers to the impact television crime programs such as the *CSI* and *Law & Order* franchises have had on the criminal justice system.[19] For example, "Many attorneys, judges, and journalists have claimed that watching television programs like *CSI* has caused jurors to wrongfully acquit guilty defendants when no scientific evidence has been presented."[20] In some cases, jurors believe the same types of forensic technologies are available to real law enforcement agencies that they see in these fictional television programs. While the stories may be "drawn from the headlines", the telling of them is fiction and yet there have been effects on audiences. How often someone watches these shows also affects how likely they are to believe what they see is real:

17 Gilboa 2005, 27.
18 Neuman 1996, 15–16.
19 Cole and Dioso-Villa 2011.
20 Shelton 2008, 2.

> As to how "real" a television program was perceived to be, our results indicated that the more frequently jurors watched a given program, the more accurate they perceived the program to be.[21]

These media effects, including the *Blackfish* effect, can be considered in terms of the agenda-setting theory of news influence, where repeated news coverage of issues puts them on the public agenda, prompting leaders and the public to consider these issues as more important and timelier to address than other issues not covered in the news cycle.[22] Therefore, agenda-*building* is a key part of advocacy organisations' goals (such as the animal protection movement) to get their topics in the news cycle in order to capitalise on this agenda-setting effect.[23] As part of promoting social change, accumulation and media effects theory can be considered along with the sociology literature on social movement activism that guides activist organisations to (i) capitalise on political opportunities; (ii) successfully mobilise resources; and (iii) strategically frame messages.[24]

How might a media effect function in animal and environmental activism? What does that mean and how might other animal advocacy efforts capitalise on noted attributes of a success such as *Blackfish*? The following sections discuss *Blackfish* (2013), its promotion, popular and academic responses, an analysis of responses to eight other related documentary films, and finally, present this information in terms of what accumulation theory would predict, hence offering a map for other activist organisations to consider when planning campaigns.

Background on *Blackfish*

The intent of *Blackfish* is evident in the synopsis, as per the website blackfishthemovie.com/about:

---

21 Shelton 2008, 22. See Gerbner (1986) for more on this effect.
22 McCombs 2004.
23 See also Carroll and McCombs 2003; Miller 2010.
24 McAdam, McCarthy and Zald 1996.

> *Blackfish* tells the story of Tilikum, a performing killer whale that killed several people while in captivity. Along the way, director-producer Gabriela Cowperthwaite compiles shocking footage and emotional interviews to explore the creature's extraordinary nature, the species' cruel treatment in captivity, the lives and losses of the trainers and the pressures brought to bear by the multi-billion-dollar sea-park industry.
>
> This emotionally wrenching, tautly structured story challenges us to consider our relationship to nature and reveals how little we humans have learned from these highly intelligent and enormously sentient fellow mammals.

Made for a remarkably small production budget, US$76,000, this feature-length documentary uses a combination of action-packed footage and talking heads interviews with experts as well as SeaWorld employees.[25] Several deaths and multiple incidents at SeaWorld, focusing on the then-recent death of SeaWorld Orlando trainer Dawn Brancheau, are discussed, but importantly, the circumstances surrounding each are contextualised within the experiences of the captive orcas: how they were captured, what their experience of capture was like, and what it might be like to live confined to a space equivalent to a human spending their entire life in a bathtub. Topics explored include the psychological damage such capture and confinement can do to an animal as well as the unnatural acts for human entertainment they are made to perform. This all provides a foundation for understanding why the animal behaved in the way that, in the case of Tilikum, he did. As David Hickman states: "Its story of dual tragedy – human and captive whale – was elegantly structured and told without recourse to sensationalism."[26]

But some of these documentary filmmaking techniques are not new. What was it about *Blackfish* that "contributed to [SeaWorld's] policy change"?[27] What factors seemed to work in terms of the *Blackfish*

25 Hickman 2015.
26 Hickman 2015.
27 Chattoo 2020, 115.

film's content and promotion to generate the kinds of changes that would result in plummeting stock values and attendance at the parks? What theory might predict its success? That is the subject of the next section.

Accumulation theory

To accumulate means to gradually gather, to amass. The concept of accumulation theory exists in Marxist economics,[28] as a theory of ageing,[29] and as an explanation for both short-term and long-term effects of mediated information.[30] In media theory, accumulation theory is the view that changes (in beliefs, behaviour, attitudes) can add up over time:

> when an increasing numbe[r] of individuals slowly modify their beliefs, interpretations, and orientations toward an issue that is repeatedly presented by several media that consistently emphasize a point of view. When this happens, significant changes take place on a long-term basis.[31]

Furthermore, it is:

> the view that the impact of any one message on any specific person may be minimal, but consistent, persistent, and corroborated (between mediums) messages result in minor changes among audiences that gradually add up over time to produce significant changes in society or culture.[32]

28 Harvey 2005.
29 Medawar 1952.
30 DeFleur and Dennis 1994/1996.
31 DeFleur and Dennis 1994/1996, 572.
32 Merskin 2000.

Posited by Melvin DeFleur and Everette Dennis in 1994/1996, this theory of minimal effects consists of four steps by which a message gains/accumulates meaning:

1. The mass media begin to focus their attention on and transmit messages about a specific topic (some problem, situation, or issue).
2. Over an extended period, they continue to do so in a relatively consistent and persistent way and their presentations corroborate each other.
3. Individual members of the public increasingly become aware of these messages, and, on a person-by-person basis, a growing comprehension develops of the interpretations of the topic presented by the media.
4. Increasing comprehension of the messages regarding the topic supplied by the media begins to form (or modify) the meanings, beliefs, and attitudes that serve as guides to behaviour for members of the audience.[33]

As a result, these "minor individual-by-individual changes *accumulate*, and new beliefs and attitudes slowly emerge to provide significant changes in norms of appropriate behaviour related to the topic".[34]

In terms of films that have affected mainstream views of animals, one that had early and long-term effects on audiences, some say to the present day, is the 1942 Disney animated film *Bambi*. Based on a 1923 novel by Austrian writer Felix Salten, in *Bambi: A Life in the Woods* the story "attempts to describe the frequently cruel reality of nature from a deer's perspective"[35] and also the cruelty of humans who hunt, evidenced by reactions to the death of Bambi's mother. The 1947 re-release of the film is considered by the American Film Institute (AFI) to be "the third greatest American animated film (*Snow White and the Seven Dwarfs* [1937] is number one)".[36] Furthermore, according to

33 DeFleur and Dennis 1994/1996, 578–9.
34 DeFleur and Dennis 1994/1996, 579, emphasis in original.
35 Grieze 2018, 7.
36 Wills 2016.

Ralph Lutts, the film "presents a poetic vision of woodland life and a powerful statement against hunting".[37] Horror writer Stephen King has said:

> the first movie I ever saw was a horror movie. It was "Bambi". When that little deer gets caught in a forest fire, I was terrified, but I was also exhilarated.[38]

Bambi impacted many Americans' views of nature ever since and played "a key role in shaping American attitudes about and understanding of deer and woodland life".[39] Other examples of child-targeted films that focus on empathy for captive/hunted/harmed animals include *101 Dalmatians* (1961, 1996), *Babe* (1995), *Charlotte's Web* (2006), *The Fox & the Hound* (1981) and *Dumbo* (1941, 2019). While anthropomorphism is used, as noted by Parkinson,[40] it can be an affective and effective method of personalising the experiences of fictional and animated animals.

Thus, in the current study, we can ask of *Blackfish* and subsequent media coverage: Was there a continuous presentation of media-provided interpretations of events and of the film? Did changes occur among audiences? Did the media transmit information about the documentary and its contents? While a study of attitudes and beliefs is beyond the scope of the current chapter and fertile fodder for additional research, discussions of the effects of the documentary *Blackfish* as a tool for activism can be contextualised within accumulation theory evidenced in part by a decline in ticket sales and stock value within both short- and long-term time frames following the initial screening. The following sections respond to the four research questions guiding this chapter.

37 Lutts 1992, 167.
38 Quoted in Clarke 2017.
39 Lutts 1992, 167.
40 Parkinson 2020.

Answering research questions

1. What key factors seemed to work in terms of the Blackfish *film's content and promotion?*

As shown in Appendix A, the premiere of *Blackfish* at the Sundance Film Festival in 2013 was not the first moment of heightened awareness of the treatment of captive orcas or the labour issues associated with working in animal entertainment. In 2010, a story appeared in *Outside* magazine by Tim Zimmerman, "The killer in the pool", that got the attention of director Gabriela Cowperthwaite. The magazine article detailed how orca trainer Dawn Brancheau was killed by Tilikum, a performing orca at SeaWorld, in February 2010. In 2011, the Occupational Safety and Health Administration (OSHA) cited SeaWorld for the Florida incident, gaining news media attention.[41] Two books followed not long after the tragedy: *Death at SeaWorld: Shamu and the Dark Side of Killer Whales in Captivity* (2012) and *Beneath the Surface: Killer Whales, SeaWorld, and the Truth Beyond Blackfish* (2015). The authors of these books appeared on television programs such as *The Daily Show* and *Anderson Cooper*, beginning the momentum building for corroboration between media forms. And the film premiered at Sundance in 2013 between the dates of these books and at other important film festivals such as Melbourne International. CNN bought the television rights at Sundance and repeatedly aired the documentary, reaching more than 21 million viewers. Netflix included *Blackfish* in its streaming options and Amazon sold the DVD. Top newspapers such as the *New York Times, Los Angeles Times, The Guardian* and others on the list, as shown in Appendix A, published reviews.

As a result of the accumulation of these efforts, SeaWorld suffered reputational and financial losses: its stock plunged 33 per cent, profits declined 28 per cent and attendance at the park was down by nearly a million visitors.[42] Major advertisers/sponsors such as Taco Bell and Southwest Airlines pulled out. Losses persisted: the entertainment

41 Hargrove and Chua-Eoan 2015.
42 Hargrove and Chua-Eoan 2015; Greenfield 2014. See also Soderberg 2021.

giant, owned since 2009 by private equity firm Blackstone, lost nearly $44 million in 2015 and $179 million in 2017. The stock lost 70 per cent of its value, and attendance continued to decrease.[43]

In 2014, the US Court of Appeals upheld the OSHA court ruling and fined SeaWorld $75,000 and placed responsibility on SeaWorld for Brancheau's death.[44] While SeaWorld countered with various proposals, they all seemed to backfire by drawing attention to their desire to continue to exploit captive orcas. Publicity also came from the joint Securities and Exchange Commission (SEC) and the US Justice Department investigation of the former CEO, Jim Atchison, who had declared the film would not have any significant impact on the enterprise.[45] In the meantime, Atchison disposed of 154,000 shares of his own stock in the company, reaping nearly $5 million profits, the amount he was later fined. By 2016, SeaWorld agreed to end their captive breeding program, which was a major advancement in the animal rights/protection movement.

2. How have animal activists capitalised on the film's success?

In their analysis of *Blackfish*, Caitlyn Burford and Julie Schutten argue that Tilikum, and other orcas in the film, were in fact "the first activists that initiated this particular environmental justice movement".[46] Fitting the prisoner metaphor, this view offers the orcas agency. Thus, the film splices together scenes of Tilikum's and other orcas' perceived reality from their perspective, unveiling a much different picture than what entertainment parks portray publicly.

The animal rights nonprofit People for the Ethical Treatment of Animals (PETA) amplified the information, and SeaWorld's denial, creating an anti-corporate campaign that included social media, public protests, and a website: www.SeaWorldofHurt.com. Momentum gained by the campaign continues today, with the use of cetaceans in entertainment being featured and analysed. Furthermore, social media

43 Munarriz 2018; *Investment Guru* 2019; Wynne 2017.
44 Hargrove and Chua-Eoan 2015.
45 Fechter 2018.
46 Burford and Schutten 2017.

accounts exploded. Twitter held a Q&A with Gabriela Cowperthwaite. Individuals tweeted about the film, and raised or renewed consciousness about orcas in captivity, and urged others to see the film.

3. Have there been similar successes for other documentary films intended to raise public consciousness about the rights and welfare of captive whales and dolphins?

To answer our research question on other related documentaries for comparison with *Blackfish* and to provide context for the broader media landscape before and after the 2013 film, we reviewed cetacean captivity documentaries in Western media in the last several decades, and identified eight to examine in terms of popularity and activism influence:

1. *Lolita: Slave to Entertainment* (2003)
2. *Saving Flipper* (2009)
3. *The Cove* (2009)
4. *Keiko: The Untold Story of the Star of Free Willy* (2010)
5. *A Fall From Freedom* (2012)
6. *Voiceless – A Blue Freedom Film* (2016)
7. *Inside the Tanks* (2017)
8. *Long Gone Wild* (2019)

For these documentaries, in October of 2021 we reviewed box office revenue (when available in searches from these online databases: Box Office Mojo and The Numbers), number of reviews and ratings on IMDB and Amazon Prime, social media presence, and news media mentions (based on searches in Factiva and Global Newsstream databases). The comparisons are primarily aimed at assessing each documentary's popularity/reach more so than qualitative content (e.g., we did not read all the thousands of reviews or compare filmmaking styles or narrative film structure). Unfortunately, there is no data that details how many viewers each documentary has reached, especially as most of these films were not theatrically released and have no easily accessible record of sales. Given our emphasis on activism, the only way we could feasibly assess how these advocacy documentaries were/are used by activists to engage in social change work was to determine this via news media coverage and the amount of social media engagement (for most documentaries it was feasible as qualitative researchers to review every media story, as there were often only 20 or fewer stories, but for *The Cove*, with almost 4,000 news stories, we had to just look at yearly trends).

The first documentary, *Lolita: Slave to Entertainment*, critiques the kidnapping of Lolita from her Puget Sound orca family in 1970 to perform at the Miami Seaquarium, where for the last decade, since her companion, Hugo, committed suicide, she languished alone in the nation's smallest orca tank in between performances. *Lolita* has high ratings on IMDB (8.2/10) based on 60 reviews, and on Amazon Prime (4.5/5) based on 133 reviews, some of which are recent and even compare this 18-year-old film to *Blackfish*. Eight news articles mention *Lolita* in film festivals, including winning several Best Documentary awards. Almost two decades after the film's release, activists nationwide and the international group PETA were still fighting to free Lolita (who is also known as Tokitae). Even in recent years, people continued to refer to that early documentary because Lolita remained imprisoned despite public outcry over her abysmal conditions. The hashtag #FreeLolita is still popular, and viewers created many social media pages on her behalf (not affiliated with the 2003 documentary, however). Celebrities sometimes advocated for her release, such as *Schitt's Creek*'s Daniel Levy, who tweeted in August 2021 sharing the link to PETA's Lolita video, with 300,000 views. Activists including organisations such as PETA gained news coverage in 2013 and 2015 that mentioned the *Lolita* documentary (and *Blackfish*) related to plans to reintegrate Lolita to her native habitat off Vancouver and the National Marine Fishery Service offering Lolita endangered species protections, making her captivity more legally problematic for the Miami Seaquarium. Tragically, Lolita (Tokitae) died of renal failure on 18 August 2023 in her tank at the Miami Seaquarium, which under new ownership in 2022 was finally working with activists and the Lumni Nation tribe to soon return Lolita to her home waters in the Pacific Northwest.[47] Her sudden death before rescue was reported across major national and international news outlets.

---

47 Lori Marino, Whale Sanctuary Project Blog, 23 August 2023.

The second documentary, *Saving Flipper*, features dolphin advocate Ric O'Barry's story of going from being the *Flipper* TV series dolphin trainer to their liberation advocate, explaining why keeping them in captivity for entertainment and public swimming opportunities is harmful to them, including mentioning the yearly Taiji, Japan, dolphin capture and slaughter.[48] *Saving Flipper* seemed to get almost no media attention and has no social media presence; it does stream on Amazon Prime but has only 18 reviews and a rating of 3/5.

A 2009 documentary on dolphins that did garner major media attention, over $1.1 million in revenue and critical acclaim is *The Cove*. This thriller, in *Ocean's Eleven* style, critiques fishermen's annual roundup, sale and/or slaughter of dolphins in a cove in Taiji, Japan, also highlighting the dolphin and whale meat industry and Western and Eastern activists' risky attempts to document and end the Taiji massacre and sale of dolphins into the global captivity industry. The film won many awards, most notably the 2010 Academy Award for Best Documentary, catapulting it and the Taiji slaughter towards global notoriety. *The Cove* is rated highly and reviewed widely, with over 48,000 reviews on IMDB (8.4/10) and over 900 reviews on Amazon Prime (4.5/5). The social media presence is mainly through Ric O'Barry's organisation, Dolphin Project, which mentions *The Cove* and Taiji frequently on Instagram (with over 339,000 followers). There are almost 4,000 news stories on *The Cove*, most of which are from 2009–2010. Since the release of *Blackfish* in 2013, 168 articles mention the films together, but some stories indicate that even before *Blackfish*, *The Cove* was influencing Western families not to support marine parks. Some of the media attention was based on cultural backlash *The Cove* received in Japan, where it was perceived as Western cultural imperialism and hypocrisy (since Westerners eat animal flesh and go to marine parks), including refusals to show the film in many Japanese theatres. News reports over the years explain how the Japanese government doubled down in defence of their historical cultural hunting practices, even making it hard for Western activists to immigrate to protest the ongoing annual hunt, with most of the

48 Note: O'Barry is often featured in many of the cetacean documentaries we studied, such as *The Cove*.

dolphins now sold to China's growing entertainment industry. Because the Taiji dolphin hunt continues, *The Cove* still has relevancy.

The fourth documentary, *Keiko: The Untold Story of the Star of Free Willy*, details the whale actor's dramatic story of capture, captivity and forced performance; precedent-setting rehabilitation; release into his native Icelandic waters; and eventual death. The documentary framed Keiko's rehab as a relative success even as many in the entertainment industry describe it as proof that captive whales cannot be rehabilitated to survive in the wild (according to the little news media coverage the film received). Meant for whale advocacy, *Keiko*'s extensive website features a section to educate kids using the *Keiko* film and details its 20 film festival screenings and awards, with translation into four languages. The film is highly rated at 4.5/5 on Amazon Prime (101 reviews) and 8/10 on IMDB (81 reviews). *Keiko* is somewhat popular on social media with 76,000+ followers on Facebook, 740+ on Instagram and almost 2,000 Twitter followers.

Also featuring the whale Keiko, *A Fall From Freedom* is a Discovery Channel documentary that has been described as a follow-up to *The Cove*. Narrated by *M*A*S*H* actor Mike Farrell, it reveals the sordid history of the whale and dolphin entertainment business, including their responsibility for the deaths of many cetaceans in marine parks like SeaWorld. Despite having no website anymore and no social media presence or news media coverage, *A Fall From Freedom* is favourably rated on IMDB at 8.1/10 (81 reviewers) and on Amazon Prime at 4.5/5 (55+ reviews).

The success of *Blackfish* in 2013 sparked some half-hour documentaries critiquing marine parks, not theatrically released or critically reviewed but available for free on YouTube and reaching large audiences. These include *Voiceless – A Blue Freedom Film* (a student-produced activist film with 424,000+ YouTube views) and *Inside the Tanks* (a journalism-style film by Jonny Meah with an amazing six million+ views on YouTube). *Blackfish* also inspired a follow-up/sequel feature-length documentary called *Long Gone Wild*, whose trailers have been viewed on YouTube almost 30,000 times (for comparison, *Blackfish*'s trailers have over four million views on YouTube). *Long Gone Wild*, the final film in our analysis, is said to pick up where *Blackfish* leaves off, detailing advances in Western marine park policies but also critiquing what remains the same and highlighting the growing market for whales in Russia and Asia, and also highlighting a solution for rehabbing and rehoming captive whales to seaside pen sanctuaries via the Whale Sanctuary Project. The Whale Sanctuary Project organisation handles much of the film's activist-oriented social media presence including over 3,600 followers on Facebook, 3,000 on Instagram, and 600+ on Twitter. *Long Gone Wild* is available for paid streaming on sites like Amazon Prime, where it is favourably rated at 4.5/5 (200+ reviewers), and on IMDB with a slightly lower rating at 6.8/10 (64 reviewers). What little news coverage exists on the film mentions how a 2020 PETA protest at the Miami Seaquarium to free Lolita recommended people watch *Long Gone Wild* to understand the potential for Lolita to live in a sea sanctuary in the Puget Sound near her native pod.

4. Is there a discernible Blackfish *effect formula that can be used to guide animal activism and filmmaking going forward, where activists can strategically "use the momentum created by a blockbuster"?*[49]

Some of the national/international activist groups mentioned in news stories and wire service press releases on these other cetacean documentaries include PETA, Ric O'Barry's Dolphin Project, The Orca Project, Save Lolita, The Orca Network, Sea Shepherd Conservation Society, Humane Society of the US (HSUS), Humane Society International, the Animal Welfare Institute, the Marine Animal Response Society and The Whale Sanctuary Project. *A Fall From Freedom* was sponsored by these animal protection groups: HSUS, Friends of Animals, American SPCA, Blue Voice and Whale & Dolphin Conservation Society. Activism – especially a need to change laws, policies and public support for marine parks – is built into the narrative of most of the cetacean captivity documentaries discussed in the previous section. Therefore, when news stories discuss these films (outside of film festival reviews/award stories), they often invite a leader of an animal activist group to speak on the issues, especially if news outlets are trying to provide a variety of viewpoints on any controversial

49 Loy 2016, 225.

cetacean practice, where the activist perspective is countered by some hunting or entertainment facility business view. A few news stories talk about animal activist street protests (especially related to freeing Lolita or ending the Taiji hunts/roundups) and reference *Lolita* or *The Cove* documentaries. Sometimes local news articles talk about a local activist who is screening the film or organising some petition or protest in their area inspired by the documentary. But the activist component of most news stories mentioning these cetacean documentaries comes more often in the form of including quotes from activists critical of cetacean exploitation, more so than covering direct-action street demonstrations or civil disobedience.

Some documentaries have a longer media life that extends beyond the first few years after their release, in cases where activist organisations file lawsuits and stage protests, or businesses and/or governments change animal policies that journalists find newsworthy as an update/follow-up in the life of the story; examples of this include: Lolita being granted endangered species status by a US government agency; lawsuits stating the dolphin slaughter violates Japanese animal welfare laws; Japan exiting the International Whaling Commission (IWC) to resume commercial whaling then selling this whale meat in Taiji; Tripadvisor banning sales of tickets to captive cetacean attractions; and Canada recently banning cetacean breeding and captivity. In some of these stories, reporters reference the earlier documentaries as an indicator of controversy or legitimate public critique of cetacean captivity as proof of an ongoing public debate over dolphin and whale parks. Thus, in news reporting, it seems as though these animal advocacy documentaries, even years after they were released, serve to add credibility and weight to the captivity issue as it goes through various newsworthy stages of legislative, business and cultural change. This is especially true for journalists referencing documentaries that are critically acclaimed and popular, like *The Cove* and *Blackfish*, that galvanised a broad public outcry and garner high name recognition with news audiences.

While highly rated in terms of content quality, most of the other cetacean captivity documentaries outlined in this chapter (with the exception of *The Cove*) prompted only a handful of news media stories, were only reviewed by about 100 Amazon and IMDB viewers each, and have social media followers only in the hundreds or low thousands (although some of the recent YouTube releases were viewed by hundreds of thousands of people, and *Keiko* has over 75,000 Facebook followers); these numbers pale in comparison to popularity numbers for *Blackfish*, which, as of late 2021 has 64,000+ reviews on IMDB, 131,000 followers on Facebook, 51,000+ followers on Twitter, almost 8,000 followers on Instagram, generated over $2.3 million in box office revenue, and prompted a mention in close to 5,000 news media stories. In terms of being influential, the only other cetacean captivity documentary that comes close to *Blackfish* is *The Cove* (generating over a million dollars in revenue and earning more than 48,000 reviews on IMDB and getting close to 4,000 mentions in news stories). However, *Blackfish* is the documentary that is more likely to get mentioned in news media as a yardstick by which to measure the advocacy success of other animal protection films, by comparing them to *Blackfish* (e.g., saying *Tiger King* is not the *Blackfish* of tiger captivity). (Also, reportedly, after being influenced by *Blackfish*, Disney filmmakers rewrote the ending to their blockbuster *Finding Nemo* sequel *Finding Dory* to avoid glamorising life in marine parks, which will leave an impression with millions of child viewers and their parents.)[50]

Yet, *Blackfish* and its immense success cannot be viewed as existing in a vacuum. Certainly, it is an excellent documentary that utilised the best combination of facts, storytelling techniques and combined human and nonhuman animal tragedy in a compelling way. Accumulation theory predicts that if a message is told consistently and persistently, and is corroborated between media forms, it is likely to have an effect, and that was the case here. The main message of *Blackfish* about the tragedy of orca capture and captivity had been told for years, if not decades, before *Blackfish* came to global media attention, via the other documentaries that we outlined in this chapter along with animal activism protests and anti-aquarium campaigns and their subsequent news media coverage over the decades (even consider that the *Marine Mammal Protection Act* was passed in 1972, declaring that US society privileges the lives of sea mammal individuals over fishes). The conditions were also ripe for a documentary like *Blackfish* to be

50 Child 2013.

especially resonant if you factor in the unprecedented death of SeaWorld trainer Dawn Brancheau being so newsworthy, and the unfolding newsworthiness of the subsequent labour working-conditions (OSHA) lawsuits aimed at SeaWorld and added press from the popular *Outside* magazine story on this fatal incident and the *Death at SeaWorld* book. And when *Blackfish* premiered, it had a promotion team behind it that made sure it was seen by major media outlets and reviewed globally at festivals and in major news outlets. Social media discussions and promotions followed. The luckiest break was CNN picking up the film to be aired so widely on its popular network. We do wonder: If not for the previous success of *The Cove*, along with the newsworthiness of this unprecedented killing of a human by this "killer whale", would CNN have found a whale captivity documentary so compelling? Once *Blackfish* had been viewed by so many hundreds of thousands of people on CNN, viewers whose consciousness had been raised could see, and experience, the impact of their decisions *not* to attend the theme park in the subsequent news stories exposing a rapid decline in ticket sales, attendance and stock value.

Considering all of this in context, we cannot view the *Blackfish* effect in isolation as one documentary that did everything right and so much better than any previous documentary. Nor can we disregard decades of pro-whale advocacy in the United States that set the stage for *Blackfish* (and its many supporters) capitalising on this strategic moment.

Recommendations

In order to maximise impact, reach the greatest number of audience members who will either encourage others to watch or influence them with word-of-mouth information sharing, there are several lessons learned, as listed by Chattoo,[51] that animal activists can incorporate when using documentary film to advocate for change. These lessons have been critiqued in this chapter by situating them within theories on media effects (accumulation) and activism: (i) amplified community

51 Chattoo 2016.

and sustained grassroots activism; (ii) strategic distribution; (iii) media coverage; (iv) social action embedded in the story; (v) emotion; and (vi) measurable impact.

These six strategic tools are now, as a result of this analysis, explained and contextualised as a potential primer or model for activists interested in using media and education to evoke change. Furthermore, we propose the following additional recommendations for filmmakers and animal advocacy groups who want to replicate something like the *Blackfish* effect on any animal protection issue.

To learn from accumulation theory, think holistically about your animal issue in the context of the past and current political, legal, sociocultural and media landscape that contributes to a favourable climate of public opinion on your issue. Is the timing ripe for your documentary? Or maybe you want to get in early to set the foundation for establishing your issue as a problem worthy of attention so that other media-makers and activists can build upon it in future years. Capitalising on political opportunities is part of the lessons activists can follow from the sociology literature on social movements, along with successfully mobilising resources and strategically framing compelling messages.[52]

For filmmakers, as part of the framing aspect of creating your documentary, first find an angle on the animal protection issue that is newsworthy or has already gained some public attention, so you know it has traction. This may mean that rather than exposing the broader issue/problem, you talk about it like a case study and home in on a specific newsworthy event/incident with compelling characters (named human and nonhuman animal individuals) that can serve as protagonists and antagonists. Because the media and political landscape is still anthropocentric, it is useful to tell a story about how a sympathetic human is victimised/exploited along with a nonhuman animal by the same animal-exploiting industry. The anthropomorphising of the victimised-but-resistant nonhuman animal helps viewers empathise with his/her viewpoint in a familiar way, similar to how we identify with the human character also suffering injustice within the oppressive system that we are called upon to reform or

52 McAdam, McCarthy and Zald 1996.

abolish. The injustice narrative and the bonds between human and nonhuman characters help distinguish it from a standard wildlife documentary and make it a more compelling and emotional story of social change. To increase cultural resonance, even when featuring nonhuman characters, you can draw upon familiar or mythic narrative tropes, shared values that motivate action (like calls for freedom) and/or sympathetic stories of (animal) families or mates ripped apart. Include some human and nonhuman heroic figures too to demonstrate agency and role models for resistance, which can also serve to add an action or thriller element of excitement beyond the typical "talking heads" dialogic documentary format.

Regarding mobilisation of resources, filmmakers should partner with a variety of animal protection, eco protection, and social justice groups for a broader coalition who financially support your documentary and promote it (and can agenda-build on your behalf), including encouraging members to review the films on IMDB, Amazon and other streaming sites. And combine this with a strong and clear call to action within the film (and on its website and social media) that the participating advocacy groups can facilitate as the years go by. Get your documentary screened at important film festivals and win awards in the hopes that this vetting helps you achieve wider acclaim and recognition that attracts the backing of a media network that can distribute your film to mainstream international audiences, as CNN so crucially did for *Blackfish*. That media company can help you reach your goal of gaining broader exposure beyond the activist community that is already onboard (extend your audience so you are not just "preaching to the choir").

In the months and years after your documentary is released, ride the momentum of the issue/story's life as it unfolds, by agenda-building in the news media every time a newsworthy achievement or setback extends the life of the story (e.g., lawsuits). Your social media following will build over the years with continued updated postings. Have advocacy groups mention the award-winning documentary in press releases to show the ongoing relevance of the film and the importance/prominence of the animal protection issue itself as something worthy of public critique and reform – reforms that will benefit both human and nonhuman animals.

Conclusion

In her book *Story Movements: How Documentaries Empower People and Inspire Social Change*, Chattoo notes that "the steady drumbeat of public criticism, negative media coverage, and unrelenting activism became known as the *Blackfish* effect. In 2016, SeaWorld announced a stunning corporate policy change – the end of its profitable orca shows."[53] This is as tidy a description of what would be predicted by accumulation theory as one might want.[54] Based on our analysis of other documentary films dedicated to eradicating the use of captive orcas in entertainment, the making, marketing and steady public commentary on the film made it unique in its effectiveness as an activist tool. But is this success limited to this one film? No. As described in the sections above, other films, social media activism and news stories then took the ball and ran with it, generating even more public awareness and accumulating through persistence and consistence the kind of momentum needed to generate actual social, psychological, economic and regulatory changes.

One might argue that *Blackfish*, and any effects, were a long time ago: a film premiere in 2013, stock and attendance response in the years immediately following, and disavowal by SeaWorld of any impact. And yet, in July 2020, "[s]ix years after SeaWorld Entertainment was sued for allegedly deceiving stockholders about the damaging impact the *Blackfish* documentary was having on theme park attendance", a federal judge awarded SeaWorld's investors $65 million in what is called the "*Blackfish* settlement".[55] This award was the outcome of a 2014 class-action lawsuit brought against the entertainment venue. SeaWorld was not required to admit to any wrongdoing; the judge noted that:

> social media reaction to "Blackfish" remained elevated. Consumers contacted SeaWorld and vowed never to visit its parks because of

53 Chattoo 2020, 110.

54 DeFleur and Dennis 1994/1996.

55 Weisberg 2020.

> "Blackfish." Additionally, "Blackfish" publicity led partners and sponsors to end or table partnerships and promotions with SeaWorld.[56]

The *Blackfish* effect was thus the culmination of these efforts that "forced SeaWorld to fundamentally change its business model in order to meet the dictates of this new ethos and to re-establish its postcrisis legitimacy".[57] Can SeaWorld regain its legitimacy? That remains to be seen but appears unlikely.

Looking at the promotional and coverage efforts through the lens of what accumulation theory predicts, we return to the following framing questions:

Did the media focus repeatedly on the issue of cetaceans' use for entertainment?
Yes.

Did the media present a consistent, "more or less uniform" view of SeaWorld?
Yes.

Did the media (television, newspaper, radio, ancillary services) corroborate with parallel reports?
Yes.

Academic literature reveals some strategies to help counteract corporate messages that should be useful for activist organisations. Waller and Iluzada, for example, argue that "three discursive factors drove [the] outcome" of undermining and displacing SeaWorld's captivity narrative: "resonance, credibility, coherence".[58] In the first instance, resonance, the timing was right – over the years the general public was becoming more aware of animal captivity, increasingly sympathetic to the plight of animals and, no doubt, worker conditions. *Blackfish* told a truth, substantiated by experts and experiences, that was more powerful than SeaWorld's efforts to defend its practices.

56 Quoted in Weisberg 2020.
57 Waller and Iluzada 2020, 267.
58 Waller and Iluzada 2020, 237.

Second was credibility. *Blackfish* included credible sources ranging from academic, scholarly experts to ex-trainers and workers. Third was message coherence – the telling of a true story that is coherent, consistent, backed by research as well as testimonials, in a way that resonates with the target audience made the documentary's message stronger than that of SeaWorld's. Furthermore, ensuing interviews, showings and social media sharings extended the momentum of the campaign in a way that was persistent, consistent and corroborated across platforms. Waller and Iluzada sum up the situation as follows:

> Words alone were insufficient to regain SeaWorld's legitimacy; ultimately, the frames of caring and educating had to be evidenced through actions that a public increasingly sensitive to animal rights would recognize as sincere and impactful.[59]

In addition, and this speaks to the notion of our growing resonance with nonhuman animals (especially whales), cultivating an understanding of the animal(s) of concern as "unique actors with intelligible behaviours"[60] is another important element for a successful activist media production.

References

101 Dalmatians (1961). Film. Wolfgang Reitherman, Clyde Geronimi and Hamilton Luske (Dirs). Distributor: Walt Disney Pictures.

101 Dalmatians (1996). Film. Stephen Herek (Dir.). Distributor: Walt Disney Pictures.

A Fall From Freedom (2012). Film. Stan Miniasian (Dir.). Distributor: Discovery Channel.

Almiron, Núria, Matthew Cole and Carrie P. Freeman (2016). *Critical Animal and Media Studies: Communication for Nonhuman Animal Advocacy.* New York: Routledge.

Babe (1995). Film. Chris Noonan (Dir.). Distributor: Universal Pictures.

Blackfish (2013). Film. Gabriela Cowperthwaite (Dir.). Distributor: CNN Films and Manny O. Productions.

---

59 Waller and Iluzada 2020, 239.

60 Burford and Schutten 2017, 9.

Burford, Caitlyn and Julie M.K. Schutten (2017). International activists and the "*Blackfish* effect": contemplating captive orcas' protest rhetoric through a coherence frame. *Frontiers in Communication* 1(16): 1–11. https://doi.org/10.3389/fcomm.2016.00016.

Carroll, Craig and Maxwell McCombs (2003). Agenda-setting effects of business news on the public's images and opinions about major corporations. *Corporate Reputation Review* 6: 36–46. http://tinyurl.com/snxu9zdu.

Charlotte's Web (2006). Film. Gary Winick (Dir.). Distributor: Paramount.

Chattoo, Caty B. (2016). Anatomy of the "Blackfish effect". *Documentary Magazine*, 23 March. http://tinyurl.com/57nav439.

Chattoo, Caty B. (2020). *Story Movements: How Documentaries Empower People and Inspire Social Change*. New York: Oxford.

Child, Ben (2013). Pixar "switched *Finding Dory* plot" after killer whale documentary row. *Guardian*, 12 August. http://tinyurl.com/muxx9pd4.

Clarke, Lynsey (2017). Disney horror show: master of horror Stephen King reveals he's scared of Bambi – as latest film version of his creepy clown thriller "It" hits cinemas. *Sun*, 4 September. http://tinyurl.com/njeh49db.

Cole, Simon A. and R. Dioso-Villa (2011). Should judges worry about the "CSI Effect"? *Court Review* 47: 20–31. http://tinyurl.com/ynsfa3kc.

DeFleur, Melvin L. and Everette E. Dennis (1994/1996). *Understanding Mass Communication*. Princeton, NJ: Houghton-Mifflin.

Dumbo (1941). Film. Samuel Armstrong, Norman Ferguson, Wilfred Jackson (Dirs). Distributor: Walt Disney Pictures.

Dumbo (2019). Film. Tim Burton (Dir.). Distributor: Walt Disney Studios.

Fechter, Joshua (2018). SeaWorld, company officials to pay more than $5 million to settle fraud charges over "Blackfish" remarks. *Houston Chronicle*, 18 September. http://tinyurl.com/3w6fh96j.

The Fox & the Hound (1981). Film. Ted Berman, Richard Rich and Art Stevens (Dirs). Distributor: Buena Vista.

Gerbner, George (1986). *Television's Mean World*. Philadelphia, PA: Annenberg.

Gilboa, Eytan (2005). The CNN effect: the search for a communication theory of international relations. *Political Communication* 22: 27–44. https://doi.org/10.1080/10584600590908429.

Greenfield, Karl Taro (2014). The whale stays in the picture: facing the backlash over the treatment of its animals, SeaWorld reveals a plan to save itself. *Bloomberg Businessweek*, 24–30 November. http://tinyurl.com/23yucybu.

Grieze, Zoe (2018). The Bambi portal. *Bachelor of Fine Arts Senior Papers* 57. https://openscholarship.wustl.edu/bfa/57.

Hargrove, John and Howard G. Chua-Eoan (2015). *Beneath the Surface: Killer Whales, SeaWorld, and Blackfish*. New York: St Martin's.

Harvey, David (2005). *A Brief History of Neoliberalism*. New York: Oxford University Press.

Hassan, Aisha (2018). The "*Blackfish* effect" is over for SeaWorld – for now. *Quartz*, 6 November. http://tinyurl.com/ycy3e3fs.

Hickman, David (2015). *Blackfish*: proof that documentary can be a powerful force for change. *Conversation*, 11 November. http://tinyurl.com/3xrb5wjc.

Inside the Tanks (2017). Film. Johnny Meah (Dir.). Distributor: Insidethetanks.com.

Keiko: The Untold Story of the Star of Free Willy (2010). Film. Theresa Demarest (Dir.). Distributor: Joshua Records, LLC.

Kirby, Steve (2012). *Death at SeaWorld: Shamu and the Dark Side of Killer Whales in Captivity*. New York: St. Martin's.

Lolita: Slave to Entertainment (2003). Film. Tim Gorski (Dir.). Distributor: Rattle the Cage Productions.

Long Gone Wild (2019). Film. Bill Neal (Dir.). Distributor: Vision Films.

Loy, Lorenda (2016). Media activism and animal advocacy: what's film got to do with it? In Núria Almiron, Matthew Cole and Carrie P. Freeman, eds. *Critical Animal and Media Studies: Communication for Nonhuman Animal Advocacy*, 221–33. New York: Routledge.

Lutts, Ralph A. (1992). The trouble with Bambi: Walt Disney's *Bambi* and the American vision of nature. *Forest and Conservation History* 36: 160–71.

Marino, Lori (2023). Tokitae the orca's legacy. Blog post for The Whale Sanctuary Project. 23 August. http://tinyurl.com/579f3s4m.

McAdam, Doug, John D. McCarthy and Mayer N. Zald (1996). *Comparative Perspectives on Social Movements: Political Opportunities, Mobilizing Structures, and Cultural Framings*. Cambridge: Cambridge University Press.

McCombs, Maxwell (2004). *Setting the Agenda: The Mass Media and Public Opinion*. Malden, MA: Polity.

Medawar, Peter B. (1952). *An Unsolved Problem of Biology*. London: H.K Lewis.

Merskin, Debra (2000). Media theories. *J201 Mass Media & Society*, 3 May. https://pages.uoregon.edu/dmerskin/theories.htm.

Miller, Barbara M. (2010). Community stakeholders and marketplace advocacy: a model of advocacy, agenda building, and industry approval. *Journal of Public Relations Research* 22: 85–112. https://doi.org/10.1080/10627260903170993.

Munarriz, Rick (2018). 3 reasons SeaWorld stock has more than doubled in 2018. *The Motley Fool*, 1 September. http://tinyurl.com/yz2xhdv2.

Neuman, Johanna (1996). *Lights, Camera, War: Is Media Technology Driving International Politics?* New York: St Martin's Press.

Nichols, Bill (2010). *Introduction to Documentary*. Bloomington: Indiana University Press.

Oxford English Dictionary online (2021). Documentary. September. http://tinyurl.com/2ffrjfd7.

Parkinson, Claire (2020). *Animals, Anthropomorphism and Mediated Encounters*. New York: Routledge.

Parsons, E.C.M. and Naomi A. Rose (2018). The *Blackfish* effect: corporate and policy change in the face of shifting public opinion on captive cetaceans. *Tourism in Marine Environments* 13(2–3): 73–83. http://tinyurl.com/22pcmh5a.

Rowley, Loretta and Kevin A. Johnson (2015). Anthropomorphic anthropomorphism and the rhetoric of *Blackfish*. *Environmental Communication* 12(6): 825–39. http://tinyurl.com/4t5cx5e5.

Saving Flipper (2009). Film. Savas Karakas and Sibel Mesci (Dirs). Distributor: Journeyman Pictures.

Soderberg, Annika (2021). The lasting impact of the documentary *Blackfish*. *Medium*. 12 December. http://tinyurl.com/2we673dh.

Investment Guru (2019). SeaWorld records positive performance after years of falling revenue. *Investment Guru*, 6 March. http://tinyurl.com/ykbjfk6f.

Shelton, Donald E. (2008). The "CSI effect": does it really exist? *National Institute of Justice* 259: 1–6. http://tinyurl.com/mthwzmdm.

The Cove (2009). Film. Louie Psihoyos (Dir.). Distributor: Participant Media.

Voiceless – A Blue Freedom Film (2016). Film. Katie Emmons and Abbie Emmons (Dirs). Distributor: Blue Freedom, Inc.

Waller, Randall L. and Christina A. Iluzada (2020). *Blackfish* and SeaWorld: a case study in the framing of a crisis. *International Journal of Business Communication* 57(2): 227–43. https://doi.org/10.1177/2329488419884139.

Weisberg, Lori (2020). Judge clears way for SeaWorld to pay investors $65 million in "Blackfish" settlement. *Los Angeles Times*, 25 July. http://tinyurl.com/ye242wwa.

Wills, Matthew (2016). The problematic influence of Disney's "Bambi". *JSTOR*, 3 March. daily.jstor.org/the-trouble-with-bambi.

Wynne, Sharon Kennedy (2017). Facing identity crisis and slumping profits, can SeaWorld rebuild? *Tampa Bay Times*, 11 August. http://tinyurl.com/478cmk4f.

Zimmermann, Tim (2010). The killer in the pool. *Outside*, 30 July. https://www.outsideonline.com/outdoor-adventure/environment/killer-pool.

9

Meat the Future

An interview with Liz Marshall

Interviewed by Claire Parkinson

Claire Parkinson (CP): Why did you become a filmmaker?

Liz Marshall (LM): I was initially drawn to image-making through photography. I bought my first camera at the age of 16. Looking back, I can see that I fell in love with framing the world from behind the lens from that day forward. Still images naturally transitioned to moving images after helping a roommate, who was a film student, with a film assignment. I had been a core member of a studio-style theatre company as a teenager and came to realise I was not really interested in being an actor. The interest in filmmaking was so immediate and clear for me that I applied to Ryerson University (now called the Toronto Metropolitan University) for an undergrad degree, and was accepted. I was told it was a very difficult process to be accepted and so that was a huge validation for me. That was 1989. I attended the BAA program and followed an instinct for non-fiction storytelling. I think that's the best way to describe my initial process, and from there moving forward one experience led to the next. I was especially drawn to social justice issues and to character-driven storytelling, and continued to develop and hone my artistry, skills, passion and knowledge to help create change in the world through the medium of film and television.

CP: Could you say more about the circumstances that inspired your interest in social justice issues?

LM: From an early age, the ethics of caring for one's neighbour, for the poor and disadvantaged, for the land, questioning capitalism and consumerism, were values passed down to me and my siblings. When my brothers wanted to play "war" with toy guns given to them, our mother forbade them to do so in her household. Being aware at such a tender age of the unjust infliction of poverty in the world meant that we naturally finished the food on our plates. We contributed part of our allowance each month to a family living with leprosy in the Philippines. My father, a natural cook, forbade sugar in his household and grew a vegetable garden. Our mother would quietly insert "Mother, Sister, Woman, She" each time "God" and "Man" and multiple other male descriptors and pronouns dominated the scriptures at the Anglican Church we attended. These early teachings made a deep impression. My form and style of activism eventually actualised through my camera and film work. When our parents were together (the first five years of my life), they were community-minded activists at the centre of a grassroots Christian movement in the late 60s to early 70s. In my 2018 feature documentary *Midian Farm*, I explore a formative piece of my history living on a back-to-the-land commune in Ontario [Canada], at the time when my father was elevated to that of a charismatic leader. In reflecting on such a childhood, and recognising ways I have carried the torch forward in my life and work, I am also wary of the shadow side to activism. In the urgency of life's many emergencies, there lies the risk of neglecting loved ones and oneself. Whereas, loving and caring for those closest to us, human and animal, is also radical in this hard world.

CP: How do you, as a filmmaker, understand your relationship to activism?

LM: The more I entered the realm of documentary, I realised it has tremendous possibility. And the appetite for documentary cinema, as a sort of renaissance form of storytelling, has been increasing over the years, which also includes impact documentaries as its own genre in a sense. Impact documentary films reach audiences at the grassroots but at every tier and all over the world, to foster dialogue, create awareness, behavioural and social change. There are many case studies that tell us this is true. It is evidence based. Animal advocacy and filmmaking is an important marriage, to educate and inspire diverse audiences about animal issues.

CP: Would you describe yourself as an animal activist?

LM: Oh, yes, I am, but rather view myself as an *intersectionalist*, one who cares equally about human and nonhuman animals and Mother Nature. I have grown into this awareness over time, largely through my body of work which has given me unique life experiences, and as such has profoundly influenced my moral compass and world perspective. I started my career with an eye on human rights issues, specifically the explosion of third-wave feminism and identity politics in the mid-90s. I documented feminist folk-punk icon Ani DiFranco as she toured parts of Canada and the US – this was a very fun and inspiring entry into filmmaking! From the early to mid-2000s I worked on global documentaries about war-affected children, censorship for writers, sweatshop labour and the HIV/AIDS pandemic across sub-Saharan Africa. These films were used for awareness campaigns, creating impact for audiences at the grassroots and also in the mainstream. The experience also deeply impacted us, the people behind the lens committed to exploring hard-hitting social justice issues. In the late 2000s I chose to slow down and take a different approach to filmmaking, and that's when I pursued independently produced feature-length documentaries, licensed and supported by the film industry. I immersed myself in environmental and animal rights themes [*Water on the Table*; *The Ghosts in Our Machine*; *Meat the Future*]. Longform storytelling demands more time to follow a story, which is what I wanted. As well, I was able to access more viable resources to produce a high production value. These films are showcased on multiple platforms, including being situated on the world stage at film festivals and through other public events. This meant connecting in very meaningful ways with industry, peers and organisations, and with those who are on the ground, championing films as tools for social engagement and change.

Coming back to your question about whether I am an animal activist: I've always been an animal person in my basic nature. As a child I had strong bonds with dogs and cats alike, and with the sheep, goats and chickens on the commune I spent formative years at, and with the wildlife and sea life I grew up with and around during visits to BC's Sunshine Coast, where I now live. In growing up in a socially conscious family focused on human liberation, we loved *National Geographic*, ate meat and never discussed animal liberation. But in 1989, after reading John Robbins' bestseller *Diet for a New America*, I instantly rejected meat and made the connection. I noticed, however, over the years I remained vegetarian and didn't understand veganism until Lorena Elke challenged me to commit myself to making a feature-length animal rights documentary – and that's when I went deep inside the issues and developed a new consciousness. In 2011, we began the journey of making *The Ghosts in Our Machine* and released the film to critical acclaim in 2013. A deep unavoidable awareness of global pervasive animal exploitation infused my life during the making of *Ghosts* and as such my ultimate goal for the film was to remove people's blinders and motivate personal transformation, because that is what happened for me in the making of that film. I am an animal activist. It's been a life journey with layers and nuance, one intrinsically linked to other liberation movements. They intersect for me.

CP: How would you describe your style of filmmaking?

LM: My methodology depends on the film, but I tend to fuse a cinematic and character-driven approach to exploring big issues and questions. I strive to work with a great team in creating that visual language; to immerse people. They're not biographies, they're social-issue films with a protagonist or a cast of human characters (participants) at the centre. To guide people to see the world in new ways. And there is a strong intellectual motivation in filmmaking because documentaries are educational tools.

CP: Could you say more about the storytelling techniques you favour in your films? Do you aim to have a 3-act structure?

LM: Yes, a 3-act structure. I do aim for commercial viability but am aware that my films do not necessarily satisfy the conventions of a 3-act structure. Instead, they tend to be open-ended, more philosophical and less polemical, not fast-paced. Generally, Act 1 is an introduction to the protagonist(s) and to the conflict or obstacle that s/he is up against. Act 2 delves into the journey of the protagonist. Act 3 aims to provide a resolution, and importantly leaves the audience with questions. External circumstances/issues impacting the protagonist are the underpinning, and it's critical to get the issue across coherently without simplifying what is inherently complex. I am equally drawn to the interiority of the protagonist, as this layer of storytelling guides audiences to personally identify. Interiority is expressed through close-ups, pacing, sound or music, and prioritising personal details. I strive for the balance between words (interviews and talking) and cinematic observation, images, tone and mood. The editing process is epic in trying to find that balance.

CP: What is it particularly about film and your own films that has enabled the public conversation about animal exploitation to change?

LM: When it comes to animal exploitation, we need a systems overhaul, and change also has to occur at the personal individual level. For example, I boycott animal industries as a daily form of practice. In making *The Ghosts in Our Machine*, I was motivated to find gentle ways to trigger people into awareness, into consciousness, to have a deep epiphany about how pervasive the use of animals is, how invisible the topic is and how complicit humanity is. With *Meat the Future*, it's really a story about awe and wonder, and viable change that is underway to transform industrial animal agriculture in our lifetime. I think *Meat the Future* will enable a concurrent conversation about animal exploitation, geared at people unwilling to give up meat.

CP: In Ghosts *and in* Meat the Future *you take the audience on a journey. How and when do you decide on the storyline for your films? What's that process?*

LM: With *The Ghosts in Our Machine*, Lorena [Elke] and I had talked, and were in conversation with each other for a number of years about trying to find an angle that I could pitch to the film industry. Approach is everything. You need to lead with a story, and a relatable person. So, when I started learning about Jo-Anne McArthur's photography, and the work she was doing at that point in her career, I found it very interesting. I love films about photographers and thought it would be a compelling entry point, to focus on a person whose images expose the animal issue through a gentle and principled aesthetic that inspires empathy. As a feminist I like to elevate women's stories, so I felt it was the right angle, I had a strong instinct for it. In Canadian history, *The Ghosts in Our Machine* is one of the first, or the first animal rights feature-length documentary to have had mainstream film industry support, and that was a message. The film was part of a zeitgeist. I learned in a very profound way about the resistance that exists in society at large for the animal issue, but also about the incredible shift that was taking place, and continues to take place. With *Meat the Future*, my motivation was to research and find a character-driven story about a potential solution. I was very interested in the news surrounding the cultured meatball prototype that Dr Uma Valeti and his little start-up Memphis Meats unveiled in early 2016. It struck me immediately that growing real meat from animal cells was ground zero of the next agricultural revolution. The world needs hopeful narratives more than ever, and alt protein innovation is a fascinating area that deserves a spotlight. *Meat the Future* is about the reinvention of meat, without the use of animals, which is mind-blowing really. It's a film infused with awe and wonder.

CP: Do you think of the two films as being companion films?

LM: Yes, absolutely. *Meat the Future* is a companion film to my body of work because industrial animal agriculture is an animal issue, a human issue and an environmental issue. Ninety-nine per cent of meat that people are consuming comes from industrialised large-scale meat production. It is the intersection where urgent big-world issues collide.

CP: So why particularly the topic of cellular agriculture for Meat the Future? *What was it particularly that attracted you and said, this is going to make a great story?*

LM: Well, I wanted to focus on something unique, something that will add to the conversation from a different angle. I chose a very novel topic; something the world doesn't know about. And, of course, it was a challenge and a risk, because Memphis Meats (now Upside Foods) could have folded and gone under, or the industry could have faded. You get to a point, I believe, where you do your research and follow your instinct. And that's what I did. Luckily the topic only continues to accelerate.

CP: Why do you think there has been increased interest in the subject?

LM: Largely, I think it's the time we are living in collectively. We need solutions to the way meat is produced, and this viewpoint is accepted more broadly than even a few years ago. That said, cultivated meat is not a solution everyone is or will be onboard with. It is a polarised topic right now. There are those who recognise cultivated meat and fish innovation as an obvious and welcome solution to the problems facing the global food system and supply, its impact on animals, the environment and human health. Others view it as unnatural and don't trust the idea of breakthrough technology and science producing animal protein without the use of animals. Some don't accept it strictly due to religious beliefs. Others are waiting to see if cultivated meat and fish indeed comes to market, becomes regulated and produced at scale. Others (maybe most?) simply want to taste it to be convinced. It is early days, and the interest and awareness will continue to grow.

CP: Did you intend for Meat the Future *to have either a pro-animal rights or a pro-environmental or pro-vegan message or all of the above?*

LM: Well, technically cultivated meat is not vegan. Yet there are many vegans behind the birth of the industry, with a mission to reduce animal use and suffering. And that is a motivation for me too. That message is inherent in the film, but it is not front and centre. The need for overall humanity and sustainability is a strong through line.

CP: With it being a subject that is so under the radar, or has been under the radar for a lot of people, how did you get it funded?

LM: Perseverance! CBC's Documentary Channel is the broadcaster behind *Meat the Future*. We also had the support of the Redford Center. For journalistic reasons, we did not accept funding for production of the film from mission-driven investors or donors.

CP: What were the main challenges in making Meat the Future?

LM: Getting the film fully financed was challenging. Because this kind of film needed to take place over time, between 2016 and 2019. And that's the strength of the film: the passage of time in witnessing the birth of an industry. Funders challenged me largely around a very valid concern, which was whether the film would come across as a promotion for a company. This is why it is essential to maintain a reasonable arm's length editorial distance from your subject, which we did. The main challenge we faced in making the film was gaining access to active and dramatic behind-the-scenes content, where we could truly witness risks and challenges and victories – the stuff that is exciting and nail-biting and fascinating to watch! Start-up territory comes with a volume of intellectual property and firewalls. That said, we successfully secured some unprecedented access.

CP: What did you learn from making this film?

LM: Aside from learning about the business and science and politics of the cultivated meat industry, I learned a lot about start-up culture. In following a CEO and his small team over time, I witnessed the risk and ambition involved in attempting to innovate something revolutionary. I already knew about conventional animal agriculture, and the world's dependence on that system for animal protein consumption, but in filming scenes at the USDA [United States Department of Agriculture] and FDA [US Food and Drug Administration], I witnessed two worlds colliding: the cultivated meat and fish start-ups, and the ranchers and farmers producing conventional meat.

CP: The Ghosts in Our Machine *had a large female audience particularly in the 18 to 24 age group. What are the differences or the similarities in the audiences for* Meat the Future *and then* Ghosts in Our Machine?

LM: They are very different films. *The Ghosts in Our Machine* has a female protagonist and the goal of *Ghosts* is to inspire empathy for nonhuman animals, so I think that automatically speaks more to a female demographic. *Meat the Future* is cerebral, has a male protagonist, is a film about science and business, and is ultimately aimed at meat consumers. I anticipate a higher interest from a male demographic, which is good because more men eat meat than women. The main similarity is that animal advocates are passionate about both films!

CP: We only briefly see some images of large-scale intensive animal agriculture in Meat the Future. *How did you decide what and how much imagery of farmed animals to include in the film?*

LM: There's not a random image, word or music note. Everything is considered. We laboured over this question tremendously; how much screen time do we give to witnessing the horrors of conventional animal agriculture? We need to see and understand what the problem is before zooming into the solution. So, it was very important to me to find a way to include that degree of dramatic tension and impact, without being polemical.

CP: In that key sequence which does show intensive animal agriculture, how did you arrive at the decision to include those particular images?

LM: So, let's unpack that sequence. There's no voiceover because I didn't want people to feel schooled or for the viewership experience to be disrupted by a cerebral narrative. I wanted at least half of the images to be drone, from above, and then to move to the ground footage, inside the factories, the barns, where we see the animals at eye level. It was a way of guiding people into the uncomfortable truth. Here it is from above. Okay, that's safe. Drones are very effective in communicating scale. And later in the sequence when the headlines appear from articles, the gory footage is in smaller boxes of animal slaughter. The approach was "less is more". By the end of that sequence, people realise; okay, boom, cultured meat could be a major solution. Right?

CP: The film is narrated by Jane Goodall with Moby as an executive producer. Can you tell me how they became involved in the project?

LM: During 2020, Moby emailed me out of the blue and asked to see the film. I was thrilled and shared a private link with him. The next day he said he loved the film and wanted to know how he could help. This was excellent timing, because while the film was on the global film festival circuit getting initial press, it had not been sold outside of Canada. We were in the heart of COVID, experiencing a depressing lull. One thing led to the next and Moby offered to be an Executive Producer, and suggested we repackage it for an international release with some celebrity narration. He then opened the door to Dr Jane Goodall, and adding Jane's iconic recognisable voice to the film was such an honour and gave us all a lot of hope. We were also able to include a few of Moby's songs, which further elevates the film. The repackaging was complete in 2021, and by April of 2022 the film was released in the US and select territories.

CP: We've seen a lot more celebrity involvement in animal activist documentaries recently. What are your thoughts on this?

LM: My answer is fairly simple, in that I think it's an effective way of elevating the message. At the same time, I wonder if the same small pool of AR [animal rights] celebrities and filmmakers will reach a dead-end with this approach?

CP: Meat the Future *was a film that was broadcast with plans for a theatrical release. Were there any challenges in trying to deal with both of those scenarios?*

LM: The film had a robust release in Canada in May and June 2020. We were on the main network of CBC during the heart of the lockdown when news reportage was covering slaughterhouse, meat-packing plant closures, but sadly we could not have a theatrical release. The COVID landscape drastically changed distribution plans for *Meat the Future* and many other documentaries being released at the same time. The Hot Docs Film Festival programmed *Meat the Future* as a Special Presentation Premiere (in 2020) and exciting plans were underway. I was speaking to one of Canada's top theatrical distributors and then boom, we were hit by the pandemic, which disrupted the path we would have liked for the film – in-person screenings with Q&As and panels, and the ability to interact with audiences around the globe. Yet *Meat the Future* is a COVID-themed topic because cultivated meat is a potential solution to future health pandemics, like zoonosis. In that regard, the film became more relevant.

CP: In the last 15 years we've seen an increase in the number of feature-length documentaries on animal rights and pro-vegan issues. Why is this? What's happening? What's changed?

LM: I think it's a combination of forces. The popularity and demand for documentary is there. Certainly, with film festivals, also with subscriber platforms and broadcast, and SVOD [subscription video on demand] and VOD [video on demand], and at the grassroots and for educational use. There's a growing appetite for uncensored truthful stories about animals. The moral imperative is stronger, and from various angles, such as the climate emergency and health pandemics.

CP: Meat the Future *and* The Ghosts in Our Machine *had campaigns that sat alongside the films. How important is it to have a campaign?*

LM: Essential. Social impact documentaries are strongest when accompanied by ancillary educational materials as well as active, intentional engagement with audiences. These tools and activities extend the film's linear narrative into the world by providing additional context, research sources, and interactivity with viewers. Typically, the film itself functions as a campaign centrepiece, and a website and social channels, premieres, live and online events, panels and interviews build an ecosystem of engagement to facilitate awareness. If a documentary has a Call to Action then it becomes a focal point. The final phase of our multi-year commitment to *Meat the Future* (during the COVID pandemic) included a global impact evaluation and impact report. We worked with a professional evaluator to produce an in-depth 66-page report. From inception (2016) to exhibition (2020) to impact (2022) we evaluated and charted the global reach, influence and legacy of *Meat the Future*. All of our findings, both qualitative and quantitative, are contained therein, available (for free) as a downloadable resource from the film's website. The mission of the film was to ignite global awareness and discussion about an idea whose time has come, and our impact report is a capstone showing how the film has reached, educated and influenced many thousands of viewers around the globe. Among our findings, we know that 100 per cent of viewers learned something new from watching *Meat the Future*. Ninety-eight per cent agreed that raising and slaughtering animals for food contributes to climate change and global warming. Ninety-five per cent agreed that cultivated meat and seafood is likely to have benefits for society. As quoted by *Forbes* magazine (2022), "With the popularity of *Meat The Future* and its impact on the sector, it's more evident how vital media is to the understanding and education needed for the mass adoption of positive sustainable developments."

CP: A while ago there was a debate around impact and having to have a campaign because it was needed to measure impact and that was important to satisfy funders. Do you think that because of this the filmmaking gets lost at all, or do you see the two things sit together very well?

LM: *Meat the Future* was part of the inaugural Climate Story Lab, produced by the Doc Society and Exposure Labs, and this was a question posed to all of us during that lab. Ultimately, your documentary needs to be a film that stands alone separate from a campaign. A campaign should augment your film, providing additional context, and the opportunity to educate and engage audiences to think and to learn. I do think some documentaries lack story and emotional depth because they are so intent on pushing a campaign agenda. The challenge with *Meat the Future* when it comes to impact is that there is not an action item for audiences. We aren't asking people to go vegan, or to buy a product. Rather, we are asking people to open their minds to what is possible. Science and food innovation has a major role to play in today's changing world, for animals, towards a humane and sustainable future for all.

CP: You spent nearly four years making Meat the Future, *followed by time involved in promoting the film. Is it difficult to move on to another project after being so immersed in one film?*

LM: It is always a bit difficult at first to switch gears after full immersion, but mostly it is liberating and rewarding to be at the stage where you can confidently move on to new projects, knowing that the film is available, and with good partners. You want to be able to step back and say, "I did all I can do, and now it will hopefully reach people for years to come." *The Ghosts in Our Machine* was five years of my life, and *Meat the Future* has been six years. It's like getting a PhD in a specific field of study. Finally, I will say that it's important to avoid burnout, which means having an exit plan.

CP: Would you ever consider making a film from the animal's point of view?

LM: Yes. I think that would be a beautiful exploration, not as a documentary but rather as fiction, as magic realism. Animals are another world, yet [they are] kin, so such a film would raise and pose many important questions. A wonderful creative and moral challenge.

References

Wilson, Josh (2022). How 'Meat the Future' helped inspire the cultivated meat trend. *Forbes*. https://bit.ly/421t5zV.

Part Three

Celebrity activism

10

From Brigitte Bardot to Pamela Anderson

Celebrity activists in France and the United States

Elizabeth Cherry

Introduction

When people in the United States and Western Europe think of vegan animal rights supporters, many different images may come to mind. First, they might actually know a vegan, as the number of vegans has skyrocketed in recent years.[1] Second, they might have a negative, stereotypical image of vegan activists due to negative portrayals of vegans in the media.[2] Or third, they might think of long-time celebrities associated with vegan and animal rights campaigns, such as Paul McCartney, Joaquin Phoenix and Pamela Anderson. In this chapter, I focus on the third image, that of vegan celebrities.

Celebrities who publicly support veganism and animal rights provide an excellent case study for understanding animal activism both on and off screen. Having made their name through the media and entertainment realm, celebrities can "migrate" to a new realm[3] to become animal activists. Their name recognition and star power can bring much-needed and wanted attention to animal issues. Celebrities

1 Šimčikas 2018.
2 Cole and Morgan 2011.
3 Driessens 2013.

may act as "cultural intermediaries",[4] helping audiences learn about a particular food issue, preparation or new food item. Previous research on the relationship between celebrities and animal activism has focused primarily on the media coverage related to celebrities' endorsements[5] and, to a certain extent, what activists[6] and targets[7] think of various animal rights tactics. Previous research has also examined tactical choices at the individual level, with "tastes in tactics",[8] and at the organisational level, with "institutional logics".[9]

In my own previous research on strategic and tactical decision-making in the animal rights movements in France and the United States, I employed the institutional logics perspective to explain how animal rights organisations made such choices at the organisational level.[10] In this chapter, I focus on what individual activists think of celebrity use as a tactic. Such a focus helps researchers better understand how and why such tactics are used, or not, and the justifications and thoughts that go into their use or dismissal as a tactic. It also helps researchers better understand the different trajectories of social movements, especially when focusing on the same social movement in different countries and cultures.

To understand the use of celebrities in promoting veganism and animal rights, I focus on activists' reactions to the tactic of using vegan celebrities: What do animal rights activists think of celebrity supporters? What use are such celebrity supporters to their work? How does the utility of celebrity supporters differ in different cultures? This chapter investigates how animal rights activists in France and the United States considered and used celebrities and the media in their activism, analysing data from 72 in-depth interviews and nearly three years of participant observation with activists in both countries. This chapter shows that while most of the activists I interviewed in both countries appreciated the tactic, it was not available to French activists

4 Piper 2015.
5 Cole and Morgan 2011; Craig 2019; Doyle 2016; Jeffreys 2016; Lundahl 2020.
6 Gaarder 2011b.
7 Mika 2006.
8 Jasper 1997.
9 Thornton, Ocasio and Lounsbury 2012.
10 Cherry 2016.

due to cultural constraints. Further, while activists in both countries shared concerns about the negative reputation of certain celebrities, the content of the concerns differed by country – US activists were more concerned with negative gender stereotyping, while French activists were more concerned with negative political associations. These findings have implications for both researchers and activists.

Media coverage of veganism and animal rights

Vegetarianism and animal protection movements have long been ridiculed in the media, starting with the early movements of the 19th century.[11] While animal protection movements have gone through many changes since this time, the "second wave" of animal rights activism that promotes veganism as a central tenet started in the 1990s.[12] During this second wave, media coverage has especially stigmatised veganism and animal rights activism – that is, when the media bother to discuss animal rights at all.

Media coverage differs by country. In the United States, from 1990 to 2014, the *New York Times* published 3,179 articles on animal rights. This was over 15 times as many articles as appeared in the nine top daily newspapers in France during that same time.[13] However, the same search in French newspapers showed that the environmental movement and the labour movement had ample representation, demonstrating the focused lack of coverage of animal rights in France.[14]

Media coverage also differs by organisation. In her analysis of coverage of animal activism in the *New York Times*, Erin Evans found that organisations with well-established identities as media "characters" that produce attention-grabbing media content are more likely to be covered by the media than other organisations.[15] Their transgressive

11 Shprintzen 2013.
12 Cherry 2016.
13 Cherry 2016, 84.
14 Cherry 2016, 86.
15 Evans 2016.

tactics, in comparison to more moderate organisations like the ASPCA or the Humane Society of the United States (HSUS), garnered them more attention, and more graphic descriptions of their grievances.

Once veganism became more prominently featured in newsprint media coverage, researchers studied how the media framed the movement. In their study of news articles on veganism in all UK national newspapers during the calendar year 2007, Matthew Cole and Karen Morgan found the coverage to be overwhelmingly negative, with nearly 75 per cent of all articles published portraying veganism as negative in some way.[16] These newspapers ridiculed veganism, described veganism as a deprivation, as difficult or, alternately, as a fad. Of vegans themselves, the news coverage called them overly sensitive to animals, or hostile.[17]

By 2014, media coverage of veganism had noticeably improved. Outi Lundahl conducted a study of one particular newspaper in England, the *Daily Mail*, to better understand the transition from wholly negative to more positive.[18] Looking at coverage from 2008 to 2014, Lundahl found the most common frame, and the frame that increased the most, was veganism as "celebrity fashion". That is, as more and more celebrities became vegan, ate at vegan restaurants or promoted veganism, the media coverage improved. The second, and related, frame was that of veganism as a "healthy diet", as opposed to previous coverage of veganism as vitamin deficient and sure to lead to health problems. The third theme, however, was a continuation of previous negative coverage – the newspaper also framed veganism as extreme and as evidence of "moral decay".

While the frames may have largely become more positive towards veganism, Lundahl found that the news coverage did not discuss any ethical, moral or political reasons for being vegan. Rather, the focus was on the celebrities and veganism as celebrity fashion. In this sense, veganism was presented as a mode of consumption, rather than a protest. Beyond the *Daily Mail*, more and more researchers found that as more celebrities became vegan, the media coverage of veganism

16 Cole and Morgan 2011.
17 Cole and Morgan 2011, 139.
18 Lundhal 2020.

changed. The coverage became more positive, but it was lacking in any discussion of ethics, morals or politics. This relationship was purposeful. Media portrayals of veganism were positive only when they focused on veganism as an individual lifestyle or dietary choice, rather than as an ethical commitment.[19] In some cases, this was because the celebrities in question were not necessarily vegan at all, much less vegan for animal rights reasons. Instead, they were temporarily following a "plant-based" diet for health or medical purposes, as prescribed by a doctor, as in the examples of Venus Williams and Bill Clinton.[20] Thus, the "plant-based" diet is portrayed as a "cleanse", not as a political statement.[21] This type of coverage may be likened to "spectacular environmentalism" in the sense that the so-called environmentalism is primarily a spectacle that distracts and depoliticises.[22] Veganism thus becomes more marketable and consumable as a lifestyle practice when it has been depoliticised in this way.[23]

These analyses of media coverage and media framing help researchers understand the various ways in which veganism and animal rights are portrayed by the media and thus, potentially, how they are understood by audiences. This direct media–celebrity relationship does not fully capture the range of ways celebrities use their influence for causes they support, like lending their likeness to social movement organisations in campaigns. This chapter aims to better understand the relationship of celebrities to activists, as activists attempt to choose among the various tactics they have at their disposal.

Celebrities as a cultural tool

As with any tactic available to activists, celebrities are a cultural tool[24] that activists can choose to deploy or not. Different tools, or tactics,

19 Doyle 2016.
20 Doyle 2016; Jallinoja, Vinnari and Niva 2019.
21 Jallinoja, Vinnari and Niva 2019.
22 Goodman, Littler et al. 2016, 680.
23 Doyle 2016; Driessens 2013.
24 Swidler 1986.

serve different purposes, and celebrities can serve a variety of purposes related to media attention. For example, PETA (People for the Ethical Treatment of Animals) began with a focus on getting their message out primarily through news outlets, and then turned to celebrity activism to bring animal rights to larger audiences, who might not consume traditional news reports, and to stay "stylistically current".[25]

These spectacular, celebrity-based approaches have been critiqued by feminist animal rights activists due to their reliance on sex appeal and the male gaze to garner attention.[26] Focus groups with non-activists also revealed that women who are not animal rights activists responded negatively to advertisements featuring nude and scantily clad women.[27] At times, Marie Mika noted, their moral shock was due to the animal rights message, such as an image of a nude woman whose body was labelled with various cuts of meat, like a cow, which is often the goal of such ads. The ads that purely used sex appeal to garner attention, such as women wearing lettuce leaves like a bikini, garnered the attention of the men respondents, who said they were only interested in the beautiful celebrities and not in the animal rights message.[28]

What do celebrities bring to social movements? Celebrities contribute authority and attention to a cause,[29] and given a platform like network television, celebrities can bring important attention to various issues.[30] In his compilation of research relating to "celebrity capital", Olivier Driessens[31] notes that previous studies found that celebrities bring attention,[32] favourability and reputational capital,[33] and media visibility.[34] This chapter shows that these potential benefits of using celebrities do not always work together, depending on the

25 Simonson 2001.
26 Gaarder 2011a; Gaarder 2011b.
27 Mika 2006.
28 Mika 2006.
29 Brockington 2009.
30 Craig 2019.
31 Driessens 2013.
32 van Krieken 2012.
33 Hunter, Burgers and Davidsson 2009.
34 Cronin and Shaw 2002; Heinich 2012.

celebrity. Many of the activists I interviewed were concerned with using particular celebrities, because of their lack of favourability.

To better understand the use of celebrities by activists, it is useful to differentiate among the different meanings of celebrity – or "celebritisation", defined by Driessens as "the societal and cultural changes implied by celebrity".[35] Celebritisation includes three different elements: democratisation, diversification and migration, all of which can be used to help researchers understand celebrities and animal rights. Democratisation refers to the democratising of celebrity itself, meaning that everyday people may become (temporarily) famous, through platforms like reality television or social media.[36] For veganism and animal rights activism, this could refer to vegan YouTubers with hundreds of thousands of followers on social media. Diversification refers to the increasingly diverse realms of celebrity beyond the areas of entertainment and sports. Now, people can be celebrities in politics or gastronomy, like celebrity chefs. For veganism and animal rights activism, celebrity vegan chef and restaurateur Chloe Coscarelli or beloved vegan cookbook author and restaurateur Isa Chandra Moskowitz could exemplify diversification.

Driessens' third element of celebritisation, migration, is most relevant to this chapter. Migration refers to:

> the process through which celebrities use both their relative autonomy as public personality and their celebrity status to develop other professional activities either within their original field or to penetrate other social fields.[37]

Typical examples here include models becoming actors or actors becoming politicians. For animal rights and veganism, actors, singers and other entertainers often become animal rights or vegan activists. Actress Alicia Silverstone and actor Joachin Phoenix are often touted as famous vegans for animal rights reasons, and even non-vegetarian basketball player Yao Ming has spoken out against shark fin

35 Driessens 2013, 643.
36 Driessens 2013.
37 Driessens 2013, 648.

consumption and for shark conservation.[38] In this chapter, I focus on this type of migration from the point of view of animal rights activists themselves. Celebrities who migrate into animal rights activism are tools for activists, another tool alongside other potential tactics. What do activists think about this potential or actual tool? Rather than reading celebrities or understanding the media's framing of them, this chapter will focus on activists' evaluation of using celebrities in their activism.

Methods

The data for this chapter came from an ethnography of animal rights activists in France and the United States. In each country, half of these organisations consisted of the largest national organisations and the other half included local, grassroots groups. In my larger project from this data, I was interested in the relationship between the broader culture in which these activists worked and the types of activism in which they engaged – their strategies and tactics.[39]

For this chapter, I focus on the activists' discussion of their decisions to use (or not to use) celebrities in their work, and I primarily use my interviews as the data, since my fieldwork in both countries primarily included grassroots organisations. From 2005 to 2007, I interviewed 37 French activists from 13 different organisations and 35 US activists from ten organisations. I used the same interview guide in both countries and the interviews ranged from one to four hours in length. I conducted and transcribed all of the French interviews in French, with the exception of four Anglophones. All translations are my own. Activists were offered the choice between public or confidential participation, and I use quotation marks around the pseudonyms for those who chose confidential participation.

I analysed the transcribed interviews and field notes with the qualitative analysis software program ATLAS.ti, using Ragin's

38 Jeffreys 2016.
39 Cherry 2016.

comparative method.[40] This comparative method was necessary for such an approach because this was a case-oriented study, best suited for addressing particular historical outcomes. Case-oriented methods are holistic, treating cases as whole entities and understanding the relations between the parts within the context of the whole. I maintained such attention to the whole of each case by analysing how each social movement worked within the extant culture of the country, as well as how each social movement organisation functioned together within the larger social movement field. Once I understood each part of the French and US social movements as a whole, I then made comparisons between the two movements. Using this analytic method also helped me explicate the macro–micro link, one often ignored in international comparative research where macro-level investigations predominate.

US activists

My interviews with US activists revealed four main themes. First, activists regarded celebrities as a positive tool for activism, recognising that celebrities were useful in promoting veganism and animal rights, such as making veganism "hip". However, the US activists I interviewed also harboured two main concerns about using celebrities as a tactic in their activism: celebrities could be a distraction from the main issue of animal rights, and celebrities with bad reputations could lead to stereotyping of activists. Finally, the activists I spoke to found celebrities to be the most useful to their work when the celebrities facilitated opportunities for activist–target interactions, such as musicians inviting activist organisations to have tables at their concerts. I elaborate on these findings below.

Positive: Celebrities help make animal rights and veganism "hip"

As noted above, a significant strand of the literature on celebrity activism argues that celebrities have been useful for making veganism mainstream. For example, the *Daily Mail*, which had been the most

40 Ragin 1987.

negative newspaper towards veganism in Cole and Morgan's 2011 study, engaged in positive framing of veganism by the time of Lundahl's 2020 study, because of the large number of A-list celebrities who had (publicly) become vegan. This change facilitated discussions about veganism and helped to destigmatise veganism.

While the US activists I interviewed worked with a variety of organisations from small, grassroots groups to large groups like PETA and HSUS, all of them engaged in various versions of "on the ground" activism in the 2000s and 2010s, speaking directly to individuals about animal rights and veganism. Fran, who worked with a small grassroots organisation, noted that people's responses were changing because she was "getting different reactions" than she used to, when the people she spoke to viewed her work "pretty negatively, like we're crazy, or we're going to attack them and yell at them for not believing the same thing that we believe". She attributed this to the increasing interest in environmentalism, which she said fit with animal rights, and she also thought it was due to the fact that "so many celebrities now are vegan, or are careful about their diet, so that is helping. Like Pam Anderson being a vegan." Fran's experience aligns with Lundahl's findings that celebrities helped destigmatise veganism and animal rights activists, moving from wholly negative reactions to more positive ones.[41]

Activists I spoke to who worked at large organisations found celebrities useful when they would sign on to petitions or support the organisations' efforts. The organisations used that celebrity support to promote their issue further, as "Sean" described:

> We have a multifaceted approach where we have a website, that you've seen, that explains the issue in basic detail, and then we put a new feature up for everything that happens, every major demonstration that takes place or a new company that decides that they are going to boycott [the product].

One of the major events they included in this campaign was celebrity support for the issue: "any number of celebrities, for instance, Chrissie Hynde wrote a letter to [the company], so we put that up on our

41 Lundahl 2020.

website". Celebrity support constituted a "major" update alongside "news releases and pictures from demonstrations", "Sean" explained. The attention brought to the issue was a positive use of celebrity activism to these activists at large organisations.

Negative: Celebrities distract from the issues

Some activists from larger organisations told me their initial attention on celebrities and media coverage ended up distracting them from other tactics that were, in retrospect, more strategically important. When I interviewed Heidi from HSUS, she told me about her experience working on a fur campaign. She contrasted her group's tactics to the fur industry's tactics:

> What the fur industry did, they were incredibly smart, they hired PR firms, they started putting out there into the public consciousness that fur is back. There were press releases that fur was back way before it was back, press releases to the fashion industry. So it was almost a self-perpetuating issue, where they were repeating it enough, it became reality. And they were very smart tactically in terms of where they were reaching out with their advertising dollars.

Heidi went on to note that the fur industry directly engaged fashion designers as well: "they were also reaching out to young designers – providing them with free fur, taking them on trips to fashion houses that designed with fur". She called the fur industry's efforts "intensive" and "long-range". In contrast, she said her organisation looked to be winning but missed a strategic opportunity:

> At that time, our successes were taking place with the media coverage, and on the streets, with the confrontational, and a little bit with the celebrities. And because it was an issue that we were, quote, "winning", I don't think we were putting a strategic effort where it needed to be pinpointed. We weren't there with the young kids who were designing. We weren't there reaching out to the

> young designers, and we weren't reaching out to the fashion press. And that was truly a mistake on our part, I believe.

Here, Heidi described a variety of tools in the animal rights organisation's and the fur industry's tactical toolkits. The fur industry focused on designers and getting fur into the fashion industry, whereas the animal rights organisation focused on celebrity support and media coverage. Heidi's experience relates to other activists I interviewed and their critiques of celebrity use – while celebrities might be a flashy tool in one's tactical toolkit, they might distract from using a wider variety of tools for longer-term strategic success. For example, "Steven", who works with a large organisation, said that celebrity use, media-focused tactics and things like "nudity, animal costumes and more publicity-stunt sort of activities" are tactics his organisation specifically avoids because "it distracts from the issue. It focuses attention on the activists, it can present the issue in more of a silly context, [and] we feel this issue is very serious." Suzanne said she specifically chose to work with her current organisation, Vegan Outreach, because they avoided celebrities as a tactic: "They don't get distracted with celebrities or weight-loss claims or any of the sort of silly things that some of the other groups do." Instead, she said, "I really like their honesty, their directness, and the simple purity of the message that this causes unnecessary suffering and unnecessary suffering should be prevented." The activists I interviewed were aware that celebrities were a powerful tool in the tactical toolkit, but many of them felt that celebrities distract from the bigger animal rights message.

Negative: Celebrities' bad reputations perpetuate stereotypes

Stereotyping has long been a concern of activists, including animal rights activists. Just as Cole and Morgan found evidence of "vegaphobia" in the British media, Jonas Lindblom and Kerstin Jacobsson found that mass media in Sweden stereotyped animal rights activists.[42] These stereotypes included activists being terrorists and misanthropes, activists being immature and unserious youth, and

42 Cole and Morgan 2011; Lindblom and Jacobsson 2014.

activists being out of touch city-dwellers who know nothing about farms, meat or animals. When I interviewed Jon, who worked with Vegan Outreach, he shared the concerns about terrorism but also brought up the issue of sexism:

> I think the American public is sympathetic to animal issues. But their view of animal-rights activists might be influenced by a lot of mainstream media outlets that like to run the more, what's the word, run the pieces where they portray animal activists as kind of terrorists or people who engage in the type of activism, like demonstrations where there is a naked woman. So, they might see animal rights activists as maybe on the fringe of society and those who have radical beliefs.

Jon's concerns were shared by other activists I interviewed, and activists featured in other studies. Previous research has shown that both activists and potential targets react negatively to sexism and gender stereotyping in animal rights activism. In her work on women animal rights activists, Emily Gaarder found that some activists responded negatively to PETA ads using sex appeal and the male gaze.[43] The activists she interviewed argued that animal rights activism should not come at a cost to other movements and should not perpetuate sexism in society. (However, it should be noted that some of the women activists she interviewed said animal rights activists should do "whatever it takes" to garner attention to the cause, so this outrage was not universal among her interviewees.) Researchers focusing on potential targets' responses to PETA ads have also found that people responded negatively to ads featuring nude or scantily clad women.[44]

Activists also worried about the reputations of celebrities associated with animal rights more generally. When I interviewed Grant, who worked with a small grassroots organisation, he wondered about the long-term strategy of using "ridiculous" celebrities to sell animal rights:

---

43 Gaarder 2011a, 2011b.

44 Mika 2006.

> Pamela Anderson, man. [laughs] I don't know, she is kind of a ridiculous character, but that kind of exposure, it's like, alright. I guess in some aspects, that's bad, because then it's like, well this idiot signed on to this cause, so it can't really be that worthwhile. Also, it's just more celebrity exposure to it, which is good, because Americans do what their celebrities tell them to do.

Grant's ambivalence echoes Gaarder's findings, where many of her interviewees had mixed feelings about PETA ads.[45] While Pamela Anderson's support might hold the promise of getting the word out to more people, her less-than-stellar reputation might taint that association. Thus, while celebrities might be able to bring attention[46] and media visibility,[47] some of the celebrities who are stalwart animal rights supporters do not necessarily have favourability.[48]

Positive: Celebrities facilitate activist–target interactions

The US activists I interviewed found celebrities to be the most useful when they simply facilitated activists interacting with their targets, rather than having celebrities be the primary spokespeople for the animal rights message. In her study of protestor–target interactions, Rachel Einwohner found such interactions to be hostile when the targets had different identities than the activists.[49] Removing celebrities from the interaction reduces such differences. When celebrities facilitated the interaction between the activists and their target audience, the activists I interviewed found these interactions to be fruitful and positive. Erin, who works with the Humane Society of the United States, said such interactions are very effective for one-on-one outreach. She said musicians will invite them to "set up a table and pass out literature" at concerts, which means: "We get to talk to hundreds

45 Gaarder 2011b, 127.
46 van Krieken 2012.
47 Cronin and Shaw 2002; Heinich 2012.
48 Driessens 2013; Hunter, Burgers and Davidsson 2009.
49 Einwohner 1999.

and sometimes thousands of people on a one-to-one basis." Erin characterised this as generally successful: "They always stop, and they are interested, they take that information." She went on to say that she would get immediate, positive responses, such as, "A lot of times, on site, saying yes, I'm going to go vegetarian. I'm not going to eat that anymore."

Similarly, "Justice", who worked with a grassroots organisation but who also volunteered for PETA2, said she would volunteer when PETA2 asked for people to help staff tables at concerts. She likewise reported positive interactions, and she attributed them to the younger target audience of PETA2's celebrity-infused campaigns:

> [PETA2] is geared at a younger audience, they do a lot of work with bands, a lot of celebrity spokespeople and PSAs [public service announcements]. They target a younger audience, who I think are often a little more impressionable and open and willing to look at alternative views and lifestyles.

"Justice" described the scene as:

> There was a lot of interest at the shows, and people would come up and take stickers and take literature, and it was really fun, and I think that it should be fun and hip and young.

Working with celebrities and especially with musicians, PETA2 facilitates activist–target interactions that are open, fun and positively received by the targets.

Other activists I interviewed who worked for PETA referred to videos narrated by celebrities, but the videos were simply a foil for getting targets' attention and facilitating protestor–target interactions, as Bruce explained:

> We have videos that talk about what happens to chickens that are narrated by Pam Anderson and Al Sharpton. … We are able to turn many people away [from going to KFC], because, in general, Americans don't know what is happening on factory farms.

Al Sharpton and Pam Anderson were not the focus of the event but merely an intermediary used to facilitate protestor–target interactions. Bruce went on to explain why he views these events as successful:

> We are able to reach people at demonstrations in a way that wakes them up and allows them to change their own behaviour to make the world a kinder place, which is, of course, very empowering.

This phenomenon can also be observed in celebrities such as Joaquin Phoenix producing documentaries about veganism and animal rights, including *The Animal People* (2019) and *What the Health* (2017). Such ventures are highly successful for facilitating activist–target interactions, and Réné Becerra has found documentaries to be one of the primary motivators behind conversions to veganism in recent years.[50]

French activists

My interviews with French activists revealed three main themes. Like US activists, many French activists believed celebrities might be useful for making veganism and animal rights "hip", but they also described a variety of reasons why celebrity use was not an option for them. These interviews also revealed two main critiques. First, some grassroots activists harboured an iconoclastic anti-celebrity sentiment, and thus were philosophically against using celebrities as a tactic. Second, like US activists, some activists were concerned about the bad reputation of celebrities associated with animal issues. I elaborate upon these findings below.

Positive and negative: "We'd love to use celebrities but they won't get involved"

In my larger project on strategic and tactical decision-making in the French and US animal rights movements, I found that US activists had a larger "tactical toolkit" than French activists.[51] That is, US activists

50 Becerra 2021.
51 Cherry 2016.

had many more cultural tools at their disposal than did French activists. They were able to use health and religious arguments for veganism and animal rights, for example, which were unavailable to French activists and actively worked against them. Celebrity use follows this same pattern. The largest theme I found in these interviews with French activists was them admitting they knew celebrity use was a powerful tool, but it was unavailable to them because of the lack of celebrities willing to lend their support to the cause.

When I interviewed "Bernadette", who worked with a large grassroots organisation in Paris, she extolled the virtues of using celebrities as spokespeople for animal rights and veganism:

> I think it's a good way for people to hear about it. They'll be reading *People* magazine, and if they hear that such and such a celebrity stopped eating meat, or has decided not to wear fur anymore, that kind of thing, then I think it's a good way for people to hear about it and maybe start wondering, "Why has my favourite celebrity decided to stop eating meat? Maybe I should look into this." It's just a good way to advertise any animal rights group. Plus, if you like a celebrity and you hear he's engaged in something, then maybe you'll think, "Why?"

"Bernadette's" response echoed the findings of researchers who found that celebrities promoting veganism helped spur a rise in veganism and in positive media coverage of veganism.[52] But, when I asked "Bernadette" for some examples of celebrities who support veganism, she said, "There are fewer celebrities who get involved in France." "Bernadette" knew celebrity support was a useful tactical tool, but it was unavailable to her in France. Similarly, when I interviewed Frédéric, who worked with Alliance Végétarienne, he said:

> Here in France, we'd love to! I think it's good to do that, but we have a hard time getting celebrity support. … Here in France, there are no stars. That's not because I think it's a bad idea, it's because we can't do it!

52 Lundahl 2020.

In subsequent interviews, I learned that it was not necessarily the case that celebrities particularly disdain animal rights. What many interviewees revealed to me was that celebrities did in fact support their organisation, but they were unwilling to declare their support publicly. Charles, one of the founders of Protection Mondiale des Animaux de Ferme, told me: "In France, the only actors who are interested in animal rights are unwilling to [declare this] publicly." Another activist said she had proof of such secretive support:

> Vegetarianism is still very poorly viewed in France, because people think that if you're vegetarian you are in a cult. So there are famous people who are vegetarian, but it's still very hush-hush. There are a lot of stars who are vegetarian, but they don't say it. I know they are, though, because I see them on the list of donors for [my organisation].

These responses show that tactical choices depend on more than activists' personal "tastes in tactics".[53] Some tactics are structurally and culturally unavailable to them.

Negative: Anti-celebrity

Some of the grassroots activists I interviewed disdained celebrity use as a tactic. These activists worked with small, philosophically radical organisations associated with punk and anarchist backgrounds. Their "anti-celebrity" approach reflects the anti-hierarchical position of anarchists.[54] When I asked "Albert" about celebrity use, he told me he was hoping I was going to ask about that issue. Rather than eagerly talking about which celebrities supported animal rights, as was the case with many of my interviewees, "Albert" went on to question why people love celebrities:

53 Jasper 1997.
54 Portwood-Stacer 2013.

> To say that a celebrity is vegetarian, that promotes the idea that celebrities are superior to us, like … they're better. What they do is no better than what other people do.

"Albert" admitted that such an approach could work, saying, "The fact of being famous, well, it might make someone interested because this person is famous, but other than that, meh." Ivora also admitted that celebrities could be useful, saying:

> Sure, there's a side that could work, but this whole thing, this star system, I don't like it at all. I have no desire to work with that. For me, the message is what's important. You could opine that you reach more people because people identify with certain celebrities, but no, I don't want to do that.

In these cases, these activists refused the tactic that was also structurally and culturally unavailable to them.

Negative: Bad reputation

Like the US activists, the French activists I interviewed worried about the bad reputation of celebrities associated with veganism and animal rights. In France, the activists I interviewed were more concerned about the political ramifications of these choices. This was especially fraught since the best known French celebrity who supported animal rights was Brigitte Bardot. While Bardot may be best known in the Anglophone world as a movie star from the 1960s, in recent decades in France, she has become known as someone who holds extreme far-right political views and who supports the National Front, the xenophobic far-right political party in France. Therefore, when pondering the use of celebrities, Sara put it succinctly: "You have to choose well."

Many of the activists I spoke to were concerned about the association of Bardot's far-right views with animal rights, especially since she was the first name that came to French people's minds when they think of animal rights, as Philippe explained:

> She's the only one who's really in the media as a well-known person, there's just her. What comes to mind to the average French person is Brigitte Bardot. She's the only one who gets in the mainstream media, who is known by her name.

Several activists brought up this issue before I even asked about celebrities. They found this to be a foundational weakness for the French movement, as Johanne explained:

> Most people, when they think of "animal rights", they think of animal protection, so SPA [Société Protectrice des Animaux] and then Brigitte Bardot, and it stops there. So, when they think of the SPA, they think of dogs and cats, and when they think of Brigitte Bardot, they think of the extreme right. Even in the animal rights movement, there are a lot of people who don't want to work with her because of the things she's said, and she's married to an extreme right-winger.

Johanne was explaining the misconceptions that everyday people have about animal rights. Rather than thinking about animal rights, people think about companion animal protection, or they think about the extreme far-right political party in France, which is not an association that any of them wanted to have with their movement. Of animal rights as a movement, Philippe explained, "[I]t's typically a movement that came from a progressive milieu. But in France, this isn't the case." In the Anglophone world, singer Morrissey is a well-known animal rights supporter who has also become known for his extreme right-wing xenophobic views. A primary difference, though, is that Bardot is *the* name French people associate with animal rights, whereas in the US, animal rights organisations have many different spokespeople from which to choose.

Conclusion

As this chapter has demonstrated, celebrity use exists as a tactic in both France and the United States, but with varying degrees of availability, success and cultural constraints. The activists I interviewed in both countries found celebrities to be useful in making veganism "hip" and mainstream, given celebrities' influence over food, beauty and health trends. However, the availability of this tactic differed between the countries. French activists said they would love to use the tactic, but French celebrities would not get involved in promoting veganism and animal rights. These differences increase with the US activists' enjoying celebrity-facilitated interactions with their targets, and the French activists' anti-celebrity iconoclastic sentiments.

Activists in both countries shared concerns about the bad reputation of celebrities who might lend their support, but the content of their concerns differed between the countries. In the US, the activists I interviewed shared concerns over gender stereotyping, with celebrities like Pamela Anderson using sex appeal in advertisements for groups like PETA. In France, the activists I interviewed were more concerned about distasteful and dangerous political associations, with celebrities like Brigitte Bardot endorsing the far-right National Front political party.

These findings have implications for researchers and for activists. Previous research on the media has demonstrated that a focus on celebrity vegans brings with it a depoliticisation of veganism.[55] When focusing on celebrities, the media present veganism as a fad, a trend or a healthy diet, rather than as a political and ethical lifestyle choice and statement.[56] None of the activists I interviewed reported being concerned about depoliticised media coverage, but they were worried about other negative ramifications of celebrity use. With more social movement organisations focusing on corporations and using celebrities as a target,[57] future research will need to address the ramifications of celebrity use as a tactic. For example, Claire Parkinson and her colleagues found non-vegans to be quite cynical about celebrities promoting veganism.[58] At the same time, they found younger participants more likely to read articles about veganism when they

55 Doyle 2016.
56 Lundahl 2020.
57 Turner 2016, 813–14.
58 Parkinson, Twine and Griffin 2019.

involved celebrities. Future research could focus on the targets of animal rights activists and how they interpret depoliticised media coverage.

The implications for activists align with my concern for producing scholarship that helps the animal rights movement. The differences shown here between the two countries in the availability of and concerns about celebrity endorsements demonstrate that not all strategies and tactics work in all arenas, and that rather than using tactics that have worked in other countries and cultural contexts, activists should adapt their work to best fit their particular cultural context. Of course, activists already do this to a certain extent, but having a clearer image of their targets, and the best tactics to reach their targets in their cultural context, can only help their future work.

References

Becerra, R. (2021). Becoming vegan, staying vegan: social ties and media. Presentation given at the annual meeting of the *American Sociological Association.*

Brockington, Dan (2009). *Celebrity and the Environment: Fame, Wealth, and Power in Conservation*. London: Zed Books.

Cherry, Elizabeth (2016). *Culture and Activism: Animal Rights in France and the United States*. New York: Routledge.

Cole, Matthew and Karen Morgan (2011). Vegaphobia: derogatory discourses of veganism and the reproduction of speciesism in UK national newspapers. *British Journal of Sociology* 62(1): 134–53. https://tinyurl.com/56spj26z.

Craig, Geoffrey (2019). Sustainable everyday life and celebrity environmental advocacy in *Hugh's War on Waste*. *Environmental Communication* 13(6): 775–89. https://doi.org/10.1080/17524032.2018.1459770.

Cronin, Blaise and Debora Shaw (2002). Banking (on) different forms of symbolic capital. *Journal of the American Society for Information Science and Technology* 53(14): 1267–70.

Doyle, Julie (2016). Celebrity vegans and the lifestyling of ethical consumption. *Environmental Communication* 10(6): 777–90. https://tinyurl.com/2dwj9xph.

Driessens, Olivier (2013). The celebritization of society and culture: understanding the structural dynamics of celebrity culture. *International Journal of Cultural Studies* 16(6): 641–57. https://doi.org/10.1177/1367877912459140.

Einwohner, R.L. (1999). Gender, class, and social movement outcomes: identity and effectiveness in two animal rights campaigns. *Gender and Society* 13(1): 56–76.

Evans, Erin M. (2016). Bearing witness: how controversial organizations get the media coverage they want. *Social Movement Studies* 15(1): 41–59. https://doi.org/10.1080/14742837.2015.1060158.

Gaarder, Emily (2011a). Where the boys aren't: the predominance of women in animal rights activism. *Feminist Formations* 23(2): 54–76. https://doi.org/10.1353/ff.2011.0019.

Gaarder, Emily (2011b). *Women and the Animal Rights Movement*. New Brunswick, NJ: Rutgers University Press.

Goodman, Michael K., Jo Littler, Dan Brockington and Maxwell Boykoff (2016). Spectacular environmentalisms: media, knowledge and the framing of ecological politics. *Environmental Communication* 10(6): 677–88. https://doi.org/10.1080/17524032.2016.1219489.

Heinich, Nathalie (2012). *De la visibilité: Excellence et singularité en régime médiatique*. Paris: Editions Gallimard.

Hunter, Erik, Henri Burgers and Per Davidsson (2009). Celebrity capital as a strategic asset: implications for new venture strategies. In G.T. Lumpkin and Jerome A. Katz, eds. *Entrepreneurial Strategic Content*, 137–60. Bingley, UK: Emerald Group Publishing.

Jallinoja, Piia, Markus Vinnari and Mari Niva (2019). Veganism and plant-based eating: analysis of interplay between discursive strategies and lifestyle political consumerism. In M. Boström, M. Micheletti and P. Oosterveer, eds. *Oxford Handbook of Political Consumerism*, 157–79. New York: Oxford University Press.

Jasper, James M. (1997). *The Art of Moral Protest: Culture, Biography, and Creativity in Social Movements*. Chicago: University of Chicago Press.

Jeffreys, Elaine (2016). Translocal celebrity activism: shark-protection campaigns in mainland China. *Environmental Communication* 10(6): 763–76. https://doi.org/10.1080/17524032.2016.1198822.

Lindblom, J., and K. Jacobsson (2014). A deviance perspective on social movements: the case of animal rights activism. *Deviant Behavior* 35(2): 133–151. https://doi.org/10.1080/01639625.2013.834751.

Lundahl, Outi (2020). Dynamics of positive deviance in destigmatisation: celebrities and the media in the rise of veganism. *Consumption Markets and Culture* 23(3): 241–71.

Mika, Marie (2006). Framing the issue: religion, secular ethics and the case of animal rights mobilization. *Social Forces* 85(2): 915–41. https://doi.org/10.1353/sof.2007.0017.

Parkinson, Claire, Richard Twine and Naomi Griffin (2019). *Pathways to Veganism: Exploring Effective Messages in Vegan Transition*. Final Report, Edge Hill University.

Piper, N. (2015). Jamie Oliver and cultural intermediation. *Food, Culture and Society* 18(2): 245–64.

Portwood-Stacer, Laura (2013). *Lifestyle Politics and Radical Activism*. New York: Bloomsbury USA.

Ragin, Charles (1987). *The Comparative Method: Moving Beyond Qualitative and Quantitative Strategies*. Berkeley: University of California Press.

Shprintzen, Adam D. (2013). *The Vegetarian Crusade: The Rise of an American Reform Movement, 1817–1921*. Chapel Hill: University of North Carolina Press.

Šimčikas, Saulius (2018). Is the percentage of vegetarians and vegans in the US increasing? *Animal Charity Evaluators*, 16 August. https://bit.ly/3U1Nlzb.

Simonson, Peter (2001). Social noise and segmented rhythms: news, entertainment, and celebrity in the crusade for animal rights. *The Communication Review* 4(3): 399–420.

Swidler, Ann (1986). Culture in action: symbols and strategies. *American Sociological Review* 51(2): 273–86.

Thornton, Patricia H., William Ocasio and Michael Lounsbury (2012). *The Institutional Logics Perspective: A New Approach to Culture, Structure, and Process*. Oxford: Oxford University Press.

Turner, Graeme (2016). Celebrities and the environment: the limits to their power. *Environmental Communication* 10(6): 811–14. https://tinyurl.com/3bjxwbdh.

van Krieken, Robert (2012). *Celebrity Society*. London: Routledge.

11

Food fights

The limits of celebrity chef activism

Brett Mills

Introduction

From 2008 to 2012, the UK public service broadcaster Channel 4 broadcast a number of programs featuring celebrity chefs examining the UK's food industries and campaigning for better animal welfare. The chefs Hugh Fearnley-Whittingstall, Jamie Oliver and Gordon Ramsay appeared individually in series including *Jamie's Fowl Dinners* (2008), *Hugh's Chicken Run* (2008), *Jamie Saves Our Bacon* (2009), *Jamie's Fish Supper* (2011) and *Hugh's Fish Fight* (2012). Collectively, the three chefs featured in the broadcaster's annual series of programs under the "Food Fight" banner, which campaigned for improved animal welfare in meat production. While television often depicts certain aspects of food production – for example, in programs such as *Food Unwrapped* (2012) and *Inside the Factory* (2015) – the programs featuring Fearnley-Whittingstall, Oliver and Ramsay are significant in their overtly campaigning tone, featuring imagery likely to shock viewers unaware of standard farming practices, and their direct call to audiences to engage in matters related to ethics, welfare and animal policy. As such, they are emblematic of public service broadcasting's role in engaging a national television audience in contemporary debates and indicate broadcasting's engagement with a growing public awareness of, and interest in, matters of animal welfare.

That said, what is significant about all of these programs is that they posit the necessity for better treatment of animals in food production, but not the abolition of the use of animals for such purposes. As such, they do not trouble the assumption that the human production and consumption of other beings is a morally legitimate thing to do, and each of the chefs persists in routinely using animal products in their recipe-based cookery programs. They have therefore been critiqued by vegan groups, with Oliver noting that "vegans hate him"[1] and Ramsay being embroiled in Twitter spats with PETA.[2] This means these programs, and the chefs involved in them, are emblematic of complex contradictory understandings of notions of animal welfare and the limits commonly placed on such ethical considerations even where the intention is to make visible the cruelty routinely enacted upon animals in the name of human consumption. Where the conclusion arising from these chefs' campaigns could well be veganism, the programs instead repeatedly refuse to countenance this not only as logical but also as necessary. This chapter, then, aims to examine this contradictory aspect of these media texts in order to outline how public, visible, far-reaching animal welfare campaigning such as that evident in these programs perversely remains wedded to anthropocentric norms which situate animals as resources to be used for human purposes. Indeed, it is possible that these programs are more problematic in terms of advancing animal welfare, for while they make visible the often-unseen experience of animals in much farming activity and invite audiences to be outraged and appalled by what they encounter, the solutions that are offered function to salve humans' disgust and anger more than make a material difference to the lived experiences of animals.

Food and morality

Fundamental to these programs, and the campaigning of the chefs associated with them, is the assumption that food exists within regimes of morality. That is, that the systems by which food comes into being

---

1 Zatat 2017.
2 Starostinetskaya 2018.

– including cultural assumptions about what does and does not constitute food – and the choices people make when buying and consuming food are not neutral acts but instead ones with consequences beyond themselves. As such, they align with debates about "ethical consumption", in which "ordinary consumers negotiate the idea of 'taking responsibility' as a consumer", placing what can be understood as everyday and necessary activities within a "moral dimension".[3] This "growing politicization of life and lifestyle practices" implies ethics which are complex for people to negotiate given the cultural norms that inform meanings of food and the fact that as a largely everyday activity, it is not something people are often invited to reflect upon.[4] Yet topics such as the contribution of food production to climate change, concerns about obesity and food waste have meant that cultural norms that function only if they remain invisible have instead become key talking points and considerable matters of concern.[5] Rethinking food choices requires changes in behaviour and norms, and ethical consumption serves as a potent motivator for such reflection. It is therefore no surprise that there is a correlation between someone's active engagement with, and reflection upon, topics such as animal rights and welfare, and the likelihood of them reducing their consumption of animals as food, such that "the animal ethics views of vegetarians and vegans are different from those of meat-eaters".[6] Action here follows ethics, and this is only possible if food consumption is itself understood within regimes of ethics, rather than as a "neutral", "natural" act. "Taking responsibility" typically requires understanding food consumption as not simply a personal act but also one with implications for "distant others, animals and the environment" rather than focusing solely on "human self-interest".[7] But this runs counter to the prevailing normalisation of "meat culture", which is made up of "a wide range of domains of production and consumption of animals" intertwined with regimes of "capitalism, consumerism and the notion

3 Grauel 2016, 865, 866.
4 Lewis and Potter 2010, 5.
5 Thompson and Haigh 2017; Rousseau 2012, 159–205.
6 Lund, McKeegan et al. 2016, 100.
7 Grauel 2016, 866; Lund, McKeegan et al. 2016, 90.

of free-will".[8] The television programs under discussion here necessarily have to negotiate these complex regimes, and invite audiences to situate themselves in relation to them. They thus serve as powerful interventions into normalised food practices; indeed, the tone adopted by a number of the programs aims to shock viewers into action, thereby assuming the information being presented is hitherto largely unknown. But these regimes also serve as limiting discourses within which the debates they present can take place, the solutions they offer and the level of responsibility they can place upon individuals. So, while these programs may make considerable efforts to make clear what the problem is, the dominance of "capitalism, consumerism and the notion of free-will" in relation to food choices means they, in the end, can only invite audiences to reflect on their choices and act accordingly, if at all.

It is into this complex interplay of contexts that celebrity chefs enter, functioning as conduits through which these debates can take place, and acting as experts bringing relevant information to watchers of the programs. This means they "have become key sites through which the ethics of 'good' shopping and eating in an increasingly industrialised and globalised food market are interrogated and mobilised within contemporary media culture".[9] This position is complex, for while such chefs often call on supermarkets and food production companies to improve their standards, they often also serve as "branded identities" as the faces of those organisations they otherwise critique.[10] A consequence of this is that they "become (wittingly or unwittingly) enmeshed in a complex politics of food production and consumption that exposes them to its many complex and sometimes contradictory features".[11] This movement from "cultural" to "political" intermediaries[12] represents a significant reshaping of the function of chefs within media culture, and a movement of the domain of their responsibility away from the purely domestic to broader debates about food in society. In doing so, they

8 Potts 2016, 2, 20.
9 Lewis and Huber 2015, 290.
10 Lewis and Huber 2015, 290.
11 Phillipov and Gale 2020, 402.
12 Powell and Prasad 2010.

problematise assumptions about where knowledge sits, and the places citizens should turn to in order to find information. Where "[f]ood labels, government guidelines, branding, advertising" are primary places for food information, chefs are powerful because they are "*people* – talking, interacting, celebratising, and performing food information across media platforms in entertaining ways engaging audiences in ways other formats do not or cannot".[13] The activity of "talk" here is important, such that these chefs can be considered "talking labels" that "cross the boundaries between science, health, governance, entertainment and consumption with ease to relay complex food and nutrition information in easily understandable and demotic ways".[14] There is a problem, though, for in insisting there are problems in the choices people make as consumers, and in assuming that the responsibility for this lies solely with people as consumers, celebrity chefs necessarily categorise many of the people they encounter as "unethical consumers", creating "distinctions between consumers we recognise as 'ethical' and those whose ethics either remain invisible or are rendered 'unethical'".[15] While these distinctions often circulate within hierarchical cultural categories – such as gender, race and class – they also constitute a problem for the chefs, and the programs they are involved in, in that they necessitate categorising some decisions and forms of behaviour as "unethical". The programs under discussion here employ a variety of tactics in order to offer evidence for the unethical nature of particular kinds of behaviours, but must also negotiate the problems of overt moralising of ethical certainties that conflict with contemporary notions of free will and choice. It is significant that these chefs function as "talking labels", for talk is an activity that invites engagement, discussion and reflection but does not mandate behaviour or proscribe outcomes. There is another context relevant here: that talk is understood as a human activity, and even though these programs are about the treatment of animals, their focus on talk renders mute the very beings whose welfare they purportedly promote.

13 Barnes 2017, 171, emphasis in original.
14 Barnes 2017, 176.
15 Bell and Hollows 2011, 189.

While the programs listed above feature multiple chefs, one chef stands ahead of the others in terms of their public visibility related to campaigning about food standards: Jamie Oliver. Indeed, Oliver's centrality to contemporary conceptualisations of celebrity chefs' activities and cultural meanings means there is a wealth of academic work on him to the extent that it is legitimate to suggest there is an analytical sub-field that could be called "Jamie Oliver studies". His early series, such as *The Naked Chef* (1999), are understood to have reconceptualised cookery programs in order to "emphasize the importance of lifestyle".[16] Here, cooking is recategorised as a "form of creative leisure", rather than a form of "domestic obligation", and so becomes an expression of the self and associated with personal identity.[17] While this approach to food might imply its status as a depoliticised act, it has instead served as a route by which cooking has become understood within the realm of ethics and morality precisely because the preparation of meals is understood to say something about the person doing it. By this account, in his programs Oliver is not simply offering viewers advice on how to make meals; he is also indicating that making meals is a route by which reflection can occur on how to be, as both an individual and a member of society. Oliver can then be understood as a "cultural intermediary" whose activities "move cultural ideas into new social and economic spheres".[18] He has, then, moved from "lifestyle expert to moral entrepreneur", applying his "culinary cultural capital to wider moral anxieties about health, social exclusion, and the ethics of provisioning and production".[19] Important here is his status as an "entrepreneur", because it persists in placing moral and ethical debates within capitalist regimes which understand food as an economic resource and invites audiences to understand themselves as consumers whose power – if any – is predicated on the choices they make when shopping. So, while Oliver's work can be understood as a powerful intervention into previously normalised food practices, and an insistence that people accept that their food

16 Hollows 2003, 230.
17 Hollows 2003, 243.
18 Piper 2015, 247.
19 Hollows 2010, 308.

choices have sociopolitical consequences, this rarely moves outside of ideas of consumption being the only way to enact citizenship. As will be evidenced below, Oliver's activism constitutes interventions into prevalent systems, rather than a critique of those systems themselves.

Oliver's focus on individual responsibility means he has been critiqued for his failure to acknowledge the sociocultural contexts within which people make decisions, especially in terms of disempowering cultural categories such as class, gender, race and ethnicity. His attempt to "help" the residents of the northern English town of Rotherham to change their food habits in *Jamie's Ministry of Food* (2008), for example, evidences his "inattention to the history, poverty and class positioning" of the people whose habits he attempts to change.[20] Furthermore, that program's focus on obesity – and its insistence that obesity is a result of personal choices alone – means the series functions to normalise "self-governance" intended to produce "compliant, model citizens".[21] Oliver's assertion that he has the right to intervene in people's food choices and indicate "better" choices for them to make is reliant on his status as an "expert", whereby "authority and legitimacy in this role" is intertwined with his celebrity status.[22] This indicates a complex set of "geographies of responsibility" in which Oliver's campaigning zeal often asserts itself as a moral imperative in which he attempts to use his celebrity status for good, yet it is often naive in terms of the kinds of conflicting responsibilities those he intends to "educate" must negotiate.[23] The assertion of a "correct" way to interact with food therefore serves to "other" different food practices, in a manner akin to the exoticisation of national food cultures in Oliver's travelogue cookery programs such as *Jamie's Italian Escape* (2005).[24] In all, Oliver's activities, the programs that depict these, and the academic writing on both, indicates the complex contexts within which food – as a material object but also as a cultural idea – circulates, with Oliver's campaigns functioning as an intervention into these. The

20 Warin 2011, 36.
21 Warin 2011, 36, 37.
22 Kjær 2019, 333.
23 Jackson 2016, 756.
24 Leer and Kjær 2015.

support and critique he receives indicates the contentious nature of these ideas, and the disruption – whether positive or negative – making normalised food cultures visible causes. If nothing else, the work of Oliver and other chefs such as Fearnley-Whittingstall and Ramsay insists that food is not something that should be taken for granted, destabilising that which is typically instead conceptualised as "natural" or "normal". And in offering alternatives – even where these are unrealistic or insensitive – they highlight that things could be other than they are, necessitating the moral engagement with food their campaigns propose.

It is therefore notable that there remain limits to this disruption. As noted above, the tools proposed within these programs for enacting moral relationships with food are ones that define citizens only as consumers, making ethical choices in terms of their own consumption but also, by extension, placing pressure on food production systems through decisions of what to buy and not buy. But these series also place limits on the extent to which moral concern is of relevance. In the programs focusing on obesity, participants are encouraged to make "better" choices about the kinds of meat they buy solely because the quality of that meat is understood to be better in terms of personal health; the ethics of consuming meat at all is not raised. Similarly, in the "Food Fight" programs which explicitly engage with animal welfare in meat production systems, these series remain wary of proposing veganism – or even vegetarianism – as a logical and moral stance resulting from the argument made in the programs. As will be shown below, key tools used in a program such as *Jamie's Fowl Dinners* are shock and disgust, with Oliver acting to actively discomfort those to whom he shows normalised treatment processes of animals in industrial meat-producing regimes. It is clear that he aims to indicate that what they encounter is immoral and must be changed; the participants' reactions overwhelmingly align with this. Yet the solution on offer is "better" welfare for animals, not the removal of animals from the systems as a whole. The moral considerations within which food is indicated to circulate, then, remains bounded, with some – seemingly obvious – solutions rendered invisible. As such, food here continues to circulate in complex "geographies of responsibility", with one outcome being the rejection of certain moral stances from consideration at all.

It is worth noting here that the academic work examining Oliver, celebrity chefs and the politics of their programs circulates too within limited regimes of consideration. As noted above, there is much critique of Oliver's work because it fails to be cognisant of the sociocultural factors that impact on individual and societal food choices. In doing so, such analyses make visible the unacknowledged discourses within which Oliver's activities take place, and are critical of the notions that all food choices are nothing other than personal and that citizenship should be acted only through consumer acts. But academic work – rightly mindful of power imbalances resulting from cultural categories such as gender, race and class – routinely fails to spot comparable regimes of speciesism, even when examining programs in which animals are killed for meat for human consumption. As veganism is absent in these programs, so is it absent in much academic analysis of food, with animals rendered of marginal or no concern in a manner akin to the very media texts under discussion. Fundamental to ideas of morality being expressed through human actions, especially where these situate humans as consumers, is a normalised anthropocentrism in which only humans have agency. While it is possible to critique these programs because they demonise categories such as obesity as social problems, this still means that the human – and debates about what is good or bad for humans – is deemed worthy of consideration. Similarly, academic analyses of these series that explore only their human contexts engage in an analytical anthropocentrism which – whatever their conclusions – serves to perpetuate human exceptionalism.

Jamie's Fowl Dinners

Analysing *Jamie's Fowl Dinners* exemplifies how celebrity chefs situate food within moral regimes yet limit this consideration such that veganism is not considered. The program begins with Oliver directly addressing the camera and therefore speaking to the audience at home, saying, "Once again we're tackling a very controversial subject; it's the story of our little chicken, and the egg." He then goes on to explain the format of the program, in which he is hosting a large banquet for invited guests who think they are there simply to enjoy the meal, but who will instead be forced to witness the treatment of the animals who end up on their plates. Oliver asks, "Will the guys, once they've seen where their food comes from, still be hungry?" The voiceover explains, "The dinner guests are hand-picked, from junk-food addicts to free-range foodies. Farmers, food producers, even the supermarkets." This format serves two functions. First, it aims to demonstrate that the majority of people are unaware of standard animal farming practices, and therefore that what they are about to be shown will be new to them. Second, it enables the program to visually indicate this learning process through reaction shots from the attendees. It is possible to imagine an alternative version of this program in which participants knew what they were to encounter beforehand; however, the surprise element is a fundamental part of the program's structure and effects, and throughout Oliver repeatedly asks attendees what their responses are to what they are newly encountering. The centrality of reactions to the program is evident in its opening sequence, which consists of rapid intercuts of chickens being handled by farmers and butchers and banquet attendees looking shocked, confused and upset. As a form of television, the program also assumes that its viewing audience will be similarly ignorant of that which they are about to see, and thus the reaction shots of the banquet's diners function as proxy versions of the intended viewing audience reaction.

Yet the program situates the living beings it is going to invite concern for as products from the outset. Oliver's first statement to the banquet's diners is: "We're going to be looking at two great British products: the chicken and the egg." The reference to them as "products" makes clear that, as far as the program is considered, reconceptualising animal welfare can be achieved without recategorising the animals as anything other than resources for humans within a capitalist system. But the division between the "chicken" and the "egg" also takes a single species and divides it into two categories defined solely in terms of their usefulness for humans as products. An "egg" and a "chicken" are understood in cooking and farming as two different things, for they serve different purposes in the preparation of food. Indeed, this distinction is so prevalent within food cultures that it constitutes one of the dividing lines between veganism and vegetarianism. Yet the two can instead be understood as the same thing, simply at different parts of a developmental process; it is food cultures that render them as related-but-distinct. From the outset, then, though Oliver makes clear his desire to encourage the diners to rethink their understandings of these "products", this is not to the extent that they are invited to reject the category of "product" as a whole. The animals are rendered "absent", through their reformulation as food products.[25]

The understanding of animals as products – and that related contexts of morality should circulate within capitalist discourse that situate animals as products – is indicated in Oliver's subsequent summary of the program's aims. He says:

> The industries behind [the chicken and the egg] have been pushed and pushed – and even bullied at times – to produce cheaper and cheaper food. So here's my theory; I believe that if we give you – the great British public – the credit, and show you where your cheap eggs and where your cheap meat comes from, next time you go shopping you'll make better choices.[26]

There is a clear invoking of regimes of morality here, given Oliver's request that "better choices" be made in the future assumes that bad choices are being made right now. Yet this remains limited; the desire is simply "better" choices, not the best ones or the correct ones. The invitation Oliver offers is that should those attending the banquet or watching at home change at least some kind of behaviour – to become, no matter how marginal, "better" – then this is enough. Furthermore, Oliver appeals to a common-sensical form of citizenship in his reference to the audience as the "great British public"; it indicates this is something that can be understood as a collective action, but only where that collective is the result of individual "choices" rather than something more concrete such as policy change. There is a critique of some of the consequences of capitalism – whereby animal food industries have been "bullied" – but not of capitalism itself and its categorisation of animals as a product whose welfare is dependent on "better" shopping choices made by individual consumers. There is no

25 Adams 2015, 21.

26 *Jamie's Fowl Dinners* (2008).

suggestion here at all that eating animals and animal products is wrong, or that the understanding of animals as products is inevitable within capitalism; instead, that humans should have systems for producing the foods they desire and have the resources to buy them – irrespective of the inevitable impact that has on the animals who become food in this process – is presented not only as logical and normal but also as a suitable route for the expression and enactment of food morality. Furthermore, that consumers will make "better" choices is understood by Oliver as inevitable; he does not countenance that consumers may decide to continue making choices he understands as "bad", and there is no framework offered here for critiquing that outcome should it occur.

Absent so far in all of this are chickens as living, fleshy beings. In order to rectify this, Oliver requests waiters bring serving plates covered by cloches to each dining table at the banquet. When these cloches are lifted, they reveal a platter of live chicks, huddled together on some straw. Reaction shots show the diners' surprise at this, but also their joy at the presence of the small, fluffy, cute animals, with some reaching out to stroke them and pick them up. Oliver reveals that they are "sexed by colour", in that due to deliberate breeding techniques the male chicks are paler than the female ones. He then asks the diners to separate the chicks by colour, putting the male ones in a glass box. The diners dutifully do so, and this is intercut with more shots of them gleefully holding and petting the chicks, and there are sounds of delighted squeals and a general hubbub of excitement on the program's soundtrack. The male chicks are then brought to Oliver at what he calls "the processing plant", and a voiceover warns audiences watching the program at home, "Tonight, Jamie will be showing his guests every single aspect of the production process. Viewers may find some of this disturbing."

The "disturbing" sequence involves what happens to the male chicks. Oliver introduces Charles Maclean, a free-range farmer, who outlines the problem of male chicks for the industry:

> Throughout the whole of the industry, there's 30 million of these chicks, and the males do not produce eggs, and we can't get any economic sense out of them. So unfortunately they are depleted.[27]

At this point Oliver lifts a sheet from a machine to their left, revealing a see-through plastic box with the label "dispatching chamber" attached to it. He then asks Mark Bodycote, who is labelled as an "animal euthanasia expert", what is about to happen. Bodycote says, "In this particular case we use carbon dioxide … and they are just starved of oxygen", while Oliver places the male chicks in the box. Oliver notes there are other methods for "depleting" the chicks, such as maceration, which he likens to a "big mincer". Bodycote says this is: "Very, very quick. Not very pleasant for the actual person doing it, though." Maclean then confirms that the killing of male chicks in egg production is standard irrespective of country or region, and within free-range as well as factory farming, calling it "a fact of life". Bodycote then turns on the machine, and the chicks are shown, firstly, to be gasping for air, then becoming unconscious, and then lying dead at the bottom of the box. The program shows many diners watching concernedly, with one shaking her head.

The program's tactics of making visible that which is largely hidden aligns with tools used by many animal welfare campaigns, and relies on making explicit the "meat paradox" in which there is an "inconsistency between an action (i.e., eating meat) and a cognition (i.e., animals suffer)".[28] In doing so, the program raises questions about how we might understand "cruel food: culinary experiences and food items in which the element of cruelty figures not as a by-product but as a vital ingredient".[29] While this concept largely points to food in which the act of cruelty is explicitly part of the pleasure of consumption, Oliver's insistence on his diners witnessing the processes that lead to the meal he is to offer them reshapes the hitherto benign into the cruel. The shots of the diners' reactions indicate how difficult they find the experience of seeing chicks they have just been handling die, and it is hard not to understand this moment as cruel. That said, the banal use of language to describe this process, where it is a "fact of life", and the prioritisation of concern for those humans who carry out the process, rather than the animals who are victims of it, serves to morally equate anthropocentric

27 *Jamie's Fowl Dinners* (2008).

28 Buttlar and Walther 2019, 73.

29 Strong 2011, 159.

concerns with ones of animal welfare. For the audience viewing the program at home, too, it is likely to be difficult to watch, and this raises significant questions about the effectiveness of such shock tactics in inviting moral concern. This is because while:

> increasing awareness of harm is a critical first step towards increasing moral concern for a cause and fostering change … an additional message of moral blame … may undermine … goals.[30]

This suggests that individuals do not like to be held personally accountable for moral harms, and tactics which intend to lay blame in this way may instead simply increase defensiveness and resistance.

This is relevant in terms of the tone this program and Oliver himself adopt throughout, which in these campaigning programs is at odds with the kinds of newer masculinity he was seen to exemplify in *The Naked Chef*.[31] He certainly does not engage in the kind of "destructive leadership" or "professional incivility" made up of "tongue-lashing, insulting invectives and continual swearing" that Gordon Ramsay employs in order to achieve change in the individuals he encounters and which may be understood as a trope of program-making of this kind.[32] That is, there is precedence in terms of such programming that would legitimate Oliver expressing forms of "incivility" commensurate with the topic at hand, given that the kinds of series he and other chefs such as Ramsay are involved in are typically unashamed about their role in changing behaviour and highlighting the moral contexts relevant to food consumption. To be sure, throughout the program Oliver expresses an urgency and righteous concern related to the topic, in terms of both his delivery style as well as his insistence that the diners witness that which is normally hidden. But the tone remains wedded to a notion of personal responsibility, with Oliver clearly understanding his function as giving individuals access to information that enables them to make "better choices", but not explicitly demanding such choices be made. The diners' right to express

30 Shulman, Shnitzer-Akuka and Reifen-Tagar 2021, 1.
31 Hollows 2003.
32 Balwant 2021; Higgins, Montgomery et al. 2011; Nilsson 2013, 648.

their citizenship through consumption choices, as well as their right to make decisions irrespective of their impact upon others, remains paramount. The potential for the explicit expression of moral leadership is muted in the face of the normalisation of the discourse of the "self-governing citizen-consumer", which is central to much contemporary political discourse and "perpetuates the individualization of responsibility".[33] This means Oliver's approach to his participants, and therefore by extension to those viewing the program at home, is stunted in its potency in the face of the prevalence of notions of personal choice. This is significant for a program such as this on a public service broadcaster like Channel 4, for it indicates the constraints that exist within such public service ideals. So even though Channel 4 prides itself as having a history that is about "always creating positive change" and trumpets one of its goals as being "to create change through entertainment" and "hold power to account", it too remains embedded in ideas of personal responsibility, addressing its public via programs like *Jamie's Fowl Dinners* as consumers first and foremost.[34]

This means the tone and approach evident in this first few minutes of the program remain consistent throughout. Oliver shocks and upsets his diners – and, by implication, his viewers at home – through his insistence on making visible the normal practices within the systems that produce the food he intends to serve. His diners express a range of emotions, with surprise and upset being dominant, such that it is clear they are indeed rethinking how the food they consume comes to be. Yet in its focus on the diners, the program persistently reasserts the humans in this process, rather than the animals whose very deaths are fundamental within meat-producing systems. And even when those deaths are made explicit – such as in the killing of the chicks – the meanings of these moments are centred on the upset and outrage of the diners, rather than the killing of the chicks themselves. The death of the animals is here significant *only* because of its effects on humans; the deaths themselves are perceived to carry no inherent moral weight. So there is a real oddity here, in which a program with the very clear and pragmatic intention of improving animal welfare shapes this as a matter

33 Derkatch and Spoel 2015; Roff 2007, 518.
34 Channel 4 2020, 4, 12, 17.

of consideration only with relevance to its impact upon humans. Where the program does insist that food is a moral issue, that is predicated on the immorality of humans being upset rather than animals dying.

Food fights

Jamie's Fowl Dinners, and the "Food Fight" array of programs of which it is a part, exemplify the complex and contradictory ways in which animal welfare campaigns are situated in mainstream discourse, such as that on a national public service broadcaster like Channel 4. Aligned with the history of the animal welfare movement, it draws on "the moral potency of opposition to cruelty",[35] explicitly situating citizens as moral agents whose behaviours have consequences. It coincides with the more recent shift that situates food choices within moral regimes, which itself is exemplified in media campaigns by celebrity chefs of which these programs are a part. The "Food Fight" series, then, can be understood as a logical intersection of contemporary understandings of food within consumer culture and the consumerist discourse which positions shopping decisions as the most effective and powerful political act an individual can undertake. But these two contexts severely limit the radical potential of food campaigns, for they prohibit the expression of unarguable moral outrage or the call for solutions that are perceived to limit choice, such as veganism. These programs are, then, indicative of "uneasy relations between animal welfare (and rights) activists and food activism campaigns" because the latter don't fight for abolition of animal consumption.[36] Veganism – or, more precisely, the call for compulsory veganism or the assertion that veganism is the logical response to animal welfare issues – remains outside the scope of consideration. And this is not just for the programs, because the chefs involved, such as Jamie Oliver, remain committed to the consumption of animal products, insisting that "part of being a meat-eater is all about respecting the animals that are bred for our food, so it's important for them to be cared for and well

35 Munro 2005, 153.
36 Rodan and Mummery 2016, 392.

treated".[37] While his book *Veg*[38] and his acknowledgement that he tries to "eat vegetarian 2–3 times a week"[39] indicate a significant move in thinking about meat consumption, it remains the case that vegans are, according to Oliver, "annoying".[40]

As such, this program aligns with dominant media discourses that employ "derogatory" terms to describe vegans and veganism and which serve to police what is understood as "mainstream" morality in terms of animal welfare.[41] The "Food Fight" series, however, is now more than a decade old, and there is evidence of veganism becoming more normalised within wider culture and in media portrayals.[42] There has been a shift from celebrity chefs such as Oliver who, though not a vegan himself, argues for improved animal welfare, to celebrity vegans who "present veganism as ordinary" and the development of veganism as a "lifestyle".[43] This situates a program such as *Jamie's Fowl Dinners* as having the potential to be understood as an important historical document within the gradual shifting of cultural ideas of veganism in the 21st century. Where the "Food Fight" programs routinely employed shock and disgust as tools of behavioural change, contemporary celebrity vegans instead position their food choices as nothing other than practices of identity-based lifestyle. To be sure, cookery programs remain overwhelmingly wedded to the fetishisation of animal products, and thus veganism remains a fringe activity in terms of that genre; furthermore, chefs such as Oliver who are avowedly committed to animal welfare continue to see no contradiction between their ethics and the killing of animals for their consumption. However, what remains evident is the notion that engagement with animal welfare issues remains a personal choice, which can be best practised through purchasing choices. As such, food – which is literally consumed – remains an exemplar of the notion that consumption is the most

37 British Hen Welfare Trust 2020.
38 Oliver 2019.
39 Quoted in Mackrell 2019.
40 Pevreall 2017.
41 Cole and Morgan 2011.
42 Christopher, Bartkowski and Haverda 2018; Sexton, Garnett and Lorimer 2022;.
43 Bertuzzi 2017; Doyle 2016, 777; Gheihman 2021.

powerful and legitimate expression of moral agency. Absent, of course, remain the animals themselves, who have no power within regimes of lifestyle, consumption and individualism. The programs in the "Food Fight" series aimed to make those invisible animals visible, and while they may have been a contributory step on the road to more contemporary conceptualisations of veganism, they remain wedded to ethics enacted by the consumer rather than the consumed. This means their disruptive power is minimal, for they inadvertently assert and normalise human agency as the one and only legitimate locus of power.

References

Adams, Carol J. (2015). *The Sexual Politics of Meat: A Feminist-Vegetarian Critical Theory*. New York and London: Bloomsbury.

Balwant, Paul T. (2021). Is there a bright side to destructive leadership? How Gordon Ramsay leads change in nightmare kitchens. *Journal of Leadership Studies* 14(4): 81–8. https://doi.org/10.1002/jls.21723.

Barnes, Christine (2017). Mediating good food and moments of possibility with Jamie Oliver: problematising celebrity chefs as talking labels. *Geoforum* 84(1): 169–78.

Bell, David and Joanne Hollows (2011). From *River Cottage* to *Chicken Run*: Hugh Fearnley-Whittingstall and the class politics of ethical consumption. *Celebrity Studies* 2(2): 178–91. https://doi.org/10.1080/19392397.2011.574861.

Bertuzzi, Niccolò (2017). Veganism: lifestyle or political movement? Looking for relations beyond antispeciesism. *Relations* 5(2): 125–43. https://www.ledonline.it/index.php/Relations/article/view/1254.

British Hen Welfare Trust (2020). Jamie Oliver. *British Hen Welfare Trust*, 1 April. https://www.bhwt.org.uk/news/jamie-oliver/.

Buttlar, Benjamin and Eva Walther (2019). Dealing with the meat paradox: threat leads to moral disengagement from meat consumption. *Appetite* 137(1): 73–80. https://doi.org/10.1016/j.appet.2019.02.017.

Channel 4 (2020). *Channel 4 Television Corporation Report and Financial Statements 2020*. London: Channel 4.

Christopher, Allison, John P. Bartkowski and Timothy Haverda (2018). Portraits of veganism: a comparative discourse analysis of a second-order subculture. *Societies* 8(3): 55–76. https://doi.org/10.3390/soc8030055.

Cole, Matthew and Karen Morgan (2011). Vegaphobia: derogatory discourses of veganism and the reproduction of speciesism in UK national newspapers. *The British Journal of Sociology* 62(1): 134–53. https://tinyurl.com/56spj26z.

Derkatch, Colleen and Philippa Spoel (2015). Public health promotion of "local food": constituting the self-governing citizen-consumer. *Health: An Interdisciplinary Journal for the Social Study of Health, Illness and Medicine* 21(2): 154–70. https://doi.org/10.1177/1363459315590247.

Doyle, Julie (2016). Celebrity vegans and the lifestyling of ethical consumption. *Environmental Communication* 10(6): 777–90. https://tinyurl.com/2dwj9xph.

Food Unwrapped (2012). TV. Rob Butterfield (Dir.). Distributor: Channel 4 Television Corporation.

Gheihman, Nina (2021). Veganism as a lifestyle movement. *Sociology Compass* 15(5): 1–14. https://doi.org/10.1111/soc4.12877.

Grauel, Jonas (2016). Being authentic or being responsible? Food consumption, morality and the presentation of the self. *Journal of Consumer Culture* 16(3): 852–69.

Higgins, Michael, Martin Montgomery, Angela Smith and Andrew Tolson (2011). Belligerent broadcasting and makeover television: professional incivility in *Ramsay's Kitchen Nightmares*. *International Journal of Cultural Studies* 15(5): 501–18. https://doi.org/10.1177/1367877911422864.

Hollows, Joanne (2010). "At least he's doing something": moral entrepreneurship and individual responsibility in *Jamie's Ministry of Food*. *European Journal of Cultural Studies* 13(3): 307–22. https://doi.org/10.1177/1367549410363197.

Hollows, Joanne (2003). Oliver's twist: leisure, labour and domestic masculinity in The Naked Chef. *International Journal of Cultural Studies* 6(2): 229–48. https://doi.org/10.1177/13678779030062005.

Hugh's Chicken Run (2008). TV. Helen Simpson (Dir.). Distributor: Channel 4 Television Corporation.

Hugh's Fish Fight (2012). TV. Will Anderson (Dir.). Distributor: Channel 4 Television Corporation.

Inside the Factory (2015). TV. Michael Rees (Dir.). Distributor: BBC.

Jackson, Peter (2016). Go home Jamie: reframing consumer choice. *Social & Cultural Geography* 17(6): 753–7.

Jamie's Fish Supper (2011). TV. Martha Delap (Dir.). Distributor: Channel 4 Television Corporation.

Jamie's Fowl Dinners (2008). TV. Susannah Ward (Dir.). Distributor: Channel 4 Television Corporation.

Jamie's Great Escape (2005). TV. Helen Simpson (Dir.). Distributor: Channel 4 Television Corporation.

Jamie's Great Italian Escape (2005). TV. Helen Simpson (Dir.). Distributor: Channel 4 Television Corporation.

Jamie's Ministry of Food (2008). TV. Emily Jones (Dir.). Distributor: Channel 4 Television Corporation.

Jamie Saves Our Bacon (2009). TV. Brian Klein (Dir.). Distributor: Channel 4 Television Corporation.

Kjær, Katrine Meldgaard (2019). In/authenticity and food/celebrity relationships in Michael Pollan's *In Defence of Food* and Jamie Oliver's *Jamie's Food Revolution. Celebrity Studies* 10(3): 332–45. https://tinyurl.com/3f8sfvxe.

Leer, Jonatan and Katine Meldgaard Kjær (2015). Strange culinary encounters: stranger fetishism in Jamie's Italian Escape and Gordon's Great Escape. *Food, Culture and Society* 18(2): 309–27. https://tinyurl.com/3y5x3psd.

Lewis, Tania and Emily Potter (2010). Introducing ethical consumption. In Tania Lewis and Emily Potter, eds. *Ethical Consumption: A Critical Introduction*, 3–23. London: Routledge.

Lewis, Tania and Alison Huber (2015). A revolution in an eggcup? Supermarket wars, celebrity chefs and ethical consumption. *Food, Culture and Society* 18(2): 289–307. https://doi.org/10.2752/175174415X14190821960798.

Lund, Thomas B., Dorothy E.F. McKeegan, Clare Cribbin and Peter Sandøe (2016). Animal ethics profiling of vegetarians, vegans and meat-eaters. *Anthrozoös* 29(1): 89–106. https://doi.org/10.1080/08927936.2015.1083192.

Mackrell, Daniel (2019). Is Jamie Oliver a vegetarian as he hosts meat-free meals TV series? *Metro*, 9 September. https://tinyurl.com/4mwaandh.

Munro, Lyle (2005). *Confronting Cruelty: Moral Orthodoxy and the Challenge of the Animal Rights Movement*. Leiden: Brill.

The Naked Chef (1999). TV. Paul Ratcliffe (Dir.). Distributor: BBC.

Nilsson, Gabriella (2013). Balls enough: manliness and legitimated violence in *Hell's Kitchen. Gender, Work and Organization* 20(6): 647–63. https://doi.org/10.1111/gwao.12001.

Oliver, Jamie (2019). *Veg: Easy & Delicious Meals for Everyone*. London: Michael Joseph.

Pevreall, Kaite (2017). Jamie Oliver finds vegans annoying despite believing vegan diet best for health. *LiveKindly*. https://tinyurl.com/26ap6x9p.

Phillipov, Michelle and Fred Gale (2020). Celebrity chefs, consumption politics and food labelling: exploring the contradictions. *Journal of Consumer Culture* 20(4): 400–18. https://doi.org/10.1177/1469540518773831.

Piper, Nick (2015). Jamie Oliver and cultural intermediation. *Food, Culture and Society* 18(2): 245–64. https://doi.org/10.2752/175174415X14180391604288.

Potts, Annie (2016). What is meat culture? In Annie Potts, ed. *Meat Culture*, 1–30. Leiden: Brill.

Powell, Helen and Sylvie Prasad (2010). "As seen on TV." The celebrity expert: how taste is shaped by lifestyle media. *Cultural Politics* 6(1): 111–24. https://doi.org/10.2752/175174310X12549254318908.

Rodan, Debbie and Jane Mummery (2016). Doing animal welfare activism everyday: questions of identity. *Continuum: Journal of Media and Cultural Studies* 30(4): 381–96. https://doi.org/10.1080/10304312.2016.1141868.

Roff, Robin Jane (2007). Shopping for change? Neoliberalizing activism and the limits to eating non-GMO. *Agriculture and Human Values* 24(4): 511–22. https://doi.org/10.1007/s10460-007-9083-z.

Rousseau, Signe (2012). *Food Media: Celebrity Chefs and the Politics of Everyday Interference*. London and New York: Berg.

Sexton, Alexandra E., Tara Garnett and Jamie Lorimer (2022). Vegan food geographies and the rise of Big Veganism. *Progress in Human Geography* 46(2): 605–28. https://doi.org/10.1177/03091325211051021.

Shulman, Deborah, Mor Shnitzer-Akuka and Michal Reifen-Tagar (2021). The cost of attributing moral blame: defensiveness and resistance to change when raising awareness to animal suffering in factory farming. *PLoS ONE* 16(8): 1–16.

Starostinetskaya, Anna (2018). Gordon Ramsay finally gives vegan thing a try. *VegNews*, 16 April. https://tinyurl.com/ycyj593b.

Strong, Jeremy (2011). A short poetics of cruel food. In Jeremy Strong, ed. *Educated Tastes: Food, Drink, and Connoisseur Culture*, 158–93. Lincoln and London: University of Nebraska Press.

Thompson, Kirrilly and Laura Haigh (2017). Representations of food waste in reality food television: an exploratory analysis of *Ramsay's Kitchen Nightmares*. *Sustainability* 9(7): 1139–49. https://doi.org/10.3390/su9071139.

Warin, Megan (2011). Foucault's progeny: Jamie Oliver and the art of governing obesity. *Social Theory and Health* 9(1): 24–40. https://tinyurl.com/nbh3zh2y.

Zatat, Narjas (2017). Jamie Oliver on vegans: "They hate me". *Independent*, 7 August. https://tinyurl.com/bdfbsen7.

12

Celebrity activism

PETA, Pamela, Porn

Toby Miller

> [A] majority of my work has been in Animal rights, protecting the environment and children – trying to use my image and abilities to speak on behalf of – human rights/Aids education worldwide – VIVA Glam campaigning etc – I have had [a] close friend say I'm "The most famous unknown person on the planet".[1]

> Let us stop bothering to appeal to PETA's better judgement. Now is the time for serious action against the organisation. Let those of us who care about the harm it is doing try to shut them down. The harm they do to both women and animals is enough to justify calling on even the most passionate animal rights activist to support us in the campaign to close this hate-filled organization.[2]

There is a fundamental difficulty with the word "activism". It once referred to volunteer and professional campaigners and analysts. From Los Angeles to London, hipsters and the not-so-hip alike introduced themselves as "activists". Their means of financial support and sources of knowledge were generally left undisclosed by this term, but it was understood axiomatically that they were not racist, anti-feminist,

1 Anderson 2013.
2 Bindel 2010.

militaristic or opposed to socialism and climate science, and participated in progressive social movements.

But those valences no longer dominate. There has been a dramatic shift over the last ten years as the right has learned tactics, strategies and subjectivities from the left. Vast numbers of activists are now precisely racist, anti-feminist, militaristic and opposed to socialism and climate science. Politicised spectacle may alert many people to environmental issues[3] but also encourage them to affiliate with fascism.[4] And the left itself is split.

This chapter examines the place and meaning of celebrity activism within a contemporary neoliberal landscape. A particular issue confronts the latter section of this chapter: can quasi-pornographic representations of Hollywood notables produced by People for the Ethical Treatment of Animals (PETA), specifically images featuring Pamela Anderson, incarnate and initiate progressive activism?

Celebrity activism

Identifying as an activist is akin to saying "I am an artist": it is a foundational identity. Activists must "live the issue", demonstrating a comprehensive "alignment between personal identity and collective identity".[5] Celebrities are rather different from common-or-garden activists, because they are famous for being famous, creatures of marketing and carefully directed gossip – fabulations of the culture industries. Activism is generally a hobby or branding opportunity for them, not a thoroughgoing self-definition. In Hollywood, for example, the three major talent agencies (United Talent Agency [UTA], Creative Artists Agency [CAA] and WME)[6] select causes with which their charges might associate, based on interest, image and status. An "A-lister" is connected to different issues from someone trying to break

3 Goodman, Littler et al. 2016.
4 Ravecca, Schenck et al. 2022.
5 Bobel 2007.
6 WME and ICM are not acronyms but company titles.

through or who has fallen from the heights; straight men may be articulated to different organisations than feminist women.

So UTA's "Culture and Leadership Division" is dedicated to "thought leadership" and "social impact",[7] while the "Politics department" at ICM, which recently merged with CAA, sought "to form the connective tissue between talent and the political landscape by cultivating and seeking out opportunities that support and amplify what our clients are most passionate about". This is because "Creativity has the power to spark change."[8] CAA promises "limitless opportunities" to "thought leaders who shape popular culture"[9] and can "ignite and champion efforts to improve the world around us … to create positive social change". Environmentalism is on the list.[10] WME lays claim to "one of the largest cultural footprints on Earth", enabling it to "influence perception and frame collective understanding … to shape and promote a better world" through "Cause Consulting".[11] Service to talent remains a lodestone – in this instance, "advising clients in their philanthropic, social responsibility, and cause-making endeavors".[12] These activities are denounced by reactionaries as the left's "grip on Hollywood".[13] But here is the deal – and it is perfectly ordinary – whereas full-time activists are organic intellectuals of the left or the right, celebrity intellectuals are curated within the culture industries.

Gramsci maintained that each social group creates:

> one or more strata of intellectuals which give it homogeneity and an awareness of its own function not only in the economic but also in the social and political fields.[14]

These "'organic' intellectuals[,] which every new class creates alongside itself and elaborates in the course of its development",[15] assist in the

---

7 Kroll 2019.
8 ICM 2019.
9 CAA 2018.
10 CAA 2019a.
11 WME 2019.
12 CAA 2019b.
13 Ng 2021.
14 Gramsci 1978, 5.
15 Gramsci 1978, 6.

emergence and success of that class, for example via journalistic or pedagogic expertise. They operate in "'civil society' … the ensemble of organisms commonly called 'private'". The task of intellectuals is to incarnate a "'hegemony' which the dominant group exercises throughout society" alongside its "'direct domination' or command exercised through the State and 'juridical' government". As a consequence of these superstructural and substructural elements, ordinary people give "'spontaneous' consent … to the general direction imposed on social life by the dominant fundamental group".[16] Environmental concerns, notably animal rights, are among the fields where celebrity intellectuals seek to counter or support aspects of this hegemony. So what Hollywood talent agencies are doing is normal. But as for being on the left, UTA and its kind are as far from socialism as one can imagine.

When we ponder stars' deployment by vanguards in the name of a connection to the wider population, it is easy to adopt a critical or celebratory reaction. Critics would say that rationality must be appealed to in discussions of climate change; competition for emotion ultimately fails; and grassroots ties are wildly imaginary or mechanistically cliché. Why? The silent majority does not like direct action; corporations outspend activists; such occasions preach to a light-skinned, middle-class eco-choir; media coverage is partial and hostile; and crucial decisions are made by elites, not in streets. This critique has particular resonance in the case of events that are always already animated by spectacle, such as celebrity appearances and declarations. For corporations are well schooled in asymmetrical actions against smaller critics, basing their strategies on successful struggles by regular armies against guerrilla forces. Activism may irritate them, but they simply implement affordable parts of the critique then move on.[17] Corporate beneficence and consumer selflessness will not solve environmental despoliation.[18]

While celebrity activism often attracts media coverage, the public doesn't show great interest in messages from such folks that are

16 Gramsci 1978, 12.
17 Marshall, Telofski et al. 2012.
18 Humphreys 2009; Seyfang 2005.

politicised rather than commercial.[19] For example, when stars urge boycotts of tourist spots in opposition to riding donkeys, eating dogs or hunting dolphin, the record is unimpressive.[20] When actors embody the fashion industry's recent engagement with environmentalism by favouring "green" clothing, they simultaneously turn habiliments into a mere "aesthetic of the wearer", one more fetishised commodity ready to be featured – as has been the case – by *Vogue*, *Elle*, *Flaunt*, *Marie Claire*, *Surface* or *Glamour*.[21] The effect is to adorn celebrities with seriousness and promote them, rather than highlight the cause in question.

Conversely, the celebratory camp would argue that a distinction between hearts and minds is not sustainable; humour ameliorates the image of environmentalists as finger-wagging scolds; corporate capital must be publicly opposed; the media's desire for vibrant textuality can be twinned with serious discussion as a means of involving audiences; and a wave of anti-elite sentiment is cresting. The lugubrious hyper-rationality associated with ecology needs leavening through a sophisticated, entertaining, participatory blend of dark irony, biting sarcasm and cartoonish stereotypes. Celebrity campaigns may have an impact when there is no party-political component. For example, stars might encourage the public to contemplate veganism, based on their assumed altruism.[22] This normalisation can be secured, ironically, through spectacle.[23]

Numerous Hollywood people, events and institutions associate with environmentalism. *The Day After Tomorrow* (2004) received Carbon Neutral status because the production paid perhaps US$200,000 to plant trees in mitigation for 9,072 tonnes of CO_2 emitted during filming. Many Hollywood events are vegan or favour "sustainable farming", which PETA welcomes.[24] Twenty-five celebrities arrived at the 2006 Academy Awards in Toyota Priuses. The 2007 Emmys red carpet was made from 95,000 recycled soda bottles. That same year, a "Hollywood Goes Green"

19 Becker 2013; Thrall, Lollio-Fahkreddine et al. 2008; Till, Stanley and Priluck 2008.
20 Shaheer, Carr and Insch 2021.
21 Doyle 2016; Winge 2008, 512.
22 Lundahl 2020; Phua, Jin and Kim 2020.
23 Abidin, Brockington et al. 2020.
24 Maness 2020.

summit meeting was held. In 2008, the Oscars cut 572 tonnes of carbon emissions from the previous year's amount.[25] Joaquin Phoenix wore the same evening attire throughout the 2020 awards season.[26] Thanks to Leonardo DiCaprio's foundation supporting ecological projects, including the documentaries *Global Warning* (2019) and *The 11th Hour* (2007), he is listed as one of the world's *Green Heroes*, a pantheon that comprises the Buddha, Saint Francis of Assisi, Charles Darwin, Peter Singer, Brigitte Bardot, Vandana Shiva, Rachel Carson, David Attenborough and Arnold Schwarzenegger.[27] Good to know. The Environmental Media Association (EMA) seeks to "harness the power of storytelling to call for environmental justice, climate action, and sustainability",[28] honours deserving celebrities with a Green Seal, and hosts IMPACT conferences. The majors – Disney, Paramount, Warner Bros., Universal and Sony – all express commitments to sustainability.

But there is another side. DiCaprio took a sabbatical from filmmaking in 2013 to "fly around the world doing good for the environment".[29] As part of this noble venture, he helped launch the World Wide Fund for Nature's "Hands Off My Parts". An accompanying press release focused on a country that had incurred DiCaprio's particular displeasure:

> I am joining WWF and others in calling on Thailand's government to show leadership on elephant conservation by shutting down its ivory market before the country hosts a meeting of 177 nations on wildlife trade.[30]

Such condescending conduct is one of the many unfortunate aspects to celebrities' brief encounters with the Third World.[31]

---

25 Maxwell and Miller 2012.
26 Serjeant and Ross 2020.
27 Erdős 2019.
28 EMA 2019.
29 *The Nation* 2013.
30 *The Nation* 2013.
31 Richey 2016. This sentence refers to Gary Trudeau's comic strip (1978) re US diplomacy. He tropes *Close Encounters of the Third Kind* (1977) via "Brief encounters with the Third World".

DiCaprio's activism is called into question not only by his jet-setting carbon footprint but by the very industry that feeds his needs. Some of the money he uses to "fly around the world doing good for the environment" comes from acting. Much of *Titanic* (1997) was shot in a Mexican water tank in Popotla, Baja California. During filming, the village was cut off from the sea and local fisheries by a 1.8 metre high, 152 metre long wall that kept citizens away from production. The studio's chlorination of surrounding seawater decimated sea urchins, which locals had long harvested, and reduced overall fish levels by a third. Meanwhile, the cost of making *Titanic* could have provided safe drinking water to 600,000 people for a year.[32]

Accusations of celebrity hypocrisy are levelled with great gusto by reactionaries.[33] One can see why when, for example, the swag for actors attending awards ceremonies includes luxury-cruise vouchers.[34] The news outlet MSNBC has admonished "green" stars for their superficiality, suggesting that pollution would be a more accurate symbol of Hollywood life, because the "trucks that carry equipment from studios to locations and back continue to emit exhaust from diesel engines", as do on-set generators.[35] "[E]nvironmental damage is wrought in the name of entertainment ... making a film eats up energy like no other art form."[36] Even *Variety* describes Hollywood as "a dirty, polluting and eco-unfriendly enterprise".[37]

A major study identified the motion picture industry as the largest producer of conventional pollutants in Los Angeles. Its dependence on electricity and petroleum is responsible for releasing hundreds of thousands of tonnes of deadly materials a year. In the state of California overall, screen drama's energy consumption and greenhouse gas emissions are akin to those of the aerospace and semiconductor

32 Maxwell and Miller 2012.
33 MRCTV Staff 2015.
34 Serjeant and Ross 2020.
35 Ventre 2008.
36 Aftab 2007.
37 Thompson 2007.

businesses.[38] A budget of US$50 million generally sees a motion picture produce about 4,000 tonnes of CO_2.[39]

The majors do not fully disclose their ecological impact, notably via offshore and interstate runaway production. The anecdotal record of nominative determinism is dubious: *Pirates of the Caribbean: Dead Men Tell No Tales* (2017) left untold its dumping of chemical waste in Australia; *Mad Max: Fury Road* (2015) enraged activists by assaulting the Namibian coastline; and *The Expendables 2* (2012) deemed a Bulgarian residence for endangered species inessential.[40]

Environmental celebrity does not have to be self-regarding or unself-reflexive. For example, Daryl Hannah travels by train when she crosses the US and has been arrested for chaining herself to the White House gates to protest a Canada–US pipeline. Such engagement sees her face media opprobrium.[41] So where do PETA and Pamela Anderson fit in this story?

PETA

In the time since PETA's foundation 40 years ago, it has become the most internationally prominent institutional advocate for animal rights. Like that movement in general, PETA's executive and nine million members are overwhelmingly female. The organisation's first decade was mostly dedicated to attracting news coverage of public events. Then it became "celebrity culture oriented".[42] That referenced a partial transformation from direct action and protest to gaining press coverage via celebrities who were already forged by the bourgeois media. PETA made its own texts in ways calculated to attract and shock in equal, combined measure.[43]

38 Corbett and Turco 2006.
39 Harper 2018.
40 Fitzpatrick 2019.
41 Goldenberg 2013; Rowlatt 2009; Wood 2009.
42 Simonson 2001, 407.
43 PETA 2021, 18; Simonson 2001.

It was taking on a weighty, if contested, philosophical underpinning to carnivorism, based on doctrines of human supremacism. Consider this capsule history and its resonance with centuries of state and capitalist plunder and propaganda.

Descartes argued that "reason or good sense … exists whole and complete in each of us", and that "makes us men and distinguishes us from the lower animals".[44] Kant regarded people as uniquely valuable because they were conscious of themselves and their place in the world: "through rank and dignity", human beings were "an entirely different being from things, such as irrational animals, with which one can do as one likes".[45] Hegel exalted in a world shaped and mis-shaped by our physical and symbolic mastery, avowing that "man" could put his "will into everything"; so an object or place "becomes *mine*".[46] This was because willpower transcended simple survival, setting humanity apart from other living things. As per Kant, the capacity to transcend our "spontaneity and natural constitution" supposedly distinguished us from other animals, legitimising "the right of absolute proprietorship".[47] Because human beings were unique in their desire and capacity to conserve and represent objects via semiosis, a strange dialectical process allegedly afforded them a special right to destroy as well.

The influence of this "human exceptionalism paradigm"[48] is evident in doctrines of imperialism, nationalism and economic growth; journalistic claims about common sense; college courses valorising "Western civilisation"; and pronouncements from entities such as the Countryside Alliance promoting "the rural way of life … in a managed landscape";[49] that is, sequestering, enslaving and assassinating animals. And hence monadic solipsism governing what should be the commons.[50]

There have always been dissenters. Hume maintained that animals, like people, "learn many things from experience", developing

44 Descartes 2007.
45 Kant 2000; Kant 2006; Kant 2011.
46 Hegel 1988, 50, 154; Hegel 1954, 242–3, emphasis in original.
47 Hegel 1988, 61; Hegel 1954, 248–50.
48 Catton and Dunlap 1978.
49 Countryside Alliance 2022.
50 Hardin 1968.

"knowledge of the nature of fire, water, earth, stones, heights, depths, etc." in addition to processing instructions as part of domestication. Rather than being merely sensate, some of our fellow creatures apply logic through inference – what he called "the reason of animals".[51] Bentham said: "The question is not, Can they *reason*? nor, Can they *talk*? but, Can they *suffer*?" A duty of care extended to all animals suffering discrimination.[52] PETA quotes him.[53]

As Engels poignantly put it, human beings mark the evolutionary point where "nature attains consciousness of itself".[54] For Marx, recognising oneself as a species could not only generate class consciousness but expand that awareness to encompass other forms of life.[55] Although they were indebted to Kant and Hegel, Marx and Engels realised that people had the ability and responsibility to observe and speak for those without voices, to protect those without power. For while our fellow animals can transform their living conditions, they do so without an evident, deliberate and elaborated codification of what this achieves or means, a cultural form that can be relied upon in a court of law or congressional hearing. That difference does not make us superordinate: with special capacities come additional expectations.

Contemporary environmental theories vary between eco-centric, eco-socialist, ecofeminist, intermediate and anthropocentric forms.[56] The five schools differ over values (which entities qualify for moral consideration and matter most), rights (protecting individuals and groups) and consequences (responsibility for diminishing wellbeing). Eco-centric ethics holds that "some or all natural beings, in the broadest sense, have independent moral status".[57] Eco-socialism highlights the incompatibility of capitalism with the preservation of nature, with earth reshaped and its lifespan shortened by industrial capital.[58] Ecofeminism identifies gender as crucial to environmental destruction due to

51 Hume 1955.
52 Bentham 1970, emphasis in original.
53 PETA 2013.
54 Engels 1940, 17.
55 Marx 1987.
56 Swanton 2010.
57 Curry 2006, 64.
58 Luxemburg 1970, 335.

masculinist commitments to "development" and "growth" and stereotyping of nature and women as "irrational".[59]

Intermediate ecological ethics accords some intrinsic value to nonhuman nature, extending moral status to other sentient beings. Anthropocentric eco-ethics privileges the human interests prioritised by Descartes and others. Nonhuman nature has no moral standing (and hence no rights) other than when people are also affected by environmental change. Anthropocentric eco-ethics endorses consumption while urging customers to buy responsibly and recycle. It dominates mainstream environmentalism and much state, capitalist and popular discourse – and PETA.

Consumerism has always been at the movement's heart. Along with promoting "a healthy vegan diet", the group's animating drive is "to shop cruelty-free". Protesting assaults on animals, from factory farms to college laboratories, was once equally important. But the triumphs listed today are reforms to circuses, fast-food outlets, cosmetics firms, government regulations and fashion labels. This "compassion in action"[60] is driven by the realisation that "animals are not ours to experiment on, eat, wear, use for entertainment, or abuse in any other way".[61] PETA has adopted veganism as a market category, with no full-throated attack on the industrial enslavement and slaughter of animals *qua* food capitalism.[62] The organisation released "22 Celebrity Quotes That Will Help You Go Vegan in 2022".[63] Prominent participants in the campaign included Mayim Bialik, Ariana Grande, Jessica Chastain, Joaquin Phoenix, Sadie Sink, Ava DuVernay, RZA, Billie Eilish, Madelaine Petsch, Michelle Pfeiffer, Lenny Kravitz and Natalie Portman. Their quotations referred to beauty, health, the ease of change, justice, global warming, animal welfare and the corruption of carnivorous industries. The tagline read: "Animals Are Not Ours."

Such celebrity environmental causes have made the world even safer for corporations by holding individuals and powerless workers

---

59 Adams and Gruen 2022; d'Eaubonne 1978.
60 PETA 2015a.
61 PETA 2021, 3.
62 Sexton, Garnett and Lorimer 2022.
63 Kretzer 2022.

responsible for meat's role in climate change and animal suffering.[64] PETA is vulnerable to co-optation by the business interests it seeks to influence, as a function of a fundamentally reformist politics: the organisation proudly lists the corporations whose practices it has helped change, and advocates shareholder activism. Such plutocratic beliefs are celebrated by *Forbes* magazine.[65]

Companies endorsed by PETA for "getting" the message routinely describe themselves as citizens; but their principal pursuit is economic self-interest. A restless quest for profit unfettered by regulation is twinned with a desire for moral legitimacy and free advertising, based on "doing right" in a very public way – while growing rich in a very private one. Under neoliberalism, much of politics has come to appear artificial, whereas consumption seems natural – the legitimation of social arrangements. In ecological and democratic terms, such beliefs lead to plutocratic arrangements – for example, if green activism is ordered around consumption, as per PETA, those who do not consume, or barely do so, are ipso facto excluded from the exercise of power, in the same way as they are marginal to decisions made by the International Monetary Fund or the World Bank, where voting is decided by financial contribution.

Pamporn

PETA's honorary board of directors includes Edie Falco, Pamela Anderson, Alicia Silverstone, Lily Tomlin, James Cromwell, Kate del Castillo and Anjelica Huston, among others.[66] Anderson, and several campaigns involving her and other pin-up figures, form the basis of what is to come.

Variety says, "she's spent more of her career as a punchline than a performer".[67] But Anderson shouldn't feel bad about the friend quoted in the opening epigraph describing her as the "most famous unknown

64 McCubbin 2020.
65 Aziz 2020; Bromberg 2021.
66 PETA 2021.
67 Rubin 2022.

person on the planet": the Total Celebrity Endorser Rating Model gave her a .337 rating[68] and *Vogue* welcomed her 2022 Broadway debut by asserting that she "has always stayed true to herself while triumphing over personal strife and the pitfalls of stardom".[69]

Renowned for her role in *Baywatch*, her pin-up past and her relationship with Tommy Lee, Anderson is also an environmentalist, animal rights maven, defender of *gilets jaunes* (yellow vests) against state neglect and violence[70] and anti-porn activist, according to a *Wall Street Journal* op-ed.[71] Such dedication has not only taken the form of discussions in the corridors of power – though she has done plenty of that work – it has also seen her in full scopophilic mode, spectacularising her body as per *Playboy*. While avowing her own feminism, Anderson finds the current iteration "a bore" that "paralyzes men" – something quoted with relish by the likes of *Fox News*, *Breitbart*, *People* and *The Federalist*.[72]

PETA calls Anderson a "[v]oluptuous vegan" and a "blonde bombshell"[73] and describes its "naked celebs" as "beautiful because they aren't afraid to stand up for animal rights" and oppose the pain that underpins wool, leather and fur. An illustrated list includes a bevy of stereotypically attractive adult women disrobed: Eva Mendes, Taraji P. Henson, Alicia Silverstone, Jenna Dewan Tatum, Olivia Munn, Daniela Alonso, Wendy Williams, Joss Stone, Roselyn Sánchez, Lisa Edelstein, Maggie Q and Joanna Krupa.[74]

The pictures veer between conventionally seductive and autotelically powerful, but always with a direct stare at the camera and a come-hither "doll-like" look tied to images and words favouring vegan, vegetarian and environmental causes.[75] The depictions borrow from a longstanding nostrum of marketing that sex sells things to straight

---

68 Knott and St James 2004, 93.
69 Valenti 2022.
70 Anderson 2018.
71 Boteach and Anderson 2016.
72 McCarthy 2018; Rose Falcone 2018; Russell 2018.
73 PETA 2017.
74 PETA 2016.
75 Villanueva Romero 2013, 161.

men, who are putatively "aroused" by soft-core images of women and stimulated to buy associated goods and services.[76]

One PETA-Pam image tropes the shower scene from *Psycho* (1960), re-creating the terror of Janet Leigh's character. Anderson is horrified not by a murderous hotelier but by the misuse of water: the advertisement notes that half the US supply goes to dairy and meat farms.[77] In PETA's "All Animals Have the Same Parts" advertisement,[78] she poses in a bikini, her body drawn on to list her rump, ribs, leg, shoulder, feet, round and breast as if she were food. The image was banned in Montréal, where officials deemed it counter to "the everlasting battle of equality between men and women". Anderson responded that:

> In a city that is known for its exotic dancing and for being progressive and edgy, how sad that a woman would be banned from using her own body in a political protest over the suffering of cows and chickens. In some parts of the world, women are forced to cover their whole bodies with burquas [sic] – is that next? I didn't think that Canada would be so puritanical.[79]

PETA accused the authorities of "confusing 'sexy' with 'sexist'".[80] *The Guardian* suggested some "might gaze at the poster for carnal gratification rather than vegetarian epiphany". Anderson replied that what she called a "butcher diagram" was "the perfect thing to parody, because it allows you to use your own body as a protest tool". PETA dubbed her its "weapon of mass distraction".[81]

Perhaps the organisation's most notorious campaign was "Boyfriend Went Vegan" (2012) in which a young woman has a neck brace and dislocated gait because her lover has become more sexually vibrant since embracing veganism, subsequently injuring her and

---

76 Kilbourne 2005; LaTour, Pitts and Snook-Luther 1990; Reichert 2002.
77 PETA 2015b.
78 PETA 2017.
79 *Us Weekly* Staff 2010.
80 *Us Weekly* Staff 2010.
81 Jones 2010.

damaging a wall during lovemaking. PETA promised that veganism's "freer blood flow to all of the major organs", along with the movement's need to be "press sluts", had encouraged the campaign.[82] Meanwhile, its "Veggie Love" video, promoted as banned from Superbowl TV, simulated sex with vegetables while boasting about vegetarian "performance" and pleasure.[83]

Reactionaries responded puritanically. For example, *Business Insider* listed "18 times PETA ads have used nudity, gore, and sacrilege to get your attention".[84] The ever-oleaginous *National Review* ordered its readers "to do exactly the opposite of what PETA demands".[85] The Catholic League and *InsideCatholic* decreed it irreligious.[86] More gravely, the FBI investigated PETA for ties to "domestic terrorist organisations",[87] the *Journal of the American Medical Association* decried it as "a significant threat to the future of medical research",[88] and Britain's Counter Terrorism Policing branded the organisation an extremist danger, alongside neo-Nazis.[89]

Progressives were also concerned – about the male gaze, proximity to pornography and limited range of body shapes on view. *Australian Feminist Studies* took the images to task for a heterosexism aimed at satisfying men that set unreachable goals for women, subordinating them to our fellow animals.[90] *Ms.* magazine re-designated PETA as "People for the ethical treatment of anyone but women".[91] *Affinity* charged it with "weaponising and exploiting the oppression of marginalized minorities".[92] *Huffington Post* accused the organisation of failing to connect fashion, beauty, animal torture and its "use of pornography",[93] of caring "very little for one animal in particular:

82 "Boyfriend Went Vegan" 2012; Kenney 2012; Ocasio 2012.
83 PETA 2019.
84 Baer and De Luce 2019.
85 Kelly 2017.
86 McKay 2016.
87 Younge 2006.
88 Vance 1992.
89 Dodd and Grierson 2020.
90 Dejmanee 2013.
91 Kenney 2012.
92 Whitaker 2017.

human beings".[94] *Salon* attacked PETA as a "sorry, misogyny-riddled excuse for an activist group" because of its "truly dysfunctional obsession with women's bodies".[95]

Controversy also arose when the group likened the Holocaust and human slavery to the treatment of our fellow animals, ignoring the specificity and humanness of those dual horrors. Such campaigns compromise the capacity to link social movements across and among oppressed groups in the interests of progressive politics.[96]

African Americans still struggle to be regarded as equal to other people, and comparing pre American Civil War human slavery to contemporary animal slavery as PETA did degrades a tradition of anti-racist action.[97] The National Association for the Advancement of Colored People responded to the organisation's "Are Animals the New Slaves?" campaign with "Once again, Black people are being pimped"[98] and Tiffany Haddish said she would wear fur every day until the police stopped killing African Americans.[99]

Such failings are linked to a longstanding criticism of animal rights organisations for racialised class structures, while ethnographic research discloses that the movement urges women to subordinate gender equality and other concerns to a purportedly greater good – a familiar leftist theme in relation to class, race, sexuality, religion, disability and trans issues.[100]

That said, the magnitude of daily, industrial animal suffering may be on a continuum with crimes against humanity, and *Feminismo/s* argues that the "animalization of women in advertising" does not only degrade; it may also empower, by drawing ironic ecofeminist attention to anthropomorphic cultural associations of women with our fellow animals and the oppression of both by semiotic clichés and literal violence.[101]

---

93 Pennington 2013.
94 Uprichard 2013.
95 Williams 2013.
96 Kim 2011.
97 Davis 2020.
98 Wright 2011.
99 BET 2018.
100 Gaarder 2011.

It is worth noting the history of women troping naked imagery for political capital: Breasts Not Bombs favouring toplessness in public; FEMEN criticising sex tourism; Pussy Riot denouncing patriarchy; Baring Witness opposing invasion and occupation; SlutWalk organising against sexual violence; and other groups disrupting parliament, marching for abortion and sex-work rights, undermining religiosity, faulting Brexit and challenging censorship. They refuse the notion of the female body as a site for moralism and exploitation.[102]

Such actions buy into two key strategies: one appealing to the rationality and intrinsic merit of a cause, the other using visceral pleasure or shock, as per PETA blending a moral argument about extending human rights to animals with an emotive one derived from stereotypes.[103] Outrage stimulates attention to a widely ignored issue. The focus is on vegan identity and animal justice over economic and political transformation.[104]

Can the efficacy of such campaigns be established empirically? Media-effects researchers have sought to discern whether it is "effective to advertise an ethical cause using unethical means" by showing PETA's sexualised and non-sexualised advertisements to young men and women. Their support for animal rights diminished if associated with soft-core dehumanisation of women, even when straight men were "aroused" by the imagery.[105] Away from artificial test surroundings, political economists will note the sheer presence of the organisation in popular culture: in 2021, 450 million viewings of PETA's celebrity videos, nearly 800 op-eds, and 73,000 bourgeois media interviews and inquiries, from *Good Housekeeping* to *Breitbart*, *Sports Illustrated* to *Women's Wear Daily*, Al Jazeera to Fox Sports.[106]

---

101 Villanueva Romero 2013.

102 Alaimo 2010; Chemaly 2014; Gupta 2017; Khrebtan-Hörhager 2015; Kreps 2019; Logan 2016–2017; Mendes 2015; Riccioni and Halley 2021; Trujillo 2017; Urbanik 2009; Williams 2019.

103 Babu 2012.

104 Atkins-Sayre 2010.

105 Bongiorno, Bain and Haslam 2013.

106 PETA 2021, 18.

Conclusion

PETA seeks to distinguish itself from po-faced, joyless environmentalism and traditional species supremacism. The organisation maintains that because "all but the most controversial voices are drowned out in a media din, our willingness to be cheeky and provocative when necessary ensures that the plight of animals does not go unnoticed" alongside less flashy activities such as research, education and lobbying.[107] The line is that "[w]hile it would be nice to hold a news conference and … wait for coverage, … this rarely happens".[108] Hence founder Ingrid Newkirk's plaintive remark:

> We're like a car crash … you have to look at us and you'll talk about it afterwards. We can't just deliver the straight facts. People want to be titillated these days. … We're stunt queens. We have to be.[109]

She argues that:

> If Pamela Anderson says something, everyone drops their sandwich. … Even if they can't stand her or only want to have sex with her, they're all going to listen. … she has a big chest but … an enormous heart inside it.[110]

Campaigns involving Anderson and other women celebrities use their bodies as signs of exploitation and reification in a structural homology with conventional thinking about animals, playing with humanness, vulnerability and beauty. This may shock and offend one kind of conservative, one kind of feminist, but draw a chuckle from a different conservative or feminist. That struggle for meaning is the hinge where PETA makes its play, in a conflictual articulation between denotation and connotation.

107 PETA 2021, 3.
108 Bekhechi 2010.
109 Younge 2006.
110 Younge 2006.

Given that we know animals are routinely used in marketing, as are women, should both be "on sale" by PETA?[111] Such a gambit inevitably references women as subordinate, as pets, as threats, as "other" in a longstanding "master mentality".[112] The question is whether the organisation enthusiastically and exploitatively endorses that mentality – or recasts it for progressive ends.[113]

PETA may have *become* a spectacle, with Anderson and her colleagues organic intellectuals of a problematic kind. Is a love of troping centrefolds and violence, of frottage with dubious corporate social responsibility, a good look for a social movement? The impact craved and the norms transgressed – and ramified – form a polysemic campaign strategy that both undermines and empowers women in a contradictory spiral of meaning and interpretation,[114] and the failure to link animal rights to other oppression isolates PETA from important social movements. A reductive focus guarantees clarity but jeopardises ties to anti-racism, ecofeminism and eco-socialism.

References

Abidin, Crystal, Dan Brockington, Mary Mostafanezhad and Lisa Ann Richey (2020). The tropes of celebrity environmentalism. *Annual Review of Environment and Resources* 45: 387–410. https://tinyurl.com/ywkhp888.

Adams, Carol J. and Lori Gruen (2022). Preface. In Carol J. Adams and Lori Gruen, eds. *Ecofeminism: Feminist Interactions with Other Animals and the Earth*, xxi–xxiii. London: Bloomsbury Academic.

Aftab, Kaleem (2007). Emission impossible: why Hollywood is one of the worst polluters. *Independent*, 16 November. https://tinyurl.com/47zudzpy.

Alaimo, Stacy (2010). The naked word: the trans-corporeal ethics of the protesting body. *Women and Performance: A Journal of Feminist Theory* 20(1): 15–36. https://doi.org/10.1080/07407701003589253.

---

111 Molloy 2011.

112 Villanueva Romero 2013, 172; also see Morris, Goldenberg and Boyd 2018; Salmen and Dhont 2021.

113 Pendergrast 2018.

114 Deckha 2008.

Anderson, Pamela (2018). Yellow vests and I. *Pamela Anderson Foundation*, 4 December. https://tinyurl.com/4ax6ujxt.
Anderson, Pamela (2013). Home from Haiti. *PamelaAnderson*, February. https://tinyurl.com/2m69skxa.
Atkins-Sayre, Wendy (2010). Articulating identity: People for the Ethical Treatment of Animals and the animal/human divide. *Western Journal of Communication* 74(3): 309–28. https://doi.org/10.1080/10570311003767183.
Aziz, Adhel (2020). Vegan materials. *Forbes*, 25 November. https://www.tinyurl.com/2bjkfch9.
Babu, Ambikar (2012). Persuasion & animal rights advocacy: an in-depth look at persuasion in PETA print ad using elaboration likelihood model. *Science Communicator: Inter-Disciplinary Journal for Science Communication and Journalism* 3(1): 64–71. https://tinyurl.com/2zvb8u9e.
Baer, Drake and Ivan De Luce (2019). 18 times PETA ads have used nudity, gore, and sacrilege to get your attention. *Business Insider*, 24 July. https://tinyurl.com/53jyhtse.
Becker, Amy B. (2013). Star power? Advocacy, receptivity, and viewpoints on celebrity involvement in issue politics. *Atlantic Journal of Communication* 21(10): 1–16. https://doi.org/10.1080/15456870.2013.743310.
Bekhechi, Mimi (2010). Peta's persistence is opening people's eyes. *Guardian*, 3 November. https://tinyurl.com/5n9yhbdy.
Bentham, Jeremy (1970). *The Principles of Morals and Legislation*. Darien: Hafner.
BET (2018). Tiffany Haddish declares war on PETA and police brutality at the same damn time. *bet.com*, 30 December. https://tinyurl.com/48eh2pv9.
Bindel, Julie (2010). Let's make Peta history. *Guardian*, 28 October. https://tinyurl.com/4saepncs.
Bobel, Chris (2007). "I'm not an activist, though I've done a lot of it": doing activism, being activist and the "perfect standard" in a contemporary movement. *Social Movement Studies: Journal of Social, Cultural and Political Protest* 6(2): 147–59. https://doi.org/10.1080/14742830701497277.
Bongiorno, Renata, Paul G. Bain and Nick Haslam (2013). When sex doesn't sell: using sexualized images of women reduces support for ethical campaigns. *PLoS ONE* 8(12). https://doi.org/10.1371/journal.pone.0083311.
Boteach, Shmuley and Pamela Anderson (2016). Take the pledge: no more indulging porn. *Wall Street Journal*, 31 August. https://tinyurl.com/ytttfr7b.
"Boyfriend Went Vegan" (2012). PETA. YouTube Video. *PETA*, uploaded 6 February 2012. www.youtube.com/watch?v=m0vQOnHW0Kc.
Bromberg, Lev (2021). Numbing the pain or diffusing the pressure? The co-optation of PETA's "naming and shaming" campaign against mulesing. *Law and Policy* 43(3): 285–313. https://doi.org/10.1111/lapo.12172.

CAA (2018). About us. *CAA*, June. www.caa.com/about-us.

CAA (2019a). Social responsibility. *CAA*, June. www.caa.com/social-responsibility.

CAA (2019b). Social impact. *CAA*, June. www.caa.com/social-impact.

Catton, William R. and Riley E. Dunlap (1978). Environmental sociology: a new paradigm. *American Sociologist* 13(1): 41–9.

Chemaly, Soraya (2014). 6 reasons female nudity can be powerful. *Salon*, 22 January. https://tinyurl.com/5ksebmpk.

Close Encounters of the Third Kind (1977). Film. Steven Spielberg (Dir.). Distributor: Columbia/Sony.

Corbett, Charles J. and Richard P. Turco (2006). *Sustainability in the Motion Picture Industry*. Report prepared for the Integrated Waste Management Board of the State of California. https://tinyurl.com/54eat87c.

Countryside Alliance (2022). Communities. *Countryside Alliance*, February. https://www.countryside-alliance.org/our-work/campaigns.

Curry, Patrick (2006). *Ecological Ethics: An Introduction*. Cambridge: Polity Press.

Davis, Janet M. (2020). The history of animal activism: intersectional advocacy and the American humane movement. In Robert William Fischer, ed. *The Routledge Handbook of Animal Ethics*, 479–91. New York: Routledge.

d'Eaubonne, Françoise (1978). *Écologie/feminisme: Révolution ou mutation?* Paris: Éditions ATP.

Deckha, Maneesha (2008). Disturbing images: PETA and the feminist ethics of animal advocacy. *Ethics and the Environment* 13(2): 35–76. https://doi.org/10.2979/ete.2008.13.2.35.

Dejmanee, Tisha (2013). The burdens of caring. *Australian Feminist Studies* 28(77): 311–22. https://doi.org/10.1080/08164649.2013.821726.

Descartes, René (2007). *Discourse on the Method of Rightly Conducting One's Reason and Seeking Truth in the Sciences*. https://tinyurl.com/2pz56jwr.

Dodd, Vikram and Jamie Grierson (2020). Greenpeace included with neo-Nazis on UK counter-terror list. *Guardian*, 17 January. https://tinyurl.com/3ubhypus.

Doyle, Julie (2016). Celebrity vegans and the lifestyling of ethical consumption. *Environmental Communication* 10(6): 777–90. https://tinyurl.com/2dwj9xph.

EMA (2019). EMA Awards. *EMA*. www.green4ema.org/ema-awards.

Engels, Frederick (1940). *The Dialectics of Nature*. Clemens Dutt, trans. London: Lawrence and Wishart.

Erdős, László (2019). *Green Heroes: From Buddha to Leonardo DiCaprio*. Cham: Springer.

Fitzpatrick, Kyle Raymond (2019). Behind every film production is a mess of environmental wreckage. *Vice*, 15 October. https://tinyurl.com/y3v647ws.

Gaarder, Emily (2011). *Women and the Animal Rights Movement*. New Brunswick, NJ: Rutgers University Press.

Goldenberg, Suzanne (2013). Daryl Hannah leads celebrity Keystone XL protest at White House gates. *The Guardian*, 13 February. https://tinyurl.com/ybsnjytm.

Goodman, Michael K., Jo Littler, Dan Brockington and Maxwell Boykoff (2016). Spectacular environmentalisms: media, knowledge and the framing of ecological politics. *Environmental Communication* 10(6): 677–88. https://doi.org/10.1080/17524032.2016.1219489.

Gramsci, Antonio (1978). *Selections From the Prison Notebooks of Antonio Gramsci*. Quentin Hoare and Geoffrey Nowell-Smith, trans. and eds. New York: International Publishers.

Gupta, Rahila (2017). The politics of nudity as feminist protest – from Ukraine to Tunisia. *OpenDemocracy*, 21 July. https://tinyurl.com/4zmhaav4.

Hardin, Garrett (1968). The tragedy of the commons. *Science* 162(3859): 1243–8. https://doi.org/10.1126/science.162.3859.1243.

Harper, Lauren (2018). Cut! How the entertainment industry is reducing environmental impacts. *State of the Planet*, 29 March. https://tinyurl.com/3w3r6mxk.

Hegel, Georg Wilhelm Friedrich (1988). *Lectures on the Philosophy of World History. Introduction: Reason in History*. Hugh Barr Nisbet, trans. Cambridge: Cambridge University Press.

Hegel, Georg Wilhelm Friedrich (1954). *The Philosophy of Hegel*. Carl J. Friedrich, ed. Carl J. Friedrich, Paul W. Friedrich, W.H. Johnston, L.G. Struthers, B. Bosanquet, W.M. Bryant and J.B. Baillie, trans. New York: Modern Library.

Hume, David (1955). *An Inquiry Concerning Human Understanding with a Supplement: An Abstract of a Treatise of Human Nature*. Charles W. Hendel, ed. Indianapolis: Bobbs-Merrill.

Hume, David (1739 [1896]). *A Treatise of Human Nature*. Lewis Amherst Selby-Bigge, ed. Oxford: Clarendon Press.

Humphreys, David (2009). Environmental and ecological citizenship in civil society. *The International Spectator: Italian Journal of International Affairs* 44(1): 171–83. https://doi.org/10.1080/03932720802693101.

ICM (2019). ICM politics. *ICM*, November. https://www.icmpartners.com/icm-politics.

Jones, Sam (2010). Pamela Anderson poster for Peta urges vegetarianism, provocative style. *Guardian*, 22 October. https://tinyurl.com/yzkdeycd.

Kant, Immanuel (2011). *Observations on the Feeling of the Beautiful and Sublime and Other Writings*. Patrick Frierson and Paul Guyer, eds and trans. Cambridge, UK: Cambridge University Press.

Kant, Immanuel (2006). *Anthropology From a Pragmatic Point of View*. Robert B. Louden, ed. and trans. Cambridge, UK: Cambridge University Press.

Kant, Immanuel (2000). *Critique of the Power of Judgement*. Paul Guyer, ed. Paul Guyer and Eric Matthews, trans. Cambridge, UK: Cambridge University Press.

Kelly, Julie (2017). PETA: cheese is sexist. *National Review*, 8 August. https://www.nationalreview.com/2017/08/peta-cheese-product-rape-and-abuse/.

Kenney, Shawna (2012). PETA: people for the ethical treatment of anyone but women. *Ms.*, 28 February. https://tinyurl.com/22fa6rb2.

Khrebtan-Hörhager, Julia (2015). *Je suis FEMEN!* Traveling meanings of corporeal resistance. *Women's Studies in Communication* 38(4): 367–73. https://doi.org/10.1080/07491409.2015.1089101.

Kilbourne, Jean (2005). What else does sex sell? *International Journal of Advertising* 24(1): 119–22. https://doi.org/10.1080/02650487.2005.11072907.

Kim, Claire Jean (2011). Moral extensionism or racist exploitation? The use of holocaust and slavery analogies in the animal liberation movement. *New Political Science* 33(3): 311–33. https://tinyurl.com/4vr98dx6.

Knott, C.L. and M. St James (2004). An alternate approach to developing a total celebrity endorser rating model using the analytic hierarchy process. *International Transactions in Operational Research* 11(1): 87–95. https://doi.org/10.1111/j.1475-3995.2004.00442.x.

Kreps, Daniel (2019). Anti-censorship: activists strip nude outside Facebook HQ to fight nudity ban. *Rolling Stone*, 3 June. https://tinyurl.com/3mb2p9k5.

Kretzer, Michelle (2022). 22 celebrity quotes that will help you go vegan in 2022. *PETA*, 3 January. https://www.peta.org/blog/inspiring-celebrity-quotes-go-vegan.

Kroll, Justin (2019). Darnell Strom to lead UTA's newly created culture and leadership division. *UTA*, 15 January. https://tinyurl.com/5euv7v9b.

LaTour, Michael S., Robert E. Pitts and David C. Snook-Luther (1990). Female nudity, arousal, and ad response: an experimental investigation. *Journal of Advertising* 19(4): 51–62. https://doi.org/10.1080/00913367.1990.10673200.

Logan, Debra L. (2016–2017). Exposing nipples as political speech. *Law and Psychology Review* 41: 173–90. https://tinyurl.com/y8mkxyy8.

Lundahl, Outi (2020). Dynamics of positive deviance in destigmatisation: celebrities and the media in the rise of veganism. *Consumption Markets and Culture* 23(3): 241–71. https://doi.org/10.1080/10253866.2018.1512492.

Luxemburg, Rosa (1970). *Rosa Luxemburg Speaks*. Mary-Alice Waters, ed. New York: Pathfinder Press.

Mad Max: Fury Road (2015). Film. George Miller (Dir.). Distributor: Warner Bros.

Maness, Rebecca (2020). Vegan menus are sweeping awards season this year. *PETA*, 23 January. https://www.peta.org/living/food/vegan-awards-shows.

Marshall, Alasdair, Richard Telofski, Udechukwu Ojiako and Maxwell Chipulu (2012). An examination of "irregular competition" between corporations and NGOs. *Voluntas* 23(2): 371–91. https://doi.org/10.1007/s11266-011-9205-5.

Marx, Karl (1987). *Capital: A Critique of Political Economy, Volume 1*. New York: International Publishers.

Maxwell, Richard and Toby Miller (2012). *Greening the Media*. New York: Oxford University Press.

McCarthy, Tyler (2018). Pamela Anderson blasts the #MeToo movement, says feminism can "go too far". *Fox News*, 5 November. https://tinyurl.com/4xfsvwn8.

McCubbin, Sandra G. (2020). The Cecil moment: celebrity environmentalism, Nature 2.0, and the cultural politics of lion trophy hunting. *Geoforum* 108: 194–203. https://doi.org/10.1016/j.geoforum.2019.10.015.

McKay, Hollie (2016). Critics blast PETA ad showing nude Joanna Krupa holding crucifix. *Fox News*, 11 April. https://tinyurl.com/yvw8e8sb.

Mendes, Kaitlynn (2015). *SlutWalk: Feminism, Activism and Media*. Houndmills: Palgrave Macmillan.

Molloy, Claire (2011). *Popular Media and Animals*. Basingstoke: Palgrave Macmillan.

Morris, Kasey Lynn, Jamie Goldenberg and Patrick Boyd (2018). Women as animals, women as objects: evidence for two forms of objectification. *Personality and Social Psychology Bulletin* 44(9): 1302–14. https://doi.org/10.1177/0146167218765739.

MRCTV Staff (2015). The 12 most hypocritical environmentalists in Hollywood. *Media Research Center*, 15 April. https://tinyurl.com/4hstmsan.

Ng, David (2021). Left-wing talent agency CAA solidifies grip on Hollywood by acquiring rival ICM partners. *Breitbart*, 27 September. https://tinyurl.com/nf37e3xp.

Ocasio, Jeanette (2012). PETA makes light of intimate partner violence. *National Organization for Women*, 25 May. https://tinyurl.com/6kzhuam3.

Pendergrast, Nick P. (2018). PETA, patriarchy and intersectionality. *Animal Studies Journal* 7(1): 59–79. https://ro.uow.edu.au/asj/vol7/iss1/4.

Pennington, Louise (2013). Has PETA gone too far? Sexism, pornography and advertising. *Huffington Post*, 9 March. https://tinyurl.com/3ph2a855.

PETA (2013). Why animal rights? *PETA*, 22 November. https://www.peta.org/about-peta/why-peta/why-animal-rights.

PETA (2015a). PETA's history: compassion in action. *PETA*, 18 February. https://tinyurl.com/3rjvac6v.

PETA (2015b). Pamela Anderson screams: meat and dairy farms drain half the nation's water. *PETA*, 21 May. https://tinyurl.com/4938b7e9.
PETA (2016). You won't believe which celebrities got naked for PETA. *PETA*, 17 July. https://tinyurl.com/5r2knhxa.
PETA (2017). Pamela Anderson shows that all animals have the same parts. *PETA*, 15 April. https://tinyurl.com/3dwjchrj.
PETA (2019). Watch "Veggie Love": PETA's sexy ad banned from the Super Bowl. *PETA*, 13 May. https://www.peta.org/features/veggie-love.
PETA (2021). *They Do Not Belong To Us: PETA 2021 annual review*. https://tinyurl.com/2k4sbd9s.
Phua, Joe, Seunga Jin and Jihoon (Jay) Kim (2020). The roles of celebrity endorsers' and consumers' vegan identity in marketing communication about veganism. *Journal of Marketing Communications* 26(8): 813–35. https://doi.org/10.1080/13527266.2019.1590854.
Pirates of the Caribbean: Dead Men Tell No Tales (2017). Film. Joachim Rønning and Espen Sandberg (Dirs). Distributor: Disney.
Psycho (1960). Film. Alfred Hitchcock (Dir.). Distributor: Paramount.
Ravecca, Paulo, Marcela Schenck, Bruno Fonseca and Diego Forteza (2022). What are they doing *right*? Tweeting right-wing intersectionality in Latin America. *Globalizations*. https://doi.org/10.1080/14747731.2021.2025292.
Reichert, Tom (2002). Sex in advertising research: a review of content, effects, and functions of sexual information in consumer advertising. *Annual Review of Sex Research* 13: 241–73.
Riccioni, Ilaria and Jeffrey A. Halley (2021). Performance as social resistance: Pussy Riot as a feminist avant-garde. *Theory, Culture and Society* 38(7–8): 211–31. https://doi.org/10.1177/02632764211032726.
Richey, Lisa Ann (2016). *Celebrity Humanitarianism and North-South Relations: Politics, Place and Power*. Abingdon and New York: Routledge.
Rose Falcone, Dana (2018). Pamela Anderson says feminism "paralyzes men," calls #MeToo movement "a bit too much for me". *People*, 7 November. https://tinyurl.com/2m44djfr.
Rowlatt, Justin (2009). Justin does Dallas! *BBC News*, 6 March. https://tinyurl.com/2v9nxm95.
Rubin, Rebecca (2022). A front row seat as Pamela Anderson's super fans swarm Broadway's "Chicago". *Variety*, 20 April. https://tinyurl.com/24fp92ys.
Russell, Nicole (2018). Pamela Anderson says today's feminism is a total bore. *The Federalist*, 19 November. https://tinyurl.com/4sc6rhkk.
Salmen, Alina and Kristof Dhont (2021). Hostile and benevolent sexism: the differential roles of human supremacy beliefs, women's connection to nature,

and the dehumanization of women. *Group Processes and Intergroup Relations* 24(7): 1053–76. https://doi.org/10.1177/1368430220920713.

Serjeant, Jill and Jane Ross (2020). And the Oscar goes to … planet earth? *Reuters*, 2 February. https://tinyurl.com/2zevs5z3.

Sexton, Alexandra E., Tara Garnett and Jamie Lorimer (2022). Vegan food geographies and the rise of Big Veganism. *Progress in Human Geography* 46(2): 605–28. https://doi.org/10.1177/03091325211051021.

Seyfang, Gill (2005). Shopping for sustainability: can sustainable consumption promote ecological citizenship? *Environmental Politics* 14(2): 290–306. https://doi.org/10.1080/09644010500055209.

Shaheer, Ismail, Neil Carr and Andrea Insch (2021). Rallying support for animal welfare on Twitter: a tale of four destination boycotts. *Tourism Recreation Research*. https://doi.org/10.1080/02508281.2021.1936411.

Simonson, Peter (2001). Social noise and segmented rhythms: news, entertainment, and celebrity in the crusade for animal rights. *The Communication Review* 4(3): 399–420. https://tinyurl.com/3w23vfwf.

Swanton, Christine (2010). Heideggerian environmental virtue ethics. *Journal of Agricultural and Environmental Ethics* 23(1–2): 145–66. https://doi.org/10.1007/s10806-009-9186-1.

The 11th Hour (2007). Film. Leila Conners Petersen and Nadia Conners (Dirs). Distributor: Warner Independent.

The Day After Tomorrow (2004). Film. Roland Emmerich (Dir.). Distributor: Fox.

The Expendables 2 (2012). Film. Simon West (Dir.). Distributor: Lionsgate.

The Nation (2013). DiCaprio calls on Yingluck to ban ivory trade. *The Nation*, 25 February. https://tinyurl.com/3end9bab.

Thompson, Anne (2007). Hollywood goes green. *Variety*, 27 April. https://tinyurl.com/mvrhfmrz.

Thrall, A. Trevor, Jaime Lollio-Fahkreddine, Jon Berent, Lana Donnelly, Wes Herrin, Zachary Paquette et al. (2008). Star power: celebrity advocacy and the evolution of the public sphere. *International Journal of Press/Politics* 13(4): 362–85.

Till, Brian D., Sarah M. Stanley and Randi Priluck (2008). Classical conditioning and celebrity endorsers: an examination of belongingness and resistance to extinction. *Psychology and Marketing* 25(2): 179–96.

Titanic (1997) Film. James Cameron (Dir.). Distributor: Paramount/Fox.

Trudeau, Gary B. (1978). *Any Grooming Hints for Your Fans, Rollie?* New York: Holt, Rinehart and Winston.

Trujillo, Graciela (2017). People around the world are using nudity as a form of protest. *Medium*, 25 March. https://tinyurl.com/2j7fbskn.

Uprichard, Lucy (2013). The problem with PETA. *Huffington Post*, 24 May. https://tinyurl.com/h9zd25pv.

Urbanik, Julie (2009). "Hooters for Neuters": sexist or transgressive animal advocacy campaign? *Humanimalia: A Journal of Human/Animal Interface Studies* 1(1): 40–62.

Us Weekly Staff (2010). Pamela Anderson's nearly naked PETA ad banned in Canada. *Us Weekly*, 15 July. https://tinyurl.com/4mtskdjy.

Valenti, Lauren (2022). "I've been rehearsing my whole life for this": Pamela Anderson on her Broadway debut, TikTok's obsession with her style, and finally setting the record straight. *Vogue*, 22 March. https://tinyurl.com/mpb8nxkr.

Vance, Richard P. (1992). An introduction to the philosophical presuppositions of the animal liberation/rights movement. *Journal of the American Medical Association* 268(13): 1715–9. https://tinyurl.com/2pknybmb.

Ventre, Michael (2008). It's not easy being green, Hollywood discovers. *MSNBC*, 23 April. https://www.nbcnews.com/id/24256817.

Villanueva Romero, Diana (2013). "Savage beauty": representations of women as animals in PETA's campaigns and Alexander McQueen's fashion shows. *Feminismo/s: Revista del Centro de Estudios sobre la Mujer* 22: 147–75. https://doi.org/10.14198/fem.2013.22.09.

Whitaker, Sebastian (2017). Here's 10 outrageously problematic things PETA has done and why you shouldn't support them. *Affinity*, 26 November. https://tinyurl.com/bp69npmz.

Williams, Mary Elizabeth (2013). PETA's ridiculous new birth control stunt. *Salon*, 3 December. https://tinyurl.com/2pusaurf.

Williams, Zoe (2019). Activism laid bare: a quick history of naked protests. *Guardian*, 2 April. https://tinyurl.com/5bkeh8tu.

Winge, Theresa M. (2008). "Green is the new black": celebrity chic and the "green" commodity fetish. *Fashion Theory: The Journal of Dress, Body and Culture* 12(4): 511–23. https://doi.org/10.2752/175174108X346968.

Wood, Gaby (2009). "I'm a little bit of a nerd". *Guardian*, 7 June. https://www.theguardian.co.uk/film/2009/jun/07/interview-daryl-hannah.

WME (2019). Endeavour impact. *WME*, December. https://tinyurl.com/39zssx29.

Wright, Danielle (2011). Another PETA exhibit compares animal cruelty to slavery. *bet.com*, 21 July. https://tinyurl.com/ectedhst.

Younge, Gary (2006). "We're stunt queens. We have to be". *Guardian*, 24 February. https://tinyurl.com/3v5bj2n5.

13

About a speech

The media's reaction to a celebrity advocacy intervention

Loredana Loy

At the 2020 Academy Awards, the American actor Joaquin Phoenix won the Oscar for Best Actor for his role in the movie *Joker* (2019). His coolly delivered yet impassioned speech represents a first in terms of public outreach, subject and content. Approximately 23.6 million people watched the ceremony in the United States alone,[1] which although it is considered a record low as far as Oscar ceremony audiences go, represents a record high in terms of exposing a large audience to an unapologetic and unveiled animal rights message. Furthermore, the speech continued to have a life of its own on numerous media platforms.[2] In terms of subject – advocacy on behalf of nonhuman animals (hereafter animals) – it was a first in the history of the Academy Awards. With regards to its content, the speech was nothing short of groundbreaking because it delivered to a large audience the idea that speciesism, or human domination of other species, can and should be included alongside other ideologies and structures of oppression.

This chapter looks at the way this speech, as an intervention by a celebrity animal rights advocate, was presented, perceived and

1 BBC 2020.
2 For example, the official ABC clip had almost four million views on YouTube in May 2022.

discussed in the media and by various groups in the United States, either to capitalise on its news value or to promote and defend specific interests. The chapter seeks to uncover what the media responses to this intervention can say about the mechanisms that legitimate speciesism in our society. It looks at how media representatives (writers, journalists, show hosts and industry defenders, among others) react when confronted with a glimpse of the realities of speciesism. By examining a collection of television and radio shows that discussed the speech, as well as articles written in the aftermath of the event by mainstream media outlets and groups related to the animal exploitation industry, this chapter aims to identify and analyse the competing and common themes linking these commentaries in the hope of illuminating the significance of a unique intervention on behalf of animals by a celebrity activist.

Joaquin Phoenix is a highly respected actor and a dedicated animal rights advocate, having previously narrated the powerful animal rights documentary *Earthlings* (2005) and having starred in advertisements for People for the Ethical Treatment of Animals (PETA). At various events on the film industry's awards circuit leading up to the Academy Awards, the actor made a number of political statements in support of different advocacy causes such as the environment and diversity and inclusion in the film industry.[3] Moreover, the Golden Globes, Oscars, Critics' Choice and Screen Actors Guild (SAG) Awards, as well as the Governor's Ball, all served plant-based menus apparently as a result of the star's lobbying efforts.[4] Phoenix also paired the ceremonies with real-life activism by attending several animal rights events while he was in the running to win these prestigious awards,[5] thus helping to garner some media attention for this important social issue.

The subsequent actions of the star, which culminated in the adoption of a calf and her mother from a Californian slaughterhouse, extended the speech's momentum and provided some more opportunities for different organisations to continue the debate. A few months later, the COVID-19 crisis had cast the speech into a new light,

3 Romano 2020.
4 Baum 2020.
5 Gardner 2020.

reopening the conversation and offering further opportunities for its consideration.[6]

I start this chapter with a quick overview of the history of political speeches at the Academy Awards, in order to convey the contentious nature of such events and provide a sense of how "controversial" causes have been received by live audiences on Oscars night. I follow that with an examination of the content of Phoenix's speech to provide the reader with a perspective on the reasons why it is significant. Then I examine how the speech was covered and interpreted following the Oscars night on television and radio shows, in the media, and by interest groups. My findings show a demarcation between the way liberal and conservative television and radio show hosts engaged with the speech. The liberal hosts merely made note of the animal rights themes, while the conservatives framed them through ideological perspectives. Furthermore, the speech ignited a vigorous response from the animal exploitation industry and its defenders, who sought to defend the industry and reframe its processes as beneficial and benign.

Political speeches at the Oscars

Political acceptance speeches by celebrities at the Oscars are nothing new. However, they are still relatively rare in the history of televised Academy Awards ceremonies, which started in 1953. The first instances of such speeches ignited intense disapproval from those participating in the events. At the 1973 ceremony, in one of the first occurrences of a social justice motivated Oscar acceptance moment, Marlon Brando sent Native American activist Sacheen Littlefeather to refuse his award for Best Actor for *The Godfather* (1972) in protest of the representation and treatment of Native Americans in the film and television industry. The audience's reaction was divided. Some in the crowd applauded and others jeered, while presenter Clint Eastwood lamented that "I don't know if I should present this award on behalf of all the cowboys shot in all the John Ford westerns over the years",[7] eliciting laughter and

---

6 See McNulty 2020.

7 Oscars 1973.

applause from the crowd. Similarly, in 1978, after winning the Oscar for Best Supporting Actress for *Julia* (1977), Vanessa Redgrave gave a political speech in defence of the Palestinian Liberation Organization. In response, presenter Paddy Chayefsky, one of Hollywood's celebrated screenwriters at the time, took it upon himself to respond:

> I would like to say, personal opinion of course, that I am sick and tired of people exploiting the occasion of the Academy Awards for the propagation of their own personal political propaganda. I would like to suggest to Ms. Redgrave that her winning an Academy award is not a pivotal moment in history, does not require a proclamation, and a simple "thank you" would have sufficed.[8]

The audience applauded frenetically and celebrities were showcased nodding in approval, with very few exceptions. These early examples are followed over the decades by other Oscar winners championing their various causes and educing divided responses from audiences.

As far as this author is aware, advocacy on behalf of the environment made its first appearance at the Academy Awards in 2007 with Al Gore's acceptance speech for *An Inconvenient Truth* (2006), a film about climate breakdown, which won Best Documentary. By the time Leonardo DiCaprio asked that we "not take this planet for granted"[9] in his 2016 acceptance speech for Best Actor for *The Revenant* (2015), both live audiences and those watching at home were more or less expecting political speeches from stars involved in advocacy causes. It also seems, judging by the reactions at the awards ceremony, that audiences have become more tolerant of political speeches over the years, either as a result of growing accustomed to them or because of a decrease in the degree to which they appear controversial.[10]

8 Fretts 2019.

9 Oscars 2016.

10 It is beyond the purposes of this chapter to track and examine the trajectory of the nature of speeches and responses, but the general trend seems to point towards either a more tolerant audience or a decrease in the degree to which these speeches are considered controversial. Naturally, the fact that

Furthermore, the Academy of Motion Pictures itself has recently embraced social-issue advocacy in the ceremony; the 2016 event included various nods to the #MeToo movement as well as to the people involved with it.

The first surprising thing about Phoenix's acceptance speech is that the actor did not make a single mention of his movie. He did not thank a list of people, as is usually customary with Oscar speeches. Instead, he used his time to deliver a thoughtful and well-crafted manifesto that aimed to bring animal rights to the forefront of social justice issues. Phoenix's speech made history for bringing forth and showcasing an issue that had not made an appearance before at the Oscars. Yet the speech displays some other notable qualities. For instance, the actor did not sugarcoat the content of his speech to make it more palatable to audiences. Thus, he did not employ "information control", the Goffmanian concept described as the effort to manage what an audience is perceived as capable of understanding, with the aim of maintaining a favourable impression in front of that audience.[11] Phoenix did not shy away from speaking out against the dairy industry and giving an example that must have seemed preposterous to many.[12] Furthermore, although he spoke directly to his peers sitting right in front of him in the auditorium, it seems that – as with any political speech – his intention was to reach beyond the walls of the Dolby Theatre in Los Angeles to disclose to viewers everywhere a dimension of the world that most had never considered.[13]

Research has shown that celebrity advocacy can sometimes be detrimental to a cause due to celebrity dilettantism.[14] For example, celebrities can commonly end up delivering misguided or diluted

---

Hollywood is predominantly liberal plays an important role, since most of the causes championed feature on liberal agendas.

11 Goffman 1974.

12 The fact that the process by which milk is obtained involves separating the mother cow from her baby in order to take the milk intended for her infant.

13 On a side note, *The Hollywood Reporter* ran a poll asking its audience to vote for their favourite speech. Phoenix's speech got 65 per cent (or 3,148 votes), by far the most votes, followed (not closely) by Best Director Oscar winner Bong Joon Ho with 16 per cent (or 789 votes).

14 Cooper 2008.

animal rights messages that seem to cater to disinterested and potentially antagonistic audiences rather than serve the cause they are supposed to support. Two possible explanations for these unconvincing efforts, in line with the aforementioned Goffmanian concept of information control, are that these efforts either stem from the messenger's inadequate understanding of the issues or are crafted around the need to protect the messenger from coming across as "crazy" or extreme to their fan base.[15] This is not the case with Phoenix's effort.

The significance of the speech

Phoenix begins his acceptance speech by expressing gratitude for the position he inhabits in the film industry. He argues that it is this position that obligates him to be a "voice for the voiceless", which could be considered a cliché if not for the fact that it has never been done on behalf of animals at such a significant event. Phoenix then frames the issues that he is about to shine a light on as *collective issues* – things that *we all* should be concerned about:

> I think the greatest gift that it's given me, and many people in this industry is the opportunity to use our voice for the voiceless. I've been thinking about some of the distressing issues that we've been facing collectively.

He then builds on the idea of the collective by linking the social issues to each other: "I think at times we feel or are made to feel that we champion different causes. But for me, I see commonality." By bridging these ideas and presenting them as collective, he lays the foundation for his main claim – that speciesism belongs together with all the other "isms":

15 For example, Jessica Chastain's point that not everyone needs to be vegan, although she claims to be one (see Lupica 2017).

> I think, whether we're talking about gender inequality or racism or queer rights or indigenous rights or animal rights, we're talking about the fight against injustice. We're talking about the fight against the belief that one nation, one people, one race, one gender, one species has the right to dominate, use and control another with impunity.

Equating the rights of people with those of animals and including the domination and exploitation of nonhumans along with all the other forms of domination and exploitation must have seemed like a radical and perhaps even outrageous idea to many of those paying attention to Phoenix's words. At this moment the camera cuts to members of the audience, who are shown watching the actor intently. It seems that Phoenix got their attention with the enumeration of conventionally accepted causes (i.e., gender inequality, racism, queer rights, Indigenous rights) and won their approval to that point. At the end of the list of human oppressions, he delivers the unexpected element – animal rights – surprising his audience while they are still nodding in approval. Phoenix also takes great care to pronounce the words *animal rights* distinctly and gravely, emphasising these words to ensure that they stand out as the focus of the sentence. A semi-modest roar of applause follows. Nearly half of the audience can be seen applauding his remarks.[16]

I can only speculate about what the lack of more vigorous support as well as the lack of boos could mean, perhaps anything from disapproval to disinterest or confusion. If the reception of works that compare the suffering of animals with that of people can tell us anything, it is that they are often met with hostility.[17]

Next, the actor delivers his indictment. He uses the notion of the collective again to make a direct call-out to everyone, but this time

---

16 Among the visible "supporters", as measured by the perceived level of enthusiasm exhibited during the applause, were Brad Pitt and Leonardo DiCaprio, both well-known environmentalists, and Penelope Cruz, who has previously worked with PETA on animal rights campaigns.

17 See Socha 2013. Two main works come to mind, *The Dreaded Comparison: Human and Animal Slavery* (Spiegel 1996) and *Eternal Treblinka: Our Treatment of Animals and the Holocaust* (Patterson 2002).

to point to the collective responsibility that we should all share. Once again, Phoenix brings in the animal rights issue, giving an example from a ubiquitous "process" that is intimate to dairy producers but mostly unfamiliar to the public that consumes the "product":

> I think we've become very disconnected from the natural world. Many of us are guilty of an egocentric world view, and we believe that we're the centre of the universe. We go into the natural world and we plunder it for its resources. We feel entitled to artificially inseminate a cow and steal her baby, even though her cries of anguish are unmistakable. Then we take her milk that's intended for her calf and we put it in our coffee and our cereal.

Phoenix then brings his plea full circle by appealing to individuals' capacity to effect personal change, making sure to point out why personal change is important – because systemic change can follow:

> I think we fear the idea of personal change, because we think that we have to sacrifice something, to give something up. But human beings at our best are so inventive and creative and ingenious, and I think that when we use love and compassion as our guiding principles, we can create, develop and implement systems of change that are beneficial to all sentient beings and to the environment.

He closes with an example of transformation that seems to be intended to ignite a sense of possibility in the audience. He speaks of his personal journey from a "scoundrel" to this "risen" Phoenix who is standing in front of his peers as a result of the redemption they extended him.

Media coverage: Television and radio shows

How was this emotional but also well-planned, smartly structured and strategically constructed speech received? First, I look at coverage from national television and radio shows in the United States on the day following the ceremony. The format and structure of these shows, which feature multiple hosts and guests and often contain dialogue among them, can help unravel some insights, not only into how the speech was covered but also how it was interpreted for television and radio audiences. Using the Access World News database, I looked for shows that mentioned the actor's name on 10 February 2021. I retrieved 26 TV show transcripts from CNN, Fox, ABC, NBC and MSNBC, and one radio show from NPR.

One theme that emerged from the data is a divide between the two main factions of the American political landscape. The liberal shows, which discussed Phoenix's speech and its various dimensions, and the conservative shows, which presented the speech as the proverbial "Hollywood pontificating to the rest of the world" moment and an attack on the American way of life. Notably, both sides agreed on one thing – that Phoenix's speech was honest and came from "a good place", as seen on Fox News,[18] "from the heart", as seen on CNN[19] and from a place of "humanity" and "empathy", as seen on ABC.[20]

The liberal shows exhibited a largely approbatory tone towards the speech and discussed how Phoenix had been political throughout the award season, for example on CNN, and how he was "using his platform for good" and was a "voice for the voiceless" for example on ABC.[21] However, the hosts chose to focus on the human dimensions of the speech, in line with the conventionally accepted causes enumerated above, such as systemic racism and inequality as well as culture and sustainability. Overall, the hosts of these shows did not engage with its animal rights dimension. When they did, it was either to express confusion about that message or to discount it as an oddity. Here's an example of dialogue between two hosts on ABC's *Good Morning America*:

> Keke Palmer: He [Phoenix] was great. There were a couple of moments in the speech where I was, like, it, it, is he not, like, where is this going? And then he brought it, but he did bring it

18 Williams 2020.
19 Holmes 2020.
20 Palmer and Haines 2020.
21 Palmer and Haines 2020.

> back. But when he would say, like a baby cow and the, taking the milk from the mom, well.
>
> Ross Matthews: You have to stay with him.
>
> Vernin Francois: So, pretty much if, if you tuned in the middle of that speech, you may be supremely confused, but, yes.
>
> Sara Haines: I was actually brushing my teeth in the bathroom, and I go, "Did he say baby cow? What is he talking about?"[22]

None of the shows on either side discussed the inclusion of speciesism among the other "isms" that the star mentioned, even though the section of the speech where this takes place was included in the video segments presented to viewers.

The popular show *The Five* on the conservative network Fox News played the section of the speech in which Phoenix references the dairy industry. The host of the show, Katie Pavlich, introduced the clip as "liberal Hollywood once again lecturing America at the Oscars with some truly bizarre rants".[23] She unwittingly, or perhaps in line with the free market ideology that occupies the conservative collective consciousness, latched on to the economic dimension of the issue by commenting at the end of the clip that "Karl Marx … also got a shout out".[24]

We know that opposition to environmental protection is a matter of ideological assertion for conservatives.[25] Here, the show host seems to have equated advocacy for ending animal exploitation with advocacy for Marxism. To get there, she appears to have lumped animal exploitation together with environmentalism, and by extension applied the same conservative tokenistic anti-environmental stance to animal rights.

It is interesting to note how natural the bundling of environmentalism with animal rights seems to be to conservatives. This is not even the case for environmentalists, who often attempt to

---

22 Palmer and Haines 2020.
23 Williams 2020.
24 Williams 2020.
25 Dunlap, McCright and Yarosh 2016.

dissociate themselves from the animal rights cause and wilfully exclude the concept from their efforts.[26] However, proponents of animal rights have long been advocating for the integration of animal rights into the broader environmental movement.[27] Most recently, this dichotomy has surfaced in climate change discourse. Whenever a shift to a plant-based food system is proposed as part of climate mitigation, it is contested by prominent progressives, environmentalists and climate scientists.[28]

On another Fox News show, *Morning with Maria*, the speech was summarised as "[Phoenix] talked about a baby calf being pulled away from his mother just so she can provide milk for your cereal and coffee" and labelled as "promoting vegan eating".[29] The host did not expand on these comments any further, and she did not qualify them either negatively or positively.

It is important to note that in contrast to the liberal shows, these right-leaning shows engaged with the animal dimension present in the speech. More research is needed to understand whether this can be explained as an extension of recent conservative trends to include food, especially meat and dairy, in their so-called "culture wars" in which they have claimed, among other things, that liberals attempt to alter diets and hence attack their way of life.[30] However, the fact is that meat and dairy have joined abortion, gun control and transgender rights as trigger conservative issues.[31] Furthermore, although the actor was vocal about other issues that also irk conservative sensibilities (i.e., queer rights), the hosts chose to ignore those points and focused on the animal rights dimension. This is perhaps further proof that this is the message that rose most prominently out of the speech.

The bigger question is why the liberal shows elected not to discuss the inclusion of speciesism in the collection of "isms"? Considering the nature of these shows, the subject could have easily been sensationalised. However, it must have been more straightforward for

---

26 See Grendstad, Selle et al. 2006; Hargrove 1992; Khoo 2009.
27 Khoo 2009; Hargrove 1992.
28 See Dutkiewicz 2020; Mann 2019; Mann and Brockopp 2019.
29 Bartiromo 2020.
30 Beaumont and Mcfetridge 2021.
31 Beaumont and Mcfetridge 2021.

the hosts to go along with themes they were familiar with, and which have been promoted by Phoenix in other speeches prior to the Oscars event, such as gender inequality and racism. Without a deeper look into their rationales, I can only speculate that the decision to ignore that part of the speech was based on the discomfort that such a discussion would entail and on the lack of awareness about animal rights issues. Research has shown that the media reception of this speech reflects discomfort towards veganism stemming from the defence of animal rights (as opposed to veganism that is health motivated) and is especially heightened when animal rights are equated with human rights.[32]

Regardless of the explanation, the issue remains that avoidance or exclusion of the topic contributes to the perpetuation of the status quo. By avoiding alternative or marginalised imaginaries, the media can block public discourse around those ideas.[33]

However, this silence is also indicative of larger trends that characterise the animal rights issue in our society. There is nothing more ubiquitous and more normalised than the exploitation of animals; it is part of the fabric of society. Information about the atrocities committed against nonhumans surface occasionally, yet there is no collective uproar. People choose to remain detached from the issue. Kari Marie Norgaard calls this type of collective distancing from disturbing information "the social organization of denial".[34] The decision to ignore the animal issue serves as a mechanism of avoidance of action. Stanley Cohen describes the choice to ignore information as implicatory denial – a type of denial based on the response and the change that acknowledging the issue would necessitate.[35] In the case of animal exploitation, the social organisation of denial and implicatory denial work together and are reinforced at both levels, structural and individual, enabling current social arrangements that allow for it to remain unperturbed.

32 Parkinson and Herring 2022.
33 Maeseele and Raeijmaekers 2017.
34 Norgaard 2006, 372.
35 Cohen 2001.

Media coverage: Industry perspectives and mainstream media outlets

For the media coverage of the speech, I retrieved articles from Nexis Uni. I searched for articles that included the actor's full name and the term "speech" anywhere in the body of the article and were written between 9 and 29 February 2020 in newspapers, magazines and journals in the United States. I retrieved 118 articles. After an initial review of all search results, elimination of duplicates and other irrelevant items, I narrowed the sample to 41 articles.

Industry perspectives

By far the most vehement engagements with the speech came from efforts representing animal exploitation industries. In a public statement, Republican House Representative Fred Keller, who represents an animal industry-heavy district in Philadelphia, labelled Phoenix's "speech about animal rights" as "offensive".[36] *The Hill* reproduced sections of the congressman's statement, particularly the part in connection with the dairy industry:

> Joaquin Phoenix winning Best Actor for playing the Joker fits him to a T because his comments would have been laughable were they not so offensive … Phoenix's rambling remarks about America's dairy industry prove how out-of-touch he is with the hardworking Americans who grow our food and create healthy communities.[37]

The *Washington Examiner* also highlighted some of Keller's comments: "Phoenix's Hollywood-elite world view has clearly blinded him to the sacrifice and struggles of America's dairy farmers".[38] The article goes on to summarise the speech, in what is perhaps its most accurate interpretation found in the media (even if conceivably unintentional):

36 Keller 2020.
37 Kurtz 2020.
38 Dibble 2020.

"Phoenix argued that people were ignoring injustices throughout the country. He focused on animal rights and criticised the dairy industry for its treatment of cows."[39]

A *New Mexico News* article featured a dairy farmer who argued that "every practice they implement, including artificial insemination, is in the best interest of the cows and calves" and that "It really goes back to the safety of the cows and it's a practice that is [i.e. exists] because we want to take better care of our cows."[40] She also took the opportunity to invite Phoenix to her "farm" in order to "research both sides of the conversation".[41]

BEEF Magazine, which sports a readership of about 100,000 readers according to its website, published two articles dedicated to Phoenix. In the first one, entitled "How Activists (& Joaquin Phoenix) are Working to End Animal Ownership", the author argues that Phoenix is a member of a domestic terrorist group (Animal Liberation Front) and makes an ardent call for the protection of freedoms allegedly in danger from Hollywood elite activism:

> These Hollywood elite may have good intentions, but at their core, their mission to impose sin taxes on meat, dairy and eggs and to regulate livestock farmers out of business really hurts the most vulnerable people of all – the food insecure and the impoverished people in our country and around the world. I'm proud to produce safe, affordable, nutrient-dense beef to feed a hungry planet, and stripping those options away from the hungry who desperately need high-quality protein isn't caring at all! I don't care if you're a vegan or carnivore – what I do care about is protecting our freedom to farm, our freedom to own property and most importantly, our freedom to choose the foods that best suit our needs, not the ideals of politicians or celebrities.[42]

39 Dibble 2020.
40 Washington 2020.
41 Washington 2020.
42 Radke 2020a.

The second article, entitled "Joaquin Phoenix: A Person is Worth More than a Scallop", capitalises on the entrenched conservative disdain for liberal movements: "Move aside Black Lives Matter and the #MeToo movement, the trendy new crusade is to go meatless to save the planet and to save the animals!"[43] The author argues that "God gives us permission to eat them [animals]" and quotes from the Bible. She uses false equivalents between sentient nonhuman animals, scallops and human animals, and argues that "despite what Disney movies would tell us, animals do not have the emotional range, depth of souls and divine value that humanity does".[44]

Also, in response to the speech, the *Milwaukee Journal Sentinel* reported that calves are taken from their mothers for their own safety. As for the "cries of anguish" that the actor mentioned in his speech, a dairy farmer interviewed for the article had this to say:

> She's going to moo for that calf a little bit, but she's not charging at us or anything. It's almost like "Woo hoo, the babysitter is here. Now I can go eat." And that is what she needs to do … Today's modern dairy cow isn't all that maternal … Occasionally we will have a cow that shows a little more maternal instinct, but it's pretty rare.[45]

Finally, *Fox Business* invited comments from a representative of the National Milk Producers Federation, who had this to say:

> If he [Phoenix] studied the commitment of dairy farmers to animal welfare and had a fuller understanding of the contribution of dairy products to a nutritious diet, especially for children, he might have a different perception of the value that dairy contributes to global health and the importance of the dairy sector to global livelihood.[46]

43 Radke 2020b.
44 Radke 2020b.
45 Barrett 2020.
46 Settembre 2020.

A few important themes are identifiable in these articles. First, there are the themes that speak to larger societal structures, such as the economic system. Here we see claims that Phoenix's rhetoric represents an attack on the freedoms that conservatives hold dear, such as property rights, the "right to farm" and the right to "choose what food to eat". These claims are tied to and justified by dominionism.[47] According to these commentators, those who promote these progressive ideas are discounted as elites who are out of touch with hardworking struggling Americans and who don't understand how "farms" function and how nutrition works.

The concept of status politics can help interpret these themes to some extent. Different social factions compete to have their own lifestyles – and food practices – become culturally dominant and seen as moral and normative.[48] Since eating animals is the status quo, plant-based lifestyles and, most importantly, a shift away from animal agriculture and to a plant-based food system are seen as threats to this dominant social frame. Thus, Phoenix's speech ignites these contestations between one group which has delineated itself using a set of group-sanctioned values and the other group embodied by those allegedly suggesting the abandonment and the transformation of these values. The offending group is often symbolic or imaginary, as in the case related to the animal issue. This is because in reality, we would be hard-pressed to find American liberal public figures who champion the radical transformation of the economic system and the abandonment of animal industries.[49] In fact, they vigorously retort when accused of doing so. This tendency has been most recently observed in the media when conservatives accused the Biden administration of trying to ban meat in order to mitigate climate change.[50] Liberals responded promptly by defending animal products and denying that such efforts

---

47 Dominionism is the belief that God has given humans dominion over animals and nature, which Lynn White (1967), in her famous essay, argues is the root of our ecological crisis.

48 Gusfield 1986.

49 One rare exception is Democratic congressman Cory Booker (D-NJ) who advocates for the reform of factory farming, although not for the end of the industry itself (see Klein 2020).

50 See Atkin 2021.

were part of the administration's plan and assuring everyone that "Biden is not coming for Americans' Big Macs, chicken wings or bacon".[51]

Second, there are the themes that speak directly to the notion of animal rights. Here we see claims that dairy and meat "farmers" are working for vulnerable people, children and health (both local and global), which conveniently ignores the fact that the actual goal of these industries is to make a profit. More importantly, industry practices are reframed as benign or being in the interest of the animals, for their protection and safety. The so-called "animal husbandry" practices such as removing the calf from the mother right after birth, which allow these industries to exist in the first place, are avoided and concealed in industry narratives.

Because dishonesty is the main characteristic in these statements, these themes are more difficult to interpret. The ease with which these "alternative facts" are produced suggests that they might be rooted in something less palpable in addition to being aimed at protecting economic interests. In his essay entitled "The Animal of Bad Faith: Speciesism as an Existential Project",[52] John Sanbonmatsu argues that participation in the inherently violent and oppressive system of animal exploitation involves disavowing one's participation in this system by concealing and disguising the truth even from oneself. Language has long been used to achieve such concealment, and indeed the use of euphemisms is common when it comes to animals. Terms such as "euthanasia" to justify the killing of healthy animals or the use of "harvest" instead of slaughter are often employed in public industry discourse. Likewise, in these industry-focused responses to Phoenix's speech we see a complete denial of what is being done to animals and a defence of reframed and altered realities.

Mainstream news and magazines

The mainstream news media articles that followed the Oscars ceremony examined in this chapter overwhelmingly ignored Phoenix's efforts to

---

51 Reiley 2021.

52 Sanbonmatsu 2014.

engage with the animal rights theme. A majority of articles simply stayed away from mentioning those themes, choosing instead to focus on the tribute that Phoenix made to his brother, River, and qualifying his speech with various hyperboles depicting his emotional state.

Even the few outlets that mentioned those themes decided to report or interpret the messages in simplistic terms. *Rolling Stone* noted that the actor "urged viewers to take better care of our planet"[53] and quoted the portion of the speech in which the actor references animal rights but did not comment on them. However, the article mentioned that Phoenix veganised the menus on the awards circuit. One of a few *New York Times* articles focused on the Oscars night stated that the actor made "oblique references to meat eating"[54] and pled for animal rights, citing the part of the speech referencing the dairy industry.

Only the specialised media outlets took a more focused interest in the speech. The *Washington Examiner*, a conservative news outlet, dedicated a more thoughtful article entitled "The Bizarre Brilliance of Joaquin Phoenix" to the actor's "tortured address" which resonated with audiences, the author thought. The article acknowledges the connection between Phoenix's comments and industrial farming operations and goes to some lengths to discuss it:

> Most people willing to look at what goes on at industrial farms understand those actions to be cruel, and Phoenix knows this, but he aimed higher than just guilt-tripping the audience over the milk in their cereal.[55]

Furthermore, the author even brought up the corruption of the meat industry:

> Just look at how state legislatures, Canada, and the European Union have colluded with the meat lobby to make it harder for plant-based meat alternative companies such as Beyond Meat or Impossible Foods to market their products on shelves alongside

53 Ehrlich 2020.
54 Deb 2020.
55 Kent 2020.

> genuine meat products. Leave it to lobbyists and bureaucrats to force veggie burgers into being labeled "veggie discs".[56]

Vox, a liberal outlet, also commented on industrial farming, stating that the actor spoke about the "trauma that the factory farming industry visits on livestock".[57] *Vulture*, also a liberal outlet, was not so generous. The article attacks Phoenix for paralleling "veganism with anti-racism"[58] and makes a mockery of the entire speech. Finally, *The Atlantic*, another liberal outlet, mentions the inclusion of animal rights along with the other "isms" without showing outrage, but also without dissecting the issue any further:

> Rather than speaking singly about racism or sexism or his long-standing activism on behalf of animals, Phoenix tied them all together. It was hard not to read the speech as the moment all his other podium petitions had been building toward – an opportunity for an actor who's deeply uncomfortable with the manufactured rigmarole of awards season to turn it into something he could stand, all without seeming too ungracious for the honors being festooned upon him.[59]

One important insight can be drawn from this media ethnography. The way the mainstream media (dis)engaged with the animal rights themes provides a much-needed perspective over the daily functioning of speciesism as the overarching ideological system of our society. The different prism through which the animal rights themes in the speech were refracted in the media show important aspects of the legitimation regime of speciesism: the conservative take, which is the most intuitively accurate and grasps to some extent the connection between animal rights and other social justice movements, and the liberal take, which is basically characterised by dismissal and condescension and

56 Kent 2020.
57 Romano 2020. Note the use of the word "livestock", an omnipresent speciesist term.
58 Harris 2020.
59 Gilbert 2020.

seems to be arising out of an effort to police the boundaries of humanism.

The practice of avoiding a meaningful engagement with the animal rights issue is present especially in the liberal outlets, as most of the outlets fail to even mention the animal-focused references. Once again, it is the conservative or conservative-leaning outlets that engage and dig deeper into the issues presented in the speech. I will only add to what I already said earlier about the way the avoidance of the topic works to perpetuate the status quo, the always relevant words of Michel Foucault, which can aid our understanding of why the animal rights themes were ignored: "Each society has its regime of truth, its 'general politics' of truth; that is, the types of discourse which it accepts and makes function as true."[60]

Concluding remarks and future research suggestions

This chapter looked at some of the public discourse surrounding the memorable Oscar acceptance speech given by Joaquin Phoenix. It discussed how this speech, as an intervention by a celebrity who happens to be an animal rights advocate, was taken up by the media ecosystem and how this ecosystem ultimately ended up legitimating and promoting speciesism.

Future research should expand on this examination by looking at complementary areas that could provide a more comprehensive perspective of the power of such an intervention. A more focused and systematic look into the way liberals and conservatives processed the speech could provide some important insights into the way the left and the right view the animal rights dimension. Also, a comparison between the coverage in the United States with other countries could inform on any geographical and cultural differences in the way people relate to the animal rights issue.

Another area that was not covered in this chapter and which warrants investigation is the reaction of the animal and environmental advocacy movements to the speech, and the ways in which groups

60 Foucault 1980, 131.

representing these movements might have used the speech to promote their cause (or not). In addition, such research could examine any tensions that might have risen between the two movements in connection with strategies to promote a plant-based future, which the speech and the public discourse surrounding it might have stimulated.

Finally, an important area not considered in this chapter is the public's response to the speech. One avenue of analysing this response is social media. Observing the reactions to the speech on Twitter, Facebook and especially YouTube might enhance our understanding of how such events are received and processed by audiences in real time.

Ultimately, Phoenix's speech champions an alternative social order. The animal rights messages contained in his speech have been ignored or treated by some cultural pundits as either a peculiarity or a nuisance, and triggered others who registered it as a threat to the animal exploitation industry or to the hierarchy of humanistic causes. One thing is clear, the speech and Phoenix's advocacy work have become part of the groundwork necessary for laying the foundation for a speciesism-free world.

References

An Inconvenient Truth (2006). Film. Davis Guggenheim (Dir.). Distributor: Lawrence Bender Productions.

Atkin, Emily (2021). Prepare for meat war. *Heated*, 27 April. https://tinyurl.com/yc7h7waf.

Barrett, Rick (2020). Stung by Oscar speech, dairy farmers suggest actor Joaquin Phoenix doesn't know what he's talking about. *Milwaukee Journal Sentinel*, 2 October. https://tinyurl.com/4bdhhzvu.

Bartiromo, Maria (2020). 92nd Academy Awards. *Mornings with Maria*. Fox Business, USA, 10 February.

Baum, Gary (2020). How Joaquin Phoenix vegan-ized awards season behind the scenes. *Hollywood Reporter*, 4 February. https://tinyurl.com/y6eff7ps.

BBC (2020). Oscars 2020: number of TV viewers falls to all-time low. *BBC News*, 10 February. https://tinyurl.com/4v77htvc.

Beaumont, Thomas and Scott McFetridge (2021). Red meat politics: GOP turns culture war into a food fight. *City News Everywhere*, 7 May. https://tinyurl.com/mvfu59at.

Cohen, Stanley (2001). *States of Denial: Knowing about Atrocities and Suffering.* Cambridge, UK: Polity Press.

Cooper, Andrew F. (2008). *Celebrity Diplomacy.* New York: Routledge.

Deb, Sopan (2020). Joaquin Phoenix pleads for animal rights in Academy Awards speech. *New York Times*, 10 February. https://tinyurl.com/ynjt3au4.

Dibble, Madison (2020). "Hollywood-elite world view": Pennsylvania congressman slams Joaquin Phoenix for speech targeting dairy industry. *Washington Examiner*, 11 February. https://tinyurl.com/598eaxh3.

Dunlap, Riley E., Aaron M. McCright and Jerrod H. Yarosh (2016). The political divide on climate change: partisan polarization widens in the U.S. *Environment: Science and Policy for Sustainable Development* 58(5): 4–23. https://doi.org/10.1080/00139157.2016.1208995.

Dutkiewicz, Jan (2020). The climate activists who dismiss meat consumption are wrong. *The New Republic*, 31 August. https://tinyurl.com/mwbmf4ak.

Earthlings (2005). Film. Shaun Monson (Dir.). Distributor: Nation Earth.

Ehrlich, Brenna (2020). Joaquin Phoenix wins Best Actor for "Joker" at the 2020 Oscars. *Rolling Stone*, 9 February. https://tinyurl.com/yejjvdt3.

Foucault, Michel (1980). *Power/Knowledge: Selected Interviews and Other Writings, 1972–1977.* New York: Pantheon Books.

Fretts, Bruce (2019). Oscars rewind: the most political ceremony in Academy history. *New York Times*, 11 January. https://tinyurl.com/3d7wzann.

Gardner, Chris (2020). Joaquin Phoenix left SAG awards for pig vigil: "I have to be here". *Hollywood Reporter*, 20 January. https://tinyurl.com/mtmcjz3m.

Gilbert, Sophie (2020). How Joaquin Phoenix disrupted awards season. *Atlantic*, 10 February. https://tinyurl.com/4drvx35r.

Goffman, Erving (1974). Stigma and social identity. In Lee Rainwater, ed. *Deviance & Liberty: Social Problems and Public Policy*. New York: Routledge.

Grendstad, Gunnar, Per Selle, Kristin Stromsnes and Oystein Bortne (2006). *Unique Environmentalism: A Comparative Perspective*. New York: Springer.

Gusfield, Joseph (1986). *Symbolic Crusade: Status Politics and the American Temperance Movement*. Urbana: University of Illinois Press.

Hargrove, Eugene C. (1992). *The Animal Rights/Environmental Ethics Debate.* Albany: State University Press of New York.

Harris, Hunter (2020). A close read of Joaquin Phoenix and Renée Zellweger's baffling Oscar speeches. *Vulture*, 10 February. https://tinyurl.com/ycxeax57.

Holmes, Michael (2020). Bong Joon-Ho's Parasite big winner on Sunday night. *CNN Newsroom*. CNN, USA, 10 February.

Joker (2019). Film. Todd Phillips (Dir.). Distributor: Warner Bros.

Julia (1977). Film. Fred Zimmerman (Dir.). Distributor: Twentieth Century Fox.

Keller, Fred (2020). "Hollywood-elite world view": Pennsylvania congressman slams Joaquin Phoenix for speech targeting dairy industry. *Fred Keller*, 11 February. https://tinyurl.com/y334fkky.

Kent, Stephen (2020). The bizarre brilliance of Joaquin Phoenix. *Washington Examiner*, 25 February. https://tinyurl.com/mxk24ndj.

Khoo, Olivia (2009). A new call to arms or a new coat of arms: the animal rights and environmentalism debate in Australia. *Journal of Animal Law* (5): 49–70.

Klein, Ezra (2020). Farmers and animal rights activists are coming together to fight big factory farms. *Vox*, 7 August. https://tinyurl.com/24uvaxds.

Kurtz, Judy (2020). Pennsylvania Republican rips "detestable" Joaquin Phoenix Oscars speech. *The Hill*, 11 February. https://tinyurl.com/282umb3y.

Lupica, Diana (2017). Oscar nominated actor Jessica Chastain speaks out about her vegan lifestyle. *Plant Based News*, 3 November. https://tinyurl.com/bdfmafmd.

Maeseele, Pieter and Daniëlle Raeijmaekers (2017). Nothing on the news but the establishment blues? Toward a framework of depoliticization and agonistic media pluralism. *Journalism* 21(11): 1593–1610. https://tinyurl.com/33s39vcx.

Mann, Michael (2019). Lifestyle changes aren't enough to save the planet. Here's what could. *Time*, 12 September. https://tinyurl.com/4n9pz4zv.

Mann, Michael and Jonathan Brockopp (2019). You can't save the climate by going vegan. Corporate polluters must be held accountable. *USA TODAY*, 6 March. https://tinyurl.com/25efvsj9.

McFetridge, Thomas and Scott Beaumont (2020). Red meat politics: GOP turns culture war into a food fight. *Chicago Tribune*, 5 July. https://tinyurl.com/5d629zsu.

McNulty, Charles (2020). Why Joaquin Phoenix's Oscar speech doesn't seem so crazy in our Coronavirus times. *Los Angeles Times*, 15 April. https://tinyurl.com/2s4bpz5p.

Norgaard, Kari Marie (2006). "People want to protect themselves a little bit": emotions, denial, and social movement nonparticipation. *Sociological Inquiry* 76(3): 372–96. doi:10.1111/j.1475-682X.2006.00160.x.

Oscars (1973). The Godfather wins Best Picture: 45th Oscars. *The Official Channel of the Academy of Motion Picture Arts and Sciences*. https://www.youtube.com/watch?v=Y1qWRdil--A&t=40s.

Oscars (2016). Leonardo DiCaprio winning Best Actor: 88th Oscars. *The Official Channel of the Academy of Motion Picture Arts and Sciences*. https://www.youtube.com/watch?v=xpyrefzvTpI.

Oscars (2020). Joaquin Phoenix wins Best Actor: 92nd Oscars. *The Official Channel of the Academy of Motion Picture Arts and Sciences.* https://www.youtube.com/watch?v=qiiWdTz_MNc.

Palmer, Keke and Sara Haines (2020). Hayley Hasselhoff, Ross Matthews – Oscars recap. *Good Morning America.* ABC, USA, 10 February.

Parkinson, Claire and Laura Herring (2022). Vegan celebrity activism: an analysis of the critical reception of Joaquin Phoenix's award speech activism. *Celebrity Studies* 14(4): 584–601. https://doi.org/10.1080/19392397.2022.2154684.

Patterson, Charles (2002). *Eternal Treblinka: Our Treatment of Animals and the Holocaust.* New York: Lantern Books.

Radke, Amanda (2020a). How activists (& Joaquin Phoenix) are working to end animal ownership. *BEEF Magazine*, 17 February. https://tinyurl.com/nn35nfsh.

Radke, Amanda (2020b). Joaquin Phoenix: a person is worth more than a scallop. *BEEF Magazine*, 10 February. https://tinyurl.com/y4nn6t34.

Reiley, Laura (2021). Biden's climate change plan may not nix cheeseburgers, but science says beef should be on the chopping block. *Washington Post*, 26 April. https://tinyurl.com/4x6j5a4e.

Romano, Aja (2020). Joaquin Phoenix's Oscars speech was a sprawling sociopolitical epic. *Vox*, 10 February. https://tinyurl.com/263mzy7n.

Sanbonmatsu, John (2014). The animal of bad faith: speciesism as an existential project. In John Sorenson, ed. *Critical Animal Studies*, 29–45. Toronto: Canadian Scholars Press.

Settembre, Jeanette (2020). Joaquin Phoenix's Oscars speech slamming cow's milk sparks backlash from dairy industry. *Fox Business*, 10 February. https://tinyurl.com/5c4yzm37.

Socha, Kim (2013). The "dreaded comparisons" and speciesism: leveling the hierarchy of suffering. In Kim Socha and Sarahjane Blum, eds. *Confronting Animal Exploitation: Grassroots Essays on Liberation and Veganism.* Jefferson, North Carolina and London: McFarland & Company, Inc., Publishers.

Spiegel, Marjorie (1996). *The Dreaded Comparison: Race and Animal Slavery.* Philadelphia: New Society.

The Godfather (1972). Film. Francis Ford Coppola (Dir.). Distributor: Paramount Pictures.

The Revenant (2015). Film. Alexander G. Iñárritu (Dir.). Distributor: New Regency Productions.

Washington, Francesca (2020). New Mexico dairy farmer calls out Joaquin Phoenix for Oscar acceptance speech. *New Mexico News*, 11 February. https://tinyurl.com/bdzm2yz8.

White, Lynn (1967). The historical roots of our ecological crisis. *Science* (155): 1203–7.
Williams, Juan (2020). The Oscars gets political. *The Five*. Fox News, USA, 10 February.

14

"That'll do, Pig!"

Critical potentials in celebrity-activist media ecologies

Eva Haifa Giraud

The final words of the 1995 film *Babe*, "That'll do, Pig, that'll do", are not only regularly referred to as one of the best cinematic closing lines of all time, but are also, reportedly, the ringtone of lead actor James Cromwell's mobile phone.[1] In the film itself, Cromwell's character, Farmer Hoggett, utters the phrase at the culmination of country sheepdog trials, in which eponymous piglet Babe not only emerges victorious in sheep-herding but – in the process – secures his transition from "livestock" to working animal. Following the trajectory of the novel from which it was adapted, Dick King-Smith's *The Sheep-Pig*, "that'll do" signifies that Babe has done "enough" to be granted a different set of rights and privileges to other members of his species.

Owing to its themes of interspecies solidarity and disruption of anthropocentric classificatory schemes, in animal studies contexts *Babe*

1 Recent references to "That'll do, Pig" as one of the finest closing lines in cinema history, for instance, include a 2018 article in the UK national newspaper *The Telegraph*, as well as entertainment websites such as *Games Radar* and *Hollywood.com*; numerous GIFs, memes and YouTube parodies also revolve around the line. In the wake of a feature on Cromwell in the *New Yorker* (Schulman 2017), Cromwell's use of the phrase as his mobile ringtone has been reported in contexts ranging from *The Internet Movie Database* to *Vulture* and *Entertainment Weekly*.

has been seen to hold complex ethical potentials.[2] My focus in this chapter, however, is not primarily on the complexities offered by the film itself, but contemporary narratives surrounding the "real life" Farmer Hoggett. Outside of *Babe*, Cromwell has a reputation less for being an individual who has to be persuaded to spare the life of a piglet and more as a vegan activist and "rabble rouser" who has faced arrest for (among other things) protesting animal experimentation and disrupting a live orca show at San Diego SeaWorld wearing a t-shirt stating "SeaWorld Sucks".[3] The mediation of Cromwell's activism is not restricted to mainstream press depictions of his involvement in direct action; over the past two decades, he has also taken a proactive role leveraging his celebrity status in support of vegan campaigns. In 2012, for instance, Cromwell narrated the 12-minute Mercy For Animals film *Farm to Fridge*, which is still circulated widely through online video-sharing platforms. In the years since, he has engaged with wide-ranging initiatives that include campaign videos and radio broadcasts for PETA and Viva and he served as Executive Producer on *Cowspiracy* (2014) as well as director Keegan Kuhn's feature-length documentary *Running for Good* (2018) about vegan marathon athlete Fiona Oakes.

Cromwell's story is deserving of particular attention in a context where environmental activism more broadly, and vegan activism specifically, has been criticised for eschewing systemic critiques of production in favour of palatable messaging about lifestyle change.[4] In contrast, as I trace throughout this chapter, Cromwell's media ecologies juxtapose well-loved imagery from children's cinema and celebrity gossip with more disruptive modes of politics, including direct-action protest as well as depictions of extreme violence towards animals. The particular relationship between these different narratives, and the varied platforms used to disseminate them, I suggest, creates visibility for media frames that actively contest existing ethical norms and practices surrounding animal agriculture; in marked contrast with more high-profile examples of celebrity veganism, which position

2 McHugh 2002, 2011; Stewart and Cole 2009; Traschel 2019.

3 Shulman 2017.

4 See Doyle 2016; Fegitz and Pirani 2018; Wrenn 2020.

"lifestyle consumption as the point of ethical intervention".[5] In media landscapes that normalise the excesses of industrialised agriculture and in which "farmed animals are commodified and framed mostly according to economic interests",[6] the celebrity-activist ecologies associated with Cromwell thus elucidate how more challenging narratives can gain purchase.

In developing these arguments, the chapter draws together and builds upon two bodies of work: scholarship concerned with popular or spectacular environmentalism and research engaging with the media ecologies of contemporary activism. I expand on the value of media ecological theories in more depth at the close of this chapter, but – simply put – this research has departed from a focus on how activists engage with or are represented by singular media platforms and texts, instead turning its attention to the political dynamics and discursive meanings that are created by the relationships between media. The mediation of Cromwell's activism, for instance, cannot be understood without taking into account video-sharing platforms, social media practices by NGOs and celebrity profiles in entertainment websites, as well as the enduring legacies of *Babe* itself as it is remediated via GIFs and memes.

Before focusing on the modes of vegan praxis articulated in Cromwell's media ecologies, I begin by setting out wider political and academic discussions of the ambivalences of spectacular environmentalisms – or spectacular veganisms – particularly narratives related to pigs. These general discussions set the stage for examining materials related to Cromwell himself, including mainstream media articles (gathered via the Nexis database), awareness-raising films, interviews and activist websites. Across these texts, I trace three distinct expressions of vegan politics – the spectacular, the shocking and the systemic – and examine the affordances of, and relationships between, these approaches in relation to Cromwell's celebrity. Finally, I reflect on what can be gained both conceptually and politically through understanding Cromwell's celebrity activism in media ecological terms,

5 Doyle 2016, 788.
6 Almiron, Cole and Freeman 2016, 373.

drawing attention not just to the relations between textual content but the platforms through which his politics is disseminated.

Spectacular veganisms and alternative pig stories

While there is a well-established body of scholarship about the dynamics of alternative and activist media use, far less research has examined environmental and animal activism operating in the terrain of the popular (though these issues are gradually being redressed[7]). Questions about popular environmental protest are important in light of the rise of "spectacular environmentalisms", a term defined by Michael Goodman and colleagues as: "large-scale mediated spectacles about environmental problems" which could include such "phenomena as the Live Earth concerts, *Vanity Fair*'s Green Issues, or celebrity environmental activity".[8] As elucidated throughout Goodman and colleagues' edited collection on these themes, while high-profile, mediatised environmentalisms might hold the potential to travel beyond activist enclaves to wider publics, they are also highly ambivalent.

The term "spectacle" is designed to foreground the ambiguity of mediatised environmental politics.[9] On the one hand, this term evokes Situationist arguments that contend mass media serve as a distraction from economic inequities. At the same time, Goodman and colleagues' reference to Situationism foregrounds a lineage of activists tactically working against social norms by turning the grammar of media spectacle against itself. Culture jamming, such as subvertising or playful and performative appropriations of public space, for instance, often appropriate spectacular logics by diverting them away from profit-making ends and towards agendas for change. Framing popular environmentalisms in spectacular terms, then, points to an interplay between radical critiques of the socioeconomic and ecological status quo and a need to reconcile these critiques with limitations imposed

7 See Abidin, Brockington et al. 2020; Parkinson 2019; Seymour 2019.
8 Goodman, Littler et al. 2016, 678.
9 For elaboration, see Giraud 2019, 145.

by the popular media contexts that these critiques depend on to gain visibility. These limitations might, for instance, range from the constraining grammar of mainstream media framings of issues to the strictures imposed by algorithmic economies of visibility.[10] What is key, in such contexts, is for activists to identify opportunities to tactically appropriate spectacular logics, without going so far that they undercut their own aims.

The tensions and potentials associated with spectacular environmentalisms are equally applicable to popular veganisms. Indeed, two articles in Goodman and colleagues' special collection focus on animal and vegan activism explicitly: Julie Doyle's analysis of the celebrity veganism of Alicia Silverstone and Ellen DeGeneres, and Alex Lockwood's discussion of the affective dimensions of the feature-length documentary *Cowspiracy*.[11] Both papers point to commonplace features of the media ecologies of contemporary vegan activism, such as uses of celebrity spokespeople – often mediated via a range of social media platforms – and appeals to biography and narrative as tools for engaging publics who might feel alienated by negative activist imagery. Yet for all their potential, as Doyle argues, in many cases spectacular veganisms foreground individual consumer behaviour as a site of agency and empowerment, wherein an emphasis on being "kind" in one's *consumption* habits often overshadows wider structural critiques related to the *production* of animal products.[12] The potentials, as well as the sharp limitations, of spectacular veganisms are brought into still further relief on considering the roles of animals themselves, who have assumed increasing prominence in spectacular campaigning contexts.[13]

Animal biographies are regularly engaged with in vegan activism, where this approach has been seen as holding a more subversive role than consumer-oriented lifestyle politics by bringing the lives of animals themselves into focus.[14] From popular fictional portrayals such

---

10 For example, Wood 2020.
11 Doyle 2016; Lockwood 2016.
12 Doyle 2016, 778.
13 Abidin, Brockington et al. 2020, 393–4.
14 DeMello 2018.

as *Babe* to "real life" rescue animals like Esther the Wonder Pig, animals are often spotlighted in vegan campaigns in order to disrupt the cultural classification of nonhuman beings and contest categorisations such as "food animals" – along with the ethical treatment this categorisation legitimises.[15] Yet, as Claire Parkinson foregrounds, while appeals to animal subjectivity are often a powerful means of crafting alternative narratives about other species – which can do valuable political work – such narratives again carry ambivalences, which can be illustrated when turning to pigs specifically.[16] As Brett Mizelle puts it, "pigs are more than just the 18 per cent ham, 16 per cent bacon, 15 per cent loin, 12 per cent fatback, 10 per cent lard and 3 per cent each of spare rib, plate, jowl, foot and trimmings that exit the modern packing plant" and new stories are required to provide "us with ways to think about our relationships with each other on this porcine planet".[17] The difficulty is finding ways to articulate these more expansive understandings of pigs, in contexts where human–pig relations are ordinarily defined – as Mary Trachsel argues – by an "industrial 'pork story' that seeks to gain narrative control of relational norms between people and pigs".[18]

High-profile examples such as Esther the Wonder Pig help to elucidate the challenges Trachsel points to. Esther was erroneously purchased from a friend under the guise of being a micro pig, but by the time her "owners", Steve Jenkins and Derek Walter, discovered Esther would likely grow to 500 lb (227 kg) she had already become an integral part of their existing dogs' pack.[19] Rather than give her away, Jenkins and Walter turned their home into a sanctuary for Esther: who swiftly became central to an entire media ecology of her own, which includes her website, Instagram, Facebook and Twitter, as well as two full-length books and a children's picture book dedicated to her journey.[20] These texts are designed to create revenue streams to

15 See Arcari 2020.
16 Parkinson 2019.
17 Mizelle 2011, 7.
18 Trachsel 2019, 1.
19 Indeed, she ultimately grew to 600 lb.
20 Giraud 2021, 96. Between writing this chapter and receiving proofs, Esther passed away on 19 October 2023, aged 11.

sustain the sanctuary and to promote veganism through questioning Esther's status as "livestock". The way Esther's story has been mobilised, however, does not necessarily sit easily with wider critiques of animal agriculture. Her website does contain a section focused on the lives of industrially farmed pigs in general, and in interviews Jenkins regularly links their experiences with Esther to more far-reaching critique: "The more we discovered about what her life could have been, it seemed crazy to us that we ate animals, so we stopped."[21] Yet, ultimately the narratives disseminated across Esther's different media platforms promoted a relatively unified story that positioned her specialness as the wellspring of Jenkins and Walter's individual decisions to enact lifestyle change. Esther's status as celebrity animal, then, did not escape the tensions highlighted by Doyle wherein celebritised veganisms tend towards individualised modes of ethics.

Babe offers equally complex potentials. It is notable, for instance, that both Trachsel and Mizelle point to the film as an instance of an alternative narrative about human–pig relations, with *Babe*'s critical and commercial success even noted on Mizelle's succinct historical timeline of the pig (which begins in 14,000 BC!).[22] The counter-narrative offered by *Babe* and *The Sheep-Pig* is that they disrupt the passage from – to use the title of Cromwell's subsequent campaign – "farm to fridge". Though Babe was originally destined to be fattened up for Christmas dinner, the plot revolves around his avoidance of this fate; central to the narrative is that Babe "hybridize[s] two categories – food animal and companion animal", with the film's threat hinging on the "reassertion of [his] primary food animal identity".[23] Over the course of this narrative trajectory, the cultural logics that legitimate Babe's status as food are exposed: such as sheepdog Fly's justification that only "stupid" animals (such as pigs) are consumed, in contrast with "intelligent" dogs,[24] or Duchess the cat's stance that the purpose of pigs is to be "eaten by people".[25] These farmyard hierarchies are ultimately rejected in favour

21 Jenkins 2017.
22 Mizelle 2011, 182.
23 Stewart and Cole 2009, 463.
24 Trachsel 2019, 9.
25 McHugh 2011, 192.

of interspecies solidarity, with the film's concluding scenes seeing sheep and border collies collaborate in order to secure Babe's televised victory – and accompanying cultural recategorisation – at the sheepdog trials.

Babe's significance, therefore, is as an instance of popular culture where ethical classifications that cast pigs as "livestock" are disrupted, and where the legitimation of these categories, which are ordinarily implicit, are brought to the surface and shown to be untenable. Like Esther the Wonder Pig, however, the wider political potentials of *Babe* are often obscured. Susan McHugh, for instance, points to Animals Australia's 2004 "Save Babe" campaign, which featured emotive pictures of cute piglets to deter people from animal product consumption.[26] These tactics, McHugh suggests, might illustrate the emotional "staying power" of *Babe*, but their political efficacy is limited by an individualised focus on a particular animal that neglects the film's wider messages of interspecies solidarity and the overturning of classifications that it offers.

Paralleling Doyle's observations about human celebrity veganism, then, emotive fictional portrayals and celebrity animals might play a role in awareness-raising and promote values that are "consistent with ethical veganism".[27] At the same time, the potential for these narratives to develop into systemic critiques of production are often undermined in order to ensure that popular texts do not alienate potential audiences with moralism and that high-profile figures – including celebrity animals such as Esther – maintain "viability as celebrity commodities".[28] While the alternative pig stories offered by *Babe* and Esther could be used to question pigs' wider cultural categorisation, because these narratives are oriented around the special qualities of particular animals – such as Babe's skills or Esther's personality – there is a risk of undercutting a more fundamental disruption of the "industrial 'pork' story".[29] The challenge, therefore, is finding ways to negotiate the terrain of the popular without sacrificing more radical imaginaries of what alternative human–animal relations might look

26 McHugh 2011, 186.
27 Doyle 2016, 787.
28 Doyle 2016, 788.
29 Trachsel 2019, 1.

like. As I argue below, Cromwell's celebrity activism offers potential routes into understanding, and navigating, some of these tensions.

Cromwell as celebrity activist

Cromwell's representation (and indeed self-representation) is significant because it combines more spectacular expressions of celebrity veganism with shocking imagery as well as structural critique of animal agriculture. More normative expressions of celebrity veganism that focus on lifestyle and consumption, in other words, circulate alongside radical contestations of institutions associated with the "animal-industrial complex".[30] Understanding how spectacular, shocking and structural articulations of vegan politics are entwined in Cromwell's media ecologies, I argue, is useful in grasping how more complex ethical narratives can emerge in the context of spectacular veganisms.

The spectacular

As described previously, spectacular veganisms operate on the terrain of the popular and tend to assume more palatable forms, with the risk of these approaches being that visibility comes at the expense of meaningful action. In the case of Cromwell, matters are still more complex because his celebrity persona is intimately bound up with *Babe*. Indeed, it is the relationship between fiction and non-fiction that constitutes Cromwell's distinct brand of celebrity activism; through his own interviews, mainstream media reports of protest actions and publicity materials related to projects he has contributed to, Farmer Hoggett is a recurring reference point. What is significant about the way fiction is mobilised in these narratives is that Hoggett's journey is used by both Cromwell himself and vegan NGOs as a framing device to render more radical expressions of vegan ethics meaningful and accessible to audiences. Still more significantly, this frame is routinely reproduced by other media sources, from mainstream press to entertainment websites.

30 Noske 1989.

In a celebrity profile in *Vice* magazine to celebrate *Babe*'s 20-year anniversary, for instance, Cromwell describes two key turning points in his biography. The first moment involved driving past animal feedlots in Texas, which prompted his decision to become vegetarian, while the second occurred during the filming of *Babe* itself:

> We had a little pig that was brought out for the last scene, during the pig contest. It had gone through the training that all the other little pigs had along the line. When that little pig was put down on that big pitch and saw the blue sky and the green grass and the sea, that pig just took off, and said, I don't want any part of this. I am out. I support that![31]

Cromwell then shifts the focus to scenes *within* the film, deliberately drawing parallels between his own transformational experiences and those of his character. In relation to one of the most well-known scenes in *Babe* – a song and dance routine to cheer up the fearful piglet after he thought Farmer Hoggett was about to slaughter him – Cromwell describes how:

> He [Hoggett] has the opportunity to readjust his point of view and learn something. Farmer Hoggett's consciousness and our consciousness – if you'll allow yourself to take the time – will arrive at the same conclusion: that we have no right to usurpation of another sentient being's destiny for our own needs and self-interests.[32]

An identical narrative of ethical transformation is deployed in other interviews:

> I love the dancing scene. It was at this moment that my character shifted from a man who would think to shoot the pig to seeing this little creature in his lap who is not only in pain but suffering.[33]

31 Cromwell in Pearl 2015.

32 Cromwell in Pearl 2015.

33 Plus Media 2014.

Here, therefore, Cromwell's own status as activist vegan is modulated through a popular scene, portraying his subjective ethical response as something that aligns not only with his character but with the audience's own investment in preserving Babe's life, as encouraged through the film's narrative structure.

This anchoring of Cromwell's celebrity-activist persona in relation to his character is not an isolated incident. For instance, five years later, in the wake of *Babe*'s 25-year anniversary, Cromwell foregrounds a different experience on set:

> [W]hen *Babe* came, we would work with the animals and the animals were trained and they were extraordinary. So I just watched these extraordinary animals do the things that they did – and then I would go to lunch … And so on the lunch table would be all the animals that I had just worked with. There was duck and there would be lamb. I thought, "Oh man, this is really horrible. I have to go vegan."[34]

Again, therefore, by situating his own activist-celebrity status in relation to Farmer Hoggett, Cromwell is able to frame veganism as a logical outcome of the film's disruption of anthropocentric classifications.

The relationship between Cromwell and Hoggett, moreover, goes beyond a brief reference point in interviews and is actively cultivated through acts of self-branding. Cromwell's Twitter account, for instance, deliberately plays with the affinities between personal and fictional ethics, in featuring a pig snout on his bio while he promotes content related to activist causes: from his recent Animals Asia documentary on the plight of moon bears, to an appearance on a popular podcast in which he connects climate change to political corruption, and his promotion of a march for public education in Los Angeles. The same appeal to character in Cromwell's construction of celebrity runs through publicity for *Running for Good*, which consistently celebrates both his role in *Babe* and his activism, with this frame reproduced by vegan websites promoting the film (such as *Plant Based News* and *Live Kindly*). As hinted at through these examples, fictional narratives

34 Cromwell in Abramovitch 2020.

thus play an important role in holding together Cromwell's celebrity activism with deep-reaching critiques of animal agriculture, something that comes to the fore in his awareness-raising films.

The shocking

Until recently, the forms of mediated vegan politics that received most attention academically were not spectacular veganisms but shock tactics, such as exposés based on footage from sites such as industrial farms, slaughterhouses and animal laboratories.[35] These tactics are commonplace in feature-length films such as *Earthlings* (2005), as well as short campaign videos by groups such as PETA, and speak to "the popular maxim that 'if slaughterhouses had glass walls, everyone would be vegetarian'".[36] The efficacy of a politics based on "moral shocks",[37] however, has increasingly been called into question, due to fears "[s]uch radical, moralized encounters can lead to exhaustion, apathy, and even cynicism".[38]

The use of moral shocks is a core feature in many of the campaigning videos Cromwell has fronted for PETA. In a 30-second video from 2012, for example, his narration over scenes of animals being beaten describes how a pig is killed "every three seconds" in large slaughterhouses, while his closing line pleads for audiences to stop eating "sensitive, intelligent animals" such as pigs. Perhaps the most famous of Cromwell's awareness-raising films, which is frequently referred to in the mainstream media as a counterpoint to Cromwell's role in *Babe*, however, is the aforementioned *Farm to Fridge*. An archetypal shock film, the 12-minute documentary includes such graphic imagery of violence towards "livestock" animals that it is age-restricted on video-sharing platforms YouTube and Vimeo. Indeed, the film has even led to YouTube influencers producing reaction videos of themselves watching the imagery in tears and with expressions of

35 Giraud 2021, 68–73; Wrenn 2013.
36 Quinn 2020, 916.
37 Wrenn 2013.
38 Lorimer 2015, 130; see also Rasmussen 2015.

horror – which Mercy For Animals have in turn embedded in their websites alongside the original documentary.

The film's content emphasises both the scale of industrialised agriculture (such as surplus chickens being thrown into bin bags, with a reminder that this process happens to a million male chicks a year in the US) and acts of spectacular violence towards animals (including adult pigs being hung from farm machinery and slowly strangled). As with media profiles of Cromwell, again references to *Babe* are difficult to avoid; in *Farm to Fridge*, however, these linkages are made via more implicit intertextual connections. The first section of the documentary, for example, is entitled "Pork" and includes scenes of piglets covered in scratches and sores; semi-conscious animals flung into bins and covered in flies; and live animals scalded in hair-removal tanks, with Cromwell's voiceover offering a reminder that the average life of an industrially farmed pig is five to six months, "a fragment of their lifespan".

In addition to Cromwell's involvement in awareness-raising campaigns, his celebrity status has resulted in direct-action protests gaining visibility in the mainstream press; most recently, he was threatened with a class-A misdemeanour – which ordinarily carries a fine and one year in prison – for successfully disrupting laboratory experiments on golden retrievers.[39] Other widely reported campaigns include pickets against Walmart's pork suppliers, a campaign against fast-food chain Wendy's (which led to Cromwell being banned from the franchise) and a protest action where he presented the Governor of Utah with a pig carcass. These initiatives are aside from Cromwell's wider environmental, labour and anti-racist activism, such as protests to preserve wetlands, anti-fracking campaigns and early membership of a defence committee for the Black Panthers. Again, *Babe* is a consistent reference point across media reports of Cromwell's other activism: NGOs use the film to frame their actions in accessible ways as well as raising their profile, while newspapers deploy it as a frame that fits with celebrity news values.

Yet, although mainstream media articles consistently link Cromwell's politics to *Babe*, they oscillate between using the film to

---

39 Cromwell in MacKenzie 2021.

make his beliefs intelligible and framing direct action an excessive response to the film. Typical examples of this shift in frames might be mentioning the ethical significance of *Babe* to Cromwell's biography, before undercutting the accessibility of this narrative by stating that he is not just vegan but "a *really hardcore* vegan" and labelling his activism a "crusade".[40] Numerous articles also make more subtle contrasts between Cromwell's "extreme" protest actions and the ostensibly more intelligible forms of empathy for nonhuman animals encouraged by *Babe*, as with the 2018 byline of a celebrity profile in UK newspaper *The Guardian*:

> The Hollywood star now has a second life as a fearless animal activist and eco warrior – and, he reveals, it all started with Babe, his film about a talking pig.[41]

For all these tensions, however, the complex relationship between celebrity and activism in Cromwell's media ecologies means that actions which directly disrupt institutions associated with the animal-industrial complex are afforded media coverage. While this coverage does certainly not embrace direct-action protest, it rarely slides into the outright negativity or incredulity that has historically been associated with popular media depictions of ethical veganism or animal activism.[42] The limitations associated with representations of Cromwell's direct action, moreover, are further ameliorated by deliberate attempts – by the actor himself and NGOs – to reframe these actions less as something grounded in an individual ethical response and instead as a structural critique of animal agriculture.

The structural

Structural critiques of animal exploitation have tended to occur less in popular settings and more in the context of social movements. Such approaches shift the focus away from acts of spectacular abuse and

---

40 Pearl 2015, emphasis in original.
41 Brokes 2018.
42 Cole and Morgan 2011; Giraud 2019, 98–117.

towards routinised violence that occurs in the process of rendering animals as commodities, as with campaigns that engage with data and statistical evidence to discuss, for instance, the scale of animal death that occurs in industrialised agriculture, emissions it creates, and its relationship with human oppression.[43] Other approaches that activists regularly use to pose structural questions entail questioning classificatory systems that inform the treatment of particular animals. Indeed, the sense that classification underpins the differential treatment of nonhuman beings is not just a commonplace assumption in activism, but central to a number of high-profile texts such as Melanie Joy's *Why We Love Dogs, Eat Pigs, and Wear Cows.*[44]

Resonating with Joy, Cromwell's own journey – again articulated with the experiences of Farmer Hoggett – is regularly deployed in campaigning contexts to disrupt the classification of pigs as edible. In relation to the Wendy's protests, for instance, newspapers reproduced verbatim Cromwell's statement that: "he changed to a vegan diet, avoiding milk and eggs as well as meat, after 'Babe,' which he said shows a human recognising a pig has aspirations and hopes".[45] Almost 20 years later, at his protests in Utah, newspapers reproduced Cromwell's request for government officials to: "consider the plot of 'Babe' – where, spoiler alert, a pig is saved from being eaten and discovers his destiny in herding sheep – and apply its principles to life",[46] while a 2017 PETA press release to promote a Cromwell-fronted anti-pork campaign was again picked up by news agencies:

> "When I made the movie *Babe*, I learned how smart and sensitive pigs are," Cromwell says in the spot. "I developed a lot of respect for them and stopped eating them. Won't you join me in bagging the bacon and giving ham the old heave-ho this Easter?".[47]

43 For an overview, see Giraud 2021, 68–77.
44 Joy 2011.
45 Greenfield 2001.
46 Harkins 2018.
47 PETA 2017.

These texts' straightforward reproduction of activists' narrative framing again foregrounds the potential for celebrity activism to enable more complex structural critiques to gain wider visibility.

At the same time, there are risks in anchoring structural critiques to the classificatory challenges posed by individual animals. As Siobhan O'Sullivan underlines in *Animals, Equality and Democracy*, it is not just the case that different species are also given differential ethical treatment (i.e., that pigs can't be pets or, in the case of *Babe*, working animals), because processes of cultural categorisation cut across species lines.[48] As O'Sullivan traces through examining legislation and media framing related to hens, rabbits, horses and dogs in Australia, members of the same species are routinely categorised in very different ways and with very different consequences. For instance: "a rabbit can be an Agricultural Animal, a Companion Animal, a Research Animal and so on", and legislation that surrounds these categories varies significantly in terms of the rights and protections it affords.[49] What O'Sullivan's work foregrounds, in other words, is that the treatment of some animals as deserving of privileges which others of the same species do not possess is something that is already a routine part of everyday life. Following this logic, Babe might have disrupted his status as "livestock", but because members of the same species are routinely given a differential ethical status (i.e., some pigs are considered pets while others are food), this does not offer a more fundamental challenge to the – already contradictory – ways the category of livestock operates in different cultural contexts.

Initial audience responses to *Babe* underline this point. Although there were widespread reports of animal product reduction in the wake of the film, as Kate Stewart and Matthew Cole note, "these were transient trends rather than catalysts for enduring change".[50] What their work also elucidates is that one of the reasons for this transience is that any counter-representations about nonhuman animals are operating within the constraints of a social landscape in which tensions between affective engagements with piglets and eating pig are routinely

48 O'Sullivan 2011.

49 O'Sullivan 2011, 112.

50 Stewart and Cole 2009, 464.

smoothed over during childhood. In what she calls "the Peppa Pig paradox", for example, Lynda Korimboccus points out that in contexts such as the UK it is commonplace for children to celebrate fictional pigs before going on to consume actual pigs.[51]

What is notable about Cromwell's media ecologies, however, is that mainstream media reports about Cromwell's direct action are not the only spaces where his celebrity activism is afforded visibility. An array of social media platforms are used both by NGOs and the actor himself to circulate content that shifts the focus away from individual animals and towards structural critique. *Farm to Fridge*, for instance, might gain visibility due to Cromwell's celebrity, and begins with a focus on pigs in a nod to this context, but it soon shifts to foregrounding the routine violences enacted towards other nonhuman animals. Indeed, even in celebrity profiles, Cromwell makes explicit that his affective response to events in *Babe* was not just about feeling a personal emotional connection with individual animals, but "about what we do to each other by pigeonholing us and other people into certain categories that protect our own sense of entitlement and position and power".[52] It is valuable, therefore, to reflect not just on the potentials and limitations of particular texts or tactics that constitute Cromwell's media ecologies but the relationship between these media.

Conclusion: The promise of Cromwell's celebrity-activist media ecologies

Building on the above arguments, I conclude this chapter by offering a more in-depth reflection of how media ecological approaches can be used to draw out the hopeful political potentials of Cromwell's activism and spectacular environmentalisms more broadly. As Emiliano Treré outlines in the book *Hybrid Media Activism*, there have been several "waves" of media ecological theory.[53] Initial uses of the term in the 60s focused on the co-constitutive relationships between technologies in a

51 Korimboccus 2020.
52 Cromwell in Pearl 2015.
53 Treré 2019, 39–41.

given media system.[54] The resurgence of media ecological thought from the late 90s, however, understood user practices, social relations and discursive formations as holding equally significant roles in shaping the dynamics of particular media environments.[55] The field in which expanded conceptions of media ecologies have proven the most fertile is at the nexus of media and social movement studies.[56] Here the recognition that media do not function in isolation has been valuable in resisting simplistic narratives that (for example) position singular social media platforms as drivers of social change. Instead, the affordances of platforms are seen as emerging through their relationship with other media used by activists – from inward-facing email lists to pamphlets – as well as modulated by the user practices that become associated with these media.[57]

The different media platforms entangled with Cromwell's activism illustrate the value of extending media ecological approaches beyond social movements, to conceptualise the equally complex dynamics of spectacular environmentalisms. Treré's *Hybrid Media Activism* already begins to hint at the potentials to apply ecological frameworks to celebrity politics, in a chapter focused on uses of digital media by Italy's Five Star movement, which was rooted in figurehead Beppe Grillo's fame. Grillo, a well-known actor and comedian in Italy during the 70s and 80s, foreshadowed tactics engaged in during Donald Trump's presidential campaigns, using digital media (such as an opinionated blog and meet-up sites to organise large public rallies) to give the impression of accessibility. The dynamic affordances of these platforms worked with populist narratives, in ways that meant – despite being part of a wealthy media elite – Grillo was able to depict himself as a man of the people, through fostering "myths of horizontality, leaderlessness, and digital democracy".[58] While Five Star is an instance of media ecologies being manipulated in support of authoritarian ends, Treré's

54 Treré and Mattoni 2016, 293.

55 Mattoni 2017, 495–6.

56 For example, Cammaerts, Mattoni and McCurdy 2013; Mercea, Ianelli and Loader 2016.

57 Feigenbaum, Frenzel and McCurdy 2013.

58 Treré 2019, 124.

analysis nonetheless illustrates the importance of analysing how media spectacle – and tactical appeals to celebrity in particular – can intersect with other aspects of media ecologies.

Cromwell's celebrity activism, for instance, cannot be grasped purely through an analysis of texts such as *Farm to Fridge*. Instead, it is important to grasp the relationship between fictional narrative and Cromwell's celebrity persona, and how this relationship is, in turn, utilised to unsettle classificatory schema and add dramatic weight to shocking activist films. Cromwell's celebrity, moreover, is not only a component of these films' narratives but something that affords these texts algorithmic visibility on video-sharing platforms. This visibility is then, in turn, taken advantage of by NGOs who embed these films in their websites, as well as the YouTube influencers who interact with them and afford further attention to critiques of animal agriculture. The uptake of Cromwell's protest actions in the mainstream press, likewise, needs to be understood in relation to the mediation of a persona that combines the news values associated with Hollywood celebrity gossip with disruptive expressions of direct action. This is not to say that the narratives surrounding Cromwell (or indeed any expression of celebrity activism) should be treated uncritically. My aim here, though, has been less to evaluate these narratives and more to conceptualise how they work. To this end, I suggest that Cromwell's activism illustrates how different modes of politics can unfold on different media platforms for different ends, while also being tactically brought together in ways that create mainstream visibility for narratives that are ordinarily excluded from celebrity activism.

I suggest, therefore, that the term "celebrity-activist media ecologies" offers a useful descriptor of the complex relationships between platforms, textual content and social practices that mediate contemporary vegan politics. But, more than this, ecological approaches are valuable in identifying how space for more radical narratives can emerge amidst the contradictions of spectacular politics more broadly. In foregrounding the tensions associated with spectacular environmentalisms and veganisms, I am not intending to dismiss the role of popular culture in fostering awareness and even (potentially) political change. As Chris Ingraham suggests in *Gestures of Concern*, though everyday acts of clicking, sharing and liking political content are often dismissed as slacktivism, they can still contribute to an "affective commonwealth" with potential to foster:

> a shared sense of what it feels like to be alive at the present time … as if that feeling were a resource anyone could draw on to make sense of their worlds and to affirm more sustainable ways of being interconnected within them.[59]

Likewise, vegan consumption is often dismissed as an individualistic, neoliberal mode of politics that offers an inadequate response to collective problems; a framing that neglects the complex relationships between individual practices, consumerism and social change.[60] It is, nonetheless, important to recognise the limits of *only* focusing on consumer-oriented lifestyle ethics and identify opportunities for deep-rooted critiques of production systems to emerge alongside and work with more popular narratives.

References

Abidin, Crystal, Dan Brockington, Michael K. Goodman, Mary Mostafanezhad and Lisa Ann Richey (2020). The tropes of celebrity environmentalism. *Annual Review of Environment and Resources* 45: 387–410.

Abramovitch, Seth (2020). Hollywood flashback: James Cromwell reflects on "Babe" 25 years later. *Hollywood Reporter*, 8 August. https://bit.ly/3HkLa2d.

Almiron, Núria, Matthew Cole and Carrie P. Freeman (2018). Critical animal and media studies: expanding the understanding of oppression in communication research. *European Journal of Communication* 33(4): 367–80. https://doi.org/10.1177/0267323118763937.

Arcari, Paula (2020). *Making Sense of Food Animals*. Singapore: Palgrave Macmillan.

Babe (1995). Film. C. Noonan (Dir.). Distributor: Universal Pictures.

Brokes, Emma (2018). James Cromwell: in jail, everyone recognises my face. *Guardian*, 27 February. https://bit.ly/3Hl4Gf6.

59 Ingraham 2020, 5.

60 Dickstein, Dutkiewicz et al. 2020; Giraud 2021, 43.

Cammaerts, Bart, Alice Mattoni and Patrick McCurdy, eds (2013). *Mediation and Protest Movements*. London: Intellect Books.

Cole, Matthew and Karen Morgan (2011). Vegaphobia: derogatory discourses of veganism and the reproduction of speciesism in UK national newspapers. *The British Journal of Sociology* 62(1): 134–53. https://tinyurl.com/56spj26z.

Cowspiracy: The Sustainability Secret (2014). Film. Kip Anderson and Keegan Kuhn (Dirs). Distributor: AUM Films/First Spark Media.

DeMello, Margo (2018). Online animal (auto-)biographies. In André Krebber and Mieke Roscher, eds. *Animal Biography*, 243–59. Basingstoke: Palgrave Macmillan.

Dickstein, Jonathan, Jan Dutkiewicz, Jishnu Guha-Majumdar and Drew Robert Winter (2020). Veganism as left praxis. *Capitalism Nature Socialism*, 1–20. https://doi.org/10.1080/10455752.2020.1837895.

Doyle, Julie (2016). Celebrity vegans and the lifestyling of ethical consumption. *Environmental Communication* 10(6): 777–90. https://tinyurl.com/2dwj9xph.

Earthlings (2005). Film. Shaun Monson (Dir.). Distributor: Nation Earth Films.

Farm to Fridge (2011). YouTube Video. Mercy For Animals. Uploaded 4 February, 2011. https://bit.ly/48TyhId.

Fegitz, Ella and Daniela Pirani (2018). The sexual politics of veggies: Beyoncé's "commodity veg*ism". *Feminist Media Studies* 18(2): 294–308. https://doi.org/10.1080/14680777.2017.1358200.

Feigenbaum, Anna, Fabian Frenzel and Patrick McCurdy (2013). *Protest Camps*. London: Zed Books.

Giraud, Eva Haifa (2021). *Veganism: Politics, Practice and Theory*. London: Bloomsbury Academic.

Giraud, Eva Haifa (2019). *What Comes After Entanglement?* Durham, NC: Duke University Press.

Goodman, Michael K., Jo Littler, Dan Brockington and Maxwell Boykoff (2016). Spectacular environmentalisms: media, knowledge and the framing of ecological politics. *Environmental Communication* 10(6): 677–88. https://doi.org/10.1080/17524032.2016.1219489.

Greenfield, Heather (2001). "Babe" actor banned from Wendy's. *Associated Press*, 17 December.

Harkins, Paighten (2018). The star of "Babe" brought a dead piglet to the Utah capital to make a point about animal cruelty. *Salt Lake Tribute*, 21 November.

Ingraham, Chris (2020). *Gestures of Concern*. Durham, NC: Duke University Press.

James Cromwell's PETA Ad (2012). YouTube Video. People for the Ethical Treatment of Animals, uploaded 30 October 2018. https://bit.ly/48VTmBE.

Joy, Melanie (2011). *Why We Love Dogs, Eat Pigs and Wear Cows*. San Francisco: Conari Press.

Jenkins, Steve (2017). "Experience: I accidentally bought a giant pig". *Guardian*, 10 February. https://bit.ly/3S2MonO.

King-Smith, Dick (1983). *The Sheep Pig*. London: Penguin.

Korimboccus, Lynda M. (2020). Pig-ignorant: the Peppa Pig paradox. Investigating contradictory childhood consumption. *Journal for Critical Animal Studies* 17(5): 3–33.

Lockwood, Alex (2016). Graphs of grief and other green feelings: the uses of affect in the study of environmental communication. *Environmental Communication* 10(6): 734–48. https://tinyurl.com/4xxzdckt.

Lorimer, Jamie (2015). *Wildlife in the Anthropocene: Conservation after Nature*. Minneapolis: University of Minnesota Press.

MacKenzie, Steven (2021). James Cromwell: there's no hope in the system, no hope for Mr Biden. *Big Issue*, 21 January. https://bit.ly/3O3qsru.

Mattoni, Alice (2017). A situated understanding of digital technologies in social movements. *Social Movement Studies* 16(4): 494–505. https://tinyurl.com/8hkdncra.

McHugh, Susan (2011). *Animal Stories: Narrating Across Species Lines*. Minneapolis: University of Minnesota Press.

McHugh, Susan (2002). Bringing up Babe. *Camera Obscura* 17(1): 149–87.

Mercea, Dan, Laura Ianelli and Brian D. Loader (2016). Protest communication ecologies. *Information, Communication and Society* 19(3): 279–89. https://doi.org/10.1080/1369118X.2015.1109701.

Mizelle, Brett (2011). *Pig*. London: Reaktion.

Noske, Barbara (1989). *Humans and Other Animals*. London: Pluto.

O'Sullivan, Siobhan (2011). *Animals, Equality and Democracy*. Basingstoke: Palgrave Macmillan.

Parkinson, Claire (2019). *Animals, Anthropomorphism and Mediated Encounters*. London: Routledge.

Pearl, Mike (2015). "Babe" is now 20-years-old, and so is star James Cromwell's animal rights crusade. *Vice*, 8 June. https://bit.ly/3O31hoS.

PETA (2017). James Cromwell Wants You to Give Pigs Like "Babe" a Break this Easter. *PETA.org*, 11 April. https://bit.ly/3O6dnxr.

Plus Media (2014). The tale of an unprejudiced heart: an interview with James Cromwell. *US Official News*, 18 December.

Quinn, Emelia (2020). Notes on vegan camp. *PMLA* 135(5): 914–30. https://doi.org/10.1632/pmla.2020.135.5.914.

Rasmussen, Claire (2015). Pleasure, pain and place. In K. Gillespie and R.-C. Collard, eds. *Critical Animal Geographies: Politics, Intersections and Hierarchies in a Multispecies World*, 54–70. New York: Routledge.

Running for Good (2018). Film. Keegan Kuhn (Dir.). Distributor: First Spark Media.
Seymour, Nicole (2018). *Bad Environmentalism: Irony and Irreverence in the Ecological Age*. Minneapolis: University of Minnesota Press.
Shulman, Michael (2017). James Cromwell's civil disobedience. *New Yorker*, 28 August. https://bit.ly/3O65o3A.
Stewart, Kate and Matthew Cole (2009). The conceptual separation of food and animals in childhood. *Food, Culture and Society* 12(4): 457–76. https://doi.org/10.2752/175174409X456746.
Trachsel, Mary (2019). Befriending your food: pigs and people coming of age in the Anthropocene. *Social Sciences* 8(4). https://tinyurl.com/ewmhcb2e.
Treré, Emiliano (2019). *Hybrid Media Activism: Ecologies, Imaginaries, Algorithms*. London: Routledge.
Treré, Emiliano and Alice Mattoni (2016). Media ecologies and protest movements: main perspectives and key lessons. *Information, Communication and Society* 19(3): 290–306. https://doi.org/10.1080/1369118X.2015.1109699.
Wood, Rachel (2020). "What I'm not gonna buy": algorithmic culture jamming and anti-consumer politics on YouTube. *New Media and Society* 23(9): 2754–72. https://doi.org/10.1177/146144482093944.
Wrenn, Corey Lee (2020). *Piecemeal Protest: Animal Rights in the Age of Nonprofits*. Ann Arbor: University of Michigan Press.
Wrenn, Corey Lee (2013). Resonance of moral shocks in abolitionist animal rights advocacy: overcoming contextual constraints. *Society and Animals* 21(4): 379–94. https://doi.org/10.1163/15685306-12341271.

Appendix A: *Blackfish* accumulation timeline

February 2010	Dawn Brancheau killed at SeaWorld Orlando, Florida
30 July 2010	Story in *Outside* magazine – Brancheau's death (seen by filmmaker Gabriela Cowperthwaite)
2013	*Blackfish* premieres at Sundance Film Festival
2013	Receives distribution via CNN, Magnolia Films, Dogwoof (UK), Madman Films for Australia and New Zealand 17 worldwide appearances Twitter Q&A with Gabriela Cowperthwaite Talks at the Apple Store in London **Available** Watch Now iTunes Amazon instant video Google Play DVD and Blu-ray **Reviews** *Awards Daily* *Daily Express* *Daily Mail*

	Daily Mirror *Empire Magazine* *Evening Standard* *FEARnet* *Huffington Post* *Los Angeles Times* *Movie Scope* *New York Daily News* *New York Times* *Sunday Telegraph* *The Guardian* *The Hollywood Reporter* *The Independent* *The Irish Times* *The Metro* *The Observer* *The Scotsman* *The Sun* *The Times* *Total Film* *Variety* *Village Voice* *Vulture* **Social media** Twitter Instagram Facebook
2014	US Court of Appeals upheld the OSHA court ruling and fined SeaWorld $75,000 and placed responsibility on SeaWorld for Brancheau's death
2020	SeaWorld ordered to pay investors $65 million

About the contributors

Núria Almiron is co-director of the UPF-Centre for Animal Ethics and a tenured professor in the Department of Communication at Universitat Pompeu Fabra (UPF). Her main areas of research include and combine the ethics and political economy of communication – particularly interest groups and persuasive communication – with critical animal studies, climate change, animal advocacy and interspecies ethics. Her work has been published in academic journals such as *Climatic Change, Journal of Agricultural and Environmental Ethics, Environmental Politics, Journalism Studies, Environmental Communication, International Journal of Communication* and *European Journal of Communication*. She is the author and editor of several books in various languages, the latest being *Like an Animal: Critical Animal Studies Approaches to Borders, Displacement, and Othering* (co-edited with Natalie Khazaal, 2021). She is the co-ordinator of the research project COMPASS (Lobbying and Compassion: Interest Groups, Discourse and Nonhuman Animals in Spain).

Olatz Aranceta-Reboredo is a PhD researcher in the Department of Communication at Universitat Pompeu Fabra (UPF), a member of the CritiCC communication research group at the same university and a board member of the UPF-Centre for Animal Ethics. Their areas of research include critical animal studies, interspecies ethics, interest groups and the representation of animals in media. They graduated in English Studies from the University of the Basque Country and hold an MA in Media, Power and Difference from the Universitat Pompeu Fabra. Olatz is the project manager of the COMPASS research project (PID2020-118926RB-I00), and they are conducting their PhD research titled "COMPASSION IN (S)PAIN: How Interest Groups' Discourse Contributes to the Perpetuation of Animal Captivity and Exhibition" within this project and under the supervision of Dr Núria Almiron.

Paula Arcari is a Leverhulme Early Career Research Fellow within the Centre for Human Animal Studies at Edge Hill University, UK (2019–2022). Her three-year project, The Visual Consumption of Animals: Challenging Persistent Binaries, examines practices relating to zoos, horse racing and greyhound racing in the UK. Paula earned her PhD in Sociology at RMIT University and holds two MAs in Geography and Environmental Science. She is the author of *Making Sense of "Food" Animals: A Critical Exploration of the Persistence of "Meat"* (2019) based on her research on the production and consumption of "ethical" meat in Australia, and is editor of a forthcoming volume exploring liberated animal futures. Paula's research focuses on understanding how both societal change and stability are constituted, particularly in relation to the oppression of nonhuman animals, the expropriation of nature, and climate and environmental change.

Elizabeth Cherry is Professor of Sociology at Manhattanville College (Purchase, NY, USA), where she researches and teaches on human–animal studies, environmental sociology, culture and social movements. She is the author of *Culture and Activism: Animal Rights in France and the United States* (2016) and *For the Birds: Protecting Wildlife through the Naturalist Gaze* (2019).

Lorena Elke Dobbie is passionate about documentary film and social justice issues, and was a researcher and consultant on the award-winning documentaries *The Ghosts in Our Machine* and *Water on the Table* by Liz Marshall. She is also the author of *If Cats Could Talk: A Holistic Approach to our Feline Companions* (1999). Lorena is a Simulated Patient Medical

Educator at the University of Toronto, Canada, where she teaches patient-centred communication skills to healthcare professionals and students and is part of an award-winning team who has presented work both nationally and internationally. She has studied film, women and gender studies and has a Masters of Education in Adult Education and Community Development from OISE, University of Toronto. Lorena has spent decades as an activist involved in animal, environmental and reproductive justice movements. She acknowledges her privilege to live and learn on Indigenous lands and is extremely grateful.

Laura Fernández is a critical animal and media studies researcher. She holds a PhD in Communication from Universitat Pompeu Fabra (UPF), she previously graduated in Social and Cultural Anthropology (Autonomous University of Madrid, 2016) and completed a Master's degree in International Studies on Media, Power and Difference (Pompeu Fabra University, 2017). In 2022, Laura obtained a Juan de la Cierva Formación 2021 postdoctoral fellowship from the State Research Agency (Ministry of Science and Innovation of the Government of Spain) to work at the Barcelona University with the Centre of Research in Information, Communication and Culture (CRICC). Her research lines include strategic visual communication, social movements, media representation of oppressed groups and the moral shock strategy in the animal liberation movement. She is the author of more than ten academic publications and a book and she is a board member of the UPF-Centre for Animal Ethics.

Carrie P. Freeman, PhD is a Professor of Communication at Georgia State University in Atlanta, USA, who researches and teaches strategic communication for activists, media ethics, environmental communication and critical animal studies, with a specialty in animal agribusiness and veganism. Her books include *The Human Animal Earthling Identity: Shared Values Unifying Human Rights, Animal Rights, and Environmental Movements* (2020) and *Framing Farming: Communication Strategies for Animal Rights* (2014). She co-edited the 2015 anthology *Critical Animal and Media Studies: Communication for Nonhuman Animal Advocacy*, and with Debra Merskin co-authors media style guidelines for respectful coverage of animals at animalsandmedia.org. She has been active in the grassroots animal rights movement since the mid-1990s, including serving as faculty advisor for the GSU student animal rights club she helped charter. For over a decade she has co-hosted an environmental radio program and podcast ("In Tune to Nature") on Radio Free Georgia.

Eva Haifa Giraud is a senior lecturer in Digital Media and Society at Sheffield University, UK, whose research focuses on the (sometimes fraught) relationship between theoretical work focused on relationality and entanglement, and activist practice. Her publications include *What Comes After Entanglement? Activism, Anthropocentrism, and an Ethics of Exclusion* (2019), *Veganism: Politics, Practice, and Theory* (2021), and articles in journals such as *Theory, Culture & Society*, *New Media & Society* and *Social Studies of Science.*

Dr Lara Herring is a lecturer in the School of Arts and Media at the University of Salford, UK. Coming from a film production background, Lara's postgraduate research centred around film industry analysis, framed by cinematic geopolitics and the role of cinema in communicating national identity. Lara's research has examined the ways in which social networking sites shaped the development of the Chinese film industry. Lara's research interests also include critical animal studies and she has worked on studies that examine the pathways and barriers to veganism. Lara's current research includes a contextual analysis of *Cloud Atlas* (2012) that seeks to address the manner in which the film critiques carnism by simultaneously connecting the meat industry with cannibalism, human slavery and sexual exploitation. Lara's doctoral thesis examined the relationship between the Chinese and American (Hollywood) film industries. Taking a film industry studies approach, Lara's research investigated this developing relationship by way of changing funding and distribution models, the emergence of co-production partnerships, studies of cross-cultural film products, analysis of the ongoing power shift between the Chinese and US film markets and the geopolitical industrial landscape that emerged as a result.

Loredana Loy is a Post-Doctoral Associate – Disinformation, Animal Agriculture, and Climate Change, with the Rosenstiel School of Marine,

Atmospheric, and Earth Science at the University of Miami, USA. She obtained her PhD in Sociology from Cornell University in 2023. She holds an MA in sociology and media studies from New York University and a BS from the Bucharest University of Economic Studies. Loredana's current postdoctoral research examines the way culture and ideology interact with political and economic power systems to shape social transformation processes related to the exploitation of nonhuman animals and the protection of the environment. Her past doctoral research refracts the challenge of environmental governance through the prism of stalled climate action in the United States Congress. Loredana's work has been published in *Science and Public Policy*, *Climatic Change*, and *Communications, Earth & Environment*. In her spare time, Loredana has been managing the social media presence of the Animals & Society section of the American Sociological Association.

Motivated by the transformative language and platform of film and television, **Liz Marshall** has dedicated her career to exploring some of the most pressing issues and ideas of our times. An award-winning Canadian filmmaker, Liz has written, directed, produced and filmed multiple impactful documentary projects around the globe, working with diverse teams since the 1990s. With a focus on change-makers and solutions, her feature-length work has been reviewed and screened widely.

Debra Merskin, PhD is Professor Emerit of Media Studies in the School of Journalism & Communication at the University of Oregon, USA. Her expertise is in the re-presentation of animals in media and popular culture and the psychological process of speciest attitudes, beliefs and behaviours. Her latest book is *Seeing Species: Re-presentations of Animals in Media & Popular Culture* (2018). She is active in the animal rights community, serving as an advisory board member for the Kimmela Center for Animal Advocacy, Predator Defense and the Humane Education Coalition. Along with Dr Carrie Freeman, she co-founded the website and media style guide site animalsandmedia.org.

Toby Miller is Profesor Visitante at the Universidad Complutense de Madrid and Research Professor in the Graduate Division of the

University of California, Riverside. He just concluded three years as Stuart Hall Profesor de Estudios Culturales, Universidad Autónoma Metropolitana Cuajimalpa, and was a professor at the UCR for a decade and New York University for 12 years. The author and editor of over 50 books, his work has been translated into Spanish, Chinese, Portuguese, Japanese, Turkish, German, Italian, Farsi, French, Urdu and Swedish. His most recent volumes are *A COVID Charter, a Better World* (2021), *Violence* (2021), *The Persistence of Violence: Colombian Popular Culture* (2020), *How Green is Your Smartphone?* (co-authored, 2020), *El Trabajo Cultural* (2018), *Greenwashing Culture* (2018) and *Greenwashing Sport* (2018). Formerly the editor of the *Journal of Sport and Social Issues, Social Text* and *Television & New Media*, he currently edits *Open Cultural Studies* and is co-editor of *Social Identities: Journal for the Study of Race, Nation and Culture.*

Brett Mills teaches and researches in television, media and film at Edge Hill University, UK, and is an Honorary Professor of Media and Cultural Studies at the University of East Anglia, UK. He is the author of *Television Sitcom* (2005), *The Sitcom* (2012) and *Animals on Television: The Cultural Making of the Non-Human* (2017). He is a member of the team that undertook two Arts and Humanities Research Council-funded (AHRC) projects on multispecies storytelling: Multispecies Storytelling: More-Than-Human Narratives About Landscape (2019–2022) and Multisensory Multispecies Storytelling to Engage Disadvantaged Groups in Changing Landscapes (2020–2022). He has undertaken Research Fellowships at Animal Charity Evaluators (2021) and the Future Matters Project (2022).

Claire Parkinson is Professor of Culture, Communication and Screen Studies, Associate Head of the English and Creative Arts Department, and founder and co-director of the Centre for Human Animal Studies at Edge Hill University, UK. She is the author or editor of eight books including *Beyond Human: From Animality to Transhumanism* (2012), *Popular Media and Animals* (2011) and *Animals, Anthropomorphism and Mediated Encounters* (2020). She recently led two Arts and Humanities Research Council-funded (AHRC) projects on multispecies storytelling: Multispecies Storytelling: More-Than-Human Narratives About Landscape (2019–2022) and Multisensory Multispecies Storytelling to

Engage Disadvantaged Groups in Changing Landscapes (2020–2022). Previous to this she led the funded projects Pathways to Veganism: Exploring Effective Messages in Vegan Transition (2018–2019) and Public Perceptions of "Dangerous" Dogs and Dog Risk (2020–2022).

Emily Plec (she/they) is Professor of Communication Studies at Western Oregon University and editor of *Perspectives on Animal-Human Communication: Internatural Communication* (2013), which received the Oravec Award from the Environmental Communication Division of the National Communication Association. They coined the term "internatural communication", teach introductory and advanced seminar courses on Animal Communication topics, and publish and present related articles, book chapters and workshops. Their work appears in journals such as *Environmental Communication and Rhetoric Society Quarterly* as well as in edited volumes such as *Critical Animal and Media Studies* (Almiron, Cole and Freeman 2015), *Rhetorical Animals* (Bjørkdahl and Parrish 2017), *Intimate Relations* (Fletcher and Dare 2021) and *Gender and Sexuality in Critical Animal Studies* (George 2021). They thank their students, especially Daisy Pratt, for inspiring the chapter that appears in this volume.

Mieke Roscher is Associate Professor for Cultural and Social History and the History of Human-Animal Relations at the University of Kassel, Germany. Her publications include *Ein Königreich für Tiere* (2009) on the British animal rights movement, the edited volumes *Animal Biography* (together with André Krebber, 2018) and the *Handbook of Historical Animal Studies* (together with André Krebber and Brett Mizelle, 2021) as well as numerous articles on animal historiography and agency, the 20th-century European zoo and gender in animal welfare. She is currently writing a monograph on the political history of animals in the Third Reich.

Index

www.ingramcontent.com/pod-product-compliance
Lightning Source LLC
Chambersburg PA
CBHW050643270326
41927CB00012B/2847
* 9 7 8 1 7 4 3 3 2 9 7 5 7 *